Building Online Stores with osCommerce:
Professional Edition

Design, build, and profit from a sophisticated
online business

David Mercer

PUBLISHING

BIRMINGHAM - MUMBAI

Building Online Stores with osCommerce: Professional Edition

First published: November 2005

Published by Packt Publishing Ltd.
32 Lincoln Road
Olton
Birmingham, B27 6PA, UK.

ISBN 1-904811-14-0

www.packtpub.com

Cover Design by www.visionwt.com

Credits

Author
David Mercer

Reviewers
Monika Mathé
Theodore S. Boomer

Technical Editors
Niranjan Jahagirdar
Nanda Padmanabhan
Abhishek Shirodkar

Editorial Manager
Dipali Chittar

Development Editor
Louay Fatoohi

Indexer
Niranjan Jahagirdar

Proofreader
Chris Smith

Production Coordinator
Manjiri Nadkarni

Cover Designer
Helen Wood

Foreword

osCommerce is *the* e-commerce solution of choice for thousands of online shop owners. That's with good reason; it is an extremely powerful tool and highly customizable. The advantage of osCommerce (Open-Source Commerce) is the availability of core code and the ability to adjust it to meet each shop's particular needs. At the same time, however, this can prove challenging for those who have no experience with HTML, PHP, or databases such as MySQL.

This is why the osCommerce community will be excited to have this new book available to them. *Building Online Stores with osCommerce* clearly details all aspects of osCommerce—from installation, to specific customization, including adding contributions—and it does so in a logical, easy to understand fashion. There is no doubt that new osCommerce users, with this book as a guide, will be capable of creating an online business that best meets their needs.

Many new users have been waiting for an excellent reference book like this, a guide that will save them countless hours of searching for solutions. *Building Online Stores with osCommerce* provides well chosen examples to assist new users to become masters in their own domain.

If you have been dreaming of having your own online store, there is nothing to hold you back now. I wish you all the best in your new venture!

Dipl.-Ing. Monika Mathé
Oracle Certified Database Administrator (OCP DBA)
osCommerce Expert

http://www.monikamathe.com

About the Author

David Mercer

David Mercer was born in August 1976 in Harare, Zimbabwe. Having always had a strong interest in science, David came into regular contact with computers at university, where he minored in Computer Science.

As a programmer and professional writer, he has written both code and books for about seven years. He has worked on a number of well-known titles, in various capacities, on a wide variety of topics. This has afforded him a singularly unique oversight into the world of programming and technology as it relates to furthering the goals of business.

David finds that the challenges arising from the dichotomous relationship between the science (and art) of software programming and the art (and science) of writing is what keeps his interest in producing books piqued. He intends to continue to write professionally in the future.

As a consultant for his own technical and editorial consultancy, David balances his time between programming, reviewing, writing, and furthering his studies in Applied Mathematics. When he isn't working (which isn't that often), he enjoys playing guitar and getting involved in outdoor activities ranging from touch rugby and golf to water skiing and snowboarding.

You can contact him at davidm@contechst.com, or alternatively, visit his consultancy's website at http://www.contechst.com/.

A big thanks to the team at Packt Publishing for giving me the opportunity to work on this book. I also thank my family and friends as well as my girlfriend, Bronagh. They have all done a great job of supporting and encouraging me over the last six months or so.
Ad astra per aspera.

About the Reviewers

Monika Mathé

Fascinated by anything combining logic and creativity, it seems that destiny found me in 1999 when I became a software developer and Oracle-certified database administrator.

It was a tough call to decide in which field to work, but landing a position in a marketing agency and working with everything from Oracle to SQL Server and HTML, ASP, and JavaScript was a fabulous decision I still congratulate myself for! I learned more about marketing campaigns, e-commerce, and CRMs than I had ever wanted to know, I mean, ever thought was possible!

I have also been taken in by the open-source community; I've become an avid believer in PHP (perhaps a bit less in MySQL), and definitely in a love affair with osCommerce. I believe almost anything can be done with it ... I challenge anyone to prove me wrong!

I am an active member of the osCommerce online community and know preemptively which questions will arise in new shop creation. Presently, I am creating as many new shops for customers as time allows, of course, while urging them to add as many custom coded modules as I see fit ... that's dessert for me!

Theodore S. Boomer

While recovering from an extended illness, I was on my computer searching for something to challenge my mind. I found HTML. At first it was very basic, but quickly it grew as competing browsers and then HTML editors progressed. I have supplemented my knowledge with additional learning through online communities, groups, some colleges, and books from Pack-IT, which have enabled me to keep an edge on software that I can incorporate to give me a competitive edge in design.

Now I have taken the many hours I have spent finding sources to complete client projects and consolidated them into my web design business and expanded to an Internet Business Technologies company that provides web development, web hosting, systems development, merchant card services, and high-speed Internet connections from entrepreneurs to Fortune 50 companies.

Table of Contents

Introduction

The modern-day entrepreneur, or indeed a business of any kind, small or large, can scarcely do without some form of presence on the Web. The pervasiveness of the Internet has brought about a new reality for business people. No longer is it sufficient to set up shop somewhere and sit quietly waiting for customers. Instead, the initiative must be taken with goods and services being marketed and sold online, reaching hitherto unheard-of sizes of consumer markets, nationally and internationally.

With the added burden of the acquisition of IT skills, many small- to medium-size enterprises have found themselves being outstripped by their larger cousins, who have the resources and manpower to harness and utilize the Internet properly. Prohibitively expensive development costs or ill-fitting off-the-shelf applications have hampered SME's ability to compete on an even footing. Up until now that is!

With the advent of osCommerce and other open-source technologies like it, the door has been opened for anyone with a bit of determination to set up a sophisticated online store that will hold its own against any other site out there. It's not surprising that osCommerce is growing in popularity as more and more people switch to the advantages of building and running their very own e-commerce website.

Unfortunately, while running and administering your own site is now within your grasp, it's not to say that you don't have to work at it. There is a lot of information you need to know, plenty to learn about installing, configuring, customizing, securing, and running osCommerce, and indeed the technologies you will be basing your business on. You can also benefit from some general wisdom and knowledge that programmers apply to their everyday work. Providing you with this knowledge is why I have written this book!

The advantage you will derive from learning about the technologies you are using, while you are building your online business, will help you to not only gain a foothold in the competitive world of e-commerce, but also ultimately to outstrip your competitors. That's what a successful business is about after all! I wish you the best of luck…

What This Book Covers

Chapter 1 discusses the not inconsiderable task of ensuring that you understand fully the resources both, in terms of time and money, that this project will require. A large part of this requires us to discuss the design and construction of your site and relate these to the needs of your business.

Chapter 2 provides an oversight of how to set up your development environment, which will provide you with a place to experiment and most importantly, learn your way around osCommerce without having to endanger your online business by working on it directly.

Chapter 3 presents a brief overview of how osCommerce works and makes use of its underlying technologies. As well as this, we take a quick tour of a standard website and then discuss how you can benefit from and be of benefit to the osCommerce community.

Chapter 4 deals with the most common configuration settings, which you will need to familiarize yourself with.

Chapter 5 gets right to the heart of the matter with an in-depth look at data in osCommerce. Here you will learn not only how to add and remove products and manufacturers as well as administer orders and customers, but also how to properly design your category/product hierarchy. Finally, this chapter also covers the addition of a community contribution, that handles automated uploads to your database, making your life a whole lot easier.

Chapter 6 is where the standard look and feel of osCommerce gets a face-lift. After reading this, you will have a sound knowledge of design and how to relate it to the dictates of your business. Additionally, we will discuss the all-important topics of stylesheet modification, images, and language and show how to deal with them effectively. Get ready to get your hands dirty as there is plenty of work in here.

Chapter 7 takes you one step closer to running an online business by comprehensively dealing with taxes, payments, and shipping. Strategies for implementing various policies pertaining to money matters are also scrutinized and by the end of this chapter, you will be well versed in your site's money matters.

Chapter 8 is arguably the most important of all. If you only read one chapter, make it this one. The integrity of your e-commerce site (and for many of you, your livelihood) rests on how well you can implement security and disaster recovery policies. Follow along here to learn how to gain a peaceful night's sleep, safe in the knowledge that your precious business is safe.

Chapter 9 looks at some advanced additions like cross-selling and up-selling features, discount and gift vouchers, as well as feed aggregation to enhance both the appeal and sophistication of your site. This chapter really narrows the gap between what you as a smaller business can produce and the large, expensive e-commerce sites with all their fancy features.

Chapter 10 introduces you to some important tools, which will no doubt make your life a lot easier in the time to come. As well as this, it takes a more lighthearted look at some neat tricks and how to make a few nice touch additions.

Chapter 11 covers moving what you have developed over the past ten chapters to the live site where it will be available to the public. Once again, there are a lot of issues involved in doing this right, so put on your thinking cap.

Chapter 12 takes you one step further by looking at how you can get ahead in the online business world. Marketing and advertising on the Web is covered in detail, as well as some handy and innovative schemes for boosting revenue and exposure. Naturally, search engine optimization is put in the spotlight here as well.

Appendix A provides you with a look at various methods that can be used to effectively deal with problems and errors. Having a programmer's perspective and embracing a sound methodology will save you countless hours and frustration and is applicable to a wide range of software, not just osCommerce.

Conventions

In this book, you will find a number of styles of text that distinguish between different kinds of information. Here are some examples of these styles and an explanation of their meaning.

There are three styles for code. Code words in text are shown as follows: "We can include other contexts through the use of the `include` directive."

A block of code will be set as follows:

```
if (substr(basename($PHP_SELF), 0, 8) != 'checkout') {
    include(DIR_WS_BOXES . 'languages.php');
    include(DIR_WS_BOXES . 'currencies.php');
}
```

When we wish to draw your attention to a particular part of a code block, the relevant lines or items will be made bold:

```
if (substr(basename($PHP_SELF), 0, 8) != 'checkout') {
    // include(DIR_WS_BOXES . 'languages.php');
    include(DIR_WS_BOXES . 'currencies.php');
}
```

Any command-line input and output is written as follows:

```
mysql> insert into user values (
    -> 'localhost',
    -> 'oscommerce',
    -> Password('password'),
    -> 'Y','Y','Y','Y','Y','Y','Y'
    -> 'N','N', 'N','N', 'N','N', 'N','N', 'N','N', 'N',
    -> 'N','N', 'N','N', 'N','N', 'N','N', 'N','N');
```

New terms and **important words** are introduced in a bold-type font. Words that you see on the screen, in menus or dialog boxes for example, appear in our text like this: "clicking the Next button moves you to the next screen".

> Warnings or important notes appear in a box like this.

Reader Feedback

Feedback from our readers is always welcome. Let us know what you think about this book, what you liked or may have disliked. Reader feedback is important for us to develop titles that you really get the most out of.

To send us general feedback, simply drop an email to feedback@packtpub.com, making sure to mention the book title in the subject of your message.

If there is a book that you need and would like to see us publish, please send us a note in the SUGGEST A TITLE form on http://www.packtpub.com or email suggest@packtpub.com.

If there is a topic that you have expertise in and you are interested in either writing or contributing to a book, see our author guide on www.packtpub.com/authors.

Customer Support

Now that you are the proud owner of a Packt book, we have a number of things to help you to get the most from your purchase.

Downloading the Example Code for the Book

Visit http://www.packtpub.com/support, and select this book from the list of titles to download any example code or extra resources for this book. The files available for download will then be displayed.

> The downloadable files contain instructions on how to use them.

Errata

Although we have taken every care to ensure the accuracy of our contents, mistakes do happen. If you find a mistake in one of our books—maybe a mistake in text or code—we would be grateful if you would report this to us. By doing this you can save other readers from frustration, and help to improve subsequent versions of this book. If you find any errata, report them by visiting http://www.packtpub.com/support, selecting your book, clicking on the **Submit Errata** link, and entering the details of your errata. Once your errata have been verified, your submission will be accepted and the errata added to the list of existing errata. The existing errata can be viewed by selecting your title from http://www.packtpub.com/support.

Questions

You can contact us at questions@packtpub.com if you are having a problem with some aspect of the book, and we will do our best to address it.

1

Introduction to E-Commerce with osCommerce

When Tim Berners-Lee first decided it would be a good idea if his computer could exchange information with his colleague's computers up the corridor, he could scarcely have known that he was setting in motion, perhaps, the most profound change in the way mankind communicates since the written word. With the advent of the **World Wide Web (WWW)**, communication underwent a kind of revolution that had an impact on our daily lives in hundreds of different ways.

Of course, it also wasn't long before someone figured out how to make money from the Web and naturally everyone jumped on the bandwagon. Enter the dotcom boom and bust! Unfortunately, for the Internet and consequently Internet-based businesses, the dotcom fiasco hurt a lot of people who perhaps, buoyed up by bullish sentiment from investment houses and brokers who understood all too well the amount of money they stood to make, invested in something they didn't fully understand. At the time, very few Internet-based businesses had shown that they were reliable, stable, and profitable. Nevertheless, the money kept flowing in and the new technology companies kept spending it—on what, no one was quite sure.

However, when the bubble burst, not all Internet initiatives collapsed. Some came through it a little worse for wear, but far more resilient, and many more learned valuable lessons about how to approach this new platform for commerce and trade. It is a testament to the exceptional value of the WWW that despite the massive losses made initially on this technology, it is now more or less taken for granted that businesses of any size require a presence on the Web: if they don't have one yet, they are going to have one soon.

Today the world recognizes that being able to retail online to potentially billions of customers on a global scale is not the panacea it was first touted to be. Instead, a more mature approach needs to be adopted. It is now the accepted viewpoint that while having the ability to interact on the Web is a critical tool for success in today's world, it is still just that—a tool! In order to be successful, your business still needs to be based on a solid idea, with a good demand or client base, backed up by either great products or great services. Just like the good old days.

By purchasing this book, you have implicitly given a vote of confidence to the Web and will, hopefully, be able to turn it to your advantage. Before we are able to begin working directly on the site, it is imperative that you are equipped with some basic information about life and business on the Internet.

This chapter discusses the following topics:

- A brief history and motivation for osCommerce and e-commerce
- The issues surrounding the business-related aspects of e-commerce
- An outline of what goes into designing a site to meet your business needs
- An outline of the process of building a site to meet your business needs

Before we continue, it is important to realize that as things stand, our global village is still undergoing a revolution in communication driven by the giant leaps in the sophistication of both hardware and software alike. While it seems that everything is becoming more advanced and therefore complicated, the one thing to remember is that pretty much everything you see around us is here to make things easier. One of the best things about advances in technology is that they give everyone the ability to leapfrog stages of development. What this means is that the companies that invest a lot of money in order to be innovative and stay ahead of the competition blaze a trail that is decidedly easier for those of us without unlimited funding to follow.

A good example of leapfrogging is happening with technology in Africa. In many countries, poor infrastructure hampers business and communication. Luckily for them, laying hundreds of thousands of kilometers of phone line is no longer necessary, as it was for countries in the West seventy years ago. Nowadays, telecommunications companies install their own towers and the public has instant access to cellular or wireless communications. In ten short years, some African states have gone from utilizing ageing, outdated copper wire systems to modern cellular communications without having to invest their resources in research and development.

This idea applies very much to software application development and in the same way, we are going to piggy-back a ride on the work of others (in this case, the osCommerce development team) to arrive at a sophisticated and functional e-commerce website without having to re-invent the wheel. This is good news for everyone concerned because it means that one no longer has to have a PhD in computer science in order to build and operate a fairly complex Internet-based software application.

For a lot of us, the urge to dive straight into the building of the site is all but overwhelming because, after all, that is where the magic happens. Don't do it! Instead, take a deep breath, grab a cup of coffee and read through this chapter before doing anything else. While it may seem like a drag now, it will save you a lot of time, frustration, and sanity later.

The What and Why of osCommerce

osCommerce has been around since March 2000 and was originally founded by Harald Ponce de Leon. The development of osCommerce is still overseen by Harald, but has also since become the domain of a full team of dedicated people. You can read about the osCommerce team on the http://www.oscommerce.com/about/team page/. At present there are about 6,000 live, registered osCommerce sites and about 70,000 registered community members. With the rising success and popularity of this remarkable piece of software, these numbers are all set to increase dramatically.

Looking at how long osCommerce has been around, it's safe to say that there has been enough time for the technology to mature and for people to be confident that it has endured plenty of use and has been reworked and debugged to the point where it is stable and reliable. If you are not someone who is readily convinced, a visit to the osCommerce community forums at http://forums.oscommerce.com/ will demonstrate that there is a lively, active community supporting this technology—proof enough that osCommerce is working for others, and that there is the interest to push osCommerce forward in the years to come.

Quite apart from all this, it is fair enough and important to ask "*Why should I use osCommerce?*" at this early stage. Part of the answer to this seemingly innocuous question goes straight to the heart of an issue that has led to a massive divergence in one of the fundamental socio-economic questions surrounding modern computing.

There are two schools of thought that divide most programmers and developers firmly into two camps, which compete against each other, in some cases quite vehemently. The issue is whether or not intellectual property (in particular, software) should be made available for everyone in the world to use, modify, and contribute to or whether it should be protected.

It is strongly urged to avail yourself of the facts when it comes to open source technology, even if for nothing other than allowing you to form a considered opinion about the software upon which your business relies. The following is a fairly good definition of the term **Open Source**:

> Open Source is defined as any program whose source code is made available—most often subject to certain conditions—for use or modification by users or other developers as they deem fit.

Open source software is usually developed as a public collaboration and is freely available. For more information on what open source is, check out http://www.opensource.org/.

So, we know that osCommerce is an open source initiative—big deal! How does this change anything or how should it influence our decision to use it? Well, let's look at some of the advantages of the open source paradigm and relate it to what you can expect from the overall osCommerce experience:

- **Totally free**: It might cost you tens or hundreds of thousands of dollars to get a software development company to build you a fully functional commercial site from scratch. Not having to pay for this development removes one of the largest obstacles that retards e-commerce growth for the small to medium enterprise.

- **Secure and stable milestone releases**: The osCommerce core has become a secure and stable environment for online commerce due of the large amount of community participation. This doesn't mean it is impervious to attack—like any other software, it has weaknesses—but you can be sure of a swift community response to any new threats that may appear.

- **Large development community**: osCommerce's source code is readily available and free to modify and so there are thousands of developers who test and improve it on a daily basis. osCommerce effectively has an unlimited development team, and with the software gaining in popularity, new code will be produced at a faster rate.

- **Large support community**: osCommerce has a large support community. This is due to the fact that the open source paradigm encourages the development of communities that feel a collective responsibility to aid others within that community.

While the above points might not seem like a big thing now, knowing that there is someone else who has perhaps struggled with the same issues that you have, and is willing to spend time to help you solve your own problems is a huge benefit that can't really be quantified in terms of cost.

Apart from the previously listed advantages that have been automatically bestowed upon osCommerce users, it is also fair to say that this is one of the world's truly valuable pieces of software that is leveling the playing ground between enterprises with large pockets and those with tighter budgets. This is because it empowers people to act on their ideas and bring their services and products to the world, via the medium of the World Wide Web, without being subject to high development costs. Removing obstacles in doing business stimulates growth and helps everyone in the long run. Hopefully, you will embrace the spirit of open source and encourage others to join in the future.

So has osCommerce done all our work for us and we only have to sit back and rake in the cash? Nice try! There is still plenty to do and unlike other more transient and perhaps gimmicky promises, which you might find on the Net, this book certainly won't get you up and running in twenty minutes. Instead, it will teach you how to develop an intelligent approach to what you do from here on. This will enable you to understand *why* and *how* you are doing things and give you control over how to develop your business with confidence in the future.

E-Commerce! What am I Doing?

Given that most readers will know all too well how many little things crop up when starting a conventional business, it should come as no surprise to find that an online venture is no different in this respect. The trick, as with many things in life and in software, is to break down your bigger problems into smaller, more manageable chunks, and deal with each chunk on its own. So while the available literature on e-commerce is extensive to say the least, we are going to look at a simple and effective way to start on the road to building a successful online business.

While there are by necessity many similarities between conventional and virtual enterprises since both have fundamentally the same goals, the differences can be devastating. Let's say, for example, you have set up a conventional business, for argument's sake, a bakery, and after one week you find that the new oven is not powerful enough to bake your bread quickly. As upsetting as it may be, you will probably have to go and buy another one. And while that problem has a painful solution, it is at least obvious.

This is where a conventional enterprise and a computer-based enterprise can vary greatly because, if instead of an incorrect oven specification, the virtual enterprise application accidentally utilized differing parameters (say, units of measurement) in some of its code, then it is entirely possible you could lose a $125 million Mars exploration vehicle just like NASA did in the late nineties. The loss of the Mars orbiter has hopefully highlighted areas where NASA's processes need to be looked at again, but the point of this is that the fault was not immediately obvious until it was too late. For those of us without a few hundred million dollars in lessons to be learned, a little planning should help ensure our more modest efforts don't suffer the same fate.

Before we dive into anything more specific, let's take a closer look at what the term **e-commerce** means, just to ensure we are all reading off the same page.

> We define e-commerce as commercial transactions occurring over computer networks, facilitated by electronic applications.

Granted, this definition is pretty vague, but given the huge number of different businesses interacting over a variety of platforms and technologies all over the globe, it serves as a good basis for our purpose. In this instance, commercial transactions can be taken to mean anything from buying and selling to marketing and distributing, and electronic applications means, in this instance, your osCommerce website.

Taking our lead from this definition, we can start looking at what needs to be done in order to join the world of e-commerce. Accordingly, the rest of this chapter looks at how the example application, a specialist computer bookstore called **Contechst Books**, was developed. It is recommended that you follow all the steps mentioned here in order to be at the same stage of development in your own site as the demonstration site, by the end of the book.

Do I Go For It or Not?

Before we decide whether or not to go for it, we should ask ourselves what it is we are going for. This can be answered very simply by stating the **goal**. Your goal is really a statement of what the desired result of this endeavor should be. Here is the goal for the example site:

> **Contechst Books' Goal:** To build and maintain an elegant and effective online bookstore that will allow customers to browse the website and purchase books and e-books for delivery or download, in order to generate extra revenue and increase competitiveness and market share by using an online medium.

The goal is pretty abstract at this stage since we don't even know what exactly is going on the site until we begin designing it. The important thing here is to state what you want the site to do in general and relate that to your needs as a business. If the first part of the goal (what the site is expected to do) relates well to the second part (how the site relates to the business) then the goal is coherent. Only you can determine whether the goal is accurate because the goal depends *entirely* on what you want for your business.

Now, there are several things to consider before we can make the choice to go ahead with investing time, money, and resources into building a complex, albeit relatively easy to implement, enterprise application. By and large though, the short answer to the question "*Do I go for it?*" is a resounding "*Yes!*". Even so, it is still worthwhile to think about whether or not to go ahead and build a site, because doing so will help to outline exactly what needs to be put into the endeavor, and also what the expected returns are.

The following sections discuss some of the main issues that need to be addressed before making a decision to move ahead.

Cost Versus Return

"What costs are you talking about? This software is free." is a reasonable question here. Well, you still have to put in the time and effort to actually build the site, even if osCommerce, and other related technologies like Apache, MySQL, and PHP are all free. Don't forget that your live site will also have to be hosted somewhere, although this is generally not a huge expense, and you will also need to buy a domain. Remember too, that you need the hardware on which you develop the site, even if ultimately it will be held on the Internet Service Provider's hard disks.

There are other expenses that are not really obvious at this stage. What will you do if you want to accept credit card payments on your site? How will you ensure the absolute security and privacy of those details? The best answer to this, for small to medium businesses, is not to handle them at all. This doesn't mean you are doomed to not accept credit card payments until you run a large multinational, but it does mean that a secure, third-party credit card payment facility will need to be involved, and with it, some expenses. As a matter of interest, we will look at the different methods for obtaining payments in Chapter 7.

Of course, monetary expense is not the only form of cost involved in this equation. You will also have to dedicate some time to building and maintaining the site. Determine now whether or not this time could be utilized better in doing other things. A big factor in deciding this, is ensuring you have a good idea of the hours required for the project. If time is not something you have in abundance, then it may be worth the expense to get a professional to build an osCommerce site for the business instead.

This leads on to the next point, which is that it may not be critical to have a site built immediately. If your business relies on word of mouth or is in its infancy, then it may be more fruitful spending time developing your client base and simply putting up an informative placeholder on the Web as opposed to a full-blown retail enterprise. Be certain that having an e-commerce site will enhance your business in the near future rather than drain resources from other more immediate concerns. The flipside is that by obtaining a sophisticated and professional online presence you might well get the head start before your competitors.

Resources and Commitment

While the goal of most computing is to automate tasks to make things easier, it doesn't automatically mean that we can upload a website and leave it to haul in cash. Unfortunately, things don't really work like this, so deciding to have an online division of your business requires a constant commitment if not quite a full-time one. Much attention needs to be given to operational sites because there are a host of things that can go awry if left unsupervised. For example, it is quite likely that you will need to track how and what your site is doing and selling on a regular basis. This alone means you will probably have to build in some form of reporting to monitor your stock and sales.

Of course, if the business in question is not already a well-known one, then making it more visible to potential customers, alas, requires more resources and time. We will look at how to use various advertising and marketing channels and tricks in order to raise the profile of your site in Chapter 12. For now though, suffice to say that you can expect to spend further time and probably money on capturing a larger client base.

There are plenty of other issues that arise from owning an online retail business, and it is up to you to identify as many of them as possible in order to determine whether you will be able to maintain a steady level of commitment to the site. This time-commitment can be reduced substantially by ensuring that sufficient planning has gone in before site development begins.

Designing an E-Commerce Site

There are several design aspects that need to be dealt with before you can begin building a website. These individual pieces of the overall picture form a cycle, which, when implemented properly, provides a consistent and well-structured approach to creating a successful online business. Furthermore, with proper planning you can ensure that your online business can change and scale to suit your real-world business needs.

That's not where the story ends at all though. In fact, in some ways, designing your site never ends precisely because the process is a cycle. And like any other aspect of your business, your online enterprise needs to be maintained and developed as time goes by, with improvements and upgrades and all the stuff that goes with them.

To begin with, however, you have to isolate your business needs, and draw up a specification of your site based on your needs. The next step would be to analyze the specification and determine the best way to do it. Once you have built your site (hopefully, in the most efficient and cost effective way) you have to test it to ensure that it performs as expected and meets the requirements of the specification. No doubt, there will be lessons learned during this stage and this is where the loop of the design cycle closes. Taking what you have learned from the testing phase, it is then necessary to go back and upgrade the site.

The following diagram illustrates the **design process**:

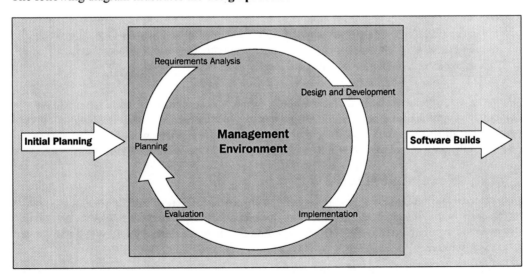

Of course, there are variations on how this cycle can be implemented. Some people prefer to do a bit of work and test it before moving on. In this way, they arrive at the final solution with a fully tested and operational application. Of course, other considerations like maintaining a good version control policy come into play when there are a lot of modifications to a site. For now, it is not necessary to get bogged down in a debate on methodology. Suffice to say that osCommerce makes life simple; provided we do a good job of planning ahead and testing the final product, we should come out just fine in the end.

Let us now look at the different aspects of designing and maintaining an e-commerce website.

Isolating the Site's Requirements

One of the first things you need to think about is what exactly you want your online business to do. This might seem a little silly at first because the chances are you already know what the business should do—it must sell books or jewelry, or it must provide a consulting service. Whatever it is, isn't it obvious that the site should be built to do just that? Well, yes and no.

For example, if you want to sell books online you could go right ahead and put a picture of all your books on a web page, with their prices and descriptions underneath. This solution certainly meets the specifications we have just mentioned—the site is selling books after all. But what happens when you want to add the ability to sell e-documents, or better yet, want to automate your stock control or implement useful marketing techniques like up-selling? Trying to append these changes onto a site after it has already gone live is often troublesome because the site wasn't initially designed with these things in mind.

Accordingly, the first thing to do is decide exactly the *type of functionality* you require from your online business. Later on you can look at how to implement those requirements and whether there are any critical problems or issues associated with your needs; for now it's time to put pen to paper.

> Please be aware that we are talking specifically about the online business here. This is not the same as writing a business plan, which may deal with investments, office location, and expenses or any number of unrelated things.

Having said that, there are several places where a formal business plan and a site specification overlap. This is of course exactly as one would expect since the virtual enterprise must reflect the needs and realities of the business in the real world. If you already have a business plan, then pull that out of the drawer and look over it as it will certainly aid you in building your site.

Business-Related Needs

Like all conscientious business people, we need to ensure that we know exactly what is required of the business before we jump in. The first thing to deal with is deciding the auxiliary requirements that need to be met in order to run and maintain the site. There are quite a lot of those little things to think about here.

The following bulleted list shows a good, generic list that has been developed for the purposes of the demonstration site. Naturally, each site or business is unique, so use this list only as a guide. There may be things that are important for you, but are not listed here, and some things that are listed here may not be important to you:

- **Find an Internet service provider**: There are a lot of options out there so rather than endorse one or two, it is better to give generic advice here. Make sure the provider is giving you enough hard disk space to safely run the business. Remember that you will probably have a lot of log files and a fair amount of images as well as data in your database. The provider must also use Apache and support PHP and MySQL since these are the technologies that make up osCommerce. Other than this, they should provide some form of SSL support, depending on what your needs will be. Beyond that, you should also look for fair pricing, reliability (specifically, look for percentage downtime), and ease of use as well as email facilities.
  Don't worry if this is slightly confusing at the moment. You only have to find a provider once you are ready to deploy your site to the Internet. Before that, you have to develop it on your own personal computer. Once that is done, you will understand your site's requirements a lot better.

- **Register a domain name**: This is easily done through an Internet service provider. If you would like to know whether or not your proposed name has been registered or not, then check out `http://www.whois.net/`. Depending on the deal you find, you can expect to pay a fairly small amount for your domain. Remember, you might want to explore domains other than `.com` depending on your customers.

- **Development environment**: At some stage you will need a computer to build the site. This means you need either a Windows or Linux machine with PHP, Apache, and MySQL installed. Complete installation and setup instructions for both platforms are covered in Chapter 2. You will also need a text editor to work with PHP files. If you don't have anything that will color code your PHP, then Wordpad will suffice. However, if you do want something that will make things a bit clearer (and it is recommend if you are going to get involved in this project in depth), you might want to consider investing in something like **EditPlus** (`http://www.editplus.com`) or **PHPEdit** (`http://www.waterproof.fr/`).

- **Integration**: If you are already running a conventional business, then ideally the aspects of the business should work in harmony to support and augment each other. Customers should be able to approach a real live person on the other end of the Web address to handle their problems or queries—human contact is not entirely redundant. Of course, changes to the business should be reflected on the site as quickly as possible to avoid dissatisfaction. For example, closing down a department without showing those changes on the site could leave a few customers quite angry if they make orders that are not honored.
  Obviously, one of the biggest tasks is to ensure that the real life part of the business (such as goods storage, ordering, availability, logistics and delivery) reflect the promises and assertions of the site. It is no good building a wonderful site that guarantees overnight delivery, if you are using normal snail mail to deliver goods.

- **Third Parties**: While this is probably not an immediate concern, at some stage you may wish to incorporate various different features that are not provided by osCommerce onto your site. In this case, you will need to learn how to deal with various other online establishments. A good example of this, for popular sites, is **Google Ads,** which allows a site to generate money by advertising related products in a panel.

The above points outline the main issues that *surround* the ownership of an e-commerce site, but don't actually impact on what the customer sees when browsing online. It is essential to understand what the site will need in order to make it a viable and useful place for people to shop. To this end, a bit of thought is needed as to what functionality to add to the site.

Site Functionality

Being diligent at this stage of the game will really pay off at a later date. A good way to decide on what exactly the site will end up doing is to build a list of tasks that it must be able to perform. Effectively, after creating a list of the various things we need, the site's architect (most probably yourself) should have a clear enough idea of the requirements to go ahead and begin working. Unfortunately, it is often hard to predict exactly what is needed by simply sitting down and writing, but a good way to start is by looking at similar sites. In other words, go to your competitors and take note of everything that is useful and desirable on their site and add this to your list.

If you get stuck or run out of ideas, it is helpful to try a thought exercise. Split yourself into two people—the first is the owner of the business who knows what the business needs are, and the second is a software architect who needs to find out what to build. Use the software architect persona to question the business owner about what has to be done. Approaching the problem from two perspectives often helps mimic real-world situations where software developers try to find out exactly what their client needs by asking probing questions before they start working on a project.

The following is a list of the requirements for developing the example site. Remember to build a list like this for your own site before moving on to the next chapter. The site should have the following features:

- The online store must be intuitive and easy to use.
- It should have SSL enabled for both customers making purchases and the administration for increased security.
- It must have an original design, look, and feel, and accurately reflect the nature of the business—both practically and aesthetically.
- It should offer shopping cart facilities.
- It should allow users to search for products using a word search or by navigating a product category tree.
- It should provide images and buying information for each product, as well as show reviews, if any.
- It should show any discounts or special offers.
- It should allow customers to create an account and have their account history tracked so that they can be made eligible for promotions and promotional discounts (perhaps based on the total amount of purchases).
- It should provide a sophisticated shipping policy for local, national, and international purchases.
- It should provide bulk email facilities for emailing members as well as automated confirmation and welcome emails.

- It should have cross-selling and up-selling facilities.

- It should be optimized for search engines to increase the business's profile on the net.

- It should possess advertising facilities for increased revenue. For example, banner advertisements and Google AdWords.

- It should follow good practices throughout like disaster recover/database backups, effective error reporting, high security, and ease of use.

Notice that some of the above bullet points are pretty vague, while others are quite specific. The reason for this is that if we were to list absolutely everything the site needs, we would spend too much time actually building the list instead of the site. Instead, we use sentences like "The online store must be intuitive and easy to use" to demonstrate that each and every aspect of the site's front end (or interface—the part that the client sees) should not be ambiguous in its meaning or use.

Other criteria are more specific, like "It should allow users to search for products using a word search or by navigating a product category tree", which really states that whatever we do, we need to build in a navigable tree structure for the products, as well as provide a text box that users can use to input text (for example, a book's name) to run against the product database.

Incidentally, no mention of the actual architecture of the site has been made in the above specification. Under normal circumstances, a huge chunk of time would be devoted to designing the business logic (the code that drives the website) and the database (the part of the application that retains all the information needed to keep things running). In our case though, all of this is taken off our hands by osCommerce, so we are free to think about what to put on the site instead of having to worry about how to actually *make* the site.

With the specification in hand, we have taken a large step towards the goal that we laid out earlier.

Analyzing the Proposed Solution

Now that we have the specification in hand, we know *what* we need. It is time to look at *how* to deliver it. Off the top of your head, it may seem as if one simply sits down and goes through the list point by point until everything has been checked off. From one perspective this is absolutely fine and certainly at some stage everything should be ticked off the list. But, if we look a little closer, the picture begins to get a bit fuzzy because we really need to go back over all the points listed and find out *what is involved* in getting each one done. Knowing what lies ahead is the best way to handle problems preemptively!

There are three main areas of concern that we need to deal with.

Feasibility

Having a wish-list is a great way to decide on what you want, but that doesn't mean it is feasible. In order to be feasible, the criteria should not involve an inordinate amount of effort relative to the benefits it will return. For example, if the site specification calls for a feature that requires a hundred hours of programming, then it is probably not in your interests to waste that time doing it, if it is not going to affect your revenue in any way. It may be better to look for a cheap and elegant alternative. One of the old programming mantras, "*There's more than one way to do it!*" holds true here.

Phone a Friend?

Look at your requirements very carefully. Are you sure you can actually provide everything that is required? If not, spend some time looking over this book, the osCommerce site at `http://www.oscommerce.info/docs/english/`, and the osCommerce knowledge base at `http://www.oscommerce.info/`, and forums at `http://forums.oscommerce.com/` to see if you can learn anything new. If you are absolutely stuck, then get on the forums and lists and ask for help. One of the great things about osCommerce is that it is what is known as a **community-driven project**, which roughly translates into, *"There are generally people around who are happy to help"*. Bear in mind that this is not a one-way relationship, and once you have some experience and knowledge to share, there are always people who are grateful for a helping hand.

Critical Versus Desirable Criteria

In order to determine the priority of tasks, it is a good idea to divide all your requirements into two categories—those that are fundamentally necessary to the success of your online business, such as finding a service provider, and those which are not, such as deciding on whether to make your hyperlink color dark blue or light blue. There are a couple of reasons for this. First off, doing this will help you allocate time and resources to certain tasks while putting others on a backburner. Secondly, and as bad as it sounds, at some stage you might find yourself in a situation where you are running out of time, or simply never really had enough time to finish everything. In both these cases, it is important to know what *has* to be finished and what can perhaps be left out or left for another day.

Building an E-Commerce Site

In order to understand how osCommerce helps us to build an e-commerce site, we can compare the creation of a website to the building of a house. Having free software is, for example, like being given the raw materials for building the house—sand, concrete, bricks, and wood—for free. This doesn't mean the whole house is free though. We still have to design the house and actually put it up. In our case, osCommerce is like a framework for the house; the overall structure is there, but we still have to put on the roof and decide what windows we need and so forth.

Using this analogy also helps to show why planning is so important. Obviously, it would be pretty startling to hear that building contractors for a house had gone ahead with construction without an architect first designing the house. Of course, this is exactly what people do when they don't sit down and plan out their site beforehand. Having worked through this chapter, we will already have completed the designing and planning phase of the project and will be ready to don our hardhats and begin with construction, or development, as it is known.

Development

Unlike building a house, development of a website takes place on a *copy* of the site instead of the real site. This means that while the site is being built, it is not available for the public to view and use on the Internet. With a bit of thought, this should make sense. Any potential client who came across the site-in-progress would probably get frustrated with bits and pieces that don't work, error messages, untidy presentation, and any number of things that could scare away valuable customers at the drop of a hat. A far more important and dangerous threat to an unfinished site that has been made live is that hackers could potentially access important information, and/or gain control over the site. An unprotected site like this is effectively a free meal for the denizens of the Web—don't think it won't happen to you!

So, all development happens on a development machine and not on the hosted site. Some readers may well be wondering what to do with their domain in the meantime, assuming one has already been purchased. The best solution is to put up what is known as a **placeholder page** that delivers a simple message that this is the right site, that development is in progress on the working site, and that customers should visit again in the near future. If you want to learn how to get a page onto your Internet site before going any further, then check out Chapter 11 on deployment, which outlines the process of moving your fully functional website onto your Web domain. The process for doing the whole site and a single page is more or less the same but naturally, moving a single page is a lot less complicated.

As mentioned earlier, we need to download and install various bits of software in order to be able to develop with osCommerce. The next chapter covers how to get all of this up and running on your home or work machine, but simply having all the right gear is not enough; we have to develop a process to use. Like any project of reasonable size, we need to make sure that things don't spiral out of control as we work on different aspects of the site. There are two principles that will save you a lot of time and prevent cases of programmer's rage:

- Save early and save often
- Maintain good version control

The first point directs us to save progress after every bit of important functionality is added. To be extra sure, you may want to save both a copy on your hard disk and a copy to a floppy disk or CD. There is nothing more frustrating than spending a day building a wonderful search engine, only to have it lost or destroyed during a power failure.

The second point talks about how we can ensure **milestones** in our progress are recorded properly. Because your development may take place over days, weeks, or months, it is important that you save a copy of the site at various milestones during development. These milestones can be anything you want. For example, once all your products have been added to the site you could save a copy and put it into a different folder. In this way, copies of the site are kept after each major step, for use at a later stage if necessary.

After each milestone is saved, development is carried out on a copy of the latest milestone so that you always end up working on new parts of the site, and progress is easily tracked and monitored. Each milestone should also contain a text file outlining what has occurred during that phase of development, as well as listing the entire functionality of the site till date. This may sound like overkill now, but it will make life easier if you are always aware of what has been done and when it was done.

In order to make your version control easier to manage and understand, you should choose suitably descriptive names for your versions. Something like `Contechstbooks_Milestone01.zip` for milestone files, which could be held in a separate `Milestones` folder in your working directory (or preferably on a removable storage device) would be sufficient here. Your current version (the one you are working on) could then be called Contechstbooks_Milestone01_Dev01. If you wished to try out development of a variety of things instead of simply working on one file you would simply create several Dev folders (Contechstbooks_Milestone01_Dev01, Contechstbooks_Milestone01_Dev02 and so on) to work in until you were satisfied with one, which would then become the next milestone.

Obviously, you need to transfer any changes you make to Dev folders that you would like to keep to the copy that will become the next milestone. In order to prevent confusion, the Dev folders that are not the ones you will go forward with should be moved to another folder, usually entitled Old, or something more appropriate. The following screenshot shows the type of structure you should consider creating for the project. Remember that your active Dev folder should be in a folder that the Apache server has access to, so that it can serve pages for you to test as you go (don't worry if you are unsure about how to do this—it will all be made clear once we begin developing):

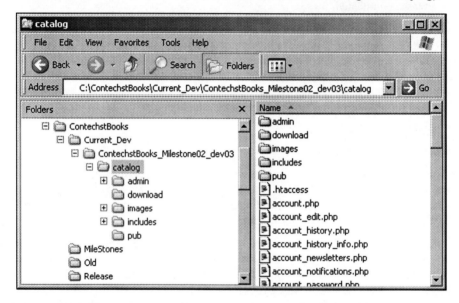

If there are going to be several people working on your site, then version control becomes even more important because it is often easy for one person to alter files that are not being worked on by others, or worse for someone to alter files that other people are not expecting to be altered. In this case, **CVS** may well be what you are looking for. CVS stands for **Concurrent Versioning System** and there is an open source option available for download at https://ccvs.cvshome.org/. Since this is not critical to the development of an osCommerce site, we will not look at this again, but you are urged to consider it if you are going to have a team of developers working on your project.

Given that osCommerce handles a lot of the complexity of the development phase, it should suffice to simply have a good working process in place and stick to it throughout the development phase. By adhering to the two points mentioned earlier, you should find that any losses due to mistakes or hardware and software failures are kept to a minimum.

Once that glorious day arrives when everything is in place and the final milestone version has been saved (in this case, the final version of the site should be saved in the form `Contechstbooks_RTP.zip` —**RTP** stands for **Release to Public**), you can deploy the fully functional site to the **URI** (**Universal Resource Indicator**) or website, in order to make the web pages accessible to the public. Apart from transferring files over to the host file system, there will be other settings and tasks to perform to make sure everything works as it should. We take an in-depth look at the deployment phase in Chapter 11. Naturally, any further development should be done on a copy of the `RTP` version on the development machine to minimize the impact of any changes that may be necessary as time goes by.

Testing and Debugging

Ensuring that your application is 'bug' or error free is a critical part of developing and building any software—and e-commerce websites are no different. There are different ways and means of isolating faults and correcting them, but before we look at those it is important to quickly acknowledge the different types of error that can make their unwelcome presence felt. Different types of errors also show in different ways and some are quite subtle and not easy to spot.

The first, and hopefully the most common, type you will encounter is a **syntax error**. A syntax error will prevent PHP from actually running your code. On the plus side, this should be relatively easy to locate. We will look at how to set error reporting levels on your test machine to print any errors to the screen for you to act on. Of course, once your site is active, you don't want the internal errors in your system being reported to the screen because this can often allow malicious users to glean information about your system.

Run-time errors are slightly worse than syntax errors because they are not quite as obvious or easy to pin down. There are quite a few different ways in which a run-time error can occur, and many of these can only be caught by thorough testing on your live site as well as your development machine. For example, file paths may change between your development machine and your live site, breaking links, losing files, or disrupting connections. While these errors won't show up when the PHP script is parsed, they will show up when it is executed.

Logic errors are quite sneaky in that they won't really show up at all. It is incumbent on you to decide whether your site is performing as it should. For example, accidentally typing a + sign instead of a - won't show up as either a run-time error or a syntax error, but will obviously affect the result of a calculation, which can have disastrous effects if it is part of your invoice calculator.

Unfortunately, there are quite a few more miscellaneous errors that can rear their ugly heads at inopportune moments, which we won't cover in much detail here. It is important at this stage to recognize that errors will creep into your application at some point and that you will need to deal with them effectively if you are to be successful. Appendix A, which deals with problems, discusses various tactics for hunting down and removing errors, as well as looking over some of the more common errors and problems that arise while using osCommerce. One thing that should give you some comfort at this stage is that since osCommerce handles so much of the underlying code for us, the number of errors you encounter should be a bare minimum.

A good strategy to identify errors early and often is to try out new developments all the time. If you make changes to your site, don't take it for granted that it will just work. Access the relevant page and try to use what you have added in as many ways as possible. In this way, you won't go through several days' worth of coding before having to backtrack to find the source of an error.

Deployment and Maintenance

By the time the site is at the deployment stage, one might be forgiven for thinking that the hard work is done. In a way it is, but that is not a license to relax and begin working on the next project. Deployment is a serious business, replete with its own problems and requisite testing. Once deployment has been carried out successfully and the site has been shown to be sufficiently error free, we can turn our attention to finding customers, promoting the site, as well as monitoring its performance and maintaining it.

The amount of work required to maintain a site is proportional to how well it has been developed. If there is a proper error-reporting facility with logs outlining the site's vital statistics and a good administration tool, then chances are you are going to have a relatively easy time debugging errors. Luckily for us osCommerce does a lot of this work automatically and it is simply up to you to decide how and what you want to monitor as well as maintain the file system.

Deployment and maintenance is such an important topic that it has its own dedicated chapter, Chapter 11, which is presented after the site has been built in Chapters 3-10.

Summary

This chapter has provided a solid backdrop to the considerable task of building a working e-commerce website. We talked about the issues that should be considered before beginning a project such as this, and then looked at how to determine whether or not this is the right project at the right time. Armed with the knowledge of how best to approach and manage a fairly large project like this, you can be sure that time that would have been wasted on inefficient processes will be saved.

As well as being able to identify the needs of your site in a semiformal manner, you also have a good understanding of what will be involved in implementing these needs. Having a good grasp of what is required in order to complete the project then plays a vital role in how you build the project. Consequently, the main issues involved with building a site were covered, completing the reader's introduction to the world of e-commerce. So, for better or for worse, you have decided to join the fray and from here on, you will find new things to learn and put to work for you and your business. Let's get cracking...

2
Setting Up the Development Environment

The first chapter highlighted the fact that all development should take place on a copy of the website on a computer to which the public has no access. This computer was called the *development machine*, and is where most of your time will be spent getting everything right before transferring the more or less finished product to the live site. In order to be able to work effectively, and ensure that the development environment provides us with everything we need to be able to deliver our website, we need to find, download, and install the following software:

- **PHP**: PHP is the language in which osCommerce is written. Recently it has received a major upgrade and is now more or less a fully functional **Object Oriented Language**, with some very powerful features. PHP is widely used on the Internet for a multitude of different projects and is renowned for its ease of use. The current version of PHP is PHP5, which is what we will use in this book for our demonstration. However, you are welcome to use version 4 because this is what most Internet Service Providers use at present. The good news is that we will not have to delve deeply into programming code in order to build our site—osCommerce handles most, if not all the complex programming issues.

- **Apache**: This is the web server we will use to serve web pages during the development phase. Apache is the most popular web server on the Internet, with millions of live sites using it every day. In fact, as the Apache website says, it is *more widely used than all the other web servers combined.*

- **MySQL**: This is what we will use to store all the information required to keep the website running. Everything from customer details to product information and a host of other things will all be stored in the MySQL database. Keeping with the trend of popularity, MySQL is also the world's most popular bit of database software with over six million active installations worldwide.

The above three pieces of software all come separately, or they come combined in packages. Many people have found that it is easier to simply download a bundled package, which installs a standard distribution of PHP, Apache, and MySQL. Our recommendation is that you install each piece of software individually.

The most important reason for installing everything separately is that it is unlikely that you can foresee everything you will need in the future. Having a package installation severely limits the flexibility you have when it comes to doing things slightly out of the ordinary. Installing everything individually not only gives you more flexibility and control over your development environment, but it is also a great way to become acquainted with the software upon which you are about to base your business. Of course, it is your prerogative to choose, so we will also show how to get hold of, and install, everything using a package.

Once all the auxiliary software is in place, we can go about installing:

- **osCommerce**: It's difficult to say it better than the website, so here is what you need to know about it: *osCommerce is an online shop e-commerce solution under on going development by the open source community. Its feature packed out-of-the-box installation allows store owners to set up, run, and maintain their online stores with minimum effort and with absolutely no costs or license fees involved.*

For now, don't worry if you are not entirely certain about how each piece of software fits together, or how they produce a working online shop. Chapter 3 will give you a brief, high-level look at the technology you are using to build a business, and will give you a solid grasp of how everything is tied together behind the scenes. At the moment, we need to concern ourselves with setting everything up and ensuring we have a good platform for the development phase. This will involve making a few adjustments to each bit of software; for example, we will need to create a username and login for the MySQL database, which osCommerce can then use to gain access.

Because all these technologies can be utilized from either a Windows or a Linux-based computer, this chapter will cover installation of osCommerce on both operating systems. Installation and setup for Apache, MySQL, and PHP will only be covered for Windows because we trust that Linux hacks will have everything installed already (or will know how it is done)—on the off chance that you don't have everything installed, a quick glance over the instructions given on the site should suffice to get you on your feet.

Before we begin, however, there is one crucial bit of advice to be given:

> Ensure that your development machine has a good, preferably lightning fast, Internet connection, as you will be downloading a fair amount of software.

For those users who have already installed various bits of software, you might find it more expedient to skip whatever sections you do not need, going over only those that are of interest. As well as providing information on installation, this chapter will also have a troubleshooting section at the end to address many of the most common errors associated with the setup process for osCommerce—advice on troubleshooting for each individual piece of software will be given in their respective sections.

Downloading Software

The method used to obtain any bits and pieces of software you may need is pretty much standard from company to company. Remember that it is in a software producer's best interest to make things as easy as possible for their clients to download and install software; otherwise they leave a gap for someone else to improve on their process. Because the best way to make things easy to understand is by providing a logical and consistent approach to obtaining their software, you will find that for more or less anything you want to get hold of, the following steps will apply:

1. Go to the producer's site.
2. Find the download page.
3. Download the software.
4. Unpack the software or run the executable, depending on the method of installation.
5. Install the software.
6. Configure your installation.
7. Test your setup.

Mostly this is the procedure followed, though not all the time. As an exercise in getting to know your way around your development environment, you might want to read over the next section, and then try to install and set up MySQL by yourself rather than follow along step by step. Admittedly, this is the slower route, but any type of exposure to this type of usage will benefit you in the coming days, weeks, or months. Ideally, by the time you get to install osCommerce, you should be familiar with the process and able to do it without the use of this text—apart from maybe the troubleshooting section, but we hope it won't come to that.

MySQL

The MySQL homepage can be found at `http://www.mysql.com/`, and it is recommended that you take some time to look over their site and learn about the MySQL project. Remember that all this work is being done to provide us with totally free software, which is made to the same standards as any commercial software—some would even contest that it is in fact better than any available commercial software.

One thing that should be noted is that we won't be using the latest beta version of the software advertised on the site. A beta version is a well-tested, trial version that has *not* been formally released to the market as the finished product. Often there are still changes to be made in the beta version before it can be considered a stable release. For our purposes, the latest stable release (MySQL 4.1) should be more than ample to provide us with everything that we, and osCommerce, need. Incidentally, if version 5.0 is out as a stable release by the time you read this book, feel free to make use of that as it won't affect the site adversely in any way.

The latest stable release for whatever platform you are working on can be found in the downloads section at `http://dev.mysql.com/downloads/mysql/4.1.html`. Please look closely at which distribution you require before downloading it. The following screenshot shows the different options you will be faced with when downloading MySQL for Windows—if you are using a different platform, for example Mac OS, then simply scroll down to the options presented for that operating system.

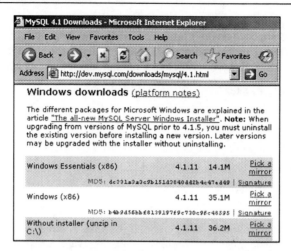

Notice that there are three options presented here, with the first one being substantially smaller than the other two. For our purposes, the Windows Essentials (x86) option is the one we want. The Essentials package is being pushed by MySQL as the recommended one because it is flexible, smaller, and provides everything that a standard MySQL setup does. Feel free to browse the link given in the paragraph below the Windows downloads heading for more information.

Click Pick a mirror and then either fill out the form presented or go straight to the downloads section. A mirror site is simply a replica of the original site, and is held on a server in another part of the world. The reason for this is to speed up your download time; if everyone wanted the same bit of software from the same server, it would be a fairly long wait before everything came through. So, pick a mirror to use—MySQL will probably suggest one that is closest, but not necessarily the fastest—and go ahead and download. Notice that you are presented with an option to download via HTTP or FTP. Either of these will do, and won't really affect anything since they are simply the different protocols, which, in this case, are simply used to deliver the requested file.

Depending on your security settings, you will be asked if you want to run the executable file from MySQL, which is in charge of overseeing your installation. Click Run in order to set the download in motion. You now have to wait for the MySQL files to be transferred across to your machine. If you have a fast internet connection, you might consider skipping to the next section to begin downloading PHP at the same time. Otherwise, it's time for a quick coffee break while you wait…

Installing MySQL

Once the package has been downloaded, it is time to install everything. Clicking Run (again) will bring up the start page of the step-by-step installation procedure. Click the Next button to bring up the first list of choices and choose the Typical option, which should be selected by default and is sufficient for our purposes. MySQL will now inform you of where it intends to install—this will be c:\Program Files\MySQL\MySQL Server 4.1\ (assuming you are installing the same version). Carry on with the installation process; there is nothing too complicated here, so we don't need to discuss it in too much depth.

At some stage, you will be asked whether you want to create a MySQL.com account. Whether you choose to sign up or not, your setup will not be affected. The final screen will inform you that the setup wizard has completed its task and gives the option to configure your server as shown here:

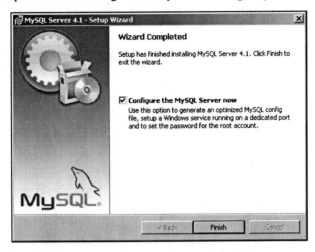

Make sure that the option is checked, as there *are* some configuration tasks that we need to perform in order to prepare for using osCommerce later. Clicking the Finish button will bring up the Server Configuration Wizard, which we will now run through quickly.

The first option presented in this wizard is whether to perform a standard or detailed configuration. Click Standard Configuration and then Next. The next window should be set up as shown in the next screenshot—it is not entirely necessary to have the Bin directory entered into the Windows PATH environment variable, but at a later stage, you will be thankful for it. Making the Bin directory available for Windows to use, via the PATH variable, allows you to execute MySQL programs from the command line without having to actually be in the Bin directory on the command line—useful if you want to test or run commands at any stage (and this will help you with our installation behind the scenes... it's really a sneaky move):

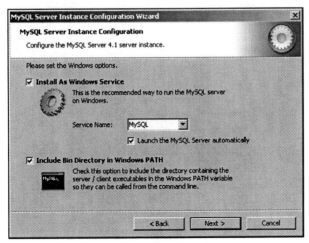

Click Next once you have emulated the above window. The next part is pretty important in terms of how MySQL is implemented and integrated into the osCommerce application. What we want to do here is create a *root* account, which you will be using as the administrator of the database. A root user is also known as a super user, with the power to do pretty much anything, so make sure you enter a password that is memorable and secure:

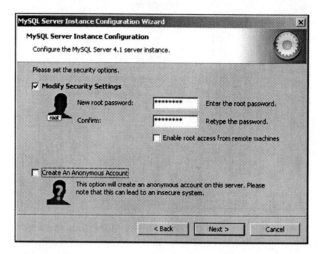

Unless you have a very good reason to enable access from a remote machine, leave the option unchecked, as it is a potential security threat. Also, notice that the option to create an anonymous user account has not been checked either. An anonymous user account means that your database can be accessed without a username and password, which is obviously not secure. Of course, if you are certain that your machine will not be used by potentially malicious users, you can go ahead and create an anonymous account for testing purposes. Once that is done, click Next to bring up the next window, and click Execute.

You should receive the following message on success:

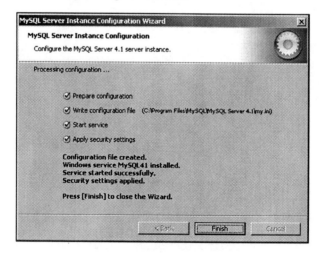

Click Finish and that's it... all done! You now have a working MySQL installation, ready to go. Of course, the first thing we need to do is verify that it is in fact working.

Testing MySQL

What do we know so far about MySQL from the installation? Well, we know that we have a root account with a password, which we have just set. What else? Recall that we were quite sneaky and told the MySQL installer to place the Bin directory in the Windows PATH variable. This is very good news because it makes it easy to test whether the server is up and running from anywhere on the command line.

If you go to the Start menu at the bottom left hand corner of your screen and open up the options therein, you should be able to see that a new program has been added to the list presented there. Click MySQL and follow the options to open the MySQL Command Line Client. This will open up a command line that will prompt you for your password. Enter the very same one you set during the installation in order to bring up the mysql> prompt, which lets you know that you are now able to run commands against your MySQL server.

Since we want to quickly ensure that everything is going according to plan, type in the following at the prompt:

```
mysql> use mysql
```

This command causes MySQL to connect to the mysql database, which holds all the tables required for administering MySQL. Since we certainly don't want to use the root account when connecting from osCommerce, we are going to create a somewhat less privileged user to do the dirty work for us. Obviously, if you have gotten this far, then your installation is working and we are merely preparing for what's to come.

Enter the following command at the prompt, substituting in whatever values for the username and password you wish—in this instance, we have chosen the username oscommerce (which is pretty easy to remember given the purpose it is to be used for) and the password as password:

```
mysql> insert into user values (
    -> 'localhost',
    -> 'oscommerce',
    -> Password('password'),
    -> 'Y','Y','Y','Y','Y','Y','Y'
    -> 'N','N','N','N','N','N','N','N','N','N', 'N',
    -> 'N','N','N','N','N','N','N','N','N','N');
```

Once that is done, your command window should look like this:

Don't fret if you are not sure what all the Ys and Ns are for (they simply grant or deny certain privileges), and don't worry about the warnings, they will not affect anything. Suffice to say that all we have done in the process of testing our installation is created a user who does not possess all the privileges of a super user. This is very important, as you will discover later on when we talk about ensuring that our application is secure.

> A good rule of thumb is to give users or programs only enough privileges to complete their intended tasks, and no more.

This is pretty much all you need to know for now, as osCommerce takes care of everything else. Of course, it is recommended that you play around a bit to familiarize yourself with everything. Chapter 3 will be useful in this regard, as it will paint a picture of how everything works together behind the scenes. As part of that, we will take a very brief high-level view of how the MySQL relational database management system works. Don't worry; it won't be a total bore, and you will be a far more formidable osCommerce developer once you have a solid grasp of your software.

You might also wish to take a quick look over Chapter 10 on *Tools, Tips and Tricks* because it highlights the use of the phpMyAdmin tool, which can be used to make the task of administering your MySQL database a breeze. For now, though, our MySQL requirements are pretty basic, and using the MySQL command line client, as we have done, is a useful tool for learning MySQL, so we need not worry about downloading and using it just yet.

PHP

Conventionally, Apache is installed before PHP. However, it will make no difference to us to install PHP now, and even makes the chapter easier to follow as we can then deal with the Apache installation and configuration in one place without having to jump around. The PHP homepage is `http://www.php.net/` and contains absolutely everything you need to know about PHP, from the various projects they have on the go, to the downloads, user groups,

Unlike MySQL, we are going to download the `.zip` file instead of the `.msi` file as shown here (if you do not currently have a utility to handle ZIP files, check out `http://www.winzip.com/downwzeval.htm` and download the trial version of WinZip. Alternatively, you can always use Google to search for a free ZIP file utility):

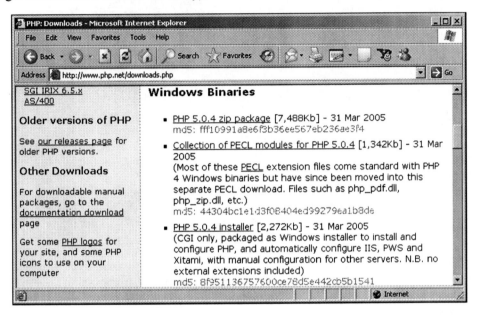

Click PHP 5.0.4 zip package to open a list of mirrors to choose from. Once you have done so, download the package, and sit back and relax while you wait.

Installing PHP

Once the ZIP file has downloaded, you will need to extract it to a suitable folder. In this case, something like `c:\PHP5` will do. Now we come to a slightly tricky bit! In order to give your system access to the relevant DLL files (a DLL file is a library file, which is used to provide functionality), we have to add the path of your PHP installation to the PATH environment variable. In order to add this file path to the PATH variable, you need to access your System Properties folder in the Control Panel.

Once you have located the System Properties window, you will notice several different tabs. Select the Advanced tab and click on the Environment Variables option. This will bring up a new window, which will show all the system and user variables that are in use. Scroll down the list of system variables until you see Path. Select this and then click Edit. This will bring up the variable in a new window and you can add the new pathname to the end of the variable (remember to insert a semicolon before the new PHP path value). Once that is done, you should have something that looks like this:

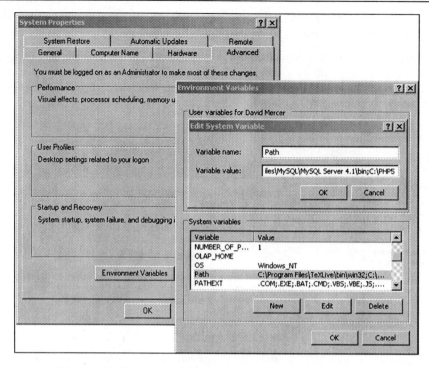

It is of course possible to edit the Path variable from the command line, but for our purposes, doing things this way is perfectly fine. The next thing is to configure the php.ini file.

Configuring PHP

Take a look in the PHP main directory. You will notice that there are two php.ini files—php.ini-dist and php.ini-recommended. Copy the php.ini-recommended file to your WINDOWS directory and rename it to php.ini. Now we have to open the file to do a bit of editing—don't worry; this won't take too long!

Here are the changes you should make to the new php.ini file in order to set things up in line with what we will be using PHP for. There is a brief discussion about why we are making these specific changes, but don't worry if you still don't understand why we are doing this for the moment; it will become apparent as we proceed:

Default value	Changed value	Description
display_errors = Off	display_errors = On	This forces PHP to report all errors it encounters to the Internet browser, allowing you to check the cause of problems. This setting should be set to off for a live site, as it could be a potential security threat.

Default value	Changed value	Description
register_globals = Off	register_globals = On	This setting is set to off by default; we need to set it to on in order to work with osCommerce. Global variables, in this case, are used to preserve information or state between page requests.
;include_path = ".;c:\php\includes"	include_path = ".;c:\PHP5\includes"	This allows PHP to access the important files stored in the includes folder. Remember to remove the leading semi-colon as this uncomments the line and allows PHP to read it.
extension_dir = "./"	extension_dir = "C:\PHP5\ext"	Extensions are used to work with different programs or software. We need this directory to be available for PHP since, among other things, it is needed to work with MySQL.
;extension=php_mysql.dll	extension=php_mysql.dll	We need to tell PHP that we will be working with MySQL; so we have to uncomment this line.
SMTP = localhost	SMTP = your.smpt.server	The ability to send emails from your test server is a huge advantage while trying out mail functions. Determine the SMTP server that is available for your computer. You can do this by looking at your account properties in Outlook if you have it.
;sendmail_from = me@example.com	sendmail_from = your@emailaddress.com	This setting is not critical, but useful for determining where emails are coming from when they are being sent from your server.

Since the php.ini file is a simple text file, you can edit it from whichever text editor you feel comfortable with. Simply perform a search for all the terms in the *Default value* column of the previous table, and convert them to the terms in the *Changed value* column. Be very careful when doing this, because some of the changes are quite small. For example, in the third row of the table, you will notice that there is no longer a semicolon present in the *Changed value* column. As mentioned, this is because semicolons are used to comment out lines of text in the .ini file so that PHP doesn't read those lines at all and skips the setting.

You will notice that some of the file paths changed from php to PHP5. This is because we want the new paths to point to the installation we have just downloaded. If you've installed everything to a directory other than PHP5, then you should make the appropriate changes instead.

Save the changes once you have completed the editing, and viola, we are finished here. Let's move on to the Apache section for the meantime. We will be able to test the PHP installation a lot easier once Apache is up and running.

Apache

Having gone through the entire process for installing MySQL and PHP, you should have a fairly good idea of what is coming next barring cosmetic differences. The Apache foundation actually has a number of excellent projects on the go, and you are urged to check out its homepage at http://www.apache.org/. At the top left-hand side of the page, there is a link entitled HTTP Server, under the Apache Projects title link. This is what we are after; so click on that to go to HTTP server project home page. Browse around to obtain any documentation or information you require. You will also be able to get through to the downloads page at http://httpd.apache.org/download.cgi..

At the time of writing, the latest stable release of Apache was Apache2.0.53, and this is the one that we will use. Obviously, you are free to choose whichever stable version is the latest at the time of reading. You know the drill... click on the download link of your choice, and click Open when prompted. It is recommended that you choose the .msi file instead of the .zip file if at all possible, as this will allow for a fast and fairly flexible installation—just like MySQL!

It's time to crank up the coffee machine or take a lunch break as the file downloads—of course, if you are lucky enough to have a high-speed connection, then a few minutes is all you will have to wait.

Installing Apache

This process is also similar to the one used for MySQL since they both make use of the MSI, or Microsoft Installer. There are a few differences which we will need to work through, however. Once the package has downloaded and you have clicked on Run to start the installation procedure, you will be faced with a license page (which you must agree to) and an information window that you can browse over. The next page, however, requires us to make a few entries as shown here:

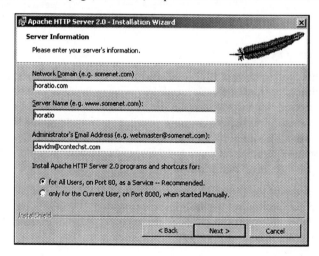

Since this is going to be a test server run only for our development machine, the network domain is not particularly important. If you are developing as part of a network and want others to have access to your pages, then you will need to enter your network domain name here. Otherwise, give your Apache web server a name, and supply it with a valid email address that can be used to pass you emails in the event of errors and such. The previous figure shows the settings used on the demo site's development machine.

The next two windows are familiar to us now. Simply select the Typical setup option and Next, followed by Next, and finally Install. If you have not already had enough coffee, it is time to take another break while the installation wizard does its business. Once this installation is complete, you should have a working Apache server.

Configuring Apache to Work with PHP

Initially, Apache has no way of knowing how you want it to interact with PHP. In order to get them on 'speaking terms', you need to navigate to the httpd.conf file in the conf folder of your Apache installation—most probably at c:\Program Files\Apache Group\Apache2\conf\—and add the following lines at the bottom of the "load modules" section. (By this I mean the DSO support section, but just look for a list of LoadModule statements and you'll be in the right place.):

```
LoadModule php5_module "c:/PHP5/php5apache2.dll"
AddType application/x-httpd-php .php .phtml .html
```

Once that has been added, save the file and close it. The next bit is very, very important!

> You need to restart the Apache server in order for any changes to take effect.

The server only picks up its settings from the configuration file on start up, and once it is running, it won't read it again. So, take a look at your system tray located at the bottom right of your screen, which shows the programs that are active at the moment. There you will notice the 🔲 icon, indicating that the Apache server is active.

Right-click on this icon and click on the Open Apache Monitor option. This will bring up—you guessed it—your Apache monitor, which lists the various things you can do with the server. Since we need to restart it, click on the Restart option, and after a short delay, you should have a screen that looks like this:

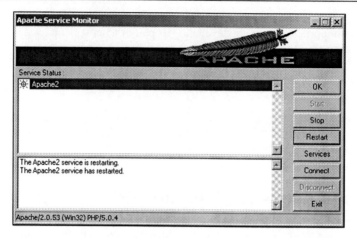

This time round, the Apache server will have picked up the modifications that we have just made to the `.conf` file, and should be geared for action. Try it out!

Testing Apache and PHP

Once the installation and configuration procedure is finished, it is time to see whether you are able to access web pages served by your brand new Apache server. The simplest way to do this is to open up a web browser such as Internet Explorer and navigate to `http://localhost/`. If you see the following page, then Apache is working just fine:

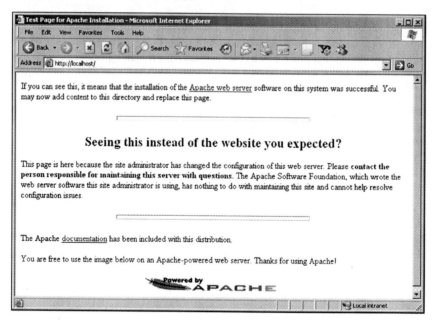

That's a relief, of course, but the big hurdle is yet to come. We now need to see whether we can serve up a PHP page. In order to do that, we will create a simple PHP page and place it into the document root of the server's directory. In your Apache directory structure, look for the htdocs folder, usually under c:\Program Files\Apache Group\Apache2\. Open this up, and in it place the following code file, entitled test.php:

```php
<?php
    echo "Good day! The date is:<br><br><b>";
    echo strftime('%A');
    echo strftime('%d');
    echo strftime('%B');
    echo strftime('%Y') . "</b>";
?>
```

If you look at the above file, you will notice that there is a <?php tag, followed by some commands, followed by a ?> tag, which tells the server that what lies in between the tags is PHP code. It is not important to know exactly what is happening here at the moment, since this will all be discussed in more detail in the next chapter. What is required at this junction is that you understand that we are utilizing PHP in order to output information to our browser, and so, if we get the desired output and don't come across any errors, then our PHP code is being handled correctly.

Now go back to your browser and enter http://localhost/test.php. You should find that you get similar results to those shown in the next screenshot:

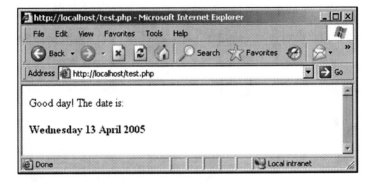

All done! If everything has gone smoothly, then you are *almost* ready to move on to installing osCommerce. Almost? Well, we know that Apache is serving PHP pages, and we know that MySQL works, but we still need to test whether all three work together—with a little luck, our rather meticulous setup process will ensure success. We'll quickly finish off this section with a short troubleshoot, before testing the entire installation.

If you have run into some problems, then the following section should hopefully be of some use. Of course, we can't cover every little possibility in this problems section, but remember that open source software often has great community support, so it is definitely worthwhile going back to the sites to look through forums and FAQs and any other literature that is made available. If you still can't find what you need, then get onto a list or forum and ask someone or take a look at Appendix A.

Why Won't the Darn Things Work?

If instead of the Apache welcome page you received a 'page not found' error or something similar, then the first thing to do is ensure that your Apache service is in fact running. If the little Apache icon in your process tray is missing or does not have the green arrow, then this is the reason. You can start the Apache service from the Start menu in Windows—it will usually be held under the main heading option of Apache HTTP Server 2.0.53 (depending on the version you are using); from there you will need to navigate to Control Apache Server and then click on the Start option to get things up and running.

You will notice that there are a host of options under the main heading in here too, allowing you quick access to the `httpd.conf` file among other things. It is recommended that you play around with this to familiarize yourself with it.

Assuming you have managed to get the Apache welcome page to display, the next problem you might encounter is a blank page when you attempt to run your first PHP file. If this happens, then it means that `.php` files are not being properly handled by Apache and that you should check that you have modified the `httpd.conf` file as per the instructions. Make sure the following line suits your installation exactly:

```
LoadModule php5_module "c:/PHP5/php5apache2.dll"
```

In other words, you should be able to find the `php5apache2.dll` file when you actually look in the `c:\PHP5` folder. If you don't find this file in the `c:\PHP5` folder, then you may have installed PHP in another directory. Find out where you have installed PHP and modify your settings to suit your installation.

Testing Everything Together

To ensure that we can access a MySQL database from a PHP program, which is served over the Apache web server, we need to write a short program that attempts to access the database. If you are confused as to why we need to perform this one final test, remember that osCommerce itself uses PHP code and a MySQL database to provide us with a web-based application. So, if we can set things up so that we can access MySQL from PHP, then we can be confident that the installation of osCommerce will be likely to succeed.

At any rate, I am sure you are all exhausted at all the set up that has gone in here, so I will simply provide you with a little file entitled `db.php`, which looks like this (remember to substitute the correct username and password, which you set up in the MySQL section earlier):

```php
<?php
$conn = mysql_connect("localhost", "oscommerce", "password");
$result = mysql_list_dbs($conn);

while($db_data = mysql_fetch_row($result)) {
        echo "<b> $db_data[0]</b><br>";
        }
?>
```

There is no cause for concern if you don't understand this code. Simply put this file in the `htdocs` folder in the Apache directory structure, and then navigate to it using your browser. Assuming that everything is set up correctly, you should receive the following output showing you what databases currently present:

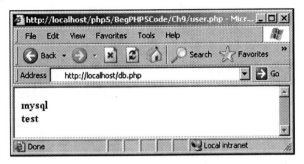

If this has worked, then you have no worries and can skip straight ahead to the installing osCommerce section. However, if there are problems, you will need to sort them out before continuing. The following section may prove valuable if you are a bit stuck.

Why Won't the Darn Things Work Together?

There are two likely errors that could arise at this stage. These errors occur because of entirely different reasons, and it is important to recognize which of the two types you have encountered if you are to isolate the problems effectively. Let's go over the less serious error first—an 'access denied' error. It usually results in a message like this:

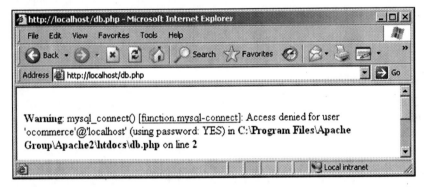

Why have I called this a *less serious error*? After all, my program is still not working! Well, the reason is this: in order for there to be an access *denied* message, PHP, Apache, and MySQL must all have communicated together in order to *attempt* to gain access to the database. This is great news, because it means the installation and setup have worked, even if this particular program has not. In order to solve this type of problem, you need to take a look at the line of code that reads:

```
$conn = mysql_connect("localhost", "ocommerce", "password");
```

Make sure that the username and password are precisely those which you gave when you set up a new user for MySQL. In this case, you should be able to spot the error—there was a typo in the username, changing it from oscommerce to ocommerce. If you read the error message in the screenshot, you will see that access was denied for user ocommerce (instead of what we intended to write: oscommerce). Simply ensuring you have the right connection parameters should sort this out.

Now onto the second type of error, which unfortunately is somewhat more serious. If you got lumped with an unfriendly screen telling you that the `mysql_connect()` function was undefined, as shown in the following screenshot, then the problem is that MySQL is not incorporated into the setup properly:

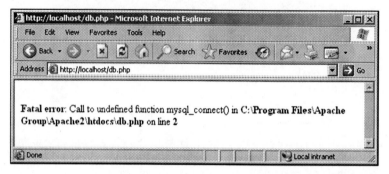

In order to rectify this, you need to go back to the `php.ini` file and check that you have uncommented the `php_mysql.dll` extension. In the old days, this problem was also caused by a missing `libmysql` file, but since MySQL's `bin` directory is automatically added to your PATH variable, this is no longer a problem.

If you have found that you cannot solve these errors by any of the means presented, then your first step is to hit the lists and forums on the individual technology's site. Google is also a useful tool here—type in the words you feel are most relevant to your problem, for example, mysql php installation problem, and see what you get.

Downloading and Installing a PHP, Apache, and MySQL Package

If you don't want to go to the trouble of installing everything individually, then there are a few bundled packages available on the Web for free download, instead. However, for the purposes of this chapter, we will use the PHP Triad option provided by SourceForge at `http://sourceforge.net/projects/phptriad/`. Navigate to this page in your browser and then scroll down until you get to the Latest File Releases section, and click on the Download link in the phptriad row. Select the download file, and then choose a mirror to start downloading. Once the .exe file is safely on its way, you can put your feet up by the fire and have a cup of coffee while you wait for it to download.

Once it has downloaded, run the executable. The first thing you will need to do is read the license agreement and ensure you agree with everything it says. Assuming you do, click I Agree to continue. PHP Triad will then begin its setup, and once it is completed, you can click the Close button.

With this done, notice that you now have a new folder called apache in your c:\ drive. This is where everything has been installed, and the htdocs folder in this directory is the *document root*, from where all the web pages will be served from. The last thing you need to do before installation can be considered complete is to read the `PHPTRIADreadme.txt` file, which you will find in the apache directory. That is all there is to it! An attractive option, to say the least, from the point of view of ease of installation.

Testing PHP Triad

Well, despite how easy downloading and installing this package has been, we can't take for granted that it is working. So, first things first:

1. Go to the Start menu and navigate to the new PHPTriad option.
2. Go to Apache Console, and click the Start Apache option.
3. Navigate to `http://localhost/` in your web browser and ensure you have the following welcome message:

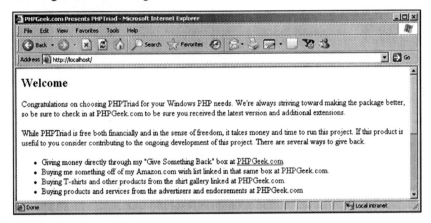

This means that the Apache setup is working perfectly.

4. Next open `http://localhost/phpinfo.php`, and you should see a formatted list of all the PHP-related settings in your setup, like this:

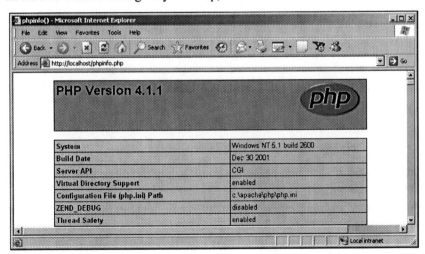

This confirms that PHP is also working perfectly.

5. To confirm that we can run MySQL commands using PHP, open a text editor and enter the following code:

```php
<?php
$conn = mysql_connect("localhost", "root", "");
$result = mysql_list_dbs($conn);

while($db_data = mysql_fetch_row($result)) {
        echo "<b> $db_data[0]</b><br>";
        }
?>
```

6. Save the file as db.php in the folder c:\apache\htdocs\.

7. Navigate to http://localhost/db.php from your web browser. If all is well, you should see the following output:

This screenshot shows you the databases that are present currently in your MySQL relational database-management system, and also means that we are able to run PHP/MySQL commands, which is precisely what will be needed by osCommerce a little later on. Since everything is handled for us in the setup, there is very little that can go wrong here, so we will not have a troubleshooting section. If, for some reason, you are experiencing difficulties, then employ the usual methods already mentioned and check the technology's homepage for FAQs or forums, or perform a relevant search or two on Google for more information.

Since our recommendation is for a separate installation of all the technologies, the rest of the book will assume individual installation instead of this package installation. However, you should have very little to no difficulties in following along with the rest of the material.

Downloading and Installing osCommerce on Windows

By this stage, your platform should be ready and waiting for osCommerce. A quick recap of what is needed in order to continue from here is as follows:

- **Apache:** Used to serve web pages. Specifically, you should be able to verify that Apache is correctly serving PHP pages that contain executable PHP code.

- **PHP:** Installed and working correctly. This can be tested through Apache. More specifically, you should have the MySQL extension enabled and should be able to repeat the results of the execution of the db.php file given in the *Testing Everything Together* section.

- **MySQL:** Installed and working with an administrator and a test user (in our case called `oscommerce`) for development purposes.

If you are lacking any of these three criteria at this stage, you must go back to the relevant section in this chapter and ensure that you have everything correctly setup before continuing.

> Since many hosts have the three pieces of software installed as part of their hosting package, it is quite likely that they also come with the option to simply enable osCommerce on your domain. For example, the demo site's hosts provide an installation of osCommerce in their scripts library. It is obviously very easy to install osCommerce on your live site this way, but development then becomes a pain because you will have to do all your work over an Internet connection. For this reason, it is still imperative to have a development machine where you can work on your site.

With that said, you should all be familiar with the process for downloading and installing software, and so without further ado, we are going to head off to the osCommerce site and grab a copy for ourselves at `http://www.oscommerce.com/solutions/downloads`. At the time of writing, the current milestone is 2.2 and this is the version you should use unless the next milestone has come out in the interim. Which version you use won't make a huge difference with respect to the material in this book.

> It is strongly recommended that you also download the documentation from this page, since you will find it full of invaluable advice, hints, and tips.

Choose whether you would like to download osCommerce from Europe or the States by clicking on the relevant link, and save the download to your My Documents folder. Notice that the download itself is only about 1.4 MB, so it's unlikely that you will have time to go and have that all-important cup of coffee while you wait—unless you are on a particularly slow dial-up connection.

Installing osCommerce

Open up the ZIP file and extract the contents to your `c:\` drive. This creates a folder called `oscommerce-2.2ms2`. In this folder, you will notice a directory contained called `catalog`. Copy this directory across to your Apache web server's root directory, the `htdocs` folder. Now open up your web browser, navigate to `http://localhost/catalog/`, and click on the `index.php` page, which you will find among the other files and folders shown. You should see the following screen presented there once you have done that (notice that your browser has been redirected to a slightly different URL):

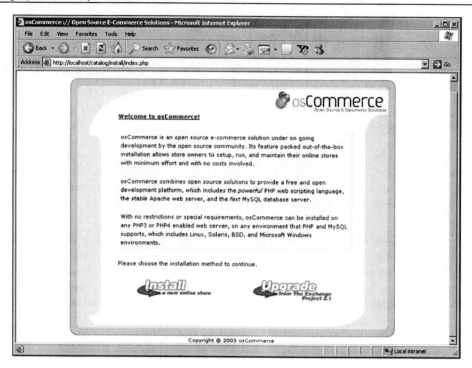

Since our hearts desire a brand new installation, we click on the left-hand option (Install a new online store) provided on the opening screen. This will bring up the next screen, which provides two options, both of which we want to ensure are selected before continuing:

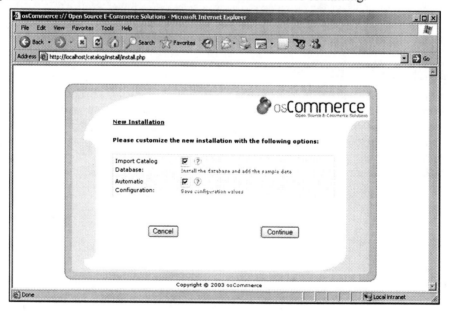

If your screen looks like the previous screenshot, then click Continue. The next page is important as it relates back to the settings we provided for MySQL earlier on in the installation procedure. Ensure that you correctly fill this out according to your set up. To give you a clue, here is how the test machine's settings were laid out:

Recall that the server was named Horatio earlier on in the game. This is because the host machine is called Horatio too. You should enter your host machine's name in here, and you can find this by going to System in the Control Panel and clicking on the Computer Name tab if you are not sure what it is already—if in doubt, use localhost, which should work fine.

Remember too that we tested MySQL by creating a username (oscommerce) and password (password) for use by osCommerce. Finally, we enter commerce_db as the name of the database we would like to use when osCommerce creates all the tables it needs within MySQL. Notice too that the Persistent Connections option is selected since we are not planning on sharing servers, but rather on developing on one machine only.

Finally, just to simplify our lives, we chose Session Storage to be maintained within the database as opposed to within files—there are both, pros and cons, to both methods of storage, but using the database is fine for our purposes.

Note that people who used the package installation can use the root username with a blank password for the meantime.

Click Continue once you are satisfied with your settings, and you should see a "success" message informing you of the following:

A test connection made to the database was successful.

All good and well! Next click Continue once again to actually get osCommerce to create your database. Once it is done, it will confirm success with another message, and clicking Continue again will bring up the next step in the installation, which will display some information about your server. Please ensure this is all correct—the test machine setup looks like the following screenshot at this stage:

Note that at this stage we don't need SSL Connections to be enabled, so we can leave that unchecked for the meantime. Click Continue once you are happy that the WWW Address and Webserver Root Directory are OK, and point to where your actual catalog directory can be found on your web browser (WWW Address) and on your file system (Webserver Root Directory). Keep clicking through the remaining pages ensuring you are happy with any of the settings mentioned—there is nothing particularly important from here on until you get to the final page:

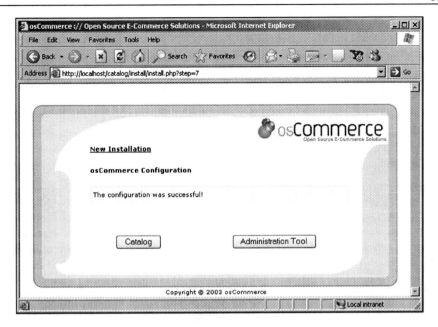

You are then presented with a "successful installation" page, which will give you two options (as shown in the previous screenshot): the first is to view the Catalog, and the second is to view the Adminstration Tool. We will look at these two options in the next chapter, and indeed both will play an important role throughout the book.

Configuring osCommerce

With osCommerce installed now, one might be forgiven for breathing a huge sigh of relief because at last everything has been done and that the universe is unfolding as it should. Of course, I urge you to click on the Catalog option on the final installation window in order to get a reality check. You will no doubt find that the page that is brought up spawns some horrid looking warnings before actually displaying anything, which could be mistaken for an online shop, much like this:

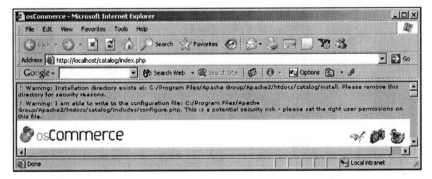

Don't worry, though! We'll quickly talk about how we can make these warnings disappear, and in the process, help secure our test environment from accidental and unintentional changes. To begin with, the first warning tells us that the install directory exists within the catalog folder, and we are asked to remove this for security reasons. Well, OK! They're the boss. Navigate to the install directory in Windows explorer and remove it from the catalog folder.

Note that you may have to rename the install folder before moving it, since there is a file called install already present in the oscommerce-2.2ms2 folder.

Once that is done, we can turn our attention to the next warning, which tells us that we have a potential security risk in the form of a writeable configuration file. Of course, we never, ever want anyone other than ourselves to be able to write to any configuration file on our own system, so this warning is certainly an important one.

Navigate over to the configure.php file in Windows explorer and right-click on it—you can find the file by reading the warning given in the browser; it will tell you the file path of the file in question. This will bring up a pop-up menu, from which you should select the Properties tag. When the Properties window opens up, you will notice (towards the bottom) an Attributes section, which gives the option of making the file Read-only or Hidden. Select Read-only, click Apply, and close the window.

With those two configuration changes made to your osCommerce installation, I'll wager that everything is now in pretty good working order; refresh your catalog index page in your browser or navigate to http://localhost/catalog/index.php if you have closed it down already. You should now find that you are presented with a demonstration site, which is free of any warnings (for the meantime). The index page should look like this assuming everything is working properly:

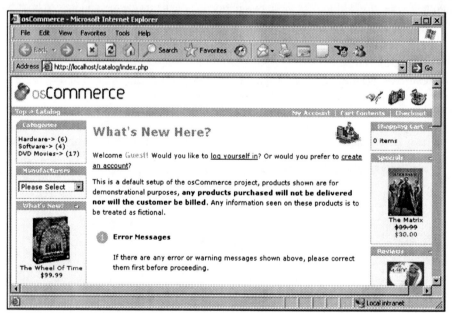

If this is the screen you have reproduced on your machine, then you can be certain that everything is shipshape and raring to go. Because osCommerce does most of its own setup, we shall not spend too much time testing everything at the moment. The only thing that is important to do is go back to MySQL and check for ourselves that the database has been set up properly. There is, however, a troubleshooting section at the end of this chapter, which will run through some of the more common problems that people encounter on the road to online success.

Before we do continue, though, you might well be curious to see what the administration tool looks like. If this is the case, either click the Administration Tool option given on the final page of the installation, or navigate to `http://localhost/catalog/admin/index.php`. In either case, you should see your admin tool, all shiny and new:

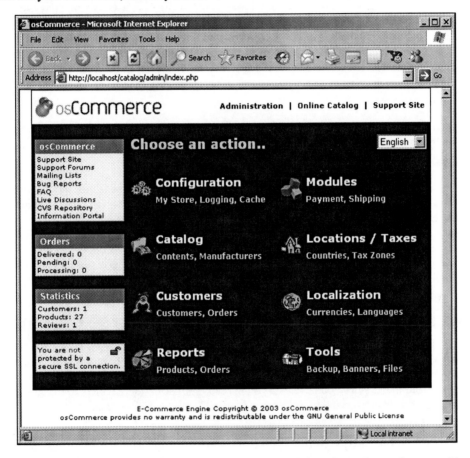

From here, you will be able to perform pretty much any administrative task your heart could desire. Everything is neatly categorized, very well laid out and intuitive to use. We will be looking at how to customize our site in Chapter 4, where we show how to use and find your way around this impressive tool. For now though, it is good enough to know that it is there ready for use.

Testing osCommerce

The following test is not really necessary to perform in terms of ensuring the wellbeing of the application. You might find it interesting though to run through it here because it will show you what osCommerce has done with MySQL behind the scenes. Open up a command-line window and type in the following command at the prompt:

```
C:\> mysql -u oscommerce -p commerce_db
password: ********
```

The word immediately following the -u in the above command should be the username you wish to log in to MySQL as, and the word following the -p is the name of the database you wish to connect to. MySQL will then prompt you for a password, so enter the user's correct password and you should find yourself given access to mysql. The fact that you can connect to this database alone should indicate that there *is* in fact a commerce_db database that can be connected to, so we already know that we have had some form of success. The thing to be curious about though is *what* has osCommerce done to the database? Let's find out by typing in the following at the mysql> prompt:

```
mysql> show tables;
```

You should see a whole list of tables that have been created. Further, you can see what is in any of the tables by issuing the following command:

```
mysql> select * from table;
```

Simply replace the word table in the above command with the name of the table (from the initial list) for which you would like to view the contents. This should demonstrate to you that during the setup phase, osCommerce was hard at work behind the scenes building the database (and populating it) so that we can pretty much begin adding and removing clients, products, or whatever we wish. Some of you may be getting nervous chills up and down your spine with visions of having to learn SQL code in order to add information to the tables. Never fear, osCommerce comes with the online administration tool for doing just that without having to learn SQL.

Downloading and Installing osCommerce on Linux

Of course, for this section of the chapter it is assumed that you have a working version of Apache, PHP, and MySQL already installed on you Linux box. If not, please visit the requisite homepages at http://www.apache.org, http://www.php.net, or http://www.mysql.com, and download a distribution from there. Once you have everything ready for osCommerce, then go to the osCommerce download page and grab a gzipped tarball from the download page at http://www.oscommerce.com/solutions/downloads.

When you have downloaded the correct distribution, you can unzip it with the following command:

```
> tar -xzf oscommerce-2.2ms2.tar.gz
```

This will create an oscommerce-2.2ms2 directory, from which you must copy the catalog directory across to your Apache web server's document root—usually at something like /usr/local/apache/htdocs/. The following recursive command will do this for you:

```
>   cp -R catalog /usr/local/apache/htdocs/
```

Next, navigate to the following URL in your browser (substituting localhost for whatever address is appropriate):

```
http://localhost/catalog/install
```

and follow the instructions given in the step-by-step installation process there. This will create your database and populate it with some dummy data, which you can play around with to familiarize yourself with the application. Once this setup process is complete, navigate to the index page of the catalog folder in your web browser. Check to see if there are any warnings given in pink backlighted text at the top of the page—if there are, then you will need to take note of these warnings and act on them appropriately. Please see the section that covers this topic for Windows, *Configuring osCommerce*, as your actions will be much the same again.

That's pretty much it! If you run into any problems, then please see the next section on troubleshooting, as it applies to osCommerce in general and is not specific to Windows or Linux machines.

Troubleshooting

Very little should have gone wrong during the setup process as outlined in this chapter. However, it is not beyond the realms of possibility that things do go amiss—hopefully due to something simple like a typo. One of the most frustrating problems can occur during the final stages in the setup of osCommerce. For example, you may have come across this:

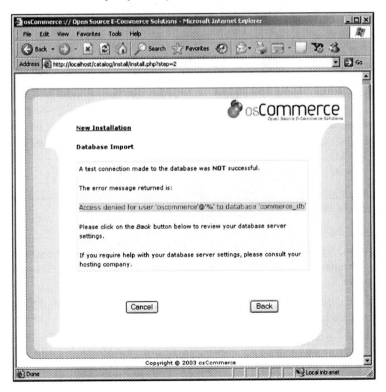

In this case, the first thing you need to do is click the Back button, check your settings and try again. If this problem persists despite you being absolutely sure that you have made no mistake, then simply refresh the window before trying again. If this still does not work, then it is OK to try to create the database as the adminstrator, in which case you would change the username and password to `root` and `<password>` and try again. If the latter option works, then the reason you were being denied access is that the user you were attempting to create the database with does not have sufficient permissions.

Again, if this does not work, then you need to go back to the *Installing MySQL* section and follow the instructions there to view the contents of the `user` table to ensure that you do have users and that they are using passwords. If this is set up fine, then you need to ensure that PHP and MySQL are *talking* nicely to each other by performing the test set out in the *Testing Everything Together* section earlier in this chapter.

Some of you may have also experienced the following difficulty when trying to access the administration tool for the first time:

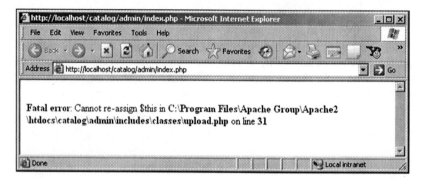

What's going on here? We certainly haven't done anything that would break the installation, so why isn't it working? The simple answer is that this may well be a bug! However, we are going to do something a bit sneaky, if not entirely naughty, and comment out the offending line by adding two forward slashes directly in front of line 31 of `upload.php` file. Go ahead and do that, using the file path given in the error message to locate the file. Once that is done, save the file and refresh your browser—you will find that your admin tool loads perfectly now.

Finally, if there are any niggling worries (or even larger worries) that have reared their ugly heads, then this is the course of action you should take:

1. Check the documentation.
2. Visit the osCommerce site, go to the knowledge base (`http://www.oscommerce.info/`) or forums (`http://forums.oscommerce.com`), and search for similar posts or problems.
3. View the bug list (`http://www.oscommerce.com/community/bugs`) to see if your problem is a reported bug.
4. If you can't find similar posts or problems, then try posting your queries on the forums, and ask someone in the community to give you a hand.

5. To supplement this, get on Google and try using relevant keywords to locate a similar problem, with hopefully a solution presented.

It may seem like a bit of a cop-out to give you a list of actions to take rather than present all the problems that may crop up. However, having a solid, robust approach for finding solutions to problems is infinitely more valuable than simply being given individual solutions to a problem. The above five points form a methodology that should help you solve *any* osCommerce-related problem you encounter ever—not just the ones that might be bugging you now!

Summary

By this stage you have a fully functional development platform, just waiting for the development that lies ahead in the coming days, weeks, and months. Having ensured that everything is not only installed, but also working properly, you can be confident that when the time comes to sit down and begin, you won't come across any unwanted surprises. The core technologies, PHP, Apache, MySQL, and osCommerce are all working together to provide a real-life environment, which will serve to slowly build and reproduce the live site as it is envisaged for your business.

Having also briefly discussed the various bits and bobs that could have gone wrong along the way, the main thing to remember in terms of troubleshooting is the five points presented at the end of the *Troubleshooting* section. These points provide a solid method for finding a solution to any problem, and not simply those concerned with installation and setup.

Armed with a solid plan of action for the development of the website according to our business needs, which were discussed and developed in Chapter 1, and equipped with a fully functional development machine, which was the subject matter of this chapter, we are now ready to move on to Chapter 3. Chapter 3 will give a brief, high-level overview of how all the interrelated technologies gel together to provide us with our online web-based retail facility. This may sound like a bit of a drag, but believe me, it is fundamentally important to how you as a site designer and developer mature and grow more confident in your abilities.

3

How osCommerce Works

I'm sure everyone is just itching to get started with osCommerce. You've got customers waiting, products to shift off the shelves, money to be earned, deals to be made, and a million other things that need to be dealt with. Why on earth, then, do we need a chapter on how osCommerce works? Why don't we jump straight ahead to the chapter on configuring osCommerce, or better yet, why not jump straight to data entry and manipulation? There are several answers to these questions, and the most important one is that I won't be comfortable if I know that there are thousands of business owners out there basing their livelihood on a technology that they don't understand. And *that's* my answer!

The answer you probably want, which is equally correct, is that by learning how to use osCommerce properly, you will become far more *efficient* and more importantly *good* at building your online retail site. In order to be efficient, you need to have a sound appreciation of how things work. Knowing how things work means that you can picture in your head the *type* of changes that you need to implement in order to effect the desired outcome.

What do I mean by this? Well, imagine that you have built your site and you notice one day that you could be making more money by advertising on your web pages. Off the top of your head, how would you go about doing that? Of course, no one expects you to know that at this stage, but if you have a good appreciation of how osCommerce works (both within your application and the community around it), then you will immediately be able to deduce where to begin and roughly what sort of cost the modification will incur in terms of time and effort. In other words, you will develop a *feel* for the technology, which is very important—this is after all part of your livelihood.

What else? Having a greater body of knowledge frees you up to experiment. Experimentation itself is a form of learning, so it is a bit of a self-fulfilling prophecy in that those who learn enough to experiment and play around with the technology are rewarded by the extra learning, which in turn allows them to experiment further. The upshot is elegantly described by the following: "*The more you know, the better your site!*"

Since it is fair to assume that everyone wants to create a retail site to the best of their individual ability, it is also fair to assume that you will need the information that will allow you to do the job with a bit of flair. This chapter then discusses all aspects that go into an osCommerce website, as well as all the issues that surround the building and maintenance of an online store. Specifically, we will look at the following details:

- osCommerce and the Internet—including PHP, HTML, and MySQL
- osCommerce architecture
- The online store
- The online community—including contributions, forums, knowledgebase, documentation, and bug and progress reports

Now don't be put off by the fact that we are going to talk about technology, among other things. We won't be fiddling around with too much code or anything. The purpose of this chapter is to help you to understand what is actually going on when your site is working. For example, when a user clicks on an item he or she wants to buy, how does the application know to add the item to the shopping cart? How does that information even get added into the system? How does the system know who is logged in? How does everything end up being nicely laid out, and is HTML solely responsible for the user interface? Basic questions like these will be answered over the course of this chapter without the need to run through reams of theory.

The technology and software side of osCommerce is really not the whole picture. Knowing how to use the online, community-based resources available to you is also an important aspect of osCommerce. Accordingly, we will look at how the osCommerce community plays a role, in the development in the *osCommerce Online Community* section. This section is especially important as it will play a large role in providing solutions to problems as well as providing off-the-shelf functionality—both of which you will use at some stage.

osCommerce and Internet Technology

To be able to give each aspect of a live website a fair look, we need to break down the overall picture into its constituent parts and look at each part individually. Before we do that, though, it is important to start at the broadest possible level and work our way down to the individual technologies that assist us in making our osCommerce site. With that in mind, the following diagram shows a basic view of how the Internet works:

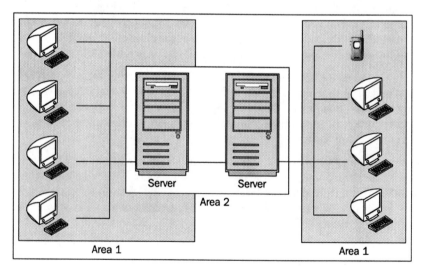

Thankfully, we don't have to concern ourselves with most of the details at this stage. It is enough for our purposes to know that in Area 1 of the diagram (with a grey background), computers (or even mobile phones and other devices) can connect to the Internet and can locate various files and data from wherever they need to. Communication between a user's laptop (or desktop) and Internet servers can occur in one of two forms; either **Hyper Text Transfer Protocol (HTTP)** or **File Transfer Protocol (FTP)**. Both are used to facilitate information exchange with servers, and you will no doubt come in contact with them in due course. More than likely, you have already used HTTP because this is the standard protocol used when visiting websites in general.

Area 2 is a fairly complex beast, which involves several different types of technologies working together to ensure that the packets of information being sent and received by machines all over the world reach their destination. This involves everything from the actual physical technologies such as laser, electricity, and radio waves, all the way through to routers and other devices used to control data flow. Thankfully, we don't need to know anything about the hardware on which all this runs, we don't need to know too much about the protocols used in order to facilitate data transfer, and we don't even need to know the physical location of our data.

What we do need to know is how osCommerce fits into this picture. Well, Area 2 in the diagram is where we should be looking. Physically, the PHP-based osCommerce files sit on a file system, which is provided by an **Internet Service Provider**—in the case of your development machine, the file system is simply your computer's file system (which is also in Area 1 since this is also where your browser is located). Other than occupying space on a server, osCommerce also requires access to a MySQL database, which may or may not reside on the same server as the PHP files themselves.

The online address of your particular file system is given by the domain, registered by you once you have decided on a suitable name for your retailer. Think of your domain name as a unique way of expressing the file system's address on the Internet. So for example, if the example site had a registered domain `contechstbooks.com`, then this URL would map to the index page of the example website. Users from all over the world would then simply have to type `http://www.contechstbooks.com/` in their browser, and the file system containing all the files that make up the website are located automatically by the various transport protocols and servers.

Of course, this is only scratching the surface. We have to take a closer look at how osCommerce, as a PHP-based application, is put to work.

osCommerce and PHP

In order to fully appreciate how osCommerce works, it is best to picture it in terms of how it deals with requests from a user. The correct way to think about any interaction between a user and your osCommerce application is in the form of requests and responses. In other words, whatever the user does (for example, click on a product thumbnail), the PHP application treats that action as a request, which may require some form of processing and then a response. In the case of clicking on a product thumbnail, the response might be to add the product to the user's shopping cart.

It is important at this stage to realize that all the processing taking place each time a user makes some form of request is handled by PHP. The only exception to this is if the user is clicking on a link, in which case there is no processing required and the link is simply followed by the browser. For every other possibility, the good people at osCommerce have written code to handle any eventuality.

The following diagram breaks the picture down into a more useful representation of an osCommerce application:

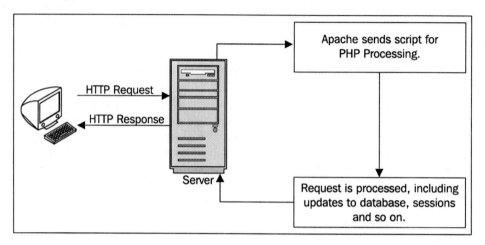

So, on the grand scale of things, whenever a customer does anything with your osCommerce site (hopefully like purchasing goods), here's what happens:

1. The relevant information is bundled off to the server in the form of an HTTP request. An HTTP request comes in two forms—either a GET or a POST. For our purposes, it is not important to understand how GET and POST work, as long as you understand that information can be captured from the user and sent to the server for processing.

2. The server receives the HTTP request and says, "*Ah! This is a PHP page that has been requested, so I need to send it off for processing by the PHP engine.*" The PHP page then gets processed and executed appropriately, and any actions that are required as a result of the user's request are performed.

3. Once that is done, an appropriate response is returned by the server to the user's browser, and the cycle continues.

The important points to remember here are that users interact with osCommerce through requests and responses to and from the server. All the processing is handled by PHP, which happens on the server side of the application—no processing is done on the user's computer. The exception to this rule is something like JavaScript, which is handled on the browser (or client) side—don't concern yourself with this for now.

Finally, since PHP is a complete, fully functional language in its own right, we are not going to attempt to specifically learn any programming in this book. However, it is strongly recommended that you do take the time to learn at least enough PHP to be able to recognize and hopefully understand what is happening in your osCommerce application in the event of any errors cropping up.

Of course, there are a few other technologies and languages that go into making up the final product, and we are going to look at all of those in more detail next.

osCommerce and HTML

We know now that PHP is responsible for the *meat* of the application—in other words, the heavy lifting and processing. But what is it that makes the site look nice? PHP is not responsible for the presentation of the site, so what is? In order for your browser to render the neatly laid out and colorful pages we are used to seeing everyday, it needs instructions on what goes where and what color to give everything. This is the domain of **Hyper Text Markup Language (HTML)**, and osCommerce is no exception in its use of HTML here.

Let's have a quick crash course on HTML before we go any further:

- **Simplicity**: From tables and frames to lists and images, as well as specifying fonts and styles, HTML is a convenient and readily understandable convention for web page creation and layout.

- **Platform independence**: HTML is platform independent, which makes sense if you think about it because the last thing you would want, as the builder of a website, is to have to cater for every different type of machine that could make use of HTML.

- **Tags**: HTML comes in the form of opening and closing tags, which tell your browser how to display the information enclosed within them. For example, the title of a page would be enclosed within the title tags like this: `<title>My Title Page</title>`. Notice that a forward slash is used to distinguish a closing tag from an opening tag.

- **Attributes**: Tags can have attributes, which can modify or define certain aspects of a tag's behavior. For example, the `size` attribute in the following HTML snippet defines the size of the font, `<font size="2">I have a font size of 2</font>`, when it is rendered in a browser.

- **Sections**: An HTML page is enclosed within `<html></html>` tags and is divided into `<head></head>` and `<body></body>` sections. The body tags enclose the bulk of the page and contain the information seen on the actual web page.

The following file, entitled `basic.html`, shows a very simple, but complete HTML web page. Make a copy of this file and save it in your document root as `basic.html`.

```html
<html>
  <head>
    <title>Basic HTML Page</title>
  </head>
  <body>
    This is a very basic <b>HTML</b> page!!
  </body>
</html>
```

Now navigate to it from your browser to see the result, which should be similar to the following screenshot.

Note that only the text contained within the body tags actually shows on the page and that we have used the <b></b> tags to make the word HTML appear in bold font. The title text is shown at the top-left corner of the browser window, which is where page titles generally reside.

Let's take a look at something straight out of osCommerce. The following code is an excerpt from the index page of the osCommerce catalog as it stands without modification:

```
<!doctype html public "-//W3C//DTD HTML 4.01 Transitional//EN">
<html <?php echo HTML_PARAMS; ?>>
<head>
<meta http-equiv="Content-Type" content="text/html; charset=<?php echo
CHARSET; ?>">
<title><?php echo TITLE; ?></title>
<base href="<?php echo (($request_type == 'SSL') ? HTTPS_SERVER : HTTP_SERVER)
. DIR_WS_CATALOG; ?>">
<link rel="stylesheet" type="text/css" href="stylesheet.css">
</head>
<body marginwidth="0" marginheight="0" topmargin="0" bottommargin="0"
leftmargin="0" rightmargin="0">
<!-- header //-->
<?php require(DIR_WS_INCLUDES . 'header.php'); ?>
<!-- header_eof //-->

<!-- body //-->
<table border="0" width="100%" cellspacing="3" cellpadding="3">
  <tr>
    <td width="<?php echo BOX_WIDTH; ?>" valign="top"><table border="0"
width="<?php echo
...
```

There are several interesting things to note about the HTML in this page. First, look closely at the second line of the code:

```
<html <?php echo HTML_PARAMS; ?>>
```

You will see that it contains opening and closing PHP tags (<?php and ?>). Everything between an opening and closing PHP tag is PHP code, and is processed by the PHP engine on the server. This is pretty nifty as it allows us to embed PHP code within our HTML in order to make dynamic pages. osCommerce uses this technique a lot, despite the trend in modern programming to separate out presentation code (HTML) and code that needs to be processed separately (PHP). As a result, you can expect to see many HTML tags mixed with PHP code when you modify your osCommerce pages.

Second, the following line mentions a "stylesheet" as part of the link tag:

```
<link rel="stylesheet" type="text/css" href="stylesheet.css">
```

What is a stylesheet? A stylesheet is basically used to define certain styles that you wish to use throughout your application. This is often important because you always want a consistent look and feel to your site, so you end up using the same styles repeatedly over all the pages of your site. Being able to write out a style once, in a stylesheet, and then reference it from your HTML file is a lot easier than writing out the style each time you need to use it in the HTML file.

We can see from the `href="stylesheet.css"` section that the name of the stylesheet in this particular instance is `stylesheet.css`. A snippet from that file is shown here:

```
...
BODY {
    background: #ffffff;
    color: #000000;
    margin: 0px;
}
...
```

What this section means is that whenever the BODY tag is encountered within the HTML file that references the stylesheet, the properties set between the braces are to be applied to that section of HTML. Incidentally, the rather odd-looking numbers next to the hash symbol are hexadecimal representations of color. You can test this by opening up `stylesheet.css` within the `catalog` folder and changing the `background` property to something like `#c0c0c0`. If you then visit the index page of your osCommerce installation, you should see something like this:

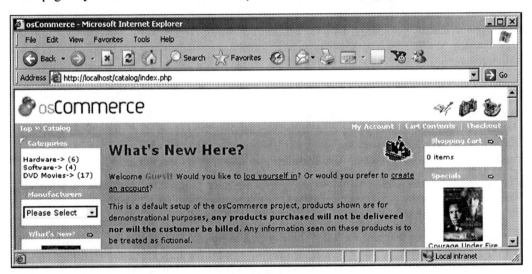

Notice how the background of the site is now a dark color as opposed to its original lighter tone. This should demonstrate the power of stylesheets, which make it really easy to modify and coordinate the presentation of your website. Not sure why? Well, visit any other page on the site, and you will see that all of them have been modified and not just the index page. So, changing a few simple characters has modified the look of every page on the site—pretty neat, huh?

Finally, the line:

```
<table border="0" width="100%" cellspacing="3" cellpadding="3">
```

mentions a table (with associated attributes). It is worth noting here that pretty much all layout work in HTML is done with the use of tables because they make it easy to divide a web page into manageable sections. osCommerce makes heavy use of tables, which is good news for us as tables are easy to manipulate. This means that adding and removing elements of a page really boils down to adding and removing elements of an HTML table. We will discuss this and all aspects of layout and design in Chapter 6.

That's all we need for the moment—you will put this information to good use in the future, once you decide how you want your site to look. The next thing we need to look over is how osCommerce uses and controls data.

osCommerce and MySQL

It is entirely likely that some of you have had a few sleepless nights already, trying to work out how to control your stock orders and keep track of all those important customers. So how does osCommerce get all of this done? Well, we know that the **presentation logic** (how the site looks) is handled by HTML and stylesheets, and that the **business logic** (the actual functionality of the application) is handled by PHP. So where does the actual accounting and storage take place? The answer is, "In the MySQL relational database management system."

That's quite a mouthful, but what does it mean for us? Luckily, we won't have to learn anything complicated about how data is organized into normal forms within a relational database. We also won't have to learn about foreign and primary keys and the relationships between tables, but what we do have to learn about is how the tables and information held within MySQL are affected by osCommerce during the course of the website's use.

There are only two or three methods of interaction with the database, which are of concern to us. One is the indirect use of data as a result of requests from the user. An example of this could be a user registering on the site for the first time. This would mean that behind the scenes, new customer records are created, containing all the pertinent information. The reason I call this use of data *indirect* is because the customer does not specifically need to be concerned with the fact that new database entries are being created—this complexity is hidden by osCommerce.

The second use is more direct in that we are specifically supplying information with the intent of modifying the database. This occurs when we use the administration tool to manually add or remove products, customers, or anything else we are working on.

We have already seen the third use when we opened a command-line prompt and interacted with MySQL directly in order to add a user to the user table. (Incidentally, using phpMyAdmin would fall under this category too). This type of interaction should really not be too common during the normal course of operation for an osCommerce site, because if the site is running correctly, then all the data can be dealt with through the administration tool instead of having to query directly using **Structured Query Language (SQL)**.

Talking of which, it is important to have a rough idea of how SQL works, because at some stage it is quite probable that you will need to look at how osCommerce is querying the database. More often than not, a basic SQL query must act upon columns or rows within a table to either retrieve information or modify the appropriate records. The best way to get a feel for something like this is in fact to see it in action. So let's take a look at some SQL queries that are used in osCommerce.

Navigate to `http://localhost/catalog/admin/customers.php` in your osCommerce installation and click the Edit button to bring up the customer-information form as shown in the following screenshot:

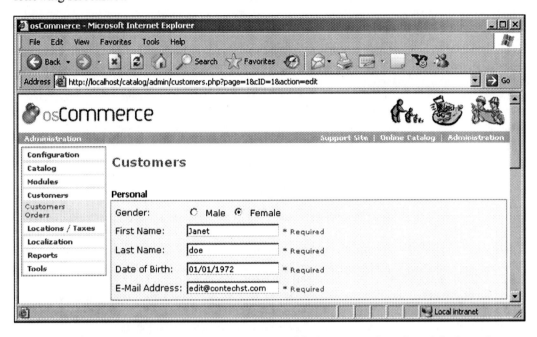

Change the values so that you can distinguish the modified customer from the original one (as you can see has been done in the previous screenshot) and click update. You will notice that the customer details have now been changed accordingly—we can check this by opening a command-line prompt and checking the database, as shown here:

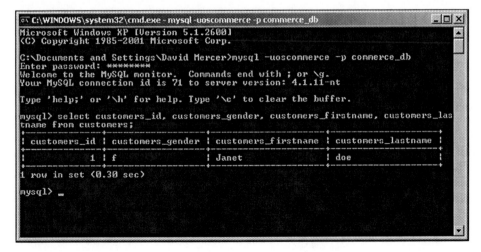

Notice in the previous screenshot that I had to log in initially using the oscommerce user and specify that I have to connect to the commerce_db database. Once MySQL verified the username and password, it connected with the commerce_db database so that I could query the database. Of course, in this case we are only interested in the customers table, since this is the one we suspect has been changed when we modified the John Doe customer, which was present by default.

In this instance we simply want to retrieve information from the database, so the SELECT statement is used, followed by a list of the column names that we want to include in the results, followed again by the name of the table we wish to pull the results from. From the data shown in the previous screenshot, we can tell that our actions in the administration tool have affected the data stored in the MySQL database, as we would expect. But how has this happened? We haven't had to issue any complex SQL statements ourselves, so osCommerce must have done it for us.

This is exactly what has happened, and the SQL statements that did all the work for us are the following (found on the customers.php page within the admin folder):

```
tep_db_perform(TABLE_CUSTOMERS, $sql_data_array, 'update', "customers_id = '"
. (int)$customers_id . "'");
tep_db_query("update " . TABLE_CUSTOMERS_INFO . " set
customers_info_date_account_last_modified = now() where customers_info_id = '"
. (int)$customers_id . "'");
```

These rather complex-looking statements are responsible for updating the information in the customers and customers_info tables using the UPDATE SQL query. The reason they look *funny* is because osCommerce has its own suite of PHP functions, which it uses to *build* SQL statements—examples of these PHP functions are shown here in tep_db_perform() and tep_db_query(). Without worrying too much about why the queries look different from the SQL we have seen so far, you should be able to recognize the following elements between the parentheses:

- An UPDATE SQL statement.

- A table upon which the SQL statement will act. (In this case, the table is denoted by the TABLE_CUSTOMERS and TABLE_CUSTOMERS_INFO constants. These constants are defined in other files.)

- A condition that tells MySQL to update only those rows where the customer ID is that of the current customer. (In both cases, the condition is given by the WHERE statement, although this is not so clear from the first statement.) This condition must be true before MySQL will execute the statement, otherwise there would be no control over which records were updated.

Due to the size and complexity of the osCommerce application, there are a lot more elements that go into running statements like this. For example, osCommerce has to check that any and all values entered into the textboxes in the administration tool are **legal values** (in other words, values that make sense). For now, though, it is important to simply realize this: if whatever action you take affects the information *about*, or contained *within*, osCommerce, it will involve the use of SQL queries which are run against the database—in much the same way as the example we have just discussed.

The osCommerce Architecture

Knowing a bit about the technologies associated with osCommerce is very useful. For example, if you were to come across an error saying that osCommerce was unable to connect to the database on a certain line of a certain file, you would know to check whether or not the database server is available and running, you would know to check the connection string and ensure that the username and password you are attempting to connect to MySQL with are valid, and finally you would know to check whether the user in question had sufficient permissions to connect to the database. You have learned all this simply by knowing a bit about how everything is laid out. Imagine being stumped by an error like that when you are not even sure what a database is.

Don't confuse this knowledge with actually knowing how osCommerce is structured. For example, if you are looking at a specific statement in a file and you find that you are not sure what it does, what will be your course of action? Knowing how osCommerce is put together can help you resolve such problems as fast as possible. Thus, you can move quickly through problem areas without getting bogged down trying to work out what has been put where. This type of knowledge only comes with experience, but it won't hurt if you get a slight head-start at this point.

To make this clear, the following screenshot shows osCommerce's entire default file structure in all its glory. Remember that the contents of images folder will obviously change quite dramatically once we have configured the site to suit our own business and products.

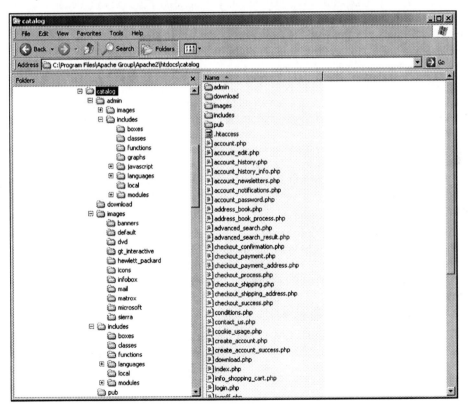

You should take a look at all the different folders to get a feel for the type of things contained therein. Knowing how the osCommerce file system is structured will save you inestimable amount of time should you ever want to indulge in a bit of manual modification once you are a more advanced osCommerce user. Talking of which, let's take a slightly more in-depth and practical look at how the knowledge of the file structure can benefit us.

What do we already know about osCommerce's architecture? We know that osCommerce as a whole is nominally divided into two sections. The first one, contained in the `catalog` folder, is the actual *online shop*, which is the client-facing part of the application. The second is the *administration tool*, held in the `admin` folder, which is not client facing—in fact, we will see in due course that it is important to password-protect this side of the application to keep it secure from potentially malicious users. Basically, we can think of osCommerce as two applications in one—an online retail store and an administration tool.

We also know, on a file level, that the presentation logic, or HTML code, is mixed up with PHP code, or business logic. This means that more often than not, a given PHP page is entirely responsible for its own functionality. This, of course, doesn't mean that all the PHP functions it uses must be defined within that file. This would be quite a serious waste of time because there are many pages that require very similar actions to be performed, and so, having certain PHP pages devoted to providing common functionality is a very, very good idea.

Let's take a look at this separation of functionality in action by means of an example. For the sake of familiarity, we will look at the `customers.php` file in the `admin` folder, which we saw in the last section. If you open up the `customers.php` file in an editor of your choice and search for `tep_db_perform`, you will be brought to the line we mentioned in the previous section. This is a good place to start looking at how the creators of osCommerce have gone about building their application.

Basically, the important thing here is to understand how to go about locating things in osCommerce, because this will give you a good feel for the overall structure and layout of the application code. Now, the function `tep_db_perform()` is not defined in this file—if you continue to search for it within the `customers.php` file, you will see that it has been used twice, but will not find the declaration anywhere. (A function declaration is how PHP registers a new function for use elsewhere in the application.) How can this be? Are we using a function that is undefined? Obviously we are not, otherwise we would have had a host of errors blaring at us when we tried to modify the John Doe customer.

Instead, we need to look somewhere else for this function declaration. Recall that earlier it was mentioned that it is possible to include other files into a PHP file. Well, this must be how osCommerce is doing it—let's look for an `include` function of some sort. The standard place to include files is at the beginning of a PHP file, and if you go to the top of the `customers.php` file, you'll see the following line:

```
require('includes/application_top.php');
```

Ah ha! This must be where the function is placed. So, let's navigate to the `includes/application_top.php` file. Notice that this is actually a relative path—in other words, a path relative to the folder the current file is in—so we need to look for an `includes` folder under which we will find the `application_top.php` file.

Sure enough, this folder does contain one such file, but if we open it, we find to our horror that there is no `tep_db_perform()` function defined here either. Before you despair, though, notice that there are a few `require` statements in this file too:

```
// include the list of project filenames
   require(DIR_WS_INCLUDES . 'filenames.php');
// include the list of project database tables
   require(DIR_WS_INCLUDES . 'database_tables.php');
// include the database functions
   require(DIR_WS_FUNCTIONS . 'database.php');
```

The first two `require` statements include filenames and database tables, which are probably not what we are looking for. The third one, however, requires that a file called `database.php` in the directory defined by `DIR_WS_FUNCTIONS` be included. Interesting! Let's find that file and open it. To cut a long story short, the `DIR_WS_FUNCTIONS` directory is defined as `includes/functions/` in the `includes/configure.php` file, and when we open that folder, we find the `database.php` file as expected.

Make sure you understand where and how the definition for `DIR_WS_FUNCTIONS` was found, by looking inside the `application_top.php` file. (Hint: Look for the statement that requires the use of the `includes/configure.php` file.)

In the `database.php` file, we find a list of PHP function declarations, including the one we have been looking for. A short snippet from this file is shown here for completeness:

```
function tep_db_perform($table, $data, $action = 'insert', $parameters = '',
$link = 'db_link') {
    reset($data);
    if ($action == 'insert') {
      ...
}
```

Of course, it is in no way important that you understand how the function works; what is important is that you have worked out how to find your way around the osCommerce application code. But why is this important? The first reason is that you now have a good idea of how files are laid out according to their function. You now know that individual pages, like `customers.php`, stand alone in the `admin` folder (or indeed the `catalog` folder), but they often require information or functionality from files in the `includes` folder.

From this example, we saw that the `functions` folder contained within the `includes` folder holds different types of *utility* files—in this case it was database functions, but if you look closely, you will notice that there are files containing general functions, HTML graph functions, session functions, and validation functions.

Above and beyond that, having this architectural understanding will also come in handy during the configuration and customization of your site. Only practice and time will give you a complete picture, so make sure that you do experiment as much as possible in your formative days. With that said, let's take a quick look at the online catalog.

The Online Store

The first thing we should do with this new-found knowledge is ensure that it is put into practice. As a result, we are going to take a quick look through the store in order to relate what we have learned to what we can do and how osCommerce is accomplishing its tasks. The best way to do this is to create an account.

Before we do this, it's worth highlighting the main sections of a typical osCommerce page. The following screenshot shows the catalog's index page after installation:

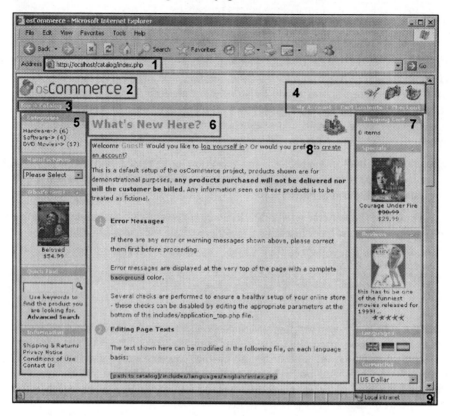

Part of the beauty of using osCommerce is that you can change any of the default behavior of the site. Despite the fact that everything might change, it is still worthwhile looking at this page now as you will need to find your way around the store during development. The following areas are of particular interest at the moment:

1. **The page URL**: This gives the address of the current page. It may also contain variables that are used to pass information or determine the behavior of a web page.

2. **The store's logo**: This is an image file that displays the company logo and provides a link to the site's homepage.

3. **The breadcrumb**: This provides a list of the hierarchy of pages followed. This is part of the navigation bar and can be used to jump to any of the parent pages up to the homepage.

4. **Quick links**: These can be used to quickly access the more important and popular customer pages on the site.

5. **Left-hand information column**: This consists of a variety of information boxes that help customers navigate the products database by a variety of methods, as well as provide other important information such as page links.

6. **The page heading**: This gives a heading, which can be changed to suit whatever page the customer is viewing.

7. **Right-hand information column**: This column contains a variety of information boxes, which also allow the user to perform a variety of tasks such as changing the store's currency or viewing the shopping cart.

8. **The page**: This area displays the content of each page.

9. **Browser's status bar**: This shows important information ranging from the target destination for links and buttons to whether a page is secure.

While it is not shown in the previous screenshot, each page also consists of a footer section, which is shown here:

In this screenshot, Area 1 is simply an information bar that gives the date and the number of requests the page has received. Area 2 is a copyright notice, and you will need to review osCommerce's conditions of use before you make any modifications to this. The last section, Area 3, is a banner that can be used to display advertising—we will discuss more about advertising in Chapters 10 and 12.

Let's put this page to use by clicking on the create an account? link in the index page. This will bring up a series of textboxes that customers use for entering their information in order to register their account at your store. This is where PHP really plays a critical part, because the information entered into the textboxes needs to be captured and stored correctly in the MySQL database using the processes outlined in the previous sections.

Go ahead and create an account, which you can then use for testing purposes later on in the book. The following screenshot shows the information used to create an account on the demonstration site:

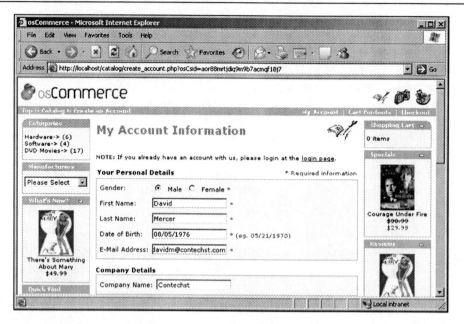

Once you have entered all the relevant information and clicked on Continue, you should receive a confirmation of success page. Now, close your browser and let's think for a second about what we expect osCommerce to have done. We know that a request has been made by a customer to create an account with the store. We suspect that the information entered into the site must have been captured and sent to the server, where it was processed. Once all the processing has been completed, a confirmation page was returned by the server.

What type of processing do we expect to have happened? Well, the most fundamental thing that PHP should have done is to have taken the customer's information and added it into the MySQL database so that the next time the customer visits the site, he or she doesn't have to re-register. If this is the case, opening a new browser and attempting to log on with the username and password we supplied should work just fine. Go ahead and try this out.

If you have logged in successfully, click on the My Account link in the navigation bar to view your account details. Click on the View or change my account information link to bring up the information that is stored in the database. You will see that everything has been faithfully recorded just as you entered it.

Almost everything that a customer does on the site is provided for as follows:

1. The Internet provides the environment in which customers can make use of e-commerce applications like osCommerce.

2. HTML provides a user interface that facilitates interaction between customers and the e-commerce application.

3. PHP deals with the requests made by the customers.

4. MySQL stores all the information required by the application to perform properly.

Knowing what you now know about the architecture of osCommerce (or PHP applications in general), it becomes easier to understand what is happening and why. This in turn helps to weed out problems that may occur, or simply helps you to define your expectations of your online store more accurately.

It is recommended that you get to know how the customer-facing side of osCommerce works quite intimately. Knowing how your customers interact with your online store is a vital part of your understanding when it comes to making decisions about how or what you are going to modify later in the development process. For now, though, let's move on and discuss an important aspect of osCommerce—the online community.

The osCommerce Online Community

Having a good technical know-how is one thing, but being able to effectively use the osCommerce community is at times equally important. Part of learning how to use osCommerce effectively must, at some point, take into account that no one needs to develop applications in isolation. The opportunity to learn from other peoples' mistakes before you fall into the same traps is a great boon for budding website developers. Even better, once you have encountered a problem, it is a pretty safe bet that someone else probably would have had that same problem and already dealt with it, which means that a solution might be available on the forums.

Apart from providing ready-made solutions to problems, as well as a huge repository of information, the osCommerce community is a *living* entity with which we can all interact. Exchanging ideas and information is an integral part of learning and the open source ethos suits the learning-as-a-collective paradigm very well. Just as important is the contributions section, which can provide you with hundreds of different add-ons to do almost anything you can conceive of without having to write the code yourself. Consequently, it is imperative that you know how to manage and use this valuable resource.

Contributions

One of the great things about programming is the ability to reuse code. This means that if some PHP guru decides he or she needs to extend the functionality provided by default with osCommerce, they can write the code that will perform the task they have in mind, and can then make that code available to everyone. Sounds almost too good to be true, but this *is* in fact true, and you can browse through the contributions section at
`http://www.oscommerce.com/community/contributions/` to take a look for yourself.

This resource provides a categorized list of all the different contributions available to users like you and me. All the contributions listed on the site are provided freely under the GNU general public license (make sure you read and understand any additional license information provided with a contribution). It's worth checking this out, and you can find a copy of the license at
`http://www.gnu.org/copyleft/gpl.html`. Other than providing a categorized list of contributions, there are also two options to search through the latest and most downloaded packages.

It is important to realize that these contributions are often developed by individuals, and while they are an excellent resource, at times they can contain bugs. You will notice that many of the download pages have multiple versions of each package—each one fixing bugs or improving on the last version. Accordingly, you should always approach the use of contributions with caution, and at all times endeavor to understand exactly how the package is working to achieve its tasks.

We will frequently use the community-based contributions in this book, so we need not discuss this any further for now. Once we start adding some advanced functionality, we will come back to this topic and run through how to download, install, and modify community contributions.

Forums

The idea behind the osCommerce forums is to provide a kind of huge noticeboard for everyone involved in osCommerce to ask questions and search for answers. It also provides a convenient way to meet other people in the same boat, which can be a useful means of sharing ideas and discussing technical issues with people at the same level of experience. Specifically, the following interesting and useful topics, among others, can be found at the osCommerce forums:

- News and announcements
- General support
- Installation and configuration
- Tips and tricks
- Contribution announcements
- Contribution support
- General chitchat
- Next steps
- E-commerce laws

With approximately 70,000 registered users and hundreds of people online at any given time, it is certain that you will find at least a part of the answer you need from the forums. However, bear in mind that like any public service, there are rules and guidelines to abide by when using these facilities. A quick read over the rules at `http://forums.oscommerce.com/index.php?act=boardrules` should avoid any infringements of etiquette.

One of the main points to remember is that you should make an honest effort to search for similar posts before adding your own post to any of the lists—obviously it is nice to keep redundancy in the lists to a minimum. This is quite a big point because it is notoriously hard to find the exact postings you are looking for. The forum gives you the option of ordering the posts based on a few criteria, searching for only those posts posted recently, and so on.

Of course, you are encouraged to register as a forum user in order to make use of the forums properly—you will find that you are able to use the search features without any problems.

Knowledge Base

The osCommerce knowledge base takes a different approach to help osCommerce users. It is more of a documentation effort taking the form of a series of articles that describe a wide variety of osCommerce issues and topics. Navigating to the homepage, `http://www.oscommerce.info/`, for knowledge base gives the following page:

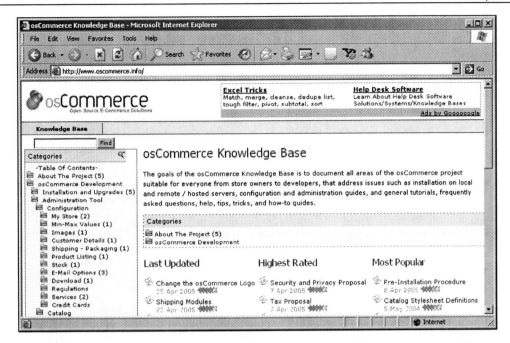

As you can see, the list on the left-hand side provides a categorized table of articles, which is really easy to use. Each article covers a single topic, and all of them can be ranked in terms of how useful you found them. The downside is that not everything has had an article written about it yet. So, while this may be the answer for your more run-of-the-mill queries, it is unlikely that it will provide you with a solution or example for more complex problems. Having said this, it is a community project, and new articles are added all the time—definitely something worth using and supporting.

Documentation

The documentation is available online *and* as a download. It is recommended that you use the downloaded version, since this will be available to you whenever you need regardless of whether your internet connection is available. The documentation uses a different method from the forums and knowledge base. This time, each aspect of osCommerce is briefly discussed in an easy-to-navigate HTML-based hierarchy. A complete listing can be found in the table of contents at `http://www.oscommerce.info/docs/english/table_of_contents.html`—perusing this is definitely worthwhile for novice and experienced osCommerce users alike, although many of you will find the information a bit terse, or even sparse in places.

Bug and Progress Reports

Another worthwhile exercise is to look at the bug reports at `http://www.oscommerce.com/community/bugs/`, which are nicely categorized, and are assigned to various experienced members of the community to either verify and act upon or to dismiss as bogus. At the very least, browsing the bug lists provides a good method of seeing whether any problems you may have been experiencing could be the result of a bug. If you do suspect a *bug* in your installation of osCommerce, you should report it, but only after you have made certain it is not simply inexplicable behavior. Obviously, every bug report needs to be looked at, so it consumes someone's time and effort to investigate a report—make reports only after some deliberation.

Progress reports can be found at `http://www.oscommerce.com/community/reports` and are very useful in terms of keeping abreast of the latest news within the osCommerce community. For example, the latest update at the time of writing contained information on the following:

- **Team reorganization**: The osCommerce team has been reorganized to have the amount of resources available optimized, and to spread responsibilities throughout the team.

- **New support site navigation menu**: A new navigation menu has been added to the support site, which now offers drop-down menu entries to the pages in each section of the support site.

- **Forum structure updates**: The forum structure has been updated to improve the usability of which postings should be made in which forum channels.

- **Daylight saving time on the forum**: To correctly set the time on the forums to reflect daylight saving time, please go to your Control Panel | Options | Board Settings and select the "Is daylight saving time in effect?" option.

- **Knowledge base update**: A table of contents page has been added to the knowledge base site to provide an overview of all knowledge base articles currently available.

- **Most downloaded contributions**: The contributions section has been updated to allow browsing the contribution packages ordered by the most downloaded.

Obviously, all pretty pertinent information for the active osCommerce community member. Talking of being an active community member, a pretty fair statement about the community, of which you are now a member, is that you get out what you put in. The online community is a great resource, and with your help it will only improve.

Summary

Without getting too bogged down in difficult coding issues, you now have a good grasp of the architecture and underlying technologies that go into the mix to produce a working osCommerce online retail site. The importance of this knowledge can't really be measured quantitatively, but you will feel the difference as you work. Knowing how things are put together will automatically allow you to make leaps of intuition concerning how to go about performing the various tasks that will be required along the way.

Sooner or later everyone requires something that is a bit beyond basic customization, and when this happens, you will be equipped with the requisite information that will make your life a lot easier as a result of reading this chapter. From an understanding of how osCommerce as an application sits within the framework of the World Wide Web, to an understanding of how PHP, HTML, and MySQL all interact to produce the final product, there will be very little that you should not feel confident in dealing with in the future.

Apart from having a firm grasp of the technical side of things, knowing how to make use of the community is also an important factor when working with software such as osCommerce. This chapter has also given you plenty of pointers on how to use the various different resources available. Keeping an eye on the goings-on in the community is an integral part of maintaining a good and up-to-date e-commerce site.

With that said, and the first three chapters now out of the way, the groundwork has been laid and we are ready to begin work on the site. Chapter 4 will take into account all the information we have covered in the first three chapters and put osCommerce through its paces as we begin customizing the site to reflect the needs of our business.

4
Basic Configuration

Take my word, there's a fair old amount to do in terms of configuring your individual osCommerce installation to suit a new business. Fortunately, the people at osCommerce have made a lot of default choices which are pretty sensible, so provided you have a good look at everything that is up for configuration, and ensure that you understand what all the settings do and mean, quite a bit of it *can* go unchanged. Apart from actually making a decision about the multitude of settings that go into defining osCommerce's look, feel, and behavior, you also have to physically implement your choices. For this, we are given the excellent administration tool (found under the admin folder in your installation), which you can think of this as osCommerce's command center.

From the administration tool, we can perform just about any configuration task our hearts desire. I say "just about" because there are always fiddly bits that aren't easily dealt with from the standard administrative interface. Consequently, in this chapter, we won't perform every bit of configuration needed to get our site up and running—that would involve a lot of work, which we don't need to concern ourselves with until a bit later on.

Basically, in order to be as efficient as possible in terms of our overall development of the site, we are going to work with the 80/20 philosophy in mind. This means we should aim to get roughly 80% of the configuration done with about 20% of the overall effort. The remaining 20% of configuration work will get done when we look at different or specialized bits of functionality, and for that we may need specialist knowledge, third-party software, or simply more time than we want to spend on configuring our setup for the moment. So what is it precisely that we are going to get done in this chapter? Well, we are going to discuss and modify the following sections found under the Configuration tab of the administration tool:

- My Store
- Maximum and minimum values
- Images
- Customer details
- Shipping/packaging
- Product listing
- Stock

- Logging
- Cache
- Email options
- Download
- GZip compression
- Sessions

What are we *not* going to look at in this chapter? Well, we aren't going to run through each and every option available in osCommerce in detail. Many of the default settings are pretty self explanatory, and require nothing more than a quick decision on your part. The ones which have slightly less clear meaning or are more complex in their action will be scrutinized more closely. More or less it's fair to say that it's the default behavior of osCommerce that's going to be modified in this section of the book. Things like changing the look and feel of the site, or populating the product database are left to their own chapters a little later.

One final thing to bear in mind is that if you still, at this stage, don't have a clear idea of what you expect from your site, you will find that it is hard to make some of the decisions concerning how you want certain aspects of osCommerce to behave. Now, it is understood that sometimes it is simply not possible to know everything in advance, so you might wish to take notes of what you are and are not modifying, and what you think you will need to come back to at a later stage. Having a quick reference of what you have and haven't done at any given junction in the development phase will make your life a lot easier if you ever do need to take a step back.

Anyway, it's certainly exciting to be finally working on the actual site; so without further delay, let's begin…

The Administration Tool

Having an online tool like the one shipped with osCommerce is of great value and advantage to us osCommerce users. If, for example, you had undertaken to build your own site from scratch, then no matter how well you built your site, it would probably be prohibitive in terms of time taken to develop a fully functional online administration center to go with it. This would mean effectively that you are doomed forever to modify your database manually, or go searching for default settings within the actual pages of your code.

Thankfully that scenario is not one we need to consider, and the only real challenges for us are to learn how to use the admin tool effectively, and to understand the behavior of all the settings. Don't be fooled, though; if we make changes to the default settings without fully understanding the consequences of the changes, there can be some unexpected and untimely surprises, and surprises in the programming world are never good! The administration tool goes a long way to helping us make our decisions though, and it even provides a sentence or two outlining what each given option means—although this is often insufficient to fully appreciate the effects of changing the setting. The following screenshot shows the administration tool, open on the My Store page of the Configuration section:

All the pages in the administration tool have several common generic features, which you should be aware of. First, There is a navigation bar running along the top of the screen, which allows us to jump to the Administration home page (this option is presented again on the far right of the bar), the osCommerce homepage (Support Site), as well as our actual osCommerce site's homepage, held in Online Catalog. Nothing too life-threatening there, but useful if you want to jump around to find information, or test the results of your modifications.

Next, all the setting options that are available for us to use are categorized and stored in the box on the far left of the screen. This chapter concentrates on only the first option, Configuration, because the other options all overlap specific topics that warrant their own chapters. Clicking on a heading category—for example, Configuration—will bring up its list of options, and clicking on these subcategories will bring up a page containing all the setting options for that category.

The category setting options are displayed in the center of the screen in a tabular format, and each option is a link that will bring up its own edit option and description on the far right of the screen. So, for example, in the previous screenshot the setting we are looking at is the Store Name, and clicking on the edit button will bring up the following page, which we can use to enter text and save the new setting:

Clicking the update button will then take us back to the settings page, which should now reflect any changes we have made. That about explains how we go about configuring the site. The rest is really about understanding what effect the changes will have. Of course, as with anything, there is also a good way and a bad way to go about making changes. Most of you should be able to guess straight off that the good way will involve some sort of verification process to ensure that our changes have the desired effect.

Now, for something as simple as deciding on the store's name, there is probably little that could go wrong, so don't feel you have to waste time verifying every single change you make. However, you should make it a point to check results after a certain number of *easy* modifications, as well as verify the more complicated settings (if possible) as and when you make them. This is really good practice—not only from a theoretical point of view, but also from a practical one—because it is likely that you will need to run exactly the same suite of tests when you deploy your site to ensure everything is working properly on the real live server.

Another important point to consider is that some of the settings you make will apply only to the development machine and will need to be modified again to suit the live system.

> You will need to make a note (a physical one, not a mental one) of the settings that are likely to change when you deploy the site to the live server. Save your notes in a file called configuration_settings.txt and leave it in a folder entitled development_notes somewhere where you will find it again.

For example, E-Mail Address in the previous screenshot will not be root@localhost when your site is live. If you have already purchased your domain, and are aware of what your email addresses, among other things are, then you can enter these settings into your development machine now. If you know that you want your emails to come from something like staff@contechst.com, then entering this value into your development version of osCommerce is fine because it will save you having to change it during deployment and won't really affect anything on your development machine.

Of course, these configuration settings are not the only things that are subject to change between the development machine and the live server. Keeping tabs on what will, might, and probably won't change is definitely a valuable practice. Of course, this book will discuss deployment in a later chapter, and will lend support in this area by providing checklists of tasks to perform in order to ensure that your live server is functioning properly. More about that in Chapter 11 on *Deployment and Maintenance*; for now, let's concentrate on the task at hand…

My Store

There are a few settings of interest in this section, and they warrant a fair investigation. For the most part, however, it is pretty plain sailing and there isn't too much in here that should cause stress. The first four items in the table—Store Name, Store Owner, E-Mail Address, and E-Mail From—are reasonably straightforward to understand, although there are a few things you might want to consider before writing in your personal details.

The Store Name property will appear in emails sent to the store owner when customers use the Contact Us page on the site. The Store Owner is most likely yourself—if you are developing for someone else, then your employer's name should go in here. Not very exciting stuff, but you will notice that the store owner's name is the name that appears in the To: field of the emails received from customers.

Talking of which, the part worth thinking about here is do you really want all customer queries (complaints, compliments, suggestions, or anything else for that matter) to land up at your personal email? The answer is probably an emphatic "No!" So what do you do? The best way to get around this is to create an E-Mail Address on your site that is used to collect all the customer emails in one place, which you can then peruse at your leisure, or pass off to an employee, or deal with in whatever manner you choose—at least they aren't clogging up your private email inbox.

So, in this instance, it is probably best to ignore the short description of E-Mail Address (The e-mail address of my store owner) given by osCommerce, and enter an address that you have access to but is not necessarily your personal email—in this case, I have used staff@contechst.com. If you wish to test out this functionality, then you will need to ensure that whatever address you enter is at least valid and can be accessed by you.

The following screenshot shows an email sent from a client (you may remember *Janet Doe* from an earlier chapter) to the store, and the reply from the store to the customer, shown below it. Take note in particular of the values in all the fields shown:

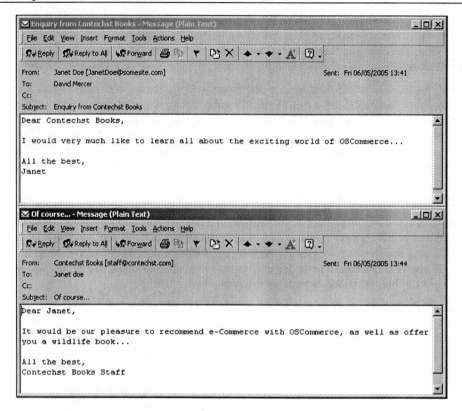

This brings up an important point, which should be mentioned before we continue:

> Just because a configurable property has a given name and description, doesn't mean you have to follow the wording precisely. It is far more important to think about *how* you want your site to work when filling in values.

Next, the Send Extra Order Email To option allows you to specify who else receives a copy of the order confirmation email sent out whenever a customer completes an order. By default this is only sent to the customer, but you may wish to set up an email address to which these order emails are sent so that you can keep track or maintain copies of orders via email—you don't *have* to do this; it is quite easy to track orders through the admin tool as well. So, assuming you had the email address orders@contechst.com, you could edit the option to send a duplicate email by typing the following in the textbox presented: Order Email <orders@contechst.com>.

At the time of writing, the Use Search-Engine Safe URLs feature was still under development, and should be left as false unless you have a newer version where this is a tried and tested feature. The Store Address and Phone option allows you to enter the details you wish to be made available to customers who are using a check or money order to pay for their goods. Apart from these options, the rest are all pretty self explanatory, and it is really up to the individual to make a decision. The following screenshot shows all the My Store settings for the demo site:

My Store

Title	Value	Action
Store Name	Contechst Books	①
Store Owner	David Mercer	①
E-Mail Address	staff@contechst.com	①
E-Mail From	Contechst Books <staff@contechst.com>	①
Country	United States	①
Zone	California	①
Expected Sort Order	desc	①
Expected Sort Field	date_expected	①
Switch To Default Language Currency	false	①
Send Extra Order Emails To	Order Email <orders@contechst.com>	①
Use Search-Engine Safe URLs (still in development)	false	①
Display Cart After Adding Product	true	①
Allow Guest To Tell A Friend	false	①
Default Search Operator	or	①
Store Address and Phone	Contechst Books 31 Wildlife Drive Wilderness California United States of America 021 555 4567	①
Show Category Counts	false	▶
Tax Decimal Places	0	①
Display Prices with Tax	false	①

Notice that the Default Search Operator and Show Category Counts options have had their values modified, while the Display Cart After Adding Product has been left as true—these simply reflect my personal preference for how a site should be presented, and I am quite certain that ten different people will have ten different opinions. The rest of these properties are left in your capable hands to decide on.

Maximum and Minimum Values

The maximum and minimum values deal with a variety of things ranging from governing customer information, to determining how many search results to present, to customer order history. Fortunately, most of these settings are pretty straightforward, so there isn't much that should cause problems here either. Before we show the default settings for Contechst Books, it is worth looking at a couple of things when determining the type of settings you want to put in place here.

The first thing to do is to navigate to the customer registration page, which you can reach by clicking on the create an account? link on the site's index page. This will bring up a page consisting of a list of textboxes that your customers will use to enter their information in order to create an account. It's a worthwhile exercise to actually fill this information out with legal and illegal values (illegal values are those which do not meet the stated minimum requirements in your Minimum Values configuration page) to check how your application behaves and to give you a better appreciation for the values you are setting.

For example, the minimum length of the date is given as 10 by default in the configuration section. Why ten? This is a bit strange because you only need six, or at most eight, characters to specify a date. Without looking at the "create an account" page, you might well change this value not realizing that osCommerce requires the user to input forward slashes to separate the days, months, and years provided in birthdates.

With that said, there is nothing we are going to modify in this section for now, since all the default minimum values represent sensible options. It is recommended, however, that you still look through each and every setting and ensure you understand what each one does, as there are still options you may wish to consider at this point. Looking at the password setting, you might consider upping the minimum length to 6 in order to encourage greater security amongst customers—obviously, enforcing longer passwords reduces the risk of customers' accounts being hijacked.

The Maximum Values section does not deal with customers, but more with how osCommerce behaves in terms of the number of items it displays in a variety of categories. While the default settings are pretty much spot on, there are a few settings worth looking over. The first two are self explanatory, although at this stage you might not be aware that Address Book Entries refers to the fact that customers can add several addresses to their account. This allows them to specify different mailing addresses depending on where and who they want purchased good to go to.

The Page Links value specifies the maximum number of links that will be shown on a results page. For example, if you set this to 5, then assuming you have enough products or results, you will get the following link structure:

1 2 3 4 5 [Next >>]

If you set it to 10, you would get:

1 2 3 4 5 6 7 8 9 10 [Next >>]

Categories to List Per Row might cause some confusion as it is not particularly clear what this refers to. To see how this influences your site, go to any one of the default links under the Categories section of the index page in your catalog site. If, for example, you go to the Hardware option, you will be presented with the following screen (notice that the background color is still darker than the original color, since we changed the setting for this in a previous chapter):

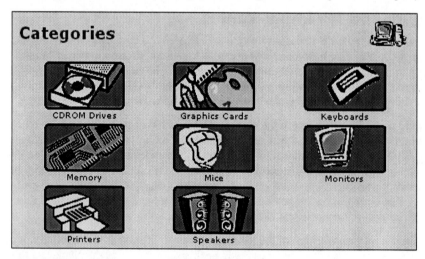

The main thing to note here, though, is that there are three columns of subcategories shown. If you don't already have a window open with your Maximum Values settings page in the admin tool, then open one up and change the default value for Categories to List Per Row to 1. Refreshing the Categories page will give you the following result:

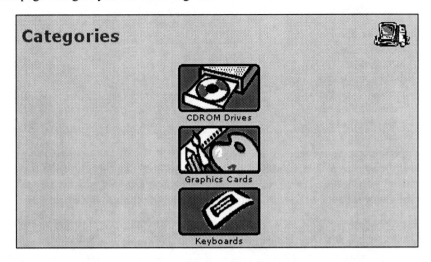

From this you can see that this setting governs how many columns are used to present the categories of products you have in your store. Simple once you know, but it can be tricky to find this out if you don't. Some things to consider when deciding on this setting are:

- How big your product category images (if any) are going to be
- How wide your page is going to be
- How many product subcategories, on average, you are going to have

Once again, the default setting is fine for the demonstration site, but this illustrates quite well that some thought should go into each and every setting—even if the end result is simply leaving the value as is.

The rest of the values in this section are pretty self explanatory, and it is left to you to go through each one and make a decision regarding what your preferences are for your own site. If you have any doubt about what a setting does, then leave it as the default. Remember, you can always come back to this section and change the values to suit your needs at any stage.

Images

Learning how to set the default values for the Images section can be a bit of a laugh. The best way to do it is to change the settings and view the results in the catalog section. Of course, ensure that you remember your default settings so that you can get things back to normal once you are done. The following screenshot shows the modified values in the Images section:

Images

Title	Value	Action
Small Image Width	10	①
Small Image Height	80	①
Heading Image Width	570	①
Heading Image Height	40	①
Subcategory Image Width	20	▶
Subcategory Image Height	57	①
Calculate Image Size	true	①
Image Required	true	①

In this case, the Small Image Width has been reduced from 100 to 10, the Heading Image Width has been increased from 57 to 570, and the Subcategory Image Width has been reduced from 100 to 20. To see the effect of these changes we will go to our catalog section and view a couple of pages. The following screenshot shows the Categories page under these modifications:

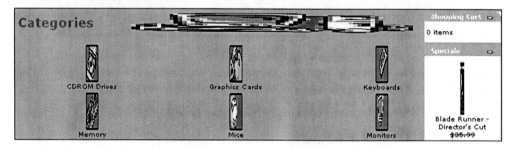

Oh dear, that's not really what we want, but it has helped to demonstrate which setting does what. The image of the Blade Runner title on the right-hand side of the screen has been squashed to only ten pixels in width—so we know how the Small Image Width affects the site. The Heading Image Width influences the image shown at the top of the page in line with the Categories title, and this image now takes up half the screen's width, which is obviously not appropriate. Finally the most obvious of the settings, the Subcategory Image Width, has been squashed to only 20 pixels, which is also not very tidy.

Playing around like this has raised some interesting questions. What size are your site's images? In other words, will they look nice with the default settings? Notice that the heading image shown in the previous screenshot is all deformed and unclear because of the stretching it has undergone. Well, it's possible that if you have made or obtained images that are of different dimensions than the default ones, then you might suffer the same fate unless you think closely about what Image values you set.

> It is possible to leave out the Width (or Height)setting for your images entirely. This will force osCommerce to size your images according to their remaining specified Height (or Width) property. Doing this should avoid any horizontal or vertical distortion as osCommerce will render the image appropriately – for this to work, the Calculate Image Size option must be set to True.

Of course, you may also decide, for example, to not have heading images at all, in which case you can leave the settings as the default ones because you will remove the images from your pages altogether when you customize your site.

Finally, it is recommended that you leave the Image Required setting as true while you are building the site, because this will allow you to spot if anything is amiss with your images—for example, if osCommerce cannot find an image, this will show up as a broken link on the screen. You can test this by modifying the name of an image in the images folder of your catalog directory and then viewing (in your browser) a page that should contain that image.

Customer Details

This is a very straightforward section, and the only setting that is modified for the demonstration site is the Company option, which has been set to false because it slows down customer registration and is not that important for our purposes. If you feel your store will benefit from knowing who your customers work for, then by all means keep it. While it is easy to understand what each setting controls in this case, you still need to think closely about what you do and don't want to store in the way of customer information.

Off the top of your head you may wonder why on earth you really need to store a customer's birthdate. After all, the more information you store about each customer, the more space you are going to use in your database. But what if down the line you decide to implement a marketing strategy that sends out a promotional discount on certain products on your customers' birthdays. Well, this is certainly a plausible marketing strategy, but one that is thoroughly impossible to implement if you haven't been storing customer birthdates from the start. The same type of argument could be made for storing gender, since certain products might be more attractive to one gender than the other, so a marketing strategy based on gender is also plausible.

At this point you should be able to see why it is so important to have a clear picture of where you want your site to go. It's a very easy slip to make saying that you don't need customer birthdates because you don't really need them at the moment. When in doubt, save the details rather than not—this will at least give you the option later on. If you know that you are really never going to use the information (like the Company value for the demo site), then remove it so as to prevent redundant data piling up in your database.

Shipping and Packaging

This section is also a pretty straightforward section, although there are several issues you need to make sure you are aware of before making any decisions here. The first two options, Country of Origin and Postal Code, can be dealt with pretty swiftly, but the next setting requires a bit of research. In order to Enter the Maximum Package Weight you will ship, you need to know the weight-to-cost scale of your shipping service provider, and find out what limits they have on their service.

Most good providers will have a list of all their expenses, and assuming you will actually be using them often will also have special rates and deals available to regular users. For example, http://www.ups.com/content/us/en/shipping/time/zones/current/select.html provides information regarding UPS' rates as well as information pertaining to their services. Whoever you choose to work with will likely have a solid support and information service to help you find your way. For example you can find out all about costs and charges at the US Postal Service at the following page, which highlights the costs of mailing packages of different weights and sizes: http://pe.usps.gov/text/dmm/R700.htm#xih82834.

Obviously, it is imperative that you look at a shipping provider of your choice in order to work out *what* your expenses are going to be, as well as the *most* cost effective and efficient solution for your business. This is something that should really have been looked at before actual development of the site—somewhere around Chapter 1. Once you know how your shipping service will work (for example, whether you are going to use a daily or weekly pick up service, whether you are going to get a special deal on international shipments, and so on), you can determine what settings are right for you.

Of course, the values you set are in pounds, and you should be aware of how much your packaging itself is going to weigh. The Package Tare Weight allows you to set a minimum value for the packaging (or throw-away) weight. If a package is large, then it is conceivable that you need to set the weight of the packaging as a percentage of the package weight instead of a single value. In such a case, osCommerce uses the percentage value given in the Larger packages – percentage increase option. The default sets the tare weight at 3 pounds and the percentage at 10, which means that for packages heavier than 30 pounds, the *percentage* value is the one which is used to calculate the package weight.

In the case of the demo site's settings, the Package Tare Weight is set to 2 pounds, and the Larger packages – percentage increase value is changed to 5 with the Maximum Package Weight being left at its default value. This means that for packages of 40 pounds or less, we are confident that only a maximum of two pounds of packaging is required—for anything above 40 pounds, we will use the percentage calculation. This is reasonable in our case since books need very little in the way of specialized packaging.

Product Listing

This section controls how you intend your products to be viewed on the site. Pretty much anything and everything from whether you actually want to display a product image at all, to whether you want to display its name or the name of the manufacturer, gets done here. This is a straightforward section with no difficult options to research—or so it would seem. Of course, depending on what you are selling, you might want different properties for your products altogether. By this I mean that if you are a book retailer, then it is unlikely you want to mention Display Product Manufacturer Name at all, but rather Display Product **Publisher** Name, or something to that effect.

Oh dear! What are we going to do if the actual properties we are configuring are not even the correct ones? Well, the quick answer is that we will get to a stage a little later on where we can configure our product attributes, amongst other things—and of course, we'll cheat by exploiting the difference between what we as the site's administrators see in the admin tool, and what the client viewing the catalog sees!

All the settings barring the last two are used to determine whether a product attribute is displayed, and if so, the value set for that attribute determines the order in which it is shown on the site. For the moment, configure those properties that you are sure you will use, and make a note of those which you believe will need to change. The following screenshot shows the settings for the demo site:

Product Listing

Title	Value	Action	Location of Prev/Next
Display Product Image	1	①	Navigation Bar (1-top, 2-bottom, 3-both)
Display Product Manufaturer Name	2	①	
Display Product Model	0	①	edit
Display Product Name	3	①	Sets the location of the
Display Product Price	4	①	Prev/Next Navigation Bar (1-top, 2-bottom, 3-both)
Display Product Quantity	0	①	
Display Product Weight	0	①	Date Added: 04/25/2005
Display Buy Now column	5	①	Last Modified: 05/11/2005
Display Category/Manufacturer Filter (0=disable; 1=enable)	1	①	
Location of Prev/Next Navigation Bar (1-top, 2-bottom, 3-both)	3	▶	

Looking through the settings shown in the previous screenshot, you can see that we want to display, in order, the product image, the manufacturer's name, the product's name, its price, and finally the Buy Now button. You might be asking yourself why—if it has already been mentioned that, as a book retailer, we don't want to Display Product Manufacturer Name—are we putting it in the line-up. The answer to this has presented itself almost too perfectly—look at the Display Product Manufaturer Name line closely in the previous screenshot. You will notice there is a spelling mistake. However, if you look at the results of these settings in the catalog:

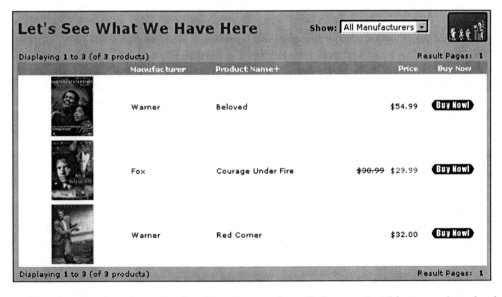

you will notice that the column heading Manufacturer is spelled correctly. This means that what is shown on the screen is not directly linked to the name given for a property in the admin tool. So, we can choose to show the manufacturer in our product listing, but this does not mean we have to make the column heading in the catalog site Manufacturer; we could, if we were so inclined, change it to Publisher. This, however, will come a bit later on in the story. What's more important than this for now is that you have related the settings made to the product listing on the site page.

The final two settings are slightly different in that they deal more with navigation than anything else. Notice in the admin tool that Display Category/Manufacturer Filter is set to 1. The resulting filter when enabled in this manner is shown above the product listing in line with Let's See What We Have Here. It is a good idea to include this, as people often have some sort of brand loyalty and would wish to search your catalog for specific brands.

Finally, Location of Prev/Next Navigation Bar is set to 3. Why have we done this, and what is the prev/next navigation bar? Well, when you get round to populating your database and enter the multitude of goodies you have for sale, you will get to a stage where the number of products in a category is greater than the number of products you are willing to display on the page. Incidentally, we have already set the number of items to display per page property in the Search Results setting in the Maximum Values section.

Once that happens, the navigation bar (at present only displays Displaying 1 to 3 (of 3 products)) will be the customer's method of hopping from one page in the product listing to another. Now, I don't know about you, but I hate scrolling down to the bottom of a page only to find that I have to go right back to the top to click on the Next page link. Conversely, if I only want to look at the first couple of items and then go to the Next page, I certainly don't want to be forced to scroll to the bottom to do so. Setting this property to 3 ensures that you will make it easier for your customer to navigate your product listings by having a navigation bar at the top *and* bottom of the page.

Stock

Deciding how you want osCommerce to deal with your stock is a very tricky business, and you will be forced to do a bit of soul searching before defining the settings in this section. Ensuring that you have a coherent game plan when it comes to dealing with stock levels and how your application deals with these stock levels is paramount to the perceived and actual integrity and reliability of your system. If you are selling products that are not in stock, and are unable for some reason to fulfill your orders... Well, I don't need to continue on with the type of things *word of mouth* will spread about your store.

With that in mind, let's take a quick look at what the demo site's settings are:

Stock

Title	Value	Action
Check stock level	true	▶
Subtract stock	true	①
Allow Checkout	true	①
Mark product out of stock	Temporarily out of Stock	①
Stock Re-order level	5	①

What do these settings mean in terms of how osCommerce will behave when a customer is purchasing an item? Ok, the Check stock level setting simply means that osCommerce will retrieve the number of items in stock before the customer checks out. The Subtract stock setting means that once an item is purchased, the database is updated by subtracting the number of items purchased from the number of items in stock. Obviously you should be able to see that this effectively automates your stock control on the purchasing side of things.

The tricky bit is the Allow Checkout setting. Since we have set Check stock level to true, osCommerce is aware of how much stock is available when a customer attempts to make a purchase. Setting Allow Checkout to true is taking a bit of a risk because it is saying that I, as the retailer, am confident that I can ship the purchased product on time despite the fact it is not in stock at the moment. Since the demo site relies on Packt's ability to ship product, we have gone with true in this instance because Packt's business model is such that they can deliver books very quickly.

You really need to determine whether you can do the same for all of your products before setting this to true. Some people may view this as a trade-off. In other words, do you make a loss from not selling the product, or do you risk having to refund the customer if you can't get stock in quickly enough. From a business perspective, this is not particularly sound reasoning since your value as a business stems partly from your reputation of reliability. This is not worth trading on, so rather take the hit from a direct loss of sales instead of proving to be unreliable and endeavor to improve your stock control.

The final two settings are pretty easy to understand, and are not life threatening in any way. You can choose these to best suit you with little effort. The following screenshot shows how these settings influence the behavior of osCommerce when ordering products that have low stock. Take note of the Temporarily out of Stock message, and the notes below the product which informs the customer of their choice to continue with checkout because of our Allow Checkout setting:

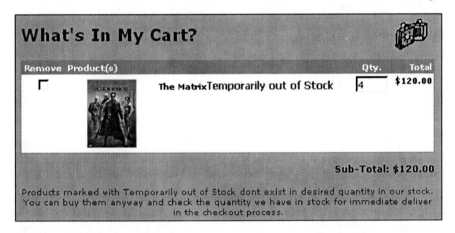

Of course, if we had set the Allow Checkout setting to false, then the second line of the checkout message would have read:

Please alter the quantity of products marked with (Temporarily out of Stock), Thank you

Finally, we will see later on in the book in Chapter 10 on *Tools, Tips, and Tricks* how to use the Stock Re-order level setting along with a community contribution to let us know when it is time to re-order an item. For now, though, we say goodbye to stocks until the next chapter, when we begin dealing with data.

Logging

Logging can be a very useful, if not critical, tool for maintaining a system's health. Logs can be used to record just about any action or change in state of an application. Most changes within an application are really of no interest to the average person, but certain things *are* useful to record in case you need that information at a later stage. Like any good system, osCommerce gives us options to create and monitor certain actions within our application. This ability comes with a caveat, however. If left untended, logs can become resource hogs, taking up gigabytes of space in a surprisingly short amount of time.

Accordingly, you need to decide what information you want to record, and then work out a good management strategy for maintaining that information. Also, logs should be kept in a secure place—you don't really need to air your database query history to the world, or worse, have it modified by someone. The options presented to us by osCommerce, along with the settings used for the demo site, are shown here:

Logging

Title	Value	Action
Store Page Parse Time	true	①
Log Destination	C:\Program Files\Apache Group\Apache2 \htdocs\catalog\admin\page_parse_time.log	①
Log Date Format	%d/%m/%Y %H:%M:%S	①
Display The Page Parse Time	true	①
Store Database Queries	false	▶

Since development is taking place in a Windows-based environment in the case of the demo site, we have added a Windows path value for the Log Destination setting. This means that the log file, which is set to store and display the Page Parse Time, will be created and held in the admin folder.

"What, oh what are you doing?" Some of you may cry out. Holding the log file in the document root will allow people to access it from the web server. Haven't we just said that the log files need to be kept out of reach of prying eyes? Well, yes, one can access this log over the web server on the development machine because we haven't secured our admin tool yet. Later, when we deploy the site (most likely to a Linux-based server) this path will need to change to something more suitable. In any event, holding it in the admin folder will still not be too much of a security risk because we need to secure this entire folder anyway.

After browsing around the site a bit, we can look at what is created in the designated log file to see the type of information we are storing. To be honest, this information is not really relevant to you at the moment, so unless there is a reason for recording logs during development, you can do without it altogether for now:

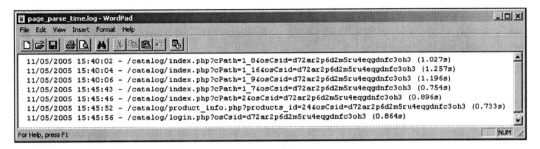

```
11/05/2005 15:40:02 - /catalog/index.php?cPath=1_8&osCsid=d72ar2p6d2m5ru4eqgdnfc3oh3 (1.027s)
11/05/2005 15:40:04 - /catalog/index.php?cPath=1_16&osCsid=d72ar2p6d2m5ru4eqgdnfc3oh3 (1.257s)
11/05/2005 15:40:06 - /catalog/index.php?cPath=1_9&osCsid=d72ar2p6d2m5ru4eqgdnfc3oh3 (1.196s)
11/05/2005 15:45:43 - /catalog/index.php?cPath=1_7&osCsid=d72ar2p6d2m5ru4eqgdnfc3oh3 (0.754s)
11/05/2005 15:45:46 - /catalog/index.php?cPath=2&osCsid=d72ar2p6d2m5ru4eqgdnfc3oh3 (0.896s)
11/05/2005 15:45:52 - /catalog/product_info.php?products_id=24&osCsid=d72ar2p6d2m5ru4eqgdnfc3oh3 (0.733s)
11/05/2005 15:45:56 - /catalog/login.php?osCsid=d72ar2p6d2m5ru4eqgdnfc3oh3 (0.864s)
```

It is recommended that you leave the Store Database Query setting as false all the time unless you have a really good reason for needing it, and you know exactly how you are going to deal with all the information being stored. These logs can grow very quickly and take up a lot of space, causing problems for your site's performance if you're not careful.

Finally, remember to make a note of all the settings, in this case the log-file path, which you will need to change come deployment time, and add the files to the development_notes folder, which you created earlier.

Cache

A cache is implemented as a directory of web pages, which are held separately from the rest of the pages. The purpose of this cache is to allow the server to quickly serve cached pages instead of querying for the page afresh each time it is requested. This has implications for the speed of delivery of pages and therefore impacts positively on the customer's experience. It is recommended that you *do* use caching on your live site for this reason.

For the development site, however, it's not a good thing, because we want to see the results of changes (configuration or customization, or straightforward hacking) that we make to our pages every time we load them. Using a cached version of a page might not reflect the changes we have implemented, as that page would not been refreshed yet. This can often cause confusion and frustration, so for now, leave the cache entirely.

Once you have deployed the site, it is a good idea to switch caching on only after *all* your testing is complete for exactly the same reason. To do so, simply set the Use Cache value to true, and pick a folder to save the files to. By default this is /tmp/, but you need to be careful in this case to ensure that you are getting the right tmp folder on the host's site. Entering something like ../../tmp will probably avoid any resource clashes with other users on the same web host—another little note to go into the development_notes folder.

Don't worry if you don't understand this completely at the moment. The only thing is to remember to leave caching off during development and testing, and switch it on, using a folder exclusive to your site once the site is live.

Email Options

Try this! Go to the last option in the administration tool, entitled Tools, click on the Send Email option, and send an email to Janet Doe, or whoever your current customer is. Ensure before doing this that the customer you are sending the email to has an email address that *you* can receive because you are going to test whether or not osCommerce is able to send emails with its default configuration. If not, you will need to go back to the Customers option and edit the email address for the customer appropriately.

Once you have sent the email, hang around for a bit to see if you receive it in good order. If so, then you can pretty much leave the email settings as they are for the time being. The only thing you need concern yourself with at deployment time is whether your site will be hosted on a Linux server (very likely) or a Windows server. If it's Linux, then all you need do is test your email configuration on the live site as is; if it's Windows, you will probably need to change the first two settings—E-mail Transport Method and E-mail Linefeeds—to their alternate settings.

The Use MIME HTML when sending Emails option should be left as false for the moment. Obviously at a later stage you might decide you would like to spruce up your emails with some HTML, but for the moment there is no need. Remember, however, that not all mail-client applications support HTML, so you might be marginalizing some customers by using this. The good news is that as time goes by, more and more people will be able to receive MIME format emails—as opposed to the just *the majority* for the moment.

You might decide that you want to check whether your customers are supplying you with email addresses that actually exist. If this is the case, then you should set the Verify E-mail Addresses Through DNS setting to true. osCommerce will then check with the relevant domain server to ensure that the given email address exists on that server and so will be able to receive the email that you are attempting to send.

You can also disable email sending entirely if you wish. For the moment this is not necessary, because at some stage we will need to test certain things relating to emails—for example, whether osCommerce is sending confirmation of order emails, and so on. It is entirely likely that you will be developing osCommerce with live data further down the line; in other words, data that reflects real live customer's details. In this case, it is unlikely that we would want them to receive erroneous emails as the result of our testing, so we simply set the Send E-Mails option to false.

If your initial attempt at sending an email didn't pay off, then try swapping the Email Transport Method setting and resending. If this fails, then I am afraid it is time for you to put the osCommerce community to good use—think of any problems like this as a chance to learn how to use the osCommerce community resource.

Download

Now we come to my personal favorite—the downloads section! One of the true wonders of the world is that we can now generate money by simply transferring information without the need for a physical medium. To this end, the demo site has a section where e-books and articles are available for purchase and download from the site. Obviously, if you are going to be retailing products that are available for download, such as software or ebooks, then this section is of particular interest to you. If not, then feel free to leave the settings as they are and continue.

To begin with, Enable Downloads should be set to true. The rest of the other settings can be left as they are for the time being. In order to demonstrate how this now works, we will need to add a product to our product database quickly. Go to the Catalog heading option and then navigate through Categories/Products till you get to the Strategy category of the Software products—it doesn't really matter where you add a product; if you feel like adding one somewhere else, go ahead—it will make no difference.

Here you should click on the new product button, and fill out the form for a new product. For this example, the new product is called My Download in order to distinguish it from the other products, as shown here:

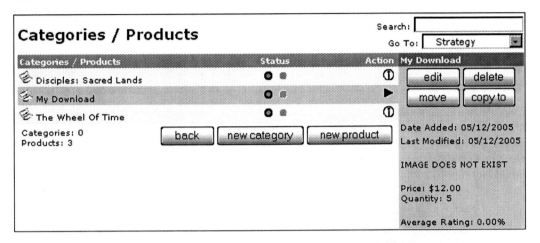

Notice the properties of My Download in the box on the right of the screen—these are arbitrary settings, and you can put in whatever you like. There is no need to hunt for an image here; this is just a quick and nasty demonstration.

Now, downloadable products in osCommerce are held in the download folder under the catalog directory, so we will need to place a file in here so that osCommerce is able to provide customers with something to download. It doesn't matter what we use for this example, but obviously when it comes to real downloads you will most likely have a zipped file with the same name as your product. In other words, if a customer downloads a computer game called unreal tournament, you will probably name your zipped download file unreal_tournament.zip to make it easy to track which files are supposed to be downloaded.

For our purposes we simply need to show that a file can be downloaded, so in this case we are going to copy account.php from the catalog folder into download. You can place any file you like in download folder, and we will attach that file to the product in the Products Attributes section in a moment. Now that the product is registered in the database, and the product file is present in the download folder, we need to set some of its attributes. For this, click on the Products Attributes link in the left-hand box of the admin tool.

At the bottom of the screen under the section Products Attributes, you will notice a drop-down list from which to select products. Find My Download from that list, add in the settings that are appropriate to the file you have placed in the download folder, and insert the product. For this example, the page looks like this:

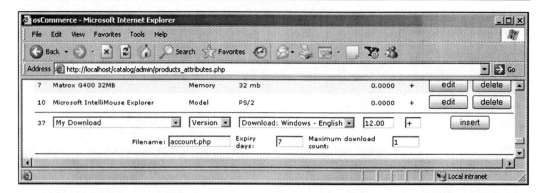

Once the product has been inserted, we can shop for it as normal on the site. If you haven't already created a customer account on the website, you will need to do so in order to be able to purchase this product. However, if you navigate to the product category in which you added the My Download product, you will notice that it is now available for purchase just like any other product. Go ahead and buy it as you would on any other site. You should end up with a page like this:

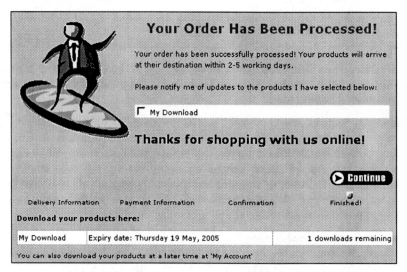

Clicking on the My Download link will allow you to begin the product download. That's all there is to it. If you are unable to download the file, then the first thing to do is check the permission settings on the pub and download folders. For Linux users, pub and download permissions should be set to 777 and 755 respectively, for Windows users, simply ensure there is no Read-Only setting in the folder properties.

At the moment, of course, you could navigate directly to the catalog/download folder in your browser and download whatever products are in there without having to pay for it. Just as bad, you may or may not have noticed that since we have not dealt with how to set up proper payments, osCommerce has made these downloads available to use while our purchase orders are still pending. Since we haven't used a credit card, this means that the download came *before* the payment. Not a very satisfactory state of affairs at the moment, but this will all be rectified a little later on in Chapter 10 on *Tools, Tips, and Tricks*, when we use a community contribution to sort things out properly. For now, though, we are able to download products if needs be.

GZip Compression

GZipping is really a good way to reduce your usage of bandwidth. Basically it allows osCommerce to send compressed files over to the customer's browser, where they are rendered as normal. Most browsers support this feature, so you should not have too many problems with compatibility if you decide to enable this setting. The only thing to look out for here is whether your server supports Zlib, and is using a version of PHP later than 4.0.4. Incidentally, if you ever need to find out how your server is configured, this simple PHP script will help you out:

```
<?
phpinfo();
?>
```

Give the script a name and navigate to it in your browser, and it will automatically print out a list of all the configuration settings (alternatively, click on Server Info in the Tools section of the admin tool). This is useful if, for example, you need to find out whether your server supports Zlib.

The Compression Level default setting is 5, and this is fine for use in general, so unless you specifically want to play around to measure performance differences, it is recommended that you leave it as is if you are going to use it. Remember that some browsers might run into problems if you enable compression, so be wary of this when your site goes live.

Sessions

Sessions can be a complicated beast to understand. The 5c explanation is that sessions are what PHP uses to retain the state of a web application. What this means is that when a customer logs on to your website, PHP assigns him or her something called a session. This session holds information about this user and allows osCommerce to keep track of various important things. For example, without the use of session, how would osCommerce know which user was using which shopping cart? Since all users have their own chosen products added to their cart, osCommerce needs to be able to tell which user is which so that it can display the correct cart for each user.

This is obviously a critical function of an e-commerce site, because where money is involved, it is paramount that the right information is recorded for each transaction. In this case a transaction could mean anything from clicking on a link to purchasing a product.

Since sessions are such a critical part of osCommerce, some thought needs to go into how you want to configure your session support. We originally asked osCommerce to use database-based session support, so the first setting in the Sessions section should not affect you. If you have configured osCommerce for file-based session support, then simply set this option to the file where you would like osCommerce to record session information. You should keep this folder in your home directory for reasons of security.

The Force Cookie Use option determines whether or not we want to use cookies. Cookies are small files that are stored on the customer's browser. The information in these files can then be used for a host of different things, including making sessions more secure. The problem is that over the years many people have abused the use of cookies to the extent that a lot of people disable their use on their browsers.

If you feel you require cookies for your sessions, then osCommerce automatically inserts a page explaining to customers why and how they should enable cookies if it detects a browser that doesn't allow their use. For the moment, though, we can leave this setting as false because it is useful for us to view session information in the URL during development. Once your site has been deployed and is live, you will most likely want to make use of cookies.

While we haven't got to the stage of worrying about securing our site using SSL and many other wondrous things, it is worth discussing the Check SSL Session ID option briefly. Since we haven't got SSL enabled on our development machine, we cannot set this value to true for the moment, but it is worth considering the performance versus security tradeoff here. Enabling this setting means that osCommerce must check and validate the customer's session ID on every page call. This increases security because it helps prevent someone else sneaking in and hijacking a session, but because of the extra work involved, it slows down your site slightly. However, assuming that the performance degradation is acceptable, it is generally wiser to opt for higher security—it's really a case of "better safe than sorry!"

Check User Agent is simply another option that adds to the security of your osCommerce transactions. Enabling this forces osCommerce to check the customer's user agent for each page request. The user agent is simply a string that identifies the requesting browser to the server, so checking this every time can increase security; if you have a hijacked session, it is likely (but not definite) that the user agent of the hijacker is different.

The Check IP Address option does pretty much the same thing as Check User Agent, only this time it looks at the customer's computer's IP address. The IP address of a computer is a unique string of digits which identifies a given computer. Due to the way some Internet Service Providers designate IP addresses, enabling this setting may cause some unwanted problems for some people—AOL customers in particular are susceptible to this.

The Prevent Spider Session option is an interesting one. This basically stops automated programs from setting up a working session in osCommerce by not issuing them with a session ID. Obviously an automated program is not a real live customer, so wasting resources on tracking its passage over the site is a pretty futile thing to do; after all, it's not like it's going to buy anything. Accordingly, it is recommended that you set this option to true.

Finally, the Recreate Session option will force osCommerce to recreate a session ID whenever a customer performs a logon or a checkout. This can help to prevent customers logging into each others accounts.

For the development site, the following session settings were made:

Sessions

Title	Value	Action
Session Directory	/tmp	ⓘ
Force Cookie Use	False	ⓘ
Check SSL Session ID	False	ⓘ
Check User Agent	False	ⓘ
Check IP Address	False	ⓘ
Prevent Spider Sessions	True	ⓘ
Recreate Session	True	▶

Once we get round to deploying the site on the live server, we will need to come back to these settings and modify them appropriately. For example, the Check SSL Session ID option will be enabled on the live site, since if something is worth using SSL over, you may as well go that bit further and guard against session hijacking. So, once you have decided what settings you want, record them in your development notes for later.

Summary

It is at this point that I should confess that I have lied to you ever so slightly. Recall that our aim in this chapter was to get 80% of the configuration done for only 20% of the effort; well, that's not really what has happened. There are quite a few more tasks to perform before we can consider the site to be more or less configured—we have done maybe 30-40% in reality, with many of the settings subject to change on the live site. That's not to say you should get despondent about how much further there is to go, because there have been some very valuable lessons learned in this chapter for very little effort.

What we have done is gone through the very basic and most general settings, which in turn has forced us to think about how we want our osCommerce application to behave in the end, which is always a worthwhile exercise. This is extremely important, as you have now been exposed to the type of things one needs to contemplate before making decisions that influence the running of the site. Furthermore, you have seen how to relate the changes in settings to the changes customers will see. Also not to be ignored is the newly learned ability to make use of the administration tool, which will form a big part of the site's development and administration in the future.

The rest of the configuration settings coincide with more specific development tasks—such as populating our product database and implementing payment facilities—and as a result are going to be discussed in their specific chapters. But for now you should feel safe in the knowledge that you have learned much about the way in which osCommerce works, and have (hopefully) built up a set of development notes that will help you pinpoint the settings to be looked at during the deployment phase.

5
Working with Data

Data is the heart of any application that needs to retain or manipulate information in any way. How to go about storing information in a database is generally a cause of consternation for developers building applications from scratch. The problem, you see, is that unlike any other part of a program, which can generally be used with little to no modification for other applications, databases must be tailored precisely to their specific application in order to be effective. You don't need to worry about this though; it's all taken care of already.

As you know, osCommerce sites use the **MySQL Relational Database Management System** to store information about products, customers, sessions, languages, configuration, orders, reviews, specials, and a bunch of other things. The structure of the database is created and built during the installation process and is ready to work whenever you decide to make changes. In fact, we have already been working with data because the configuration properties set in the last chapter are of course all retained by storing them in the database.

In this chapter, we are going to be working on adding, removing, and updating business-related information in the database. What type of information is this? Well, for a start, we need to learn how to add and remove customers, their orders, and most importantly, products from the database. Discussing how to add and remove products will take up the bulk of this chapter simply because it is more than likely the type of data you will work with most often. The only issue we will leave for another time is database security since you are (hopefully) still working on your development machine, and the topic of security merits its own chapter.

It must be said—despite its apparent obviousness—that ensuring your data is accurate is just about the most important thing you can do because corrupt data is worse than worthless, it's actually detrimental. So, along the way, we will talk about the right approach to dealing with your information. This is important because, believe it or not, it is actually quite simple to produce data that is not accurate, and in order to give you a better understanding of how your actions affect the underlying data we will often show important results in the actual database and not just on the website or administration tool.

Specifically, in this chapter, we are going to talk about:

- Working out how to store your data
- The preparations involved before adding products
- Adding, removing, and updating data from the Catalog, Customers, and Reports sections in the administration tool

- Viewing reports
- Using community contributions to work with data

Finally, it is important to realize that while it is essential that you understand how to use the administration tool effectively in order to build and maintain your site, it is not the be all and end all. Towards the end of the chapter we will look at some more advanced options for getting large numbers of products into your database without having to follow the time-consuming and quite repetitious process of entering each one in manually using the administration tool. So it is advisable that you follow along with the text to learn how to use the administration tool, but do not act on any of the information provided until the end of the chapter.

How Do I Categorize My Data?

Categorizing your products involves choosing a strategy for displaying a navigation structure on the website. This is what determines how your customers search and hopefully find products they are looking for. On a different level, you also need to have a clear idea of how your products are going to be displayed, in other words, what type of attributes are relevant for your products. This will be discussed in the *Product Attributes* section later in this chapter.

If you look at the Categories/Products data in your administration tool, you will notice that it is organized into a hierarchical structure that reflects how customers navigate it on the website. For example, we have three categories, Hardware, Software, and DVD Movies, in the Categories/Products section by default. Within these categories are subcategories such as movie genres like Action, Comedy, and Drama in the DVD Movies section. As you might predict, if we open up one of these genres, we find the types of movies we would expect to see, such as Lethal Weapon in the Action genre.

Why is this important? Structuring the data to reflect the real world is the crux of modern-day data storage. We want to mirror the real world as closely as possible when we create our database. So if you wanted to, let's say, sell jewelry from your osCommerce site, you would need to think about the best way to classify your products in order to make it as intuitive as possible for customers to locate what they are looking for.

You could have categories such as Earrings, Diamonds, and Necklaces, which customers could browse through, and certainly these categories might logically encapsulate all the products on your site. This means that you wouldn't be left with a product that doesn't seem to fit into any category very well. But are these the best categories to use? What happens if a certain young lady decides she wants to purchase a new pair of diamond earrings? Does she go to Diamonds, or to Earrings? Most people will answer that both should be equally good routes to locating the product, and so they should.

Consider, however, that you would then need to instruct osCommerce to either duplicate the data so that it showed up under both categories, or you would have to make a link from one or the other category to that product. As it so happens, both of these tasks can be accomplished quite easily by osCommerce, but there should be a better way to classify your products so that you don't have to worry about linking and copying products unnecessarily. After all, if we chose categories such that every product had to be duplicated, we would waste a lot of space. The answer, of course, is 'yes'; there is a better way to categorize the products. The exact method you choose really depends on the type of data you have, but in this case you could choose to make the main categories Earrings, Bracelets, Necklaces, and so on, and have appropriate subcategories if necessary.

So, how do you go about choosing how to categorize your products in a generic manner? The best answer is to think carefully about how this data is going to be used. In other words, think about how customers are going to search for products on your site and relate that to the actual data you have. We could simply classify everything from its highest level of abstraction, in which case we would have something like the following structure (this is just a quick demo, so we aren't going to list every category under the sun):

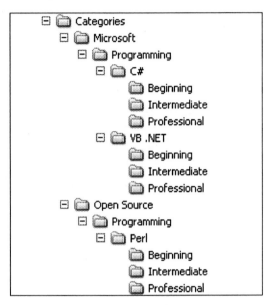

This might seem pretty logical because you certainly won't get lost with a structure like this—after all, if you are looking for a programming book you should probably know the difference between Microsoft and Open Source. But there are several problems with doing things like this from a pragmatic point of view. First off, there are only two main categories at the top level, so regardless of what the customers want to buy, they are forced to decide on Microsoft or Open Source before they do anything. They then get to the Programming level (while only programming is shown here, other topics at this level of abstraction would be things like Networking or Web Development) where they would have to make another choice, before being presented again with a choice of languages like Perl or C#, before again being presented with a choice of level of coverage.

You can see that this is pretty tedious because we have a *deep* structure to navigate. Surely our lives would be easier if we had more choices to begin with so that we only have to go through one or two levels of category before finding the products we want. Certainly, for the weary customer, being able to find what they want without going through three or four level of categories would be wonderful, but how do we decide on the actual categories?

The answer here again is to think carefully about the average customer. A customer who is shopping for a computer book is likely already to know more or less the area of their interest. A Perl programmer, for example, would really want to click directly on Perl, and view the available books. So, our conclusion is that we want to make our directory structure as flat as possible and as intuitive as possible, while efficiently encapsulating all the products. This means we should go with a large selection of categories over a deep structure because it is quicker for someone to search a list than to click on several categories and wait for the page to refresh each time.

The final thing to bring into the equation is, of course, to consider what types of products you have, and more importantly, what you intend to have in your catalog in the future. What you are going to have in the future is a huge concern. It is relatively easy to add categories and products as and when you need to. What's not easy is retrieving customers who have decided to shop elsewhere after having a torrid time with your navigation structure.

Categorizing Contechst Books Products

The selection of categories for the demo website is fairly complex. Contechst Books is a specialist retailer of computer books, and as you know, the term 'computer books' could be stretched to mean just about anything to do with technology. What about the books themselves? There are ebooks as well as hardcopy books, which may or may not come in paperback or hardback, as well as journals and articles to come in the future. So how do we go about choosing which categories are the best ones? Well, based on what we have just discussed and our current catalog, the following directory structure can be used:

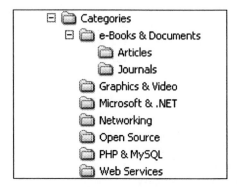

This is quite an interesting structure because it incorporates elements of everything we have discussed so far. In the end you will find that whatever you choose when developing a fair sized directory structure, you end up making trade-offs. For example, the PHP & MySQL category should fall under Open Source since that is what it is—open-source software. However, because of their immense popularity on the Web, we suspect that many people will buy specifically those types of books, and so to cater for a fair chunk of our clientele, we make things easier by upgrading PHP & MySQL to main category status.

What's the trade-off here? Well, we have moved from a purely logical structure to one that takes into consideration our perceived client base. It means things aren't nice and neat in terms of structure, but hopefully it is better in terms of customer satisfaction.

What else can we note from this structure? The e-Books & Documents section has a few tricks up its sleeve. First off, it isn't a single category, it's two in one. We have merged two logically distinct products, e-Books and Documents, into one category because they both share the property that they are downloadable, and so customers who are looking for something to download off the site don't have to search all over the show to find what they are looking for. A neat trick, but don't overuse it because over merging categories causes your structure to lose meaning. This is because the more vague a category heading, the harder it becomes for customers to work out what they will find in there.

Also, notice that e-Books & Documents has two subcategories that lie on the same level as the actual ebook products, so we have mixed products and categories into the same level. This is actually a smart move because if there are no products in a given category, osCommerce will show all the subcategories on the category's site page. This is really a beginner's mistake from a marketing point of view because it means that we are showing the customer a screen without any products to sell. Given that you only ever have about a minute or so to impress a customer into buying something, if the stats are to be believed, this is a heinous mistake.

An interesting point takes us back to the very beginning of this discussion where we talked about trying to avoid product linking and duplication. While we certainly want to avoid large amounts of redundant data through duplication and would like to keep our structure as simple as possible by avoiding large amounts of linking, some linking will be required if we are going to have a shallow directory structure like the one shown. For example, Web Services can be implemented using Microsoft & .NET as well as Open Source technologies, so it is more than likely that some of the books would need to be linked from Web Services into one of the other categories—or even vice versa.

Of course, this structure is only useful for a relatively small bookstore such as Contechst Books. If we had several thousand books in the Open Source category, then we would need to further classify and break up the books into smaller more easily browsed groups. The larger your product database, the more you need to think about how to break up the information there in order to make it easily accessible. That said, you now know how to do it, so go ahead and design your site's navigation structure.

Preparing to Add Product Data

Many of you will already have a list, or at least a partial list, of all the products you intend to sell via your website. You may be an established business with a full catalog that you need to enter into your osCommerce site, or you could have a single product to begin with that you want to sell. Whatever your situation, there are certain things that you will need to get in order before you can create an online catalog that will actually promote the sale of your goods. So what are these things? Well, the best way to find out is to let osCommerce answer that.

Open up the administration tool to the Catalog section, choose the Categories/Products link and navigate all the way down till you reach a product and click edit—it doesn't matter which product for the moment. You will be presented with a screen that looks something like this:

Looking up and down this page you can see that there are a number of *properties* assigned to this product. Most are pretty intuitive to deal with, Products Status is easy enough to decide, and the Date Available also should not present you with too many difficulties. If you set the Date Available property to some time in the future, then a friendly note pops up on the product's page on the website informing the customer that This product will be in stock on Friday 21 October, 2005 (or something similar depending on the date you set).

Of course, with the Out of Stock option set, the website will not show any product at all.

Products Manufacturer is an interesting attribute in the case of the demo site. We don't want to list the manufacturers for our products, but we require the publishers to be listed. However, rather than redesigning the internals of osCommerce to represent this requirement, we can replace Manufacturer with Publisher in our mind's eye and simply add publishers names to our list of manufacturers so that they can be displayed on the site as normal.

In order to add a manufacturer, you would simply go to the Manufacturers tab in the Catalog section and add one from there. All this will all be discussed in detail once we get to the *Catalog* section later in this chapter, so don't worry about it for the moment.

Products name, Tax Class, Products Price (Net), Products Price (Gross), and Products Description are also pretty straightforward. Of course, you will need to research whatever special tax requirements you may be subject to before you go ahead and set that information. The default one on the site, which is set in the Locations/Taxes section, is left for the time being since the product shown is not the one that the demo site will sell. We will deal with the tax options later on in Chapter 7. For now though, simply be aware that you will need to know where you stand with taxes in order to make the right choices when it comes to adding products.

Another interesting thing to note here is the fact that everything is, by default, given in three languages. If you think that you will need to include more than English into your site then obviously you will have to either hire someone to do the translations for you, or if you are a polyglot, you can simply copy out the product info into the language of your choice. Setting the languages you would like to use gets taken care of by the Localization section of the administration tool, and this will be dealt with in the chapter on customization. If you are only going to sell to a predominantly English-speaking customer base, then simply leave the other language options blank.

Take a look at the Products Description text area on your own product page. You should notice that there are HTML formatting tags in this text. This is because osCommerce will render whatever you enter into this text area directly to the browser. Without adding the relevant HTML formatting you could be left with descriptions that aren't nicely laid out—in this instance, the <br> tags simply give each sentence a new line.

Products Quantity is simple enough, and osCommerce will automatically reduce this when there are purchases *if* you have enabled stock control (see the previous chapter for more info on this). The Products Model gets displayed in the site's navigation breadcrumb bar. So whatever you would like to show in the navigation bar is what you should enter here. For example, changing the model to Frantic_DVD will produce the following breadcrumb trail when viewed on the site (we will see later that the Product Model is a very important value and you should ensure that it is never left blank and is never repeated):

With that done you can turn your attention to the Products Image, and the Products URL. Now, we will be dealing with images in detail in the next chapter, so don't fret too much about this. However, recall our earlier discussion about how osCommerce is laid out; because of the way things are set up, osCommerce automatically looks in the images folder under catalog for its images. It is recommended that you look at how the default image structure is laid out, and select one that will suit your store (there will be recommendations made in the following chapter).

> Keep your images in the image folder because if you put them outside the catalog directory, all your image links will break when you deploy your site to the live server.

Setting the Products URL will give customers the option to visit the product maker's website while viewing the product information in your store. Leaving this blank will simply cause the option not to be presented. Finally, Products Weight is easy enough to deal with, given a suitable scale to measure with.

Now that you have a good idea of what information you need to gather on each of your products and how to categorize them, we can begin adding to the store.

Catalog

The Catalog section of the administration tool is a pretty nifty piece of content management software. You can control your stock with a fine tooth comb from here, and although it is not complete on its own, using some of the community contributions to extend the default functionality provided should give you all the help you need to run and maintain the stock on your site.

Before we begin by looking at the subsections of the Catalog administration tool, there are a few things that you should know before hand. Above and beyond the standard functionality provided, osCommerce also gives you a drop-down navigation list to help find your way around your data directory structure, as well as a search tool. If you open up the Catalog page, you will be presented with something like this:

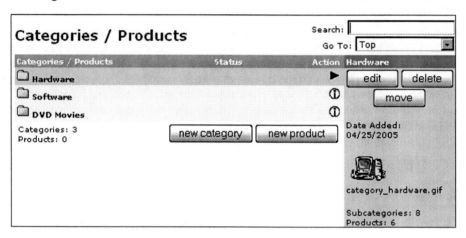

Use the Search textbox (type in the name of the product or category and hit *Enter*) to find products or categories quickly, or use the drop-down list to navigate to various sections without having to click on the individual category links. Apart from this, you should be familiar with the way the tool works from your experience while configuring osCommerce. Let's go ahead and look through each of the sections in the Catalog section.

Categories/Products

By now you should have a clear idea of what your directory structure looks like as well where your products are going to fit within that structure. Assuming this is the case, we can now go ahead and make that structure a reality and even add some data. However, we won't show more than a product or two since we have not dealt with the subject of images, which are obviously a fairly important part of the site. There are quite a lot of issues surrounding how best to make use of images, and accordingly this is given the full coverage in the next chapter.

Once you have learned how to perform the various basic product operations (like adding and removing) you should continue on through the chapter before entering in your entire product database. This is because some options for inserting a large number of products in one go are presented towards the end of the chapter. You might find that this is a better way of doing things rather than entering each one by hand.

Adding and Deleting Categories and Products

At any rate, you know the drill, so click on the new category button to add your new categories. You will notice that you have the option to fill in the Sort Order while adding the new category. Adding an integer here will define where in the navigation list the current entry should appear. Leaving this blank means that osCommerce will sort the categories in alphabetic order. For example, Contechst Books wishes the e-Books and Documents category to appear last, so it is given a high sort order while the other categories are left blank.

Once you have defined all your categories—including adding subcategories by navigating to a category and clicking the add category button to add a new folder there—check your site to view the changes made. The demo site at this stage looks like this:

There are several things to note here. First, the new categories and subcategories have been added (you can tell that e-Books & Documents has subcategories because of the arrow to the right of the title) and that obviously, there are as yet no products in the Graphics & Video section, which is the currently selected category. Secondly, you will notice a broken picture link to the immediate left of the shopping cart box. This is because we have not yet added any category images to the `images` folder. You may even decide to do away with these images altogether so wait until next chapter where they are covered in detail before making a choice.

Notice also that we have not yet gotten rid of the default categories. This is because removing all these products now will leave us with a pretty dismal looking website and make it harder to ascertain what changes have had what effect and where. There's no rush to remove them for the moment, so leave them as they are for now.

Next, let's add a new product to the database. Go to a product category and click on new product. This will bring up the product's buying info page, which we discussed earlier. Fill out the details of the product and click preview, you will then be shown what your product listing will look like on the site. For example, we have added a book entitled VirtualDub Video: Capture, Processing and Encoding with all its accompanying details. The result on the site is:

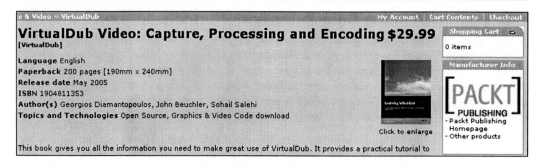

From this you should be able to tell the following:

- A small image for the product has been uploaded here. Assuming you haven't uploaded an image file for the product you will have a broken link instead.

- HTML formatting tags have been used to lay out the information nicely. For example, the book's specification information has been bolded using the <b> and </b> tags, and blank lines have been inserted using the <br> tag. All in all, the effect is pretty striking. If you want to try some special effects, remember that you have a stylesheet, which you can use to fiddle around with, and if you wish to learn more about HTML, search Google with the term HTML example.

- The Products Model has been entered as VirtualDub; you can see this by looking at the breadcrumb at the top left of the page.

- If you look closely, you will note that a manufacturer image (Packt Publishing) shown in the Manufacturer Info box on the left has also been added.

That is really all there is to adding products to the database. Of course, you can remove them just as easily by clicking the delete button on the products administration page. This is how the new products administration page looks like:

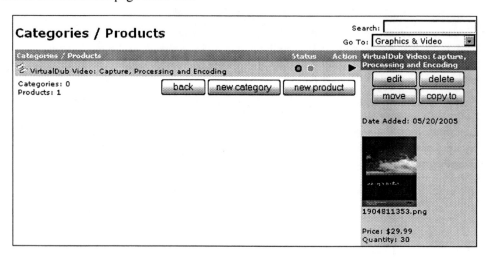

Notice that there are now two more buttons available apart from edit and delete that you are already familiar with. These two options relate to where and how the product is stored and accessed in the database.

Along with all the buttons are two 'lights' under the Status heading towards the middle of the screen. These are used to activate and deactivate products without having to go through the trouble of adding them or removing them from the database. So, if there is a product that you don't want to make available on the site for some reason, but also don't want to play around with its settings, you can simply set it to inactive by clicking on the pink button.

Moving and Copying Categories and Products

Let's say that it so happens that the VirtualDub title is available for download (it isn't, but let's just assume that it is). This being the case, it would make sense to have it appear under the e-Books & Documents folder too. Now, we don't really want to navigate to that category and re-enter all that information, so rather than that, simply click on copy to, and the following options are presented:

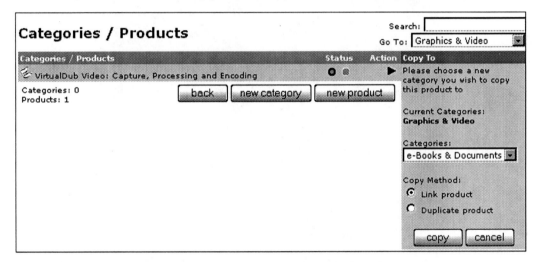

Now we can choose whether or not to Duplicate product, which will create an entirely new record in the database under the stipulated category, or alternatively, choose Link product, which will simply link the product to the stipulated category. Since we don't want to create unnecessary redundant data it is a far better idea to link the product than duplicate it. Doing this means that when we navigate to the e-Books and Documents category on the site, we are presented with the same VirtualDub product.

This has quite far-reaching consequences for stock control because if you choose to duplicate the product you now have to worry about two sales channels for the same products and ensure that you have enough stock for both. If you simply link the product then you only have one product being sold and your stock control continues as normal.

You can always confirm what is happening under the hood by checking in your MySQL database. For example, open up the MySQL console with the following command (and remembering your password):

```
c:\>mysql -uoscommerce -p commerce_db
password: **********
mysql>
```

You can find out the product ID of the new product by querying the products table like so:

```
mysql> select products_id, products_model from products;
```

This should return something like the following:

From this you can see that VirtualDub has been assigned the product ID value of 31. So, armed with this information, we can now query the products_to_categories table to see which categories this product is assigned to:

```
mysql> select * from products_to_categories;
```

We get the following results in this case:

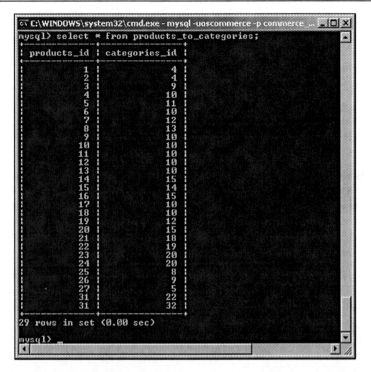

From this we can see that the product with `product_id` 31 is linked to both category 22 and category 32. This agrees with what we have done so far. The paranoid among you may wish to query the `categories_description` table to further find out the names of the two categories in question just in case they don't match our expectations. This is left as an exercise to the reader.

The other option, move, will simply move that product to the category of your choice. The product then no longer exists in its original place, but only in the new category.

It should be mentioned that you can also move categories although you aren't able to copy to. For categories, move works in exactly the same way as for products, by simply adding the category entry to the target category and removing it from the present one. It is recommended that you experiment with these features since there are other default behaviors you should learn about. For example, what happens if you try to move a product to a folder that already contains that product?

Product Attributes

Don't get the product attributes confused with the properties we covered in the *Preparing to Add Product Data* section earlier. What we have looked at is effectively the 'buying information' that is used to inform customers about a product on the website. The product attributes that we will look at later deal with a different type of information. For example, in the last section there was no way to indicate whether the product you added was available for download.

Depending on what it is you are selling you will obviously need different product attributes to be reflected in your application. For example, should you wish to become the largest retailer of Bonsai trees in the northern hemisphere, it is unlikely the default attributes of color, size, model,

Memory, and version will be of much use to you. By the same token, making up a couple of categories on the fly will probably also not help because there are a few tricks up osCommerce's sleeve that should be exploited—we will come to this while looking at how to use the Product Attributes section of the administration tool in a little while.

Assuming you were the aforementioned horticulturalist, then product attributes such as species, style, and age are probably of more use to you because they apply directly to the type of product you are selling. Furthermore, you would need to be able to offer price ranges based on these attributes. For example, the older a tree gets the more valuable it would become so you could have a range of age options presented to the buyer with their corresponding prices.

For Contechst Books, the matter is slightly different. The type of attributes we are really concerned about are things like whether the cover is soft or hardback, whether the book comes with an accompanying CD, whether it is downloadable, or whether it has more than one edition. Obviously, you will need to understand the range of options inherent in your specific selection of stock before working on this section. You only need to concern yourself with those attributes that have a range of options that should be made available to the customer.

Once you have a list of all the attributes that could have more than one value, you should enter meaningful names into the first group of textboxes under the heading Product Options on the Products Attributes page as shown here:

From this it is quite clear that we have added options 6 and 9, which will apply to some, if not all, of the books we are selling. Remember that the attributes you set in this section don't have to apply to a wide range of products; even if there is a single product that comes in a variety of flavors, you will need to add it in here in order to have the options presented to the buyer. You may recall that we also talked about whether a book would be downloadable; well, this attribute falls neatly under the Version title, so we have not added a new Product Option for downloads.

> Due to the way in which osCommerce and the download controller community contribution works, it is recommended that you look at the *Working with Downloadable Products* section of Chapter 10 before attempting to set up a working downloadable product site.

One you have your options safely entered, move across the screen to the Option Values section. This section deals with the specifics of each of the options declared in the first section. So, for example, we would define two values for Cover here, namely Hardback and Paperback. The following screenshot shows the rest of the settings used for the demo site's products:

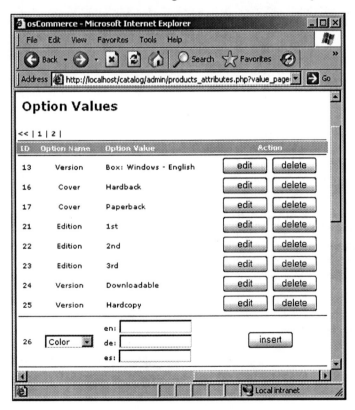

Make sure you can do this yourself by first selecting an option to work on from the drop-down list (shown in the previous screenshot as ID number 26) under Option Values, then add the option value to the text box and click insert.

Now, should the issue arise, we would be able to provide a user with the options of purchasing either the Hardback or Paperback covers (if a book comes in both), or the 1st, 2nd, or 3rd edition of the book (obviously if there is only one edition of a book you simply don't associate this attribute with that book), and finally if there is a Downloadable version as well as a paper version of a book, then customers can decide which they prefer.

The final stage is to actually tie these settings to the relevant title. So, say for example, the VirtualDub book we talked about earlier had two editions as well as being bound in both hardback and paperback. We would need to ensure that the buyers could stipulate their preference while making purchases. In order to do this you scroll down to the final section, which is entitled Product Attributes as shown here:

Products Attributes

<< | 1 | 2 |

ID	Product Name	Option Name	Option Value	Value Price	Prefix	Action	
10	Microsoft IntelliMouse Explorer	Model	PS/2	0.0000	+	edit	delete
32	Unreal Tournament	Color	16 mb	0.0000	+	edit	delete
26	Unreal Tournament	Version	Download: Windows - English	0.0000	+	edit	delete
27	Unreal Tournament	Version	Box: Windows - English	0.0000	+	edit	delete
35	VirtualDub Video: Capture, Processing and Encoding	Cover	Hardback	4.0000	+	edit	delete
37	VirtualDub Video: Capture, Processing and Encoding	Edition	1st	0.0000		edit	delete
34	VirtualDub Video: Capture, Processing and Encoding	Edition	2nd	5.0000	+	edit	delete
38	VirtualDub Video: Capture, Processing and Encoding	Cover	Paperback	0.0000		edit	delete
39	VirtualDub Video: Capture, Processing and Encoding	Version	Downloadable	7.00	-	insert	

Filename: [   ]   Expiry days: [7]   Maximum download count: [5]

At the bottom of the table you are presented with a drop-down list of all your products as well as the product options, values, and resulting modification to the price. This is really where you get down to business and associate the attributes with their respective products. As you can see in the above figure, the VirtualDub title has had two Edition options added, with 1st and 2nd as their values, as well as Hardback and Paperback Cover options too.

The Value Price column heading holds the value of the change to the standard price, and the Prefix column shows whether or not this change is positive or negative. If you leave out these values when adding a product attribute, then osCommerce defaults to no change in price. You should be able to tell that in this case, that the Hardback version will cost $4 more than a normal book, and the second edition is $5 more expensive than the first edition. Notice that the Downloadable Version of the book (the Product Attributes in the process of being added) is actually $7 cheaper than its standard counterpart.

The upshot of all this is, that when a customer decides to buy a copy of VirtualDub, they have a series of choices that affect the type of product they purchase. In this case, let's say the customer wanted a first edition hardcopy, hardback version of the book. Well, in this case they would make the selections as shown below:

And the total price would, as we expect, be $29.99 plus $4.00, which it duly is when we view the cart contents:

Notice that the actual options specified when the choice is originally made are now displayed underneath the product's name. The price is $33.99 as we expected, but had we bought the downloadable version it would have been $7.00 cheaper. Many of you should be frowning at this stage because *something just isn't right*! What could it be?

I must confess that you have been led astray slightly in order to demonstrate the need to plan ahead. Adding attributes such as the ones we have shown here will lead to inconsistent charges because we have failed to carefully identify the nature of each option. Obviously, if we categorize related attributes differently we can set up inconsistencies in the way the products present their options. In this case, we should not be able to choose a downloadable hardback book because it is *impossible* to have such a thing.

So where did we go wrong? The answer is quite simple! The hardback, softback, and downloadable product attributes are related in that they specify the type, or version, of book we are offering. Sure, the first two are a type of cover as well, but this is why it can be tricky to just jump in and make decisions like this. In order to rectify this problem we need to realize that a book cannot be a combination of hardback, softback, and downloadable, while it can be a combination of softback and edition one or two, hardback and edition one or two, or downloadable and edition one or two.

Accordingly, the solution is to go back and remove the category Cover, and insert Hardback and Paperback into the Version option, so buyers have to pick one of the three, but no more. Of course, trying to delete Cover will result in the following message from osCommerce:

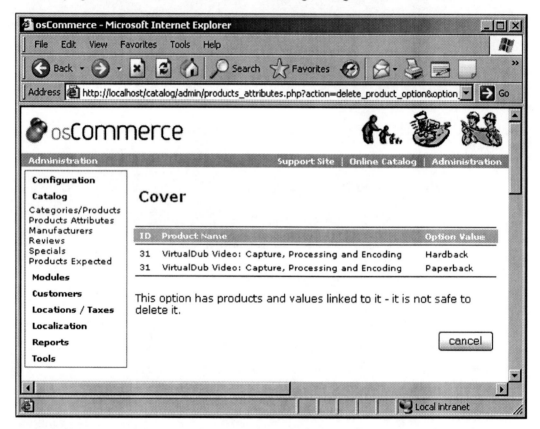

osCommerce quite rightly forces us to think carefully about what we are removing in order to maintain a valid and accurate list of product attributes at all times. This means we have to remove the settings from the Product Attributes section first, followed by the Option Values section before finally removing the Cover attribute entirely. Once this is done, the two cover options can be added to the Version attribute and associated with the book again. Now when the customer attempts to purchase the book, they are presented with *sensible* options, like so:

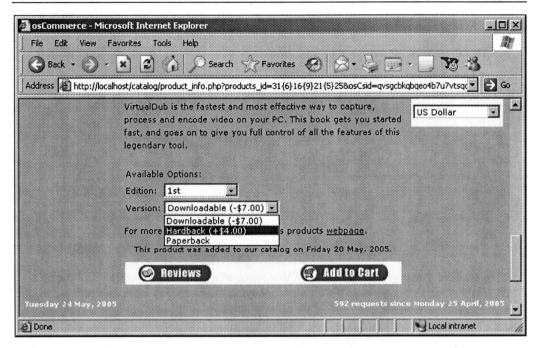

One thing to note before we move on is that it can be quite a pest to perform a large number of operations one at a time using this interface, so careful planning and using the drop-down list (at the top center of the screen) to toggle between listing the attributes by ID or alphabetically will help keep frustration to a minimum.

Manufacturers

The Manufacturers section is pretty straightforward. Using this section is a case of adding or removing the names and logos of the companies who make your products. Recall that the manufacturers declared in this section play a role in adding a product to the database since one of the drop-down lists available in that section links the manufacturers to the product. Apart from this, it is easy to add a manufacturer; simply click on insert and type in the name of the manufacturer, a link to the location of the logo image, which will be held somewhere in your images folder, and then insert the URLs for the company's site(s), like so:

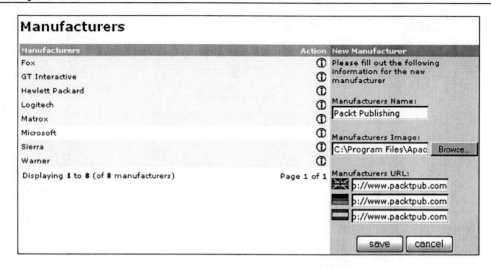

Clicking on **save** should bring up a screen similar to the following one. (Note that if you are not dealing with images yet, instead of the nice green message along the top of the screen there will be an alarming pink one with a warning that no file was uploaded.)

Of course, it is no problem if you want to come back at a later stage and edit your manufacturers. Simply clicking on edit will bring up the same screen as the insert button, which will allow you to change whatever you need to. Recall that in the case of the demo site, the manufacturers are in fact publishers and we are going to modify the site to reflect this in the next chapter. Doing this will serve as a nice example of how to get your hands dirty by making modifications directly to the PHP files that make up osCommerce's customer interface.

Finally, there are a few options that you should consider closely while deleting a manufacturer. The first is whether or not to delete the manufacturer's image, and the second is whether or not to remove all trace of the manufacturer's products including reviews, specials, and upcoming products. How you decide on these is really up to you, but unless you have a major fallout with the sales rep for a particular company, it is unlikely you will need to use this option that often.

Reviews

As with all good websites, the administrator has the final say on what reviews actually remain on the site. So when rival companies begin writing reviews like "*So and so's products are designed by baboons*" all over your site, you have the ability to delete or edit these reviews appropriately. Remember that reviews will be added by customers on the website, so this facility should really only be used for a moderator type role. It is easy enough to click on edit and insert text or modify the star rating, or delete a review by clicking on delete so we won't discuss this any further here.

Specials

At some stage you will no doubt want to offer specials to boost sales or clear old stock. Whatever your reasons, this section makes it easy to add whatever products you want to the specials list and specify how long they are to remain on special offer and how much to take off (either a set amount or a percentage), like so:

```
Specials

Product:        VirtualDub Video: Capture, Processing and Encoding ($29.99) ▾
Special Price:  10%
Expiry Date:    05  07  2005  ▷

Specials Notes:

  • You can enter a percentage to deduct in the Specials Price field, for example: 20%
  • If you enter a new price, the decimal separator must be a '.' (decimal-point), example: 49.99
  • Leave the expiry date empty for no expiration
```

Like so many other things in the administration tool, you can, of course, edit and delete specials with ease. The upshot of adding a special, however, is that predictably, every once in a while (depending on how many products you have on special), your new product will pop up in the specials box as well as displaying its new price in a different color like so:

One final thing to note is that you can activate or deactivate any specials by using the pink and green buttons on the specials homepage.

Products Expected

At first glance, this section might seem slightly superfluous because it is easy enough to set when a product is in or out of stock and when it is expected to arrive from the Categories/Products section, which we looked at earlier in the chapter in the *Preparing to Add Product Data* section. Actually, its function is exactly the same as the adding a product page; it simply provides an interface to show all the expected products in one place. Useful if you have several hundred products coming in at any one time!

When a new product is entered into the catalog, it is not necessary for that product to physically be present at your place of work yet. Accordingly, you can set a date from the pop-up calendar that stipulates when the product is expected to arrive. Provided the product has an arrival date in the future, the product will appear in the Products Expected page. There is only one option given for the products in the Products Expected page, and that is edit.

Clicking on edit simply brings up the same page used to add the product to the database in the first place, and from here you can make any necessary changes. For example, if your product has arrived early, you can set the date expected to the current date and the product will no longer be listed in the Products Expected page. Anything with an expected date prior to the current date will not show up on this list.

Apart from making life easy when trying to keep track of when all your expected products are to arrive, setting expected arrival dates will also cause osCommerce to inform customers of the expected date on the actual site, with notes, for example, such as this one:

This product will be in stock on Thursday 26 May, 2006.

As well as this, upcoming products are displayed at the bottom of the index page on the site along with their expected date.

Customers

The customers section provides a tool that can be used to search for registered customers by name, view and edit their details, check their orders, delete them from the database, and email them if necessary. By and large most of this information is taken care of by the site; the customers can register their details themselves and can keep them updated as and when necessary from the account page provided for all customers by osCommerce. The following figure shows the default customer account page from which customers can look after their details:

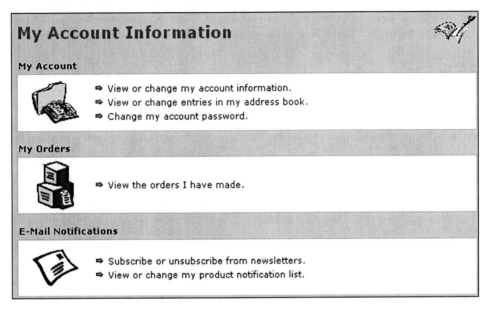

This is effectively the same functionality that the administration tool offers you as the administrator. For example, if you click on edit you are shown all the users' details in pretty much the same manner as they see them on the website. The only interesting bit of information that you may find useful here is that if you are using a fresh installation of osCommerce, and your user, or the default user, has not placed any orders on the system, then clicking on order might bring up the following page:

> **Orders**
>
> Order ID: [   ]
> Status: [All Orders ▼]
>
> 1064 - You have an error in your SQL syntax; check the manual that corresponds to your MySQL server version for the right syntax to use near '-20, 20' at line 1
>
> select o.orders_id, o.customers_name, o.customers_id, o.payment_method, o.date_purchased, o.last_modified, o.currency, o.currency_value, s.orders_status_name, ot.text as order_total from orders o left join orders_total ot on (o.orders_id = ot.orders_id), orders_status s where o.customers_id = '3' and o.orders_status = s.orders_status_id and s.language_id = '1' and ot.class = 'ot_total' order by orders_id DESC limit -20, 20
>
> [TEP STOP]

While this is certainly a hideous message to behold, it is nothing particularly serious and certainly nothing to give up the whole thing and go home over. It's a bit of a bug in the system in that there is no nice, user-friendly message telling you that no orders have been placed yet. As soon as you log onto your site, and place a dummy order, this message will disappear and you will be shown the order.

You should note that if you wish to delete a customer from your database for some reason, you may want to delete the orders associated with that customer first (assuming you don't want them to remain on the system) because otherwise you will be left with a bunch of customer-less orders floating around—at least, these orders will be inaccessible from the Customers section. Of course, it is often useful to keep all the orders on your system regardless, for sales figures and so on.

Orders

A working Orders page provides quite a lot of functionality, and looks like the following screenshot. Notice that there is no option to search through the orders according to the customer's name. This is because you can view all the orders of a particular customer by pressing the orders button in the Customers section—in this way both searches by name and order ID are provided:

There is a drop-down list that provides a filter for which results are to be displayed depending on the status of the order. It is more than likely that you will use this or the Order ID text box to cut down the size of your results since the number of orders will grow (hopefully) quite large with time. These two options provide a particularly good way of finding otherwise well-hidden orders, especially if you need to perform some form of manual processing.

There are four options for dealing with a specific order once it has been located. These include edit, delete, invoice, and packing slip. Of these, edit is by far the most interesting, so let's look at that first. On the edit page, you are presented with the order's relevant details such as the customer's address, email address, shipping and billing address, and payment method. The actual products purchased are also shown followed by information on the status of the order, as shown here:

Customer:	David Mercer 31 Hamilton Rd Claremont Cape Town, 7708 WP, South Africa	Shipping Address:	Billing Address:	David Mercer 31 Hamilton Rd Claremont Cape Town, 7708 WP, South Africa

Telephone Number: 021 671 6700
E-Mail Address: davidm@contechst.com

Payment Method:

Products	Model	Tax	Price (ex)	Price (inc)	Total (ex)	Total (inc)

1 x VirtualDub Video: Capture, Processing and Encoding
  - Edition: 2nd (+$5.00)
  - Version: Downloadable (-$7.00)
	VirtualDub	0%	$24.99	$24.99	$24.99	$24.99

Sub-Total: $24.99
Total: $24.99

Date Added	Customer Notified	Status	Comments
05/25/2005 16:05:09	✔	Pending	

Comments

[text area]

Status: Pending ▾   [update]
Notify Customer: ☑   **Append Comments:** ☑

[invoice] [packing slip] [back]

The important bit comes right at the bottom of the screen where you are given a text area to enter some comments, a drop-down list to change the status of the order, and a checkbox to notify the customer of any changes in the Status of the order, as well as one to Append Comments to the order. Being able to change the status of an order manually is critical for those shops that accept payments by check or in some other form that is not easily automated, and being able to add comments is important if you wish to keep a customer updated about the state of his or her purchase.

The invoice and packing slip options simply pull up a new page with invoice or packing slip details that you can print out and use if you so wish. Please be aware that both, the invoice, and packing slip have the osCommerce logo on them and you will obviously want to replace this when you have created your own site's logo. We will leave this for now since we haven't dealt with images yet, but remember to do this at some stage before invoicing customers; all you need to do is open up the invoice.php and packingslip.php files and find the line which reads something like this:

```
tep_image(DIR_WS_IMAGES . 'oscommerce.gif', 'osCommerce', '204', '50');
```

Replace this with something more suitable:

```
tep_image(DIR_WS_IMAGES . 'contechst_books.gif', 'Contechst Books', '375',
'50');
```

In this case, the image folder in question is actually the `images` folder contained in the `admin` folder and not the main `images` folder in the `catalog` directory. Make sure you place your GIF file in the right place otherwise you will end up with a broken link.

Finally, the delete command gets rid of the specified order, and rather usefully, enquires as to whether or not you would like to re-add the stock associated with the order back to your store's stock. This is, of course, very useful if, for example, a customer's credit card has proved invalid.

Viewing Reports

The reports section provides a nice method of ascertaining which products are viewed the most often, which products are the most popular by sales, and which customers are the biggest spenders—certainly all useful information for the conscientious business owner. Obviously this information can be of vital importance while determining how to order new stock, or working out which demographics are the biggest spenders in your store—possibly for creating targeted promotions and so on.

Actually viewing the reports is basic stuff so we need not cover it in too much depth here other than to say that the information provided here is only a fraction of the information that is actually saved by your system and, of course, the layout of the data doesn't come with colorful graphs and so on. If you are looking to capture more or different types of info, as well as have access to different methods of presenting the data, then the community contributions are the way to go. In fact, in Chapter 10 we will look at how to generate custom reports for low stock levels. You might find that you need a variety of different reports, so going over this example will set you up to add whatever reports you like in future.

Talking of community contributions, it is time to actually use one now in order to add products to the database wholesale rather than one by one!

Easy Populate

Ok, till now we have really stayed on the nerdy, safe side of things by sticking to the default administration tool options, which, while they will get the job done, are pretty boring and slow. Its time to role up the sleeves and perform the first of many enhancements to osCommerce. You can look at community contributions as a way of extending or enhancing the native functionality provided by osCommerce, and it's largely due to the osCommerce community that osCommerce itself is such a success.

Having an easily extensible product is one of the great advantages of modern computing, and you are about to see why. If you have already tried to enter more than a few tens of products at a time then you will appreciate how automating that task is a real lifesaver. Specifically, **Easy Populate** (EP) allows you to populate and update products in many categories using data from any of the following:

- Excel spreadsheet
- OpenOffice spreadsheet
- Filemaker database

- Access database
- Delimited text file

One thing to note about all community contributions is that they are written by people who are simply helping the community. They don't really have access to large amounts of funds that they can use to employ teams of top developers to write their contributions. Instead, they work at doing the best they can, and offer you the contribution not as a guaranteed product, but as something that may help you achieve your goals—you can take it or leave it.

In this case, Easy Populate does not work well with the latest version of PHP, which is PHP5. If you find you have trouble with it, you have several options open. Remember that your host site will probably not yet be using PHP5, so you can use Easy Populate to populate your database after deployment to the live server. Alternatively, you can use the PHPmyAdmin tool, which is discussed in Chapter 10.

For these reasons, you should always try out new contributions on your development server to ensure that you can get everything up and running correctly and that you have a good grasp of how the contribution works. Otherwise, you could make yourself susceptible to bugs or faulty code that might harm your store and this is not the fault of the contributor.

Further, you might often notice that you can make donations to the developers of contributions—this is certainly encouraged since they have helped you generate revenue (by helping you to achieve business related tasks) so it is only fair you return the favor. Plowing funds back into the community will also help boost community development and increase the general quality of contributions. It's a case of everyone scratching everyone else's back so that everyone wins.

Downloading and Installing Easy Populate

Head on over to the osCommerce website, navigate to the community contributions section at `http://www.oscommerce.com/community/contributions` and locate the Easy Populate package (you will probably find it in the Top Downloads sections on the right of the screen). Download this from whichever server is most suitable for you, and extract the package to a directory—something like `c:\osCommerce_Contributions` should do nicely since this will not be the only contribution that you end up using.

Now, the Easy Populate contribution actually integrates with the administration tool, so there is a bit of setting up to do. The package comes with `readme` files and documentation, which you are encouraged to go over at your own leisure. However, for completeness the main steps to installation are repeated here:

- Copy the files `easypopulate.php` and `easypopulate_functions.php` into the `admin` directory.
- Edit the `admin/includes/boxes/catalog.php` file (in your favorite editor) by adding this exact line:

```
'<a href="' . tep_href_link('easypopulate.php', '', 'NONSSL') .
'" class="menuBoxContentLink">Easy Populate</a><br>'.
```

after the line:

```
'<a href="' . tep_href_link(FILENAME_PRODUCTS_ATTRIBUTES, '',
'NONSSL') . '"class="menuBoxContentLink">' .
BOX_CATALOG_CATEGORIES_PRODUCTS_ATTRIBUTES . '</a><br>' .
```

- Create a directory called catalog/temp, and ensure that its permissions are set to allow write access.

That is more or less all you need to do unless you have modified the default structure of your installation. If you experience any problems, please go over the readme files that provide more comprehensive instructions as well as more general information regarding Easy Populate.

Once you have that done, navigate to the Catalog section in your administration tool and you should now have an Easy Populate option available for you to use, like this:

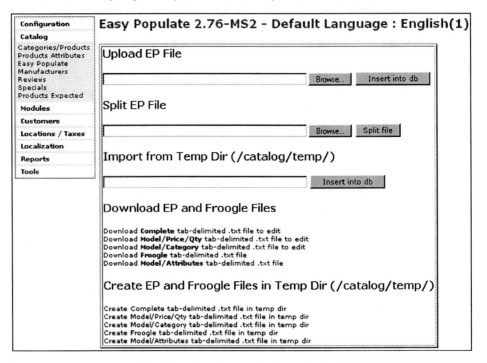

There is one further recommendation to be made before you dive straight in and begin using this new tool. You *must* open easypopulate.php and read the section marked *Configuration Variables*. It will allow you to adjust EasyPopulate's operation for your store.

There are settings in here that need to be modified if the tool is to work properly. For example, if you want to make use of Froogle (if you are unsure about what Froogle is but wish to find out, then check http://www.google.co.za/froogle/about.html and all will be revealed), then you will need to modify the following two variables to reflect your setup:

```
$froogle_product_info_path = "http://localhost/catalog/product_info.php";
$froogle_image_path = "http://localhost/catalog/images/";
```

Or, in the case of the demo site, it was necessary to modify the tempdir variables, as well as the separator, to the following in order to get things working properly:

```
$tempdir = "temp/";
$tempdir2 = "temp/";
$separator = "\t";
```

There are also quite a few other bits and bobs of information that you may or may not find important in easypopulate.php, but more than likely you will need to make several modifications before you are happy. At any rate, let's continue on…

Finding Your Way Around Easy Populate

Before we begin using this tool to add data to the database, it's worthwhile looking over the various sections presented in the Easy Populate tool. Go through each section so that you have a clear idea of what we are trying to achieve when we do get round to using it with the database.

Looking at the figure shown previously, you will notice that the two textboxes shown involve operations on EP files, Upload EP file and Split EP file. An EP file is a structured data file that Easy Populate parses (reads over and understands) in order to insert the data contained therein into your database. You will notice that both options provide the user with the ability to browse the file system in search of files.

Use the first option when you have an EP file that contains the correct data to be uploaded to the database. Here is a small and not exhaustive checklist for determining whether you are happy to have the data entered into your database:

- The file is small enough to upload properly (usually less than 300 products).

- You have a product_model field that is unique for each product.

- All the lines end with the EOREOR delimiter.

- You have the header row in place (we will look at header rows shortly).

- Any dates in the file are formatted correctly (YYYY-MM-DD).

- Certain characters can mess things up. If you are using a tab-separated file, then you need to be careful how you deal with values that contain tabs since these might be interpreted as new values.

- Be aware that backslashes (/) can also confuse EP and the database because the backslash character is the escape character for strings in MySQL.

Of course, this list assumes that the data is accurate. Remember that anything you add on the site should be exhaustively tested for errors before deployment. Make sure you view all the results of the addition directly on the live site if you are using the tool on your hosted server.

The first bullet point mentions that your file needs to be relatively small. This is no good if you have an established business and want to add your entire catalog of 2,500 products to your site. In this case, you need to split the file, which can be very tedious. The reason for this having its own special option is that, by and large you will work with files based in the temp directory because this is where EP puts files it creates. Luckily, the second option does exactly this for you, so use it if you are having problems with very large files. Splitting them up will cause EP to save the new, smaller files to the temp directory and save them in the following format EP_Split1.txt, EP_Split2.txt. You can then use the first option to add each file's data to the database.

The final text-box option, Import from Temp Dir, does the same thing as the first option, only this uploads directly from the temp directory that you created.

Following the text-box options are two series of link options, namely Download EP and Froogle files and Create EP and Froogle files in Temp Dir. The first option allows you to download several files for editing purposes, while the second creates these files anew from the data in the database.

The different file options are relatively easy to understand. If you use the Download/Create Complete tab-delimited .txt file option, you will get every bit of information about the product you can possibly imagine. This can create a number of columns if you have plenty of product attributes in several different languages.

The following example file (which can be opened in Excel) was created using the Create Model/Price/Qty tab-delimited .txt file in temp dir option. The file name is generated by EP, which uses the time and date to create it and should be found in your temp directory once it has been created:

EP2005May25-1907.txt

	A	B	C	D
1	v_products_model	v_products_price	v_products_quantity	EOREOR
2	VirtualDub	29.99	31	EOREOR
3				
4				
5				
6				

EP2005May25-1907

From this it is quite clear that the product database is nearly empty because there is only one product present. However, since Contechst Books is a new venture, this is not a problem as we will populate the database with all the new books using EP. The important thing to notice here is that as promised, the only information present is the Model/Price/Qty information for each product.

That's pretty much all you need to know about the basics. There is far more you can do by using the special configurations and hacking the code to customize EP's behavior. For now though, you have the general gist and it is time to add some data to the site.

Using Easy Populate to Add Product Data

The first thing you should do at this point is make a copy of your database – see the section entitled *Back Up Your Database* in Chapter 8 if you are unsure how to do this. This is because more than likely you will need to experiment with the setup and with importing different files before you end up getting everything right. As a result of this experimentation, your database could become a little unwieldy or inaccurate, which you do not want.

Unfortunately, having a wonderful tool like Easy Populate doesn't mean we are exempted from entering large amounts of data into the machine at some stage. In order to get the information into Excel, it needs to be entered or imported from a database. If you are going to import it from a database, then at some stage it had to be entered into the database. This rather annoying turn of events can be alleviated for those of you who already have a product database, perhaps because your business has been already using an Access database or spreadsheets to record all your information.

Now let's discuss how to add data to our oscommerce database. First, get EP to create a new and complete data file by clicking **Create Complete tab-delimited .txt file in temp dir**. Go to the `temp` dir and you should find the new file there. Open it in Excel and take a look through each of the headings in the header row. The header row is the first row that appears in the file and it contains all the names of the columns available to receive values for any given product. At this stage, you may want to delete all the superfluous data on your site so that the header row is kept to only what is relevant to your products.

> If you are only going to use English as your site's language, then it is a good idea to remove all other languages from your system before generating the `.txt` file. This is because having a product attribute listed for each product in each language adds a lot of columns to your file, which is totally unnecessary.

Now, in order to add a product, you can simply insert the relevant data into each row. One row contains data of only one product and you should be sure that you enter the correct data under the correct column heading. For this example, the data file had a couple of new products added to it as shown here:

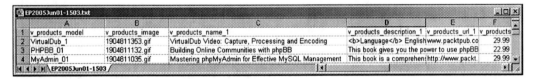

Next, we save and close the file. Then we use the **Import from Temp Dir** option to upload the file to the database. Naturally, the first thing you need to do is check that the operation has performed as you expected and that the information is added to the site and is intact. In our case, we get the following (assuming we have the image files present in the correct folder):

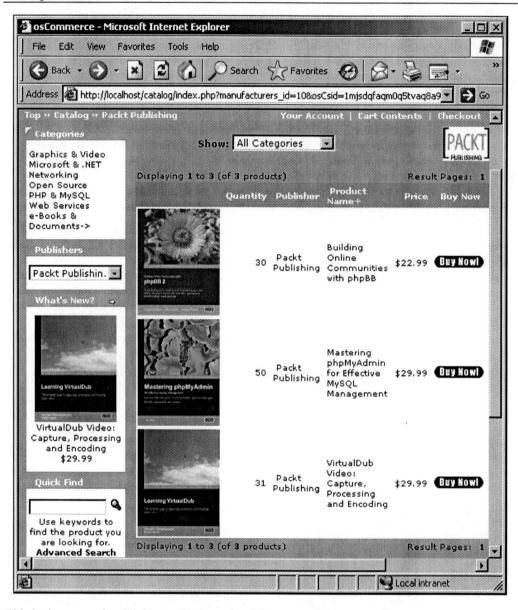

This looks neat and well laid out. We have the right product in the right category with the right quantity, and also the right price and manufacturer/publisher. However, you would still have to check whether or not the description is displayed properly on the product's page. Checking the results in the administration tool is also a good idea since that is where you will have to make any necessary changes.

You won't be able to upload all the right information all the time, and sometimes EP may get confused by various character sequences in your data. If this is the case, then you can easily make the changes you need using the administration tool. After all, you have pretty much uploaded the vast majority of the data to your site. If you have to spend some time tweaking the results, then it is no big deal.

Remember that it is far more efficient to modify your data in Excel or something similar rather than the administration tool because you don't have to wait for the page to reload each time you click a button. For example, if you have a non-osCommerce database containing your products' names and prices, but not everything else you need such as the products' descriptions, then you will end up having to add data manually through the admin tool unless you first add it in Excel or something similar.

Summary

Designing and implementing your product data structure is one of the most vital jobs involved in setting up your osCommerce store and hopefully you now find it quite easy. Consequently, you should feel pretty relaxed at this stage because you have almost all your data related needs sorted out, or at the very least, understand exactly *how to* deal with your data.

From this chapter, you have learned that categorizing your products and setting their attributes is not quite as straightforward as it may seem on the surface. Provided you think before you act, you will be just fine with regards to these and many other concepts. Of course, dealing with data can be fairly tricky even if you have a good structure, and we have seen how osCommerce helps us handle data updates and changes by giving us various options such as linking or duplicating, or warning us if we are trying to delete something with dependencies.

Having covered most of the administration tool's data-related options we took a look at how one of the community contributions can extend osCommerce's functionality and provide us with a great way of making our data entry tasks far more efficient.

Of course, this is not the end of the data story! How do you ensure that your data is safe in the unlikely event that an *act of God* wipes your working database clean? In Chapter 8, we will take a look at one of the methods of keeping data secure by backing it up in a separate place.

With that said, it is time to give our site a full facelift and nose job. The next chapter talks about customization, and it is here that we will finally discuss how to properly deal with the images you want to put up on your site.

6
Customization

I will grant that up 'til now, the site as shown in many of the screenshots looks pretty mangy, with a grey body area, broken image links, box headings that don't match the background, default text, which means nothing in the context of the new site, and so forth. All of this needs to be changed to a professional and aesthetically pleasing interface, which will help encourage and facilitate the purchase of your goods.

Sounds easy enough, doesn't it? Well, in a way it is and in a way it isn't. The reason we still have designers with jobs is because by and large the average person on the street finds it difficult to produce a site that looks like it has had money invested in the design. But as much as they would tell you differently, designers (or *creatives* as I believe they are called) aren't mythically endowed with superhuman senses to help them decide what does look good and what doesn't. Anyone can do it, to varying degrees, by following the usual *think before you act* paradigm and applying a *process* to how they go about the business of designing a site.

There are volumes and volumes of material written about how to perfect designs, but we don't have time to go over all that information here. What we will do instead is take a good look at how to decide what type of look and feel to go for relative to the business you are running, followed by a discussion on the different types of design and how to apply them properly. Once you have gone through this section, you will need to apply that information to gain a good idea of how everything is going to look and work before you begin changing things yourself.

Of course, I don't want to take all the fun out of it. Playing around with different combinations of color and layout is always worthwhile, and often teaches you more about the *best* way to do things than any process or book. You also have the luxury of having a website set up for you, which frees you to simply make changes here and there to achieve your design goals rather than develop the HTML from scratch. To some extent, this luxury actually restricts you because anything short of a total rewrite of the pages will mean your site retains some of the osCommerce *flavor*. But that's not a bad thing at all!

Once we have done with the arty side of things, the tangible work begins, and we will look at the following topics:

- Working with boxes and columns
- Dealing with images
- Modifying the style sheet
- A few miscellaneous customizations

I should warn you before we continue that there is quite a lot involved with coming up with an entirely fresh, pleasing, and distinct look to a site. There are lots of fiddly little bits to play around with, so you should be prepared to spend a bit of time on this section because after all, your site's look and feel is really the face of your business.

Another thing to remember before we begin is that you should take some time to look at what is already out there. Many issues that you will encounter while designing your site would have already been successfully dealt with all over the show—not only by osCommerce users of course. Also, don't be scared to treat your design as an ongoing process—while it is never good to drastically change your site on a weekly basis, regular tweaking or upgrading of your interface can keep it modern and looking shiny new.

Form Follows Function

The tenet *form follows function* is widely applied in many spheres of human knowledge, ranging from evolution to biokinetics and engineering. It is a well understood concept, which basically says that the way something is built or made must reflect the purpose it was made for. This is an exceptionally sensible thing to think, and applying it to the design of your site will provide you with a yardstick to measure how well you have designed your site. If you, or preferably everyone you ask, can honestly say that your site looks like a site that is meant to sell whatever it is you are selling, then you are doing a good job.

That's not to say that your site should look like every other site that sells the same products. In fact, if anything, you want to make your site as distinctive as possible without stepping over the bounds of what you believe your target customer will consider *good taste* or *common sense*. For example, if you are selling accounting software, it is reasonable to assume straight away that you should not spend time coming up with creative gimmicks to sell your products—as much as it appears that many accountants subscribe to the philosophy of creative accounting these days. That's just my little joke, but you get the picture—the visual and functional design of the site, along with the language you use, should instill confidence in your business and your product.

How do you do that? Well, the trick is to relate what you have or do as a business to your specific target market. This, of course, assumes you have a target market-specific product. If you are selling something that has appeal to both sexes of all ages across all nationalities and race or religion, then obviously you should go with something that everyone can use. If anything, this would be a slightly flavorless site since you wouldn't want to marginalize any group of customers by explicitly making your site user friendly to another group—luckily, though, to some extent your target market will be slightly easier to define than this, so you generally can make some concessions for a particular type of buyer.

Bear in mind that while these following sections refer to visual or functional design, what you are really thinking about is the visual or functional aspect of the *interaction* design, which encompasses all visual and functional design. The interaction design is how you envision your customers using and interacting with your online store. This is an important distinction because thinking about everything from the perspective of the user will help to define your choices as you go along.

Visual Design

There's no beating about the bush on this issue. Make the site appear as visually simple as possible without hiding any critical or useful information. By this I mean, don't be afraid to leave a fairly large list of items on a page if all the items on that list are useful, and will be (or are) used frequently. Hiding an important thing from a user—no matter how easy it appears to be to find it on other pages—will frustrate customers, and your sales might suffer. A consequence of this is that you should not be afraid to have quite long pages that users must scroll down—rather have information available at the bottom of the page than have a complex navigation structure (which will mess up your functional design).

How you make your site look can also have a big impact on how customers understand the site to work. For example, if you have several different fonts that apply to different links, then it is entirely likely that users will not think of clicking on one type of link or another because of the different font styles. Think about this yourself for a moment! If you were reading a page of text and the links were all given in the same font as the writing, how would you know on which words to click? Make sure your site is visually consistent and that there are no style discrepancies from one page to the next.

There are quite a few so-called rules of visual design, which you could apply to your site. These are largely theoretical, and you may or may not wish to read up on these further—might I suggest Google for some good reading matter. Some that might apply to you are: the rule of thirds, which states that things divided up into thirds—either vertically or horizontally—are more visually appealing than other designs; the visual center rule, which states that the visual center of the page (where the eye is most attracted to) is just above and to the right of the actual center of the page. Of course, deciding where this is on a page that can change size is a neat trick.

Functional Design

Humans are funny old things. One study stated that the reported download speeds of ten sites by a test group of users bore no relation to the actual speed of the sites. Instead, the correlation appeared between whether or not the users completed the task they set out to do. Interesting! This should give you a great insight into how to go about designing the functionality of the site—make it easy for the user to find what they want.

I have mentioned several times before that your site must be intuitive. What does this really mean? Well, for a start, you need to ensure that whatever a button or a link says it will do, it does! So if you have a button that says back, make sure it is clear *which* context this is working in. Does it mean back to the start page, or just back one page? Apart from this it also means that you should shy away from fancy tricks, which while most certainly fancy, might cause confusion, and in the end, lost sales.

You also need to worry about download times. There are several aspects to this, ranging from ensuring your host has reasonably quick servers, to making sure that you don't have very large pages, which take ages to download. Having overly complex pages can also lead to slow performance, and keeping a customer waiting is bad business sense. Hand in hand with avoiding slow download times goes avoiding excessive page calls. Don't make your customers wade through deep navigation structures waiting each time they click on a button—this has actually been discussed in the previous chapter on data.

Basically, it's all about usability! If it's not a pleasure to use your site, redesign it…

Language

Now this is a truly interesting part of your site's design, and the art of writing for the Web is a lot more subtle than just saying what you mean. The reason for this is that you are no longer writing simply for human consumption, but also for consumption by machines. Since machines can only follow a certain number of rules when interpreting a page, the concessions on the language used must be made by the writers (if they want their sites to feature highly on search engines).

Before you worry about making your site's text highly optimized for searching, there are a few more fundamental things that you need to get right. First off, make sure your language is clear and concise! This is the most important; rather sacrifice racy, sales-oriented copy for more mundane text if the mundane text is going to elucidate your important points better. The less clear your writing, the more likely you are to frustrate customers and lose out on sales.

You have to ensure all the text on your site is accurate of course. Leaving outdated or incorrect information on your site can have some rather hair-raising consequences if you are someone who takes customer support to heart. Another part of providing accurate information is not clouding it over with reams of superfluous information.

Apart from actual content of your language, the visual and structural appearance of the copy is also important. Use bold or larger fonts to emphasize headings or important points, and ensure that you space your text out nicely to make the page easier on the eye and therefore easier to read and understand.

Finally, maintain a consistent style of writing throughout the site and then try and follow the guidelines for **Search Engine Optimization (SEO)**, which are laid out for you in Chapter 12 on *Building Your Business*. This will provide an in-depth discussion about how to make your site fully search-engine compliant, including a discussion on how to use meta tags, why it's not worth cheating the search engines, and how to go about getting your site noticed in general. For now, let's leave the design considerations and get on with actually implementing the site.

Language Definitions

Obviously, there are quite a lot of modifications that need to be made to the default language in osCommerce. You may or may not want to change the headings of boxes, error messages, page text, and pretty much anything else that involves language on the site. In order to do this you need to edit the language of the various files presented in the Define Language section under Tools in the administration section. Navigating to this will bring up a screen with a host of different files available for editing (note that you can also do this through the File Manager section, but this will expose all the code in the file to you, which may well make it harder to do a simple language edit):

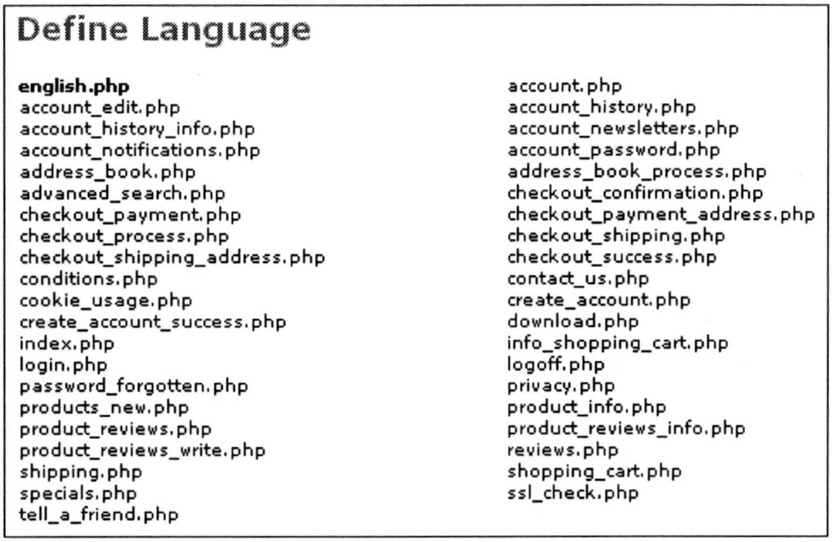

```
Define Language

english.php                         account.php
account_edit.php                    account_history.php
account_history_info.php            account_newsletters.php
account_notifications.php           account_password.php
address_book.php                    address_book_process.php
advanced_search.php                 checkout_confirmation.php
checkout_payment.php                checkout_payment_address.php
checkout_process.php                checkout_shipping.php
checkout_shipping_address.php       checkout_success.php
conditions.php                      contact_us.php
cookie_usage.php                    create_account.php
create_account_success.php          download.php
index.php                           info_shopping_cart.php
login.php                           logoff.php
password_forgotten.php              privacy.php
products_new.php                    product_info.php
product_reviews.php                 product_reviews_info.php
product_reviews_write.php           reviews.php
shipping.php                        shopping_cart.php
specials.php                        ssl_check.php
tell_a_friend.php
```

You can choose which language you want to work on by selecting it from the drop-down list at the top right of the screen. Please note that we will only deal with English in this book, since all the principles that apply to *one* language apply to *any* language—as well as this, Contechst Books only publishes English-language books, so it make sense to only have the website in English.

Now, as you might have guessed, your job is to now go through each and every one of the files to modify the site to suit your needs. Editing a file is very simple: simply click on the name of the file and make the appropriate changes directly to the text. Let's take a look at some of the more important files in this section by way of example.

english.php

Recall that Contechst Books does not have manufacturers, but would rather use the term "publisher" on the site. Well, in order to make these changes, we open up english.php and change the occurrences of Manufacturer to Publisher, as shown in the following screenshot:

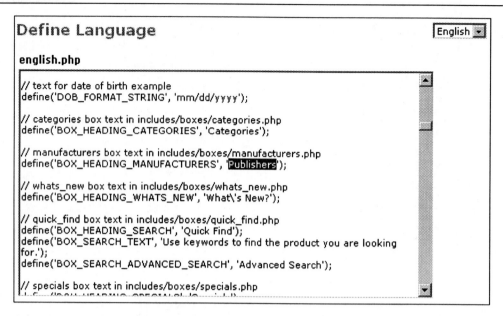

The highlighted text shows where the term **Manufacturers** has been changed to **Publishers**. Can you guess what effect this change will have on the site? Well, if you look at the line immediately above the one that was changed, which is a PHP comment line, you will see that this setting affects the `includes/boxes/manufacturers.php` file. This is because the `english.php` file actually holds information on all the generic language used on the site. Looking at it from another point of view, all expressions used only once, by one special file, should be or are in *their appropriate file*, and all other expressions that are used several times are in `english.php`.

As well as this, bear in mind that each file in the `catalog` folder has its partner file in the `includes/languages/english` folder to define the language terms there. Accordingly, rather than using the editor that is provided by osCommerce, you might want to open up the `english.php` file (or any other language file, for that matter) in a nice editor such as EditPlus in order to make it easier for you to edit the files. We will show the files being used from the admin tool for demonstrative purposes, but you will probably find you prefer to use a proper editor.

Now, look at the `define` statement again. It declares that the `BOX_HEADING_MANUFACTURERS` constant, which is used in the `includes/boxes/manufacturers.php` file is the word **Publishers**. From this you should suspect that the heading of the manufacturers' box, which is shown on all the pages of the site will now be **Publishers** instead of **Manufacturers**. Taking a quick glance at the site confirms this (Look at the box on the bottom left):

Categories

Graphics & Video
Microsoft & .NET
Networking
Open Source
PHP & MySQL
Web Services
e-Books &
Documents->

Publishers

Please Select ▼

What's New Here?

Welcome Guest! Would you like to <u>log yourself in</u>? Or would you prefer to <u>create an account</u>?

This is a default setup of the osCommerce project, products shown are for demonstrational purposes, **any products purchased will not be delivered nor will the customer be billed**. Any information seen on these products is to be treated as fictional.

This, of course, is not the only occurrence of the term Manufacturer on the site! There are other candidates to replace, so we can continue searching our english.php file for the term Manufacturer. Before we do, though, make note of one very important point:

> These are PHP statements which you are modifying, so you need to be aware that any changes to the actual code, such as removing a semi-colon by accident or adding in a single quote without escaping it with a backslash, will result in problems.

Take a look at the setting below the one we changed in the earlier screenshot to see an example of how a backslash escapes a quote in the text part of a define statement. As it so happens, we need only make one more replacement of the term Manufacturer, as well as converting this line:

```
define('HEADER_TITLE_MY_ACCOUNT', 'My Account');
```

to this line:

```
define('HEADER_TITLE_MY_ACCOUNT', 'Your Account');
```

and we are done with this file for now (the last change rewords the account login presented at the top right of the screen simply because I prefer this wording). Before we move on, though, it is useful to make note of the main files and parts of the site covered by english.php:

- header.php.
- footer.php.
- Box text.
- Error messages.
- Customer-information text.
- Navigation text.
- Image button text.
- Personalized greeting text.
- Footer text—you will probably want to remove this or change it to your own copyright notice. (Please read the conditions for modifying this text, given in the comment above in the english.php file.)

Remember to always check that whatever changes you make to these files don't cause errors or unexpected results on the site. Apart from that, you simply need to implement whichever changes you require as you go along. Most of the default text is pretty standard and shouldn't need too much attention.

index.php

When you first log on to your osCommerce site, the index page provides you with lots of helpful information about how to do things and where to go for help. This obviously needs a complete overhaul, and specifically in the case of the demo site, we don't want to waste readers' time with a whole lot of information. Since we are a specialist bookstore, we expect the customer who is visiting to be looking specifically for technical books, so rather than introduce ourselves and tell them what we do (because they more than likely know), we want to display our newest and upcoming products.

Accordingly, the first change we make to the file is change the first line of code to the following:

```
define('TEXT_MAIN', '');
```

Now remember: this may not be suitable for your store! You may wish to add some introductory information, especially if you are retailing a product that merits a bit of explanation. If this is the case, create your text based on the guidelines of good language design and insert it in between the empty quotes in the TEXT_MAIN define statement. Remember to add HTML tags where appropriate to emphasize important points and so forth, as well as escape any single quote characters with a backslash.

Apart from this change, we have also had to replace a few occurrences of Manufacturer, with Publisher on the following lines:

```
define('TABLE_HEADING_MANUFACTURER', 'Publisher');
define('TEXT_ALL_MANUFACTURERS', 'All Publishers');
```

and since we don't wish to have the chirpy Let's see what we have here text at the top of our product category pages, the relevant line was changed to this:

```
define('HEADING_TITLE', '');
```

Please bear in mind that while this means that no text will be shown because of the empty string provided in the HEADING_TITLE define statement, it doesn't mean that the space allotted to this text disappears. If you want to remove this space completely, then you need to work with the HTML that is responsible for this section of the page directly.

A category page, in this case PHP & MySQL, after these modifications looks like this:

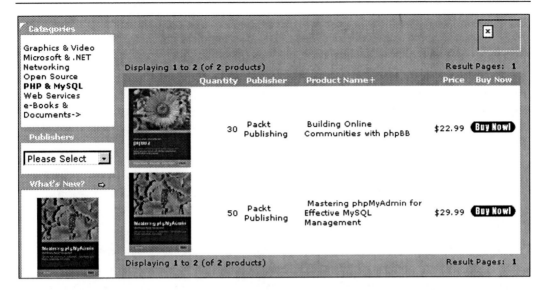

Notice that the box heading in the category listing now reads Publisher instead of Manufacturer, and that the usual Let's see what we have here text is absent. Of course, we still have a horrid broken link at the top right of the screen, but this will be dealt with in the *Images* section later in this chapter.

The rest of the files by and large deal with cosmetic touches and will not really impact the running of your site barring one or two exceptions. For example, you will need to insert your own information into the conditions.php and privacy.php files in order to present accurate legal information about your store.

Incidentally, when you look at a product listing such as the one shown in the previous screenshot, you will notice that there is a plus sign next to the Product Name column heading. This is because, along with the other headings in the product listing, you can order the results in ascending or descending form. I leave it to you to play around with this to get the hang of it—if you don't think that this functionality is obvious, then perhaps you could do something to ensure that your customers know it exists. A note about it on the page, or highlighting the links might work in this case.

Using HTML for Language Formatting

Since we are on the topic of language, there is a useful little trick that you may as well learn here since these two files (conditions.php and privacy.php) are closely related. Often on the conditions and terms of use page of a site, there is a heading called privacy, with a link to a page that holds all the privacy information. This happens because intuitively the privacy conditions should come under the conditions heading, but there is often too much information to present on a single page and anyway it helps to distinguish the two logically. Accordingly you will need to know how to create a link from one page to the other.

The conditions and terms of use page on contechst.com uses a link to take the reader to the privacy page within the actual body of the text. This is accomplished using the HTML <a> tag, with an href attribute. The actual line in the text looks like this:

```
<a href=\'http://localhost/catalog/privacy.php\'>here.</a>
```

This tells the browser to render the word here as a link, which the user can click on to open up the page specified by the href attribute—in this case http://localhost/catalog/privacy.php. Notice that the single quotes that are used to delimit the URL have to be escaped with a backslash for the benefit of osCommerce.

> **Important**: While the method shown here is pretty standard, you might want to consider the fact that it is possible that this will not propagate your customer's session ID. Make sure you check that sessions are maintained. If they aren't, then you will need to use the tep_href_link function like so:
>
> ```
> <a href="'.tep_href_link(FILENAME_PRIVACY, '', 'NONSSL').'">'.'here'.'</a>
> ```

So, we can now go from the conditions.php file as shown here (at present the formatting for the link is similar to the background color, so the here part of the sentence under Privacy doesn't show up well):

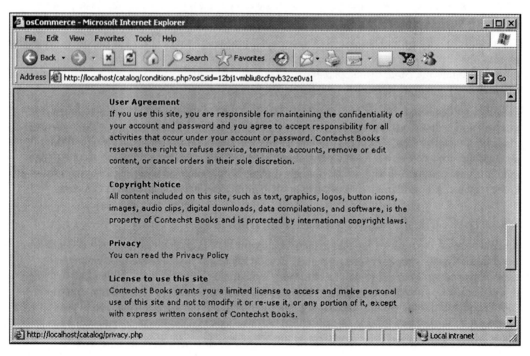

to the privacy policy page, `privacy.php`, which is shown here:

Privacy Notice

Use of your Personal Information
We use your personal information for the following purposes:

- To deliver goods to you that you ordered directly from us
- To deliver electronic services, such as newsletters or downloads that you request
- To help us create and publish content most relevant to you.
- To alert you to amendments, corrections, special offers, updated information and other new services from Contechst Books, if you so request.
- To allow you access to limited-entry areas of our site as appropriate.

Notice that quite a lot of formatting has been done to this text using HTML. The only way you will learn how to achieve the language formatting you desire is by practicing and practicing. As a matter of interest, the HTML for the section of the Privacy Notice, which is visible in the previous screenshot, is shown here:

```
<b>Use of your Personal Information</b>
<br />
We use your personal information for the following purposes:
<br />
<br />
<ul>
    <li>To deliver goods to you that you ordered directly from us  </li>
    <li>To deliver electronic services, such as newsletters or downloads that
you request  </li>
    <li>To help us create and publish content most relevant to you.  </li>
    <li>To alert you to amendments, corrections, special offers, updated
information and other new services from Contechst Books, if you so request.
</li>
    <li>To allow you access to limited-entry areas of our site as appropriate.
</li>
</ul>
```

Specifically, the bulleted list was achieved by using the `<ul>` tag, which renders an unordered list, and its corresponding bullet points are created using the `<li>` tag, which stands for list item. We don't have time to go into a full-on tutorial on HTML (you have already been introduced to it in Chapter 3), but you are certainly encouraged to play around with it enough to become proficient.

Working with Boxes and Columns

As you will have noticed over the course of the book so far, the site consists of a central column reserved for text or product images and information, surrounded on either side by columns of boxes, which hold anything from the navigations structure to a keyword search. Naturally, you might wish to change this general structure in favor of something that suits your site better. There is really an unlimited amount of possible changes, and you could quite easily alter the structure sufficiently to eradicate most if not all the evidence of the original layout.

For the first time, we are going to put down the administration tool and get involved directly with the PHP code within the site's files, and to get the ball rolling, we will start by removing a box. You know by now that contechst.com retails only English-language books and so there is now no longer any need to have a box showing the various languages available on the site. As a result, we would like to erase this box from the right-hand column entirely because it no longer serves any function. This is about the simplest operation we can perform on the site; it involves commenting out only a single line per box removed.

Removing a Box

Go to the includes/column_right.php file in your catalog folder and open it up using your favorite editor. This file is responsible for including all the boxes found in the right-hand column of the site's web pages. Now, look around the file until you find the following lines:

```
if (substr(basename($PHP_SELF), 0, 8) != 'checkout') {
    include(DIR_WS_BOXES . 'languages.php');
    include(DIR_WS_BOXES . 'currencies.php');
}
```

What do you think this statement is saying? Well, if you look at the first line involving an if statement, you can read it to mean:

If the substring of the variable $PHP_SELF, which holds the pagename of the current page, from the first character to the ninth, is not equal to the checkout string, then include the two files written here.

This is because, by default, the only time that you don't want the customer to be able to change the language of the page is when you are already checking out any purchases he or she has made. For all other times, the languages box is displayed. Now, because we want to modify this behavior to never show the languages box, we simply want to prevent PHP from reading the include statement that inserts the box. We can do this with a simple comment, which will modify the statement to the following:

```
if (substr(basename($PHP_SELF), 0, 8) != 'checkout') {
    // include(DIR_WS_BOXES . 'languages.php');
    include(DIR_WS_BOXES . 'currencies.php');
}
```

Now, as always, we need to save these changes and go to the site to ensure that the modification has had the expected results. Looking at an arbitrary page that is not part of the checkout-process page (because the box is never displayed here anyway), we can see that the languages box is no longer shown down the right-hand side:

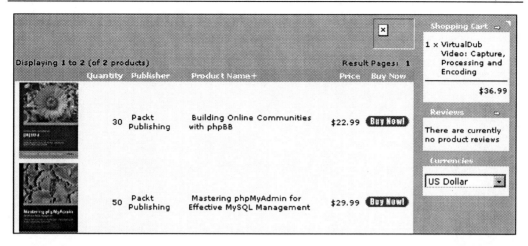

The process is really the same for removing any other box on the site. But what happens if you now want to move a box so that it appears before any other box—or even move it to the other column?

Moving Boxes

To move a box around, you simply have to move the statement that includes the box in the code. If you wanted to change columns, then you would have to move the code statement to the relevant column file—either the `column_right.php` or `column_left.php` file, depending on whether you wanted it on the left or right.

For example, let's say you want to move Currencies to appear above the Reviews box in the right-hand column. Copy and cut the following statement (which we have already seen):

```
if (substr(basename($PHP_SELF), 0, 8) != 'checkout') {
    // include(DIR_WS_BOXES . 'languages.php');
    include(DIR_WS_BOXES . 'currencies.php');
}
```

and paste it as shown here in the same file:

```
if (isset($HTTP_GET_VARS['products_id'])) {
    if (basename($PHP_SELF) != FILENAME_TELL_A_FRIEND) include(DIR_WS_BOXES .
'tell_a_friend.php');
} else {
    include(DIR_WS_BOXES . 'specials.php');
}

if (substr(basename($PHP_SELF), 0, 8) != 'checkout') {
    // include(DIR_WS_BOXES . 'languages.php');
    include(DIR_WS_BOXES . 'currencies.php');
}

    require(DIR_WS_BOXES . 'reviews.php');
```

Save the changes, and view the results in an arbitrary file, once again avoiding the checkout pages. You will notice that the boxes have swapped around as intended:

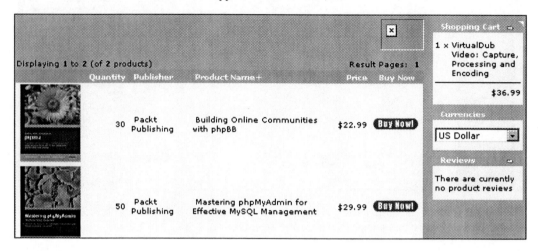

It will be left to the reader to swap boxes between the left and right columns as desired. However, this should really only be an exercise because the left-hand side is already well organized as part of a tool to help customers locate the products they are searching for. What would be really nice now is if we could add a short note to the Currencies box to explain to customers that the exchange rate is not a live exchange rate, but has a lag of, say, up to two days.

Modifying Box Content

There are a couple of ways to go about modifying boxes, and one is more correct that the other. "What could he possibly be on about saying that one method is *more* correct than the other?" you may ask. Surely if both work then both are equally correct! This is perfectly true, but when I refer to degrees of correctness, what I mean is that the designers of osCommerce have gone about building the site in specific way, and if you modify the code in your site, you should at all times try to maintain the same conventions as the original site, because if you don't, it will be nearly impossible to *guess* how you made certain alterations when you come back to them in a year or so.

Sticking to the same conventions used by the osCommerce team will keep your code neat and easy to follow for anyone who has to look over it in the future. However, depending on what it is you need to do, it may not be possible to always stick to the coding convention. Because of this, I will show two methods of changing the Currencies box to insert a little note above the drop-down list of currencies—one involving the direct manipulation of code in the box file, and the other using osCommerce's in-place convention.

The first method is more straightforward and is easier to implement. However, the second is the more *correct* method and is the one that is recommended.

Open up the code file that is responsible for creating the Currencies box, includes/boxes/ currencies.php. Look for the code that is used for populating the box's content. It looks like this:

```
$info_box_contents[] = array('form' => tep_draw_form('currencies',
tep_href_link(basename($PHP_SELF), '', $request_type, false), 'get'), 'align'
=> 'center', 'text' => tep_draw_pull_down_menu('currency', $currencies_array,
$currency, 'onChange="this.form.submit();" style="width: 100%"') .
$hidden_get_variables . tep_hide_session_id());
```

Don't worry about understanding everything here—it's not important or relevant to you at the moment. What is important is that you can see that we have a variable called $info_box_contents, which is being filled with the information given on the right of the assignment (=) operator. From the name you should be able to deduce that this is the variable that will contain the contents of the Currencies information box.

Now, we want to add the note above the drop-down list, so we append it to the front of the text contents with the . operator and enclose it in quotes to denote that it is a string, like so:

```
$info_box_contents[] = array('form' => tep_draw_form('currencies',
tep_href_link(basename($PHP_SELF), '', $request_type, false), 'get'), 'align'
=> 'center', 'text' => 'NOTE: Prices given in any currency other than US
dollars are calculated from an exchange rate which is determined weekly. <br>'
. tep_draw_pull_down_menu('currency', $currencies_array, $currency,
'onChange="this.form.submit();" style="width: 100%"') . $hidden_get_variables
. tep_hide_session_id());
```

Checking out the results on the site show us that we have made the changes successfully, but there is a problem in that the message doesn't look neat because it is simply too long:

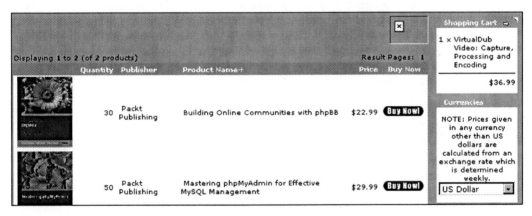

This shows that at least we can add text as we choose, but you would probably be better advised to put this type of information in your conditions.php file. However, this is fine for the purposes of this example, and so we will continue on and demonstrate the *better* way to perform this same change.

Delete any changes you have made to the box and return it to its original format. (Remember that you should really be making a backup of any files that you are worried you may break during the course of your work.) Now navigate to the Define Languages section of the admin tool and open up the english.php file discussed earlier in this chapter. Recall that one of the functions of english.php was to define a whole lot of text for various bits and pieces of the site. One of these bits is in fact the information boxes.

Navigate down to the section that deals with the Currencies box, as shown here:

```
// currencies box text in includes/boxes/currencies.php
define('BOX_HEADING_CURRENCIES', 'Currencies');
```

Now, this section is reserved for defining constants that can be used by the box files. For example, the box heading which we know to be Currencies is defined here. What we would like to do is follow this convention by providing a constant declaration that can be used by currencies.php to output our message to the site. Add the following line like so:

```
// currencies box text in includes/boxes/currencies.php
define('BOX_HEADING_CURRENCIES', 'Currencies');
define('BOX_CURRENCIES_TEXT', 'NOTE: Prices given in any currency other than
US dollars are calculated from an exchange rate which is determined weekly.
<br>');
```

Now go back to the currencies.php file in your editor and append the constant we have just modified to the text key of the $info_box_content variable like this:

```
$info_box_contents[] = array('form' => tep_draw_form('currencies',
tep_href_link(basename($PHP_SELF), '', $request_type, false), 'get'), 'align'
=> 'center', 'text' => BOX_CURRENCIES_TEXT .
tep_draw_pull_down_menu('currency', $currencies_array, $currency,
'onChange="this.form.submit();" style="width: 100%"') . $hidden_get_variables
. tep_hide_session_id());
```

Now when you save the changes to both files and view any of the pages that include the Currencies information box, you will see the note correctly displayed. So why is this second way more correct than the first way? Take a look over the english.php file—you will notice that all the constants used in the information boxes are defined here, so this is the logical place to add that information in the future too. Otherwise you will end up having information defined all over the show and it soon becomes quite hard to keep track of everything.

What if instead of modifying the default information boxes, we need a new box?

Adding a Box

We will actually need a new box on our site for some advanced functionality that we will add later on in the book, but we may as well take a look at how to add the box to the site now, even if the actual functionality and content will be added later on. Incidentally, this box is going to present a live RSS feed on new technology developments that may be of interest to our customers. Don't worry if you don't know what an RSS feed is yet: you will see a little later on.

For now, let's simply add a new box to the right-hand column of the site. The new box will be called Tech Feed, and will be based on a modified version of the currencies.php file. Make a copy of the currencies.php file in your includes/boxes folder, and call it feed.php. Then go to the column_right.php file and add this file at the bottom of the code (before the closing ?> tag), like so:

```
require(DIR_WS_BOXES . 'reviews.php');
require(DIR_WS_BOXES . 'feed.php');

?>
```

Save the file and take a look at your site. You will notice that you now have two Currencies boxes. The reason for the duplication is of course that we haven't modified feed.php to reflect the fact that it is now the Tech Feed box and not Currencies. So, to rectify this, open up feed.php in your editor and modify it so that it looks like this:

```
<!-- This is a custom box to house the contents of an RSS Feed. Originally
created on 05/30/05 -->

<tr>
  <td>
<?php
    $info_box_contents = array();
    $info_box_contents[] = array('text' => BOX_HEADING_FEED);

    new infoBoxHeading($info_box_contents, false, false);

    $info_box_contents = array();
    $info_box_contents[] = array('align' => 'center', 'text' =>
BOX_FEED_TEXT);

    new infoBox($info_box_contents);
?>
  </td
</tr>
```

Of course one shouldn't forget to use the english.php file to define the constants we are going to use for the feed box. So you will need to make the following additions to the english.php file—the best place to add this is directly after the code for the last box, as this is an intuitive place to look for it when you need to modify it in future:

```
// languages box text in includes/boxes/feed.php
define('BOX_HEADING_FEED', 'Tech Feed');
define('BOX_FEED_TEXT', 'This is the future site of the RSS Web Feed!');
```

Notice several things here:

The feed.php file uses the constants BOX_HEADING_FEED and BOX_FEED_TEXT which are defined in english.php and are presented using the same convention as the rest of the files in osCommerce.

There are HTML tags before and after the PHP code in the feed.php file. This is necessary because of the way in which osCommerce handles information boxes. These tags simply tell the browser to create a new table cell within a table. The result of all this work should be much the same as the following screenshot:

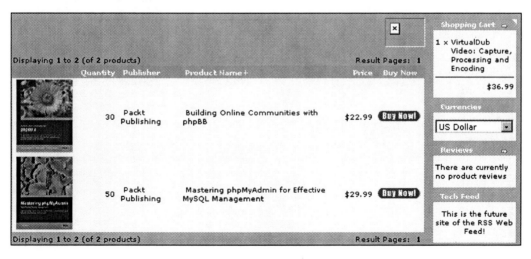

149

Of course, this box doesn't do anything useful yet, but that will happen once we get to the more advanced chapters later in the book. You can do quite a lot with boxes now, and while most of the boxes presented on the site by default are pretty useful, you now at least have the option of chopping and changing things as you see fit. Of course, we don't have to stop at modifying just boxes, we can also perform operations on the columns themselves.

Removing a Column

Working with columns is a bit of a hassle because there is no single code file that will influence the entire site. Each change you make to the columns has to be made to every page on the site. Having a column down the left-hand side of the page is generally a good idea because users are used to navigating pages from the left of the screen. Also, many sites do not have a column down the right-hand side, preferring to let their content fill the page or even show adverts down the right-hand side in any extra space.

In order to rid yourself of the right-hand column (remember you can always add any boxes you want saved to the left-hand column or any other part of the page for that matter) you will need to go to each and every page that contains the right-hand column and look for the following code:

```
<!-- right_navigation //-->
<?php
require(DIR_WS_INCLUDES . 'column_right.php');
?>
<!-- right_navigation_eof //-->
```

As you might well guess, the only change needed for removing the column entirely is to comment out that line like this:

```
<!-- right_navigation //-->
<?php
// require(DIR_WS_INCLUDES . 'column_right.php');
?>
<!-- right_navigation_eof //-->
```

This was done by way of example for the index.php file, and the results are as follows:

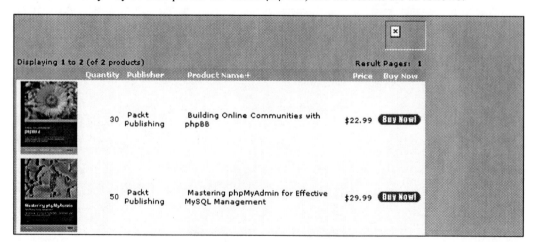

Of course, the right-hand column has disappeared, but the space it occupied has not. In order to close this space, you would need to modify the HTML on each page to remove the space allotted to this column, which should be shown directly above the column declaration. The line above the relevant column declaration reads:

```
<td width="<?php echo BOX_WIDTH; ?>" valign="top"><table border="0"
width="<?php echo BOX_WIDTH; ?>" cellspacing="0" cellpadding="2">
```

Change it to:

```
<!--
<td width="<?php echo BOX_WIDTH; ?>" valign="top"><table border="0"
width="<?php echo BOX_WIDTH; ?>" cellspacing="0" cellpadding="2">
-->
```

At any rate, this will give you the following result:

Of course, you may well want to use the space given over to the old column for something else entirely, in which case you would simply modify the `require` statement that calls the `column_right.php` file so that it calls your own file, which you have placed in the same folder as the `column_right.php` file. So:

```
require(DIR_WS_INCLUDES . 'column_right.php');
```

would become something like this:

```
require(DIR_WS_INCLUDES . 'custom_column.php');
```

This requires that you have created the `custom_column.php` file, perhaps based on the code from the original column, and that it is suitable to *fit* into the allotted space. An in-depth discussion on the page layout will come later in this chapter under the heading *Miscellaneous Customizations*. For now I am certain you will be glad that we are finally going to talk about images.

Dealing with Images

Working with images for the Web is very much an art! I don't mean this in the sense that generally you should be quite artistic in order to make nice pictures. I mean that actually managing and dealing with image files is itself an art. There is a lot of work to be done for the aspiring website owner with respect to attaining a pleasing and meaningful visual environment. This is because the Web is the one retail environment that is most reliant on visual images to have an effect on customers because sight and sound are the only two senses that are targeted by the Internet, for now.

In order to have the freedom to manipulate images as required by your site, you really need to use a reasonably powerful image editor. Photoshop or Paint Shop Pro are examples of good image editing environments, but anything that allows you to save files in a variety of different formats and provides resizing capabilities should be sufficient for a simpler looking site. Of course, if you have to take digital photographs of your products yourself, then you will need to ensure you make the photos as uniform as possible, with a background that doesn't distract from the product itself—editing the images to remove the background altogether is probably best.

There are several areas of concern when working with images, all of which need to be closely scrutinized if you hope to produce an integrated and pleasing visual shopping environment (not all of these relate to what your customers actually see, funnily enough):

- One of the biggest problems with images is that they take up a lot more memory than text or code. For this reason you need to have an effective method for dealing with large product images (or any other images), which will be required for your site—simply squashing large images into thumbnails will slow down your site because the server will still be uploading the entire, large file to the customers machine, even if it is only showing a thumbnail on their page.

- One common mistake people make when dealing with images is not working on them early on in the process to make them as uniform in size and type as possible. If all your images are of one size and of the same dimension, then you are going to have things a lot easier than most. In fact, this should really be your aim before you do anything involving the site—*make sure your product images are all uniform.*

- Of course, deciding what type of image you actually want to use from the multitude available can also be a bit of an issue because some image types take up more space than others, and some may not even be rendered properly at all in a browser. By and large there are really only two image types that are most commonly used—GIF and JPG.

- The intended use of the image can also be a big factor when deciding how to create, size, and format the file. For example, icons and logos should really be saved as GIF files whereas photos and large or complex images should be saved in the JPG format.

Two types of image files were mentioned in the bulleted list. Let's take a quick look at those here:

GIF, or Graphics Interchange Format, is known for its compression and the fact that it can store and display multiple images. The major drawback to GIF is that images can only use up to 256 distinct colors to display their data. For photographic-quality images, this is a significant obstacle. However, you should use GIFs for:

- Images with a transparent background
- Animated graphics
- Smaller, less complex images requiring no more than 256 colors

JPG, or JPEG (Joint Photographic Experts Group), should be used when presenting photo-realistic images. JPG can compress large images while retaining the overall photographic quality of the image. JPG files can use any number of colors, so it's a very convenient format for images which require a lot of colors. JPG should be used for:

- Photographs
- Larger, complex images requiring more than 256 to display properly

With that knowledge under our belts, we are now going to deal with each type of image used by Contechst Books one by one, but before we do, it's appropriate to take a quick refresher on the structure of the images folder, as this is where all the magic will happen.

The images Folder

Recall that it was recommended earlier that you maintain the same conventions when altering code as the original developers of osCommerce. That lesson applies very much to images in that it is safest to keep to the same convention as the default structure when storing images and naming folders. Doing this will promote an intuitive and well-managed folder and naming structure, which will be easy to add to and modify if needs be.

Taking a look at the default images folder, you can see that there are several folders devoted to manufacturers' products, among other things, as well as a whole bunch of small GIF images. The emphasis, of course, on the GIF images is that they are small—anything more than a few KB and you are asking for speed-related problems when customers download pages:

Name ▲	Size ▲
banners	
default	
dvd	
gt_interactive	
hewlett_packard	
icons	
infobox	
mail	
matrox	
microsoft	
sierra	
account_notifications.gif	2 KB
account_orders.gif	3 KB
account_personal.gif	3 KB
arrow_down.gif	1 KB
arrow_east_south.gif	1 KB
arrow_green.gif	1 KB
arrow_south_east.gif	1 KB
box_products_notifications.gif	2 KB
box_products_notifications_remove.gif	2 KB
box_write_review.gif	2 KB
category_dvd_movies.gif	1 KB
category_hardware.gif	2 KB
category_software.gif	2 KB
checkout_bullet.gif	1 KB
header_account.gif	1 KB
header_cart.gif	1 KB

There are a few other miscellaneous folders: there's one folder (the infobox folder) for images used in the information box headings to give them a rounded feel, another folder for your banner ads (to be discussed later), and so on. The one thing to note (although it isn't visible in the above screenshot) is that the manufacturer images are not housed within the manufacturer's image folder, but rather directly under the main images folder—where you store these is entirely up to you, so long as your choice is consistent.

Deciding on your folder structure is, of course, up to you, but for the sake of the demo site, we have mimicked the default setup and have gone with the product image structure (no other folders or images have been changed as yet) shown in the next screenshot:

> **Warning**: By default osCommerce saves all uploaded image files to the images folder. Moving them elsewhere will break the image links. You may either hold all your images in the images folder, which will not affect the performance of your site in any way, or read over some of the modifications to the code shown in the next section on *Saving Product Images* to see how to get osCommerce to save files in the manufacturers' image folders.

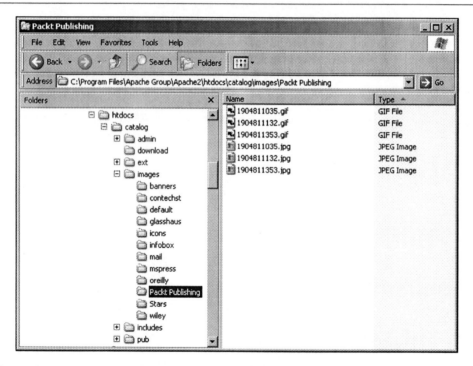

Make a quick note of the fact that under the images folder we now have a list of publishers who will have books retailed through the demo site—including *Glasshaus*, *Microsoft Press*, and *Packt*. These folders will then store all the thumbnail images of our books in GIF format and all the full sized images in JPG format. Why on earth do we need to do this—surely storing two versions of each file will take up more space?

The short answer is yes, storing a thumbnail GIF file and a full size JPG file will certainly increase the amount of disk space taken up by our images. But, I took a look at the size of the JPG files in the previous screenshot (about 60KB) and compared that to the size of the GIFs in the screenshot before—there is an order of magnitude difference. This means that if we returned say ten products using a 60KB picture displayed in the thumbnail, the page size would be about 620KB, which is far, far too big to be practical.

The problem with the other side of the coin is, if you store all your images as 5KB GIFs, then a customer clicking on a thumbnail image in the hopes of seeing it enlarge will be horribly disappointed, as osCommerce proudly opens up a new window to show them a thumbnail image again. So the answer is to allow the site to use small GIF images for all the pages except the ones that are meant to show the full-size image in a pop-up window. This means that you retain your small page size, and hence download speed, while still being able to show off full-color large images when requested. But how?

Well, in order to answer that, we'll trace all the steps it takes to get a product's imagery onto the site. However, before we do that, we quickly need to have a discussion about two other aspects of images—name and size.

Sizing and Naming Images

Apart from where you save your images, you need to think very carefully about what you call them. The reason I say this is because you should really be aiming for a uniform, meaningful, and intuitive naming convention to make things easier should you ever have to deal with images programmatically in the future. As it just so happens, books have an obvious product-image name ready made because they all have an ISBN number that uniquely identifies them—accordingly, the demo site will use the book's ISBN number to identify the images in either GIF for thumbnail images or JPG for full-size photos. You should choose whatever is most appropriate for your products—so long as everything is consistently named, you should be fine.

So, now that we know where to save images and how to name them, we need to look at how big or small to make them—both in terms of size and dimensions. This is not as easy as it sounds, and whether you like it or not, there is really no set formula for dealing with this. Remember that osCommerce can modify the dimensions of your thumbnail images, and these are set in the Images section of the administration tool. So, the first thing for you to do is take a look at the dimension of your thumbnail images and set the values in Images appropriately—for example, the settings in the demo site are:

Small Image Width   100

Small Image Height 125

because this suits the size of the thumbnail images being used *as well as* the purposes of the image.

Note that at this size not all the cover writing is legible, but it is more than clear what the title is and what the cover looks like in general, which is all that is needed, since customers would simply enlarge the thumbnail to get a close look at the cover. If you recall, the default settings had quite different dimensions from the ones listed here, which would distort the current images quite severely. As a result, a bit of trial and error time was spent finding the best thumbnail sizes.

Saving Product Images

Let's continue by taking a look at how product images were added to the Contechst Books site. To start with, the following tasks were performed (as discussed earlier in this section):

1. Create a new images folder structure based on the conventions used originally.

2. Obtain GIF thumbnail images of the books and save them to the relevant publisher's folder.

3. Obtain full-size JPGs of the books and save them to the relevant publisher's folder.

4. Set the Images width and height settings for your thumbnails in the admin tool appropriately.

5. Associate your product with its corresponding thumbnail image in the Categories/Products section of the admin tool.

The fifth task in this list may prove to be somewhat difficult for you if you intend to keep a nice neat images folder structure. Why do I say this? Well, upload a thumbnail file onto your site, so that you receive the "file uploaded successfully" message, and you can view the image when you are editing the product. Being able to view the product's image in the admin folder or on the site means that it has uploaded successfully and osCommerce is locating it with no problems. Now, go to the images folder and look for the name of the image file you have just uploaded—you will find that it has been uploaded there instead of the correct manufacturer's image folder as we want.

The reason this has happened is because osCommerce uploads all image files directly to the images folder, but after that, does no sorting based on manufacturer, category, and so on. The result of this will be a pretty large images folder containing every single product image file. This in itself is not a problem, but it makes for an un-neat site, and it is better to categorize images to avoid any potential naming conflicts (in this case, ISBNs are globally unique, but other products might suffer from naming clashes).

So, we need to make a couple of modifications to osCommerce's code. Open up categories.php in your favorite editor and perform the following replacement after locating the line that reads $products_image = new upload('products_image'); at about line 314 in the file:

```
/**
This modification allows for the categorized storage and retrieval of images
by manufacturer.
Original code:

        $products_image = new upload('products_image');
        $products_image->set_destination(DIR_FS_CATALOG_IMAGES);
        if ($products_image->parse() && $products_image->save()) {
            $products_image_name = $products_image->filename;
        }
**/

        $manufacturers_query = tep_db_query("select manufacturers_name from "
. TABLE_MANUFACTURERS .  "  where manufacturers_id = '" .
$HTTP_POST_VARS['manufacturers_id'] . "'");
        $manufacturers = tep_db_fetch_array($manufacturers_query);

        $products_image = new upload('products_image');
        $dest = DIR_FS_CATALOG_IMAGES . "$manufacturers[manufacturers_name]/";
        $products_image->set_destination($dest);
```

```
if ($products_image->parse() && $products_image->save()) {
    $products_image_name = $manufacturers['manufacturers_name'] . "/".
    $products_image->filename;
}else{
...
```

Basically this code queries the database to find out which manufacturer this product is made by. It then uses this information to insert the correct file path (under the `images` directory) target for storing the image file, and then saves the image name with the relative file path appended to it so that it can be retrieved correctly again (for example, `Packt Publishing/1904811353.gif` instead of `1904811353.gif`). It just means that instead of osCommerce saving a file to the `images` folder and then looking for it there again, it saves the file to the relevant manufacturer's folder in the `image` directory and looks for it there again instead of in `images`.

> **Caveat**: Generally it is good practice to use lowercase names with no spaces or special characters in your file names. For example, `Packt Publishing` would become the `packtpublishing` folder. I have used spaces and uppercase names to make everything clear and easy to read for the purposes of demonstration as it works fine on most servers as is.

Once this is all done, you can navigate to your products on the site, and once you have ensured your images all correspond to the correct product, click to enlarge one of them... Did you get a pop-up window with another thumbnail image? Clearly this is no good—we need to find a way of associating the full-sized JPG with the new pop-up window. Oh dear, this is going to involve some changes to the code again, but where do we start?

Well, when you roll your mouse over the thumbnail image, take a look at the status bar, which appears along the bottom of your browser when you have it enabled. The URL in the status bar shows which file—in this case it is `popup_image.php`—is targeted on clicking the image or the click to enlarge link. Obviously, this is where we will need to look in order to get things done the way we need.

For this, open up `popup_image.php` in your favorite editor and take a look through it for a line that reads:

```
echo tep_image(DIR_WS_IMAGES . $products['products_image'],
$products['products_name']);
```

This line is responsible for pulling up the image that will be shown in the pop-up window. The rest of the code is not really relevant to us for now. You should be able to understand after a little thought that this is simply pulling an image by the same name of the thumbnail file from the relevant directory—if you want to verify this, simply write in the following line above it:

```
echo DIR_WS_IMAGES . "$products[products_image]";
```

Save this file and then click on a product image on your site to view the results. You should get something like this:

images/Packt Publishing/1904811132.gif

Parse Time: 0.274s

OK, so we know that it is simply pulling the GIF file out of the right folder, which is close, but not exactly what we want. In order to get osCommerce to pull up the correct file we will need to make the following modifications to the code. Instead of the line:

```
echo tep_image(DIR_WS_IMAGES . $products['products_image'],
$products['products_name']);
```

You will need to insert the following code:

```
/**The following modification was made to allow full size jpg file pop ups to
show while still presenting smaller GIFs on the site. The original line was
echo tep_image(DIR_WS_IMAGES . $products['products_image'],
$products['products_name']);
**/
$product_substr = $products['products_image'];
$product_substr = substr($product_substr,0, strlen($product_substr) - 3) .
"jpg";
echo tep_image(DIR_WS_IMAGES .  $product_substr, $products['products_name']);
```

What this new snippet of code is doing is stripping the filename of its .gif extension and giving it a .jpg extension—obviously you will need to modify this to suit whatever file types you are using. The osCommerce tep_image function has then been called as normal except using the modified product image name. This means that instead of searching for the following file, for example:

```
images/<publisher's name>/1904811035.gif
```

osCommerce will now search for:

```
images/<publisher's name>/1904811035.jpg
```

Notice that in both code snippets there are informative comments explaining exactly what it is that has been changed. Maintaining a record of your changes like this is absolutely vital if you are to maintain a healthy system in the years to come.

Now when we click to enlarge an image, we are shown a nice full-sized JPG file (assuming it exists in the correct folder). There are a few things to make note of here:

- The code changes shown here are the author's own work and are merely presented for use as an example—you should feel free to make changes or improvements as you see fit.

- The code will not work if you have not saved the JPG files with the same name as the GIF files. Further, you need to hold the JPGs and the GIFs in the same manufacturer's image folder. While these are perfectly reasonable criteria, forgetting them after making these modifications will have undesired results.

- The names of your manufacturers' folders in your images directory must match exactly the names of the manufacturers as declared in the Manufacturers section of the admin tool. For example, when adding a manufacturer to your site, say *Packt Publishing*, you might also want to add this exact folder name to your images directory to avoid any problems later on.

- Regardless of whether you choose to use this method of presenting images or not, the importance of ensuring you have a consistent naming convention for files and folders should be made apparent by our little coding example here.

You should be aware that while the changes made here will work nicely if you are uploading files using the admin tool, you will need to come up with ways of ensuring that files get to the right folder when using other methods such as contributions. For example, if you are uploading all your files using Easy Populate, then you need to ensure that instead of simply mentioning the product's image name, the relative file path is also included, like this:

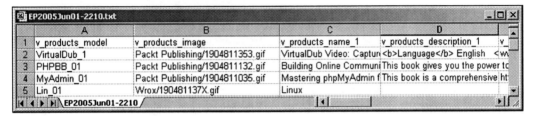

Linux users should note that there will need to be small modifications to the proposed changes here and there to suit the specifics of your operating system. However, being Linux users, it should be immediately clear to you how to make these simple changes, so we won't go into them here.

To conclude this discussion on saving product images, please note that you should upload only the GIF files using osCommerce. The larger JPG files can simply be added to the relevant folder because osCommerce doesn't need to store any information about them in its database—it simply looks them up based on the stored file path, which was modified in this section.

Graphics—Logos and Icons

To a large extent, dealing with images that are not associated with products is a lot easier than what we have seen. You really have a few well defined choices with regards to logos and icons, and once they are made, it is pretty forward to implement. Your main concern, to begin with, is whether or not you think your site will benefit from the use of graphics or not. If yes, then you need to design a suite of your own graphics to complement the rest of the site—alternatively, of course, you can use the graphics that are supplied by default with osCommerce, but in this case you are sacrificing individuality for ease of use.

Once you have made up your mind to use graphics on your site, then the two remaining questions are *where* shall I put them, and *what size* shall I make them. The second question can be easily answered by fiddling around with the image settings in the admin tool to make the space allotted for icons on the site fit the dimensions of your particular graphics. The settings for the demo site are the following because it fits in nicely with the publishers' logos, and any other graphics can be made to order (in other words, you can always pick a size, and design graphics for that exact size):

Heading Image Width   65

Heading Image Height   40

The answer to the first question really relies on your sense of taste. Obviously placing functional graphics, in other words, those which possess links or perform some sort of task, is quite an important aspect because it needs to be very obvious exactly what their function is. As well as ensuring that functional graphics are placed in easily visible spots, the actual graphic should intuitively reflect its function. Take a look at the graphics provided by osCommerce to see how they have linked function to form. For example, they have two shopping bags:

which take customers to their cart content as shown—nice and simple, but certainly intuitive!

To some extent, it is impossible to escape the use of graphics, because you will at the very least need a company logo of some sort, somewhere towards the top of the page to brand the site and give it some sort of identity. As well as this, there are buttons, which generally need some form of graphic in order to make them look realistic.

Contechst Books is not going to make much use of graphics above and beyond those needed for corporate branding and navigation (although Chapter 10 on *Tools, Tips, and Tricks* will show how to add animated GIFs to your site as a nice touch), but by way of example, we will demonstrate how to change graphics from their defaults to the new business-specific ones (we'll cover some of the design considerations that going into this too) as well as showing how to move graphics on the page to suit your needs.

Creating and Inserting New Graphics

The demo site will obviously require a new business logo to be inserted at the top of the page. Accordingly, this section is going to concentrate on how to create and insert just such a graphic. To begin with, the original page looks like this:

We would like to create something that will fit in this space nicely and provide an elegant brand or company image, which will be displayed here instead of the osCommerce logo. So, the first thing to do is set about designing the new company image. In order to do this, it has to be taken into account that this is a retailer of computer technology books and so it is likely that the clientele will be hard-working adult programmers or business people.

Because of this, the company image should be sophisticated and elegant, and should avoid garish or loud tones. That's not to say it can't be striking in some way, but it should not look like someone has graffiti'd the name onto the site. Of course, this might all sound quite boring to you, but bear in mind that your site may well have a different clientele—perhaps a marketing- or advertising-based clientele that would expect a flamboyant logo.

If you are an established business, then you already know what your company logo is going to be, and you simply need to reproduce that image for insertion here. Of course, if your company already has a color scheme, then you can alter the colors presented on the site quite easily (the next section on *Modifying the Style Sheet* will cover this). Another consideration, assuming your business doesn't already have a color scheme, is that this logo will need to fit in with the site as well. But how do you know how to design your logo when the site itself hasn't been laid out?

The answer to this is, of course, that you should already have a pretty clear image of what you want your site to look like. In your head you should have the fundamental design already worked out, so you should know roughly what is required from your graphics in terms of look and feel. Now, the Contechst site, of which the bookstore demo will become a part, looks like this:

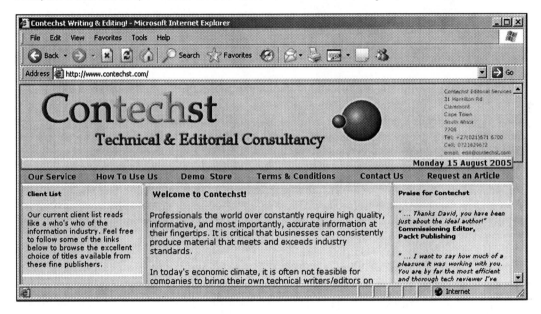

Because the store is going to become part of this site, it is obvious that we already have a rough idea of the color scheme and layout of the site. More importantly, there is a solid basis for designing the Contechst Books logo, and after no small amount of consternation the new logo is unveiled (I decided on a slightly different color since the demo site is not directly related to parent business):

Now, this still look a bit boring on a plain white background, but all that can all be rectified by judicious use of the style sheet and background images, which we will look at later in this chapter. For now, though, let's concentrate on this logo and how it was placed here. First off, because we have not yet designed the site, and because we would like the site to be as flexible as possible, we created this logo (as we will all other graphics) with a transparent background.

This is always a wise choice unless there is a specific compelling reason to do otherwise, because having a transparent background allows you to make underlying changes to the layout and color scheme of the site without affecting the graphic itself. Just think what a nightmare it would be if all your graphics had a specific color background, and you decided to change the background color of your store—you would have to go and change every single graphic individually to reflect this change.

Now, actually inserting this new GIF file can be a bit of a pest if you don't know where to look. Fortunately, with a bit of searching you will realize that the `header.php` file, which is housed in the `includes` folder, is where this particular log is declared. So, open up this file in your favorite editor and search for the line that reads:

```
<td valign="middle"><?php echo '<a href="' . tep_href_link(FILENAME_DEFAULT) .
'">' . tep_image(DIR_WS_IMAGES . 'oscommerce.gif', 'osCommerce') . '</a>';
?></td>
```

and replace it with the following line (or whatever the name of your new logo is):

```
<td valign="middle"><?php echo '<a href="' . tep_href_link(FILENAME_DEFAULT) .
'">' . tep_image(DIR_WS_IMAGES . 'contechst_books.gif', 'Contechst Books') .
'</a>'; ?></td>
```

As you should be able to tell, this change forces osCommerce to look for the file `contechst_books.gif` instead of `oscommerce.gif`, and render that to the browser. The second modified value is simply the text that will pop up when the mouse is hovered over this image—in this case we want the name of our store instead of osCommerce.

The same idea applies for inserting any other graphic on the site—you need to find out where it is referenced in the HTML, and then swap the old GIF file for the new one. If you are going to work on your site's logos, then you may as well remember to do the graphics for your packing slips and invoices now too.

Moving and Removing Graphics

Let's begin by talking about how to remove graphics, as this is the easier task to perform. Generally, it involves two steps: find the HTML that inserts the graphic, and then comment it out. Since Contechst Books is not too keen on the use of graphics to echo the functionality offered by text-based links, the three graphics at the top right-hand side of the page, which are used as shortcuts to Your Account, Cart Contents, and Checkout, are going to be removed.

If you haven't closed `header.php` already, then go to the HTML just below the line we modified in the last section and comment it out like so (once again, you may prefer to use PHP comments instead):

```
<!--
    <td align="right" valign="bottom"><?php echo '<a href="' .
tep_href_link(FILENAME_ACCOUNT, '', 'SSL') . '">' . tep_image(DIR_WS_IMAGES .
'header_account.gif', HEADER_TITLE_MY_ACCOUNT) . '</a>  <a href="' .
tep_href_link(FILENAME_SHOPPING_CART) . '">' . tep_image(DIR_WS_IMAGES .
'header_cart.gif', HEADER_TITLE_CART_CONTENTS) . '</a>  <a href="' .
tep_href_link(FILENAME_CHECKOUT_SHIPPING, '', 'SSL') . '">' .
tep_image(DIR_WS_IMAGES . 'header_checkout.gif', HEADER_TITLE_CHECKOUT) .
'</a>'; ?>  </td>
-->
```

This removes the table cell that contains the images and their links so that when you navigate to any page in the site, the heading section will look like this:

Contechst Books

That is really all it takes to remove a graphic from your site—simply find it and comment it out!

Moving graphics can be slightly trickier because you need to fiddle around with the HTML that is responsible for placing it. Let's say, for example, that you had inserted a couple of images onto a page—the following screenshot shows the ebooks and documents section with some new graphics in place:

Now, these graphics are nothing fancy, and I'm sure with a bit of time and effort you will be able to make some that will really uplift the visual aspects of your site. On the development side of things, notice that there is some lightening around the "e" at the top right at the moment. This type of issue will be common while you develop, and I have purposefully left the image like this because the background color will be a lot lighter in the final product, and this effect will disappear—the point being, always develop with the end goal in mind!

Now, let's assume that we feel that the word Categories is redundant and we wish to replace that with the category image instead. Making this assumption is not unreasonable, since the user will be able to intuit what page they are looking at from its content and layout. All that is left after the text has been removed is to move the graphic across the page to appear on the left of the central column. The same principles apply no matter where you want to place an image; it's simply a case of putting the right HTML in the right place!

Open up index.php in your editor and locate the line that reads:

```
<td class="pageHeading"><?php echo HEADING_TITLE; ?>
```

You should be able to recognize by now that HEADING_TITLE, which in this case holds the word Categories, is defined elsewhere, so there are several options we can use for making that word disappear. You can find out where HEADING_TITLE is defined and change it, or you can remove the entire echo statement, or you can comment out the entire HTML line. So what's the difference? The main difference is really whether you want to keep the same table structure or not. If you don't mind losing the cell, then comment out the whole thing; if you want to keep that cell because you want to place something else there, then perform one of the other operations.

For our purposes it is perfectly OK to remove the line entirely, so the new code looks like this:

```
<!-- <td class="pageHeading"><?php echo HEADING_TITLE; ?> -->
```

Now of course comes the big moment, when we move the graphic to its new home on the left-hand side of the screen. The line directly after the one that you have just commented out, reads as follows:

```
<td class="pageHeading" align="right"><?php echo tep_image(DIR_WS_IMAGES .
$category['categories_image'], $category['categories_name'],
HEADING_IMAGE_WIDTH, HEADING_IMAGE_HEIGHT); ?></td>
```

Notice that this is simply a new table cell, with the td align attribute set to right. Well, since we want the icon on the left, let's change that attribute and take a look at how this changes the site. The new line should now read:

```
<td class="pageHeading" align="left"><?php echo tep_image(DIR_WS_IMAGES .
$category['categories_image'], $category['categories_name'],
HEADING_IMAGE_WIDTH, HEADING_IMAGE_HEIGHT); ?></td>
```

Saving these changes (plus and comments you wish to insert about the changes) and then viewing the site shows the results just as we had hoped:

Now that that's done, the only thing left to do is insert graphic files for all the other categories, and your layout work is all done! Well, that's not entirely true... Click on another category—one that doesn't have subcategories. You will see that the icon has been realigned on the right—this means for those categories the alignment is set somewhere else. The best thing to do is search the index.php file for the string align="right", and sure enough, you will find the culprit, which can then be modified to show the graphic on the left-hand side of the screen.

Of course, there are countless possibilities for placing graphics wherever you want. All that's required is a bit of patience and some time to play around with the HTML. There is however one other type of image which is going to play a role in the Contechst Books site and we look at that next.

Background Images

One of the nicest things about designing sites (in my humble opinion) is that you can use whatever image-making software you choose for designing unbelievable pictures, which can then be very easily incorporated into your site. This ability to design on specialist software and then add to your HTML is a critical feature, without which it would soon become quite distressing to create pleasing background images.

Backgrounds themselves can be quite tricky to get right if you are using them for sections of pages which resize. If you know a page section will always be the same size, then you can design your background to order and there need not be any further fuss. If your page is going to resize, then you need to keep this in mind when creating the background image so that you don't end up with terribly distorted or ill-fitting pictures.

Now, Contechst Books would like to create a background image for the site's heading. Obviously, if your background image relied on knowing the width of the page section you were catering to (say, the left-hand column), the first thing to do is find out how wide that column is. Incidentally, by default it is set to 125 pixels, which is slightly too narrow for Contechst's liking. So, locating the BOX_WIDTH setting in the application_top.php file and setting it to 150 will give us a slightly wider box to work with and also tells us how wide to make our background image at the same time.

There are a few things to keep in mind when creating a background image apart from the width of the page section. Length is also a concern because if you have a really long page, you will end up repeating the image, which can look really un-neat if it is not planned for. One solution is to create a large background that will cover all the possible area your site could expand to, but then you need to think carefully about how large this image is going to be—remember, anything over a handful of kilobytes is too much and will contribute to slowing down your site.

You can, of course, create small background images that can be repeated over and over to fill up the screen, but by and large it is best to use background for areas you are certain will not change drastically. In our case, the heading section looks pretty boring as it stands, so we are going to create a background that will fill up the empty (for now) space in the heading section:

As you can see, this has quite a nice effect on the bar, and the background image can be made as small as you like because it simply repeats every time it runs out of width—since it doesn't change on the horizontal, it looks like one seamless striping of the main navigation bar. Of course, it is quite possible that the main navigation bar will undergo changes, but changing the background image to reflect this is very easy to do.

Notice also why it was important to make the background of the company's title logo transparent. Without doing that, the area under the title would appear as whatever background color was set, and not as the background image. Let's quickly look at how to work with button images before moving on to the section on customizing the style sheet, where we will actually insert the background image we created in this section.

Button Images

Of course, there are plenty of ways to create buttons, and you might find you want to use Flash or some other software to create exciting, dynamic buttons for your site. Remember too that some special effects can also be achieved through the use of the style sheet, so you are not totally doomed to using static-looking buttons if you don't want to go through the trouble of learning how to use other software products.

The buttons provided by osCommerce are fairly innocuous, and will certainly do the trick if you are happy to go ahead and use them. However, you should at least take a look at all the available options, which can be found online and in the community contributions. Working on the buttons yourself will also be a great exercise and will certainly boost your graphics-related experience and Chapter 10 discusses how to make attractive button templates. The flip side is that there are plenty of nice buttons out there which are free for you to use, so why not just use them instead of reinventing the wheel?

For those of you who *do* wish to work on your buttons by hand, you will find the relevant images in the `includes\languages\english\images\buttons` folder instead of with the rest of the images. This is because the buttons themselves depend on the language the site is working in, of course, and you will have to make the same modifications to all the buttons in all the languages you wish to present your site in. Simply create a button image for each type of button which is already in place, back up the current button files, and replace them with the new ones.

For the Contechst Books site, some buttons that are available under the GPL, or the Gnu Public License, were used to smarten up the feel of the site. These particular ones were available, at the time of writing, at `http://kalsey.com/2003/10/oscommerce_button_set/`, and were made available by Adam Kalsey. A screenshot of the site, with the new buttons, will follow in the next section.

Customizations Using the Style Sheet

As mentioned in Chapter 3, the pages in the osCommerce site obtain their style-related information from the associated style sheet entitled `stylesheet.css`, found in the `catalog` folder. Using style sheets gives you excellent, fine-grained control over the appearance of your web pages, and even allows you to produce some great effects. The appearance of pretty much every aspect of the site can be controlled from here, and all that is needed is a little knowledge of fonts, colors, and style sheet syntax.

Before we go any further, it will make life easier if you have a readymade list of the type of things you should look at setting using the style sheet. The following is a list of the most common areas (defined by HTML elements) where style sheets can be used to determine the look and feel of a site:

- Background
- Text
- Font
- Border
- Margin
- Padding
- List

As well as being able to change all these aspects of HTML, you can also apply different effects depending on "whether or not" conditions like a mouse hovering over the specified area—this will be demonstrated a little later on. You can also specify attributes for certain HTML tags, which can then be used to apply style sheet styles to those specific tags instead of creating application-wide changes. For example, if you had one paragraph style with a `class` attribute set, like so:

```
<p class="center"></p>
```

then you could specify this type of paragraph in your style sheet explicitly by saying something like:

```
p.center { color: green; }
```

Analyzing this line highlights the structure of the standard style-sheet code block, which appears in the form:

- Selector: in this case `p.center`
- Property: in this case `color`
- Delimiter: always `:`
- Value: in this case `green`

All the property/value pairs are contained within curly braces, and are ended with a semi-colon. Now, without getting too carried away in the niceties of style sheets, let's finish off the bulk of the modifications to the visual part of the site using the style sheet. In your favorite editor, open up `stylesheet.css`, and let's begin…

Inserting Background Images

In order to insert the background image that was shown in the last section, the following modification was made to the style sheet:

```
/* Background image added */
TR.header {
    background: #ffffff;
    background-image: url('images/heading_background.gif');
}
```

Make a similar change to your style sheet using your background image—or any image for that matter, since you just want to ensure that something is inserted into the background. Take a look at your site, and you should notice that the header of each page now has a background image. Simple? Not always… It can be quite tricky to know which modification to make and at what place. For this, you have to find out how all the HTML elements have been created. For example, open up `header.php` and look for the line:

```
<tr class="header">
```

Can you see why this above modification affected only the header section of the page? It's because the class declaration for this particular `tr` HTML tag has been given the class `header`, which is then defined in the style sheet using the `TR.header` selector. Adding background images anywhere in your code is therefore simply a case of locating the right HTML tag and shoving it in. Remember, though, that not all tags have the same properties—a paragraph tag `<p>` doesn't have a `background-image` property, for example.

As an exercise, try inserting an image into one infobox heading without having it placed in all of them.

Changing Colors and Fonts

There are a lot of interesting things to be done on the color front. You can change the color of any area of the screen (as we saw in Chapter 3) with only minimal effort. Since the demo site needs to fit in with its parent site, we are going to go with the grey, black, and red color scheme with only minor hints of other colors here and there. There is not really much point in rattling off a long list of all the modifications made to get the color scheme to this point:

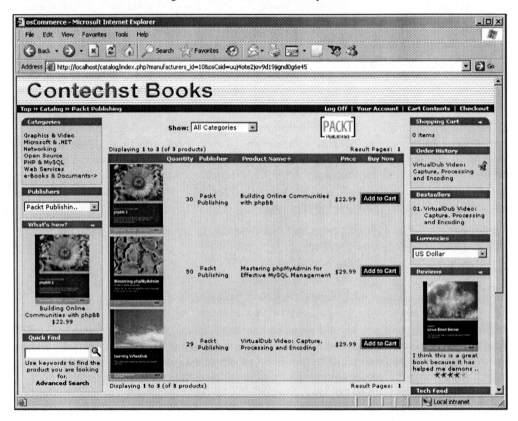

Notice some of the more interesting modifications to the style sheet (as well as the addition of the new buttons).

The body background color:

```
BODY {
  background: #EAEAEA;
  color: #000000;
  margin: 0px;
}
```

The header section:

```
TR.header {
  background-image: url('images/heading_background.gif');
}
```

The navigation bar:

```
TD.headerNavigation {
    font-family: Verdana, Arial, sans-serif;
    font-size: 10px;
    background: #003366;
    color: #ffffff;
    font-weight : bold;
    border: 0px;
    border-bottom-width: 1px;
    border-style: solid;
    border-color: #B7B7B7;
}
```

The infobox content sections:

```
.infoBoxContents {
    background: #E0E0E0;
    font-family: Verdana, Arial, sans-serif;
    font-size: 10px;
}
```

There are quite a few other changes that were made, but the above list should show you enough to get the idea. For more information on using style sheets, try Google, or go to http://www.w3schools.com/css/. Now, there is one thing concerning changes made to the background colors, which needs mentioning quickly.

In order to get that rounded effect on some of the infobox heading bars, graphic images were used. Namely, corner_left.gif, corner_right.gif, corner_right_left.gif, and arrow_right.gif, which are housed in the images\infobox folder. So, if you wish to change the color of the background for the TD.infoBoxHeading HTML elements, you will need to change these GIF files accordingly lest you end up with odd looking corners.

Fonts get much the same treatment as the colors used in the site in general. One of the really interesting effects for text which is used in HTML links is the hover effect. Take a look at the style sheet at the code block which reads:

```
A:hover {
    color: #AABBDD;
    text-decoration: underline;
}
```

Given the color scheme of the demo site, we really want to change this color so that when the mouse is hovered over a link, the color changes to something more apparent. Modify the code to look like this, and then point your mouse over the navigation links on a refreshed page:

```
A:hover {
    color: #F79418;
    text-decoration: underline;
}
```

Since that color does not really suit the color of the link in the navigation bar (don't ask me why, it just doesn't), you can try the following changes to the hover property of the navigation text:

```
A.headerNavigation:hover {
    color: #F79418;
}
```

This gives the link text a *Packt*-ish kind of feel (in other words, orange), which we all like!

Of course, you can always change the actual font properties of the font, instead of simply playing around with the colors. You can bold and underline to your heart's content. Such changes should really be done to taste, and if you get stuck, search for the answers online. For now, the demo site is quite happy with the fonts as they are.

Before we leave style sheets, remember that it is very important to test your entire site thoroughly; it is almost impossible to predict what effect every single little change will have on your site. You might find that error messages, for example, pop up in a totally different color and font than the rest of your site because you never modified them earlier—this is an easy mistake to make, because not all text or HTML elements are visible all the time.

Even worse, a few colors are not defined in the style sheet but are instead done using <span> tags directly in the language files. This happens, for example, on the login-page default text. You simply have to look over your site very carefully and ensure that you have modified everything accordingly.

Miscellaneous Customizations

There are an indefinite amount of adjustments or additions that you can make to the site—your imagination is the real limit in this respect. However, there are a few which deserve special mention because they are the most common. Remember that while we have only a bit of space to talk about some of the more important customizations, someone else has probably had to solve whatever customization problem you might have already. Make sure you use the online community to help you out if you get stuck.

Resizing Pages

The demo site needs to limit the size of the current pages to a determined width in order to provide space for some advertising, which is to appear down the right-hand side of the page. You might find that you wish to limit the width of your pages to keep everything compact and neat—especially if you have decided on a minimalist page design, which would look sparse on a large screen. Many companies do limit their page sizes for a variety of reasons, so it is important to have some control over your site's page sizes.

In order to accomplish this task, we need to say goodbye to the style sheet and begin working directly on the page HTML. For the sake of demonstration, we will work on the index page and allow the central column to resize up to a limit of 600 pixels. After that the page will stop expanding, and users who are viewing the page on full screen will instead be able to view adverts running down the right-hand side (the ads will be discussed later on in the book in Chapter 12).

Keep in mind that osCommerce does not have a unified page sizing facility. In other words, whatever page modifications you make to one of you pages, you will need to record and implement on all the other pages that you wish to have the same behavior. This is a bit of a drag, but it really isn't difficult to do with a bit of copy and pasting.

To begin with, open up index.php in your editor and search for the line that reads:

```
<table border="0" width="100%" cellspacing="3" cellpadding="3">
```

somewhere around line 49. This tag controls the overall width of the page, which you can see by examining the width tag, which is set to fill out the entire screen by always being 100%. You have another option in that you can set an absolute value in terms of the number of pixels to be used. For example, change the line to the following and then examine you page in a variety of different sizes:

```
<table border="0" width="800" cellspacing="3" cellpadding="3">
```

You will probably notice a problem with this page immediately. If you increase the page size above the 800 pixel mark, then the header and footer sections keep expanding leaving your page looking something like this:

This is pretty untidy, and we obviously would like to make the page stop expanding at the same point above and below. This means we are going to have to edit the header.php and footer.php files to reflect this change in width. So, open up both pages and in header.php look for the lines that read:

```
<table border="0" width="100%" cellspacing="0" cellpadding="1">
```

and:

```
<table border="0" width="100%" cellspacing="0" cellpadding="2">
```

somewhere near lines 55 and 63 respectively, and change them to the new width like so:

```
<table border="0" width="800" cellspacing="0" cellpadding="1">
...
<table border="0" width="800" cellspacing="0" cellpadding="2">
```

Then, in the footer you will need to change three table widths instead of two. Notice that unless the tables are set to the same width, the copyright message and the banner will shift further and further to the right as the page width increases. Accordingly, you should change the width attribute for all the tables (not just the first one) in the footer.php file to 800 pixels. This is because the alignment of the text and banner content is set to be center, and unless these table are all set to have the same length, the footer can end up looking skewed—like this:

Once those changes are all made, go along to the conditions of use page (`conditions.php`) and take a look—you should see something like this:

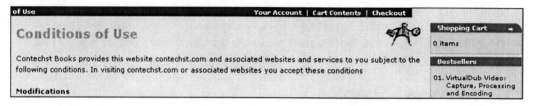

Oh dear! That's not very good… Remember that you have to modify the HTML for every different page to reflect the changes made to the site. Once you have worked out how to make the changes to one page, simply copying them over to all the others is an easy task.

What we have demonstrated here is a pretty simple modification to your standard site pages. Of course, you may wish to effect far more grand or sweeping changes to your site, and whatever changes to the HTML you need to make, the process is exactly the same as the one we have outlined—with one additional warning!

> Be aware that each PHP page may contain several versions of the same page, depending on the state of the session. If this is the case, you need to modify all the versions of each page within the same PHP file, so make sure you check everything thoroughly.

A case in point is in fact the index page, which displays a default page, as well as other information based on user requests. Some changes to the HTML will only be applied to one version only, and not the page as a whole, so you need to check the presentation on both the default and result versions of that page.

Adding Pages

Of course, it is pretty likely that at some stage, as your online site grows, you will find that you want to present more pages than the ones provided by default. In such a case, you need to add a new page with all the correct layout information and HTML elements in place. The best way to do this is to copy a page that most closely resembles what you want the new page to look like, and then save it in the `catalog` folder under its new name.

For this example, we will take the `shipping.php` file and turn it into the `feed.php` file, which will be linked to from either a click on the feed box (once we have the feeds up and running later in the book) or from the Information box on the bottom left of the page. Open up `shipping.php` and save a copy as `feed.php` in the `catalog` folder. That's it! You now have a new page, which you can confirm is working by modifying its content as follows:

```
<td><table border="0" width="100%" cellspacing="0" cellpadding="0">
    <tr>
        <td class="pageHeading"><?php echo "What's New In Technology"; ?></td>
        <td class="pageHeading" align="right"><?php echo tep_image
            (DIR_WS_IMAGES . 'table_background_specials.gif',
            HEADING_TITLE, HEADING_IMAGE_WIDTH, HEADING_IMAGE_HEIGHT); ?></td>
```

and navigating to it in your browser:

At the moment, this isn't too helpful, and we have done something *wrong* in terms of developing with osCommerce conventions in mind. Can you tell what it is? Instead of allowing the new feed.php page to call the HEADING_TITLE constant, which all the other pages do, we simply inserted our own What's New In Technology text to prove we had the right page. It's no biggie, but we should make the proper changes anyway. So, return the feed.php file to its original state, and open up the shipping.php file in the includes/languages/english/ folder, save a copy as feed.php, and make the following changes:

```
define('NAVBAR_TITLE', 'Technology Feed');
define('HEADING_TITLE', 'What\'s new in Technology?');
define('TEXT_INFORMATION', 'This is the future site of the RSS tech feed.');
```

Once this is done, close this file and open up the feed.php file in the catalog directory. We need to tell feed.php where to look to pick up the definitions we have just created, and this involves making changes to the following line:

```
require(DIR_WS_LANGUAGES . $language . '/' . FILENAME_SHIPPING);
$breadcrumb->add(NAVBAR_TITLE, tep_href_link(FILENAME_SHIPPING));
```

Of course, these constants are the ones used for the shipping.php file, and are defined in the includes/filenames.php file. We need to make our own definitions for this file within the filenames.php file, so we open that up as well and add the following line to the bottom of the page:

```
define('FILENAME_FEED', 'feed.php');
```

Save that change and then modify the feed.php file to pick up the includes/languages/english/feed.php file via the FILENAME_FEED constant, like so:

```
require(DIR_WS_LANGUAGES . $language . '/' . FILENAME_FEED);
$breadcrumb->add(NAVBAR_TITLE, tep_href_link(FILENAME_FEED));
```

Now when you navigate to the feed page, it should have no traces of its former self left:

Notice that the bread crumb now reflects the fact that this is the technology-feed page, and the heading is being picked up via the constant instead of the original message typed directly into the file. With this done, the page is ready to be used as you wish, but we will only begin working on it later. The only thing left to do (if you wish) is add this page to the information bar. This can be done quite easily by a few simple modifications.

First, open up english.php in the Define Languages section of the admin tool, and make the following addition:

```
// information box text in includes/boxes/information.php
define('BOX_HEADING_INFORMATION', 'Information');
define('BOX_INFORMATION_PRIVACY', 'Privacy Notice');
define('BOX_INFORMATION_CONDITIONS', 'Conditions of Use');
define('BOX_INFORMATION_SHIPPING', 'Shipping & Returns');
define('BOX_INFORMATION_CONTACT', 'Contact Us');
define('BOX_INFORMATION_FEED', 'Technology Feed');
```

Save that and then in the includes/boxes/information.php file, make the following changes:

```
  $info_box_contents[] = array('text' =>
'<a href="' . tep_href_link(FILENAME_SHIPPING) . '">' .
BOX_INFORMATION_SHIPPING . '</a><br>' .
'<a href="' . tep_href_link(FILENAME_PRIVACY) . '">' . BOX_INFORMATION_PRIVACY
. '</a><br>' .
'<a href="' . tep_href_link(FILENAME_CONDITIONS) . '">' .
BOX_INFORMATION_CONDITIONS . '</a><br>' .
'<a href="' . tep_href_link(FILENAME_CONTACT_US) . '">' .
BOX_INFORMATION_CONTACT . '</a><br>' .
'<a href="' . tep_href_link(FILENAME_FEED, '', 'NONSSL') . '">' .
BOX_INFORMATION_FEED . '</a>'
```

Now when you view the Information box in your browser, you get the following:

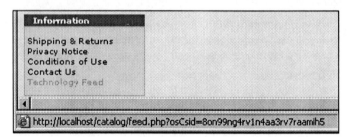

Notice that the status bar at the bottom of the screen shows that the highlighted link Technology Feed will take the customer to the feed.php file as expected. What you actually use the page for now is entirely up to you, but the process is the same for any page added.

Emails

Emails are an important interface between the customer and your business, and of course you will need to make some changes here and there to suit your site. Several different types of emails can be sent out from your store. These are the purchase confirmation, tell a friend, and welcome emails as well as the newsletters. The first three are very easy to change by simply editing them in the Language Definitions section of the admin tool—the files to modify are checkout_process.php, tell_a_friend.php, and create_account.php respectively.

The newsletter is slightly different in that you work with it through the Newsletter Manager in the admin tool. Open that up, and if you end up getting this error message:

Newsletter Manager

1064 - You have an error in your SQL syntax; check the manual that corresponds to your MySQL server version for the right syntax to use near '-20, 20' at line 1

select newsletters_id, title, length(content) as content_length, module, date_added, date_sent, status, locked from newsletters order by date_added desc limit -20, 20

[TEP STOP]

---

it is most likely because of an empty table set. This can be easily rectified by going into MySQL on the command line and inserting some dummy data like so:

```
mysql> insert into newsletters values (
     > newsletters_id = 1,
     > title = "first one",
     > length(content) = 10,
     > module = 1,
     > date_added = 20050303,
     > date_sent = 20050403,
     > status = "active",
     > locked = "N");
```

Once this is added, refresh the Newsletter Manager page, and you should find it all works swimmingly. Note that the data in this SQL query is not important because you will simply create the newsletter you want from the admin tool instead and then delete this one.

Using the tool is pretty easy; simply click on New Newsletter and add the information you want. You can choose one of two types of newsletter modules by default from the drop-down list in the New Newsletter editor. Choosing newsletter makes life simple because the store already knows which customers have chosen to receive the newsletter. Once you have written it out, you can preview, edit, delete, or send it provided it is locked. If it is unlocked, you can only preview or lock it; you can't change it in any way.

If you choose product_notification, then you need to inform osCommerce which product(s) this notification is linked to so that it can send it off to the right people. As a result, when you click on send, you are brought to the following page:

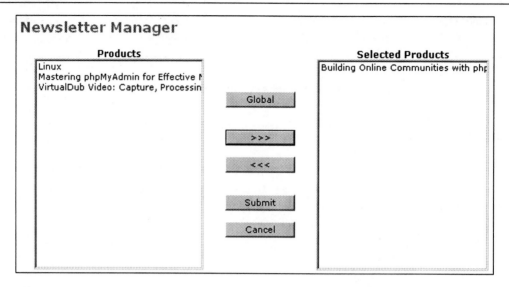

From here, you can select which products this notification is linked to—there is also a Global option to send it to all if need be. Once you have made your choices and clicked on submit, you will get the following confirmation screen, which you can use to check everything one last time before sending it on:

Of course, you may not always be happy sending out plain text emails. What happens if you would like to start sending out images of your new products in a monthly newsletter? The answer is to simply go along to the contributions section and add a WYSIWYG (what you see is what you get) editor for your newsletters. One package that you might want to look at, to begin with, is the MS2 HTML WYSIWYG Editor, Product Desc, Email + contribution, which can be found in the Features section or with a search on the term newsletter.

Summary

This chapter represents a great percentage of the overall work required to get your site looking like you want it. Once you are finished with this section, you will hopefully be satisfied that you are well on your way to deploying a working site, which will hopefully contribute to increased revenue through instilling confidence with the site's professionalism and design, as well as providing a pleasing environment in which customers can make purchases.

The knowledge gained from working with images and HTML, as well as the application of the design principles discussed will help not only with your osCommerce site, but with any other web-based application that you end up working with. Having gained an appreciation for the various different types of design, as well as having to work closely with GIF images, will free you up to create more ambitious graphical user interfaces in the future.

7
Taxes, Payments, and Shipping

Having reached this section of the development phase of your online store, you are permitted now to rub your hands together in a greedy fashion. Fundamentally, we all need to ensure a stable, if not always hugely profitable, source of income from our endeavors if we are to be able to realize our goals. Providing an excellent online avenue for sales, which makes it easy for customers to purchase goods from the comfort of their own homes, and which gives you, the merchant, the mouth-watering opportunity to sell to customers anywhere and any time is what e-commerce is all about.

To this end, osCommerce comes with a host of installable modules, which handle the complexities inherent in securing a variety of different payment types. As you would expect from software such as osCommerce, much thought and knowledge has gone into making the payment side of things as easy and efficient as possible. Try to imagine how much work would be involved in obtaining sensitive customers information, validating it all, protecting it from other parties, and integrating it with the rest of your application if it wasn't for our good friends at osCommerce.

> Despite the fair amount of work required to get a new osCommerce installation up and running, the fact that building a fully fledged e-commerce site is now within the grasp of the average businessman is an excellent contribution to the world of commerce as a whole, and especially to those with limited resources.

Watch out though—hidden dangers lurk at every corner for the unsuspecting online merchant, and unless you know precisely what you are doing, you should really stick to the more secure forms of payment rather than attempting to run a full-blown merchant account and unwittingly allowing malicious intruders access to sensitive financial information. On the other hand, the last thing you want to do is come all this way only to have to force customers to pay by check or bank deposit and so on. So where is the balance?

This chapter will attempt to give you the right balance in terms of the approach it takes in covering this material. For completeness, we will discuss all of the most common methods of receiving revenue from sales, but emphasis will be placed on the use of PayPal, since this is easy, well known, and well respected, and also supports a range of payment methods. All other options are recommended behind PayPal, with some, like handling your own merchant account, not being recommended at all for reasons of security and safety.

Of course, getting paid is not the whole story. You still have to make sure that you can get the product to the customer as well as make it as painless as possible on their wallets. This naturally requires a bit of thought about who will be buying what and from where, but once you have a good idea, it is not too hard to get all your ducks in a row.

Accordingly, this chapter will discuss:

- Getting paid
- Locations and taxes
- PayPal payments
- Credit card payments
- Checks and money orders
- Alternative forms of payment
- Shipping

Really what we are aiming for when we set up the various methods of payment is to have the transactions executed securely, reliably, and with some form of recovery in case things go awry somewhere along the line. Managing your payments effectively and reliably, as well as incorporating the correct shipping method and charges, is obviously one of the largest contributing factors to generating even more successful business transactions as well as happy customers along the way. Pay very careful attention to this section because you can really hurt your business by not being on the ball when it comes to taking people's hard-earned money.

Getting Paid

Generally, getting paid is one of the most satisfying aspects of running a business, especially for the small-to-medium level businessman or entrepreneur. Of course, the process of getting paid when you sell your products from a store, or directly, without the use of the Web, barely needs thinking about—the customers decides to purchase a product, they give you enough money, and you let them take it home. It's pretty simple!

This process is exactly the same on the Web except that each stage now needs to be closely monitored and tracked in order to ensure all the transaction information is correct. Further, you need to be able to handle pretty much any eventuality you can imagine programmatically so that you don't end up getting people paying for something they don't receive, or not paying for something they do receive, or any other number of hair-raising events.

As you would expect, osCommerce handles much of the complexity of doing this, but there is still quite a bit to think about. Furthermore, each type of payment comes replete with its own set of concerns and worries, which need to be comprehensively addressed if you are to be confident that your operation can handle things adequately. Despite the large variety of individual concerns, which need to be dealt with, there is an overall process that you can follow as a general guide to setting up payments in one form or another.

Preparation

There are several *types* of preparation you need to take up before attempting to implement a form of payment. What do I mean by this? Well, you need to ensure you have an excellent working knowledge of how a particular method of payment works. In other words, go to the provider of that method, be it a bank, specialist in online payments, post office, or whatever, and make sure you understand everything, including the legalities. You might think you know how a check works, and you probably do, but do you know enough about the intricacies of the checking system to base your business on them?

For example, do you know what an *adverse-claim* statute is? It shouldn't ever affect you, but the point is that there are often issues surrounding common forms of payment, and they don't arise until you are using them for your business. I guess in this respect, people reading this book will know plenty about checks, but my point was meant in general; I could just as easily be talking about the niceties of PsiGate, or some other online merchant service company.

Doing research on the form of payment that you are going to use is only half the problem. Once you understand how the system works, you need to work out how much it is going to cost, and what it will take to ensure that your site handles these types of transactions properly. Armed with this knowledge, you can then move confidently on to the next step.

Implementation

You need to work out exactly how payment is going to be implemented and integrated with your site. In most cases, this has been taken care of by osCommerce, since it provides default modules for the following payment methods:

- Authorize.net
- Credit Card
- Cash on Delivery
- iPayment
- Check/Money Order
- NOCHEX
- PayPal
- 2CheckOut
- PSiGate
- SECPay

However, if one of your chosen paths of revenue intake is not on this list, then you might have a slightly harder time going about implementing it. The first thing you should do as part of your preparation is check the Payment Modules section of the Contributions list on the osCommerce site as there were, at the time of writing, nearly four hundred packages available there.

So, during this stage you need to obtain or buy accounts from the various service providers (if necessary), and ensure that they are properly linked to your site—the process will differ from method to method. Then you need to make certain that your site can respond to the various different eventualities that can occur when using the payment method although this should really have been taken care of by the underlying code supplied with osCommerce or the contribution in question.

Finally you need to make sure that your business will respond correctly to payments. For example, the last thing you want to do is allow someone to download a product immediately when they are paying by check. This is a more specific case of the general one, which is concerned with ensuring that the funds required for the product and its delivery are irrevocably yours before you release the product.

Hand in hand with the last point is the ability to return payments should they be justifiably returnable and you may prefer to set up a different method for this entirely. For example, you might need to wait for a product to be returned before you can make payment, in which case you might want to simply pay by check rather than use online methods.

Once you have a payment system that is capable of handling the entire payment cycle, including returns, you can move to the next step.

Testing and Maintenance

As always, testing should be included in any undertaking in the electronic world. This means subjecting your store to all manners of different situations, which should reveal the correct functioning of the payment method, and highlight any problems at the same time. Remember that it is not sufficient to test your site for the case where the site is used as intended. You will be absolutely amazed at how users can *mess things up* in the real world, and your payments, especially, need to be robust enough to handle this.

To go along with this, a little research is also useful in this stage. Go look for problems that other people have had and see if you can reproduce them. If you can, then you know you have a problem that needs to be fixed. You might also learn how to preemptively guard against dangers or pitfalls that others have stumbled into.

Despite your best efforts to build a perfect system, you will find that you need to maintain your systems of payment: from simple things such as ensuring that you have paid your service fees to more serious things like locating any irregularities and determining their cause and effect.

Locations and Taxes

It is appropriate at this point to discuss the Locations/Taxes section in the admin tool because the settings here impact directly on your payment and shipping policies. By this stage, you have had plenty of practice using the admin tool, so I won't hold you up too much with a long discussion. Instead, we will look at the available settings and relate them to what you need for your business.

The default page, Countries, simply gives a list of all the ISO country codes. It's a useful reference if you decide to use a zone-based shipping policy, because you will need to enter various country codes into your zone-based shipping table. We will look at how to set this later on in the chapter in the sections entitled *Zone Rates* and *Contechst Book's Shipping Policy*.

The next page, Zones, gives a list of the more common zones or regions in Europe and North America, which are useful for osCommerce users. For example, there is a zone code for each of the states in the US, including some overseas territories. These can be used when determining which zones you will ship to, or what tax policy to implement—you will see an example of this later on when we deal with zone rates.

The next option is worth looking at in a little more depth because it can be slightly confusing how to work with Tax Zones.

Tax Zones

By default we are given a zone called Florida, which has the description Florida local sales tax zone. But what if you don't live in Florida and don't need to worry about Florida's tax laws? By way of example, let's assume we are in California and wish to enter that region into the system for tax purposes.

On the Tax Zones homepage, click on insert, and in the textboxes provided, give a name and description for your new tax zone. The following screenshot shows the result of the demo site's modification:

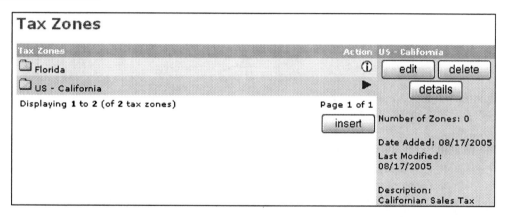

We aren't done yet, because this has not actually associated any zone with the name and description we have just entered. In order to do this, we must click on details and then select the subzone, or subzones, which fall under this category. Click on insert when the next page comes up, and then enter the country and zone you wish to link to this tax zone's name. I don't suppose you need to be told to make the name as accurate as possible so that you know which tax zone is associated with which zones. In our case we have, quite intuitively, added California as shown here:

Tax Zones

Country	Zone	Action	Edit Sub Zone
United States	California	▶	Please make any necessary changes

Displaying **1** to **1** (of **1** countries)   Page **1** of **1**

Country:
United States

Zone:
California

update   cancel

Of course, you can associate more than one subzone with each tax zone you name, and how you set things up should be the result of a bit of trial and error along with some research. For our purposes this is fine, and if you want to have a quick peek at how this zone can now be used, then go along to the Table Rate shipping module in the Modules section of the admin tool and install (if it's not already installed) and edit the module. You will notice you have a shipping option as follows:

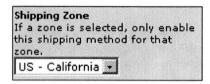

This is not the only place where a zone set by you comes into play. For example, in the payment modules you will find the following option:

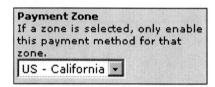

Of course, setting tax zones is all good and well, but up till now we haven't looked at how to actually classify various products in terms of tax. The next section deals with precisely that…

Tax Classes and Rates

Setting your tax class works in much the same way as setting the tax zone. You need to come up with a tax class name along with a good description for it. Once you have saved that, simply click on Tax Rates to bring up the page that allows you to set your tax percentage for that particular category. For example, the demo site added the DaylightRobbery tax in Tax Class, and then after clicking new tax rate on the Tax Rate the page was edited to get the following results:

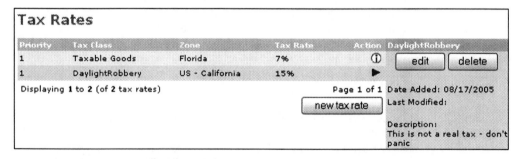

Now, if you have products that fall under the DaylightRobbery tax scheme, then you can tell osCommerce to add this tax to the product's gross price when you edit the product's attributes in the Catalog section of the admin tool, like so:

```
New Product in "PHP & MySQL"

Products          ⦿ In Stock  ○ Out of Stock
Status:

Date Available:   [                  🔽]
(YYYY-MM-DD)

Products          [Packt Publishing ▾]
Manufacturer:

Products          🏴 [Building Online Commu]
Name:

Tax Class:        [DaylightRobbery ▾]

Products Price    [22.9900              ]
(Net):

Products Price    [26.4385              ]
(Gross):
```

Observe now that the highlighted value gives the gross product price based on a calculation of 15% of $22.99, which is what we would expect from our DaylightRobbery tax. In this way you can exert fine-grained control over the taxing of all your products, which is especially useful if you are working with exotic products.

Depending on your geographical location, nationality, and the types of products you are dealing with, you will need to think carefully about how to deal with your tax responsibilities. Remember that your internal revenue service can be of assistance as well as the osCommerce community in this regard. With that done, let's move on to far more happier thoughts like…

Getting Paid with PayPal

Businesses of any size can benefit from the reliable and trusted PayPal brand. Using PayPal for osCommerce transactions is also one of the easier modules to work with. In fact, you can have a more or less working PayPal facility up and running in no time at all. The hard work comes from ironing out the wrinkles along the way and ensuring the smoothest operation of your payments in the future.

If you are happy with the most basic setup, then all you need to do is create your own PayPal account, and enable the PayPal module in osCommerce using the admin tool. Then, when customers attempt to purchase goods, they will have the option to pay with PayPal and be redirected to the PayPal site, where they can make the transaction.

There are a couple of cons to doing things this way! The main thing is that customer's making payment might simply close their browser, without continuing back to the store. In this case, the order is simply not recorded in the database. This is clearly quite a problem because straightaway you will be unsure as to who has paid for what without manually checking your records. Secondly, customers must have a PayPal account in order to complete the transaction—this is not necessarily the case if you decide to implement PayPal functionality on your own because PayPal has now introduced Account Optional facilities.

As of milestone 2, version 2.2, there is a contribution that uses the PayPal IPN system to make transactions secure and reliable. This is what we are going to use for the example site, so head on over to the contribution's homepage and download it from `http://www.osCommerce.com/community/contributions,2679`.

> This is a community contribution, and is is subject to upgrades and changes. As a result of this, you may not use exactly the same version as shown here. At the time of writing, the recommended version is the one uploaded on the 6th of August by judebert.

Some of you may be asking, "What is an IPN?"

Well, very briefly, let's quickly go over the payment transaction process for PayPal to get a good idea of what is going on under the hood. From the PayPal website, the definition of an IPN is:

> *Instant Payment Notification (IPN) is PayPal's interface for handling real-time purchase confirmation and server-to-server communications. IPN delivers immediate notification and confirmation of PayPal payments you receive and provides status and additional data on pending, cancelled, or failed transactions.*

Basically, an IPN is sent to your server as soon as a payment is made, allowing you to incorporate information sent with this notification into your programming. On receiving the notification, your server will send the information, including the encrypted code, back to a secure PayPal URL. PayPal will then authenticate the transaction and send your server a *Verified* or *Invalid* response, which you can use to fulfill an order after you have performed a few checks.

Now, you don't even have to have any form of security enabled to do this because there is no sensitive client information being passed back and forth between your server and PayPal. But while this is an option, you shouldn't really treat it as such—consequently, from your point of view, you either need to have encryption enabled to work with PayPal or you must have a secure server which can be targetted by PayPal.

As well as this, in order to get the IPN system functional you need to be able to supply PayPal with a valid URL, which it will use to send its messages to. So, what this all boils down to is that you need to ensure your hosts can provide you with encryption functionality (or a secure server); you might also wish to read through the following chapter on security, as well as this one, in order to get a better feel for security issues before you get the PayPal payment method up and running.

For now, though, let's begin with setting up a PayPal account…

Setting Up PayPal on osCommerce

It's very easy to set up your PayPal account. Simply head along to `http://www.paypal.com`, click on Sign up, and select the type of account you wish to create—more than likely a business or premier account. You will then have to furnish PayPal with a bunch of details about yourself and your business, and confirm all this before you will be given an account. Once that is done, you will be presented with a screen that looks much like this:

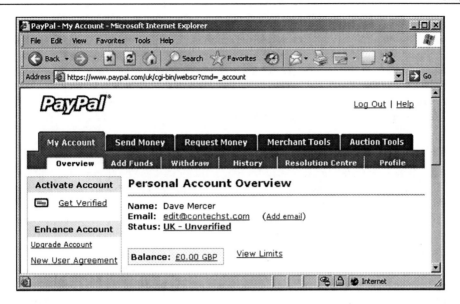

At some stage you will need to have your account verified, which will allow you to lift the limit on the amount of funds that can be withdrawn from your new account. Everything in this interface is reasonably self explanatory, and you are advised to spend some time learning your way around it before continuing. Assuming you have got your account to the status and state you need it in so as to run your business, you can turn to the admin tool and install the PayPal module in the Modules/Payments section, like so:

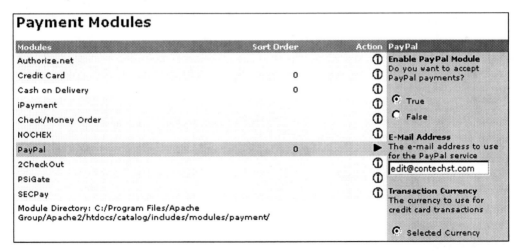

With that done, you can check to see whether everything is working by purchasing an item off the site and ensuring you are taken to the correct PayPal page to make the payment. Unless you have a couple of accounts, you will either be unable to pay yourself, or you will end up having to pay from your own account into your business account, so it isn't recommended you take it any further than this at this stage.

Unfortunately, this is not the end of the story because in order to make sure that the payments work smoothly without us having to verify orders manually, we are going to have to use the PayPal IPN contribution. To do this you will need to have a deployed site in order to work with PayPal correctly. So, for this section we are using the fully deployed site to show you how this is done despite the fact that the actual deployment chapter will follow only later on in the book. It is recommended that you get as much as you can done here while reading along before putting in the final touches once you have read the deployment chapter.

Connecting osCommerce and PayPal

The first step here is to install the IPN contribution, which requires you to copy files into the `catalog` directory. Please read the instructions supplied with the contribution to ensure that you copy everything across properly. Once this is done, you can simply go to the Payment page in the Modules section of the administration tool and click install. (Remember to remove the other PayPal module at the same time). This will bring up a list of options which you will need to edit.

> For simplicity's sake we will show you how to get a live site up and running (so you know it can be done). In reality you will need to do some testing before using the live PayPal server. In order to perform some testing you need to register as a developer with PayPal, at `http://developer.paypal.com`, and make use of their sandbox site. There is plenty of advice and documentation to help you on your way, so we won't cover it further here.

You can use the PayPal IPN contribution to choose whether to use the live site or the developer's sandbox to process transactions by simply changing the Gateway Server option to Testing instead of Live. Remember that when you do your testing work you will need to create several accounts—one to act as the receiver of payments, and a few buyers.

Let's get back to the live site. By now you should have the IPN contribution installed and the default module disabled. You should edit the module appropriately according to your circumstances. For example, you might have something like the following setup:

Property	Setting
Enable PayPal IPN Module Do you want to accept PayPal IPN payments?	This is obviously set to True.
E-Mail Address The e-mail address to use for the PayPal IPN service	The email address of your PayPal account at which you wish to receive your store's payments.
Transaction Currency The currency to use for transactions	This was left as Select Currency, but you will need to decide this based on your payment criteria.
Payment Zone If a zone is selected, only enable this payment method for that zone.	Since we are happy to receive payments via PayPal from anywhere in the world, this was left as none.

Property	Setting
Set Preparing Order Status Set the status of prepared orders made with this payment module to this value	This was set to Preparing [PayPal IPN]Processing in order to distinguish it from the default module.
Set PayPal Completed Order Status Set the status of orders made with this payment module to this value	This was set to Processing, but can be changed to any of the values in the drop-down list depending on how you want to structure your payments. For example, you might want to take certain actions based on the status of an order, in which case set this (along with other the status of other payments) to the status you desire.
Set PayPal Denied/Refunded Order Status Set a specific status to denote that something has gone wrong	A new status, Denied, was used here. You can add it to the drop-down list by going to Localization | Orders Status in the admin tool and adding a Denied status there. This option is then available for you to use in all your payment modules.
Gateway Server Use the testing (sandbox) or live gateway server for transactions?	You will obviously use the sandbox for some time until you are happy everything is working as it should. For the purposes of this demonstration, though, it has been set to Live.
Transaction Type Send individual items to PayPal or aggregate all as one total item?	This was set to Aggregate since we want entire orders processed in one go.
Page Style The page style to use for the transaction procedure (defined at your PayPal profile page)	You can set the look and feel of your personal PayPal payment page from the your account's page by selecting the Custom Payment Pages option in the Seller Preferences category of the Profile section—in this case it has been set to contechst, which you will see shortly.
Debug E-Mail Address All parameters of an Invalid IPN notification will be sent to this email address if one is entered.	Decide on an email address on which you can receive notifications of any IPN irregularities.
Sort order of display Sort order of display. Lowest is displayed first.	This is a standard option and simply governs which order on the payment information page the modules are presented.

Incidentally, due to the nature of dealing with downloadable products, many of the order status settings shown in the preceding table will be changed in Chapter 10 in the section entitled *Working with Downloadable Products*.

It is strongly recommended that you take a look at Chapter 10 before finalizing your order statuses even if you aren't going to work with downloadable products. This is because the way in which order statuses can be manipulated is covered in some detail there and will provide you with a more sophisticated way of controlling your purchases.

Also, we haven't covered the encryption section of this module's settings because we will deal with that on its own in the following chapter on security. Saving the above settings to their appropriate values and ignoring the rest, we can move to the next task. Common wisdom has it that you need to tell PayPal where it is that it should be sending its notifications... or do you? Actually, this contribution is really meant to take pretty much all responsibility off your hands, and you don't even have to tell PayPal where it needs to send its IPN.

This may seem slightly confusing to some of you who have already worked with PayPal previously because it is recommended that you supply a target address under the Profile section of your PayPal account page. I will show the standard process here because it highlights a couple of points, but please bear in mind that you *don't need to do this* if you are using the PayPal IPN module.

Under other circumstances, you would set things up on the PayPal side by clicking on the Profile link on your PayPal account page and then navigating to the Instant Payment Notification Preferences under the Selling Preferences heading. Once you are there, edit the settings like so (obviously substituting the correct values for your server):

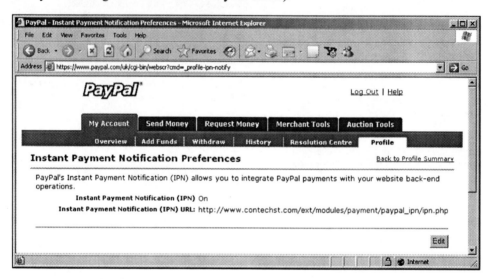

Two things you will notice here:

The first is why we needed a live site to work with PayPal—obviously your development machine has no way of receiving IPNs from PayPal, so only a working URL (shown here as http://www.contechst.com) will do. Second, we have told PayPal to send payments to the ipn.php file in the ext/modules/payment/paypal_ipn/ folder. This location might change depending on the version of the IPN contribution you are using.

Now, in contrast to this, the target URL for PayPal is actually passed to PayPal by the IPN payment module as part of the request, which is why we don't need to perform any actions other than installing the module. A customer can then select this payment method off the site, be redirected to PayPal, and can make the payment. You can verify this by observing the various stages of the order in the Orders section of the admin tool.

Working with PayPal

That's everything you need to do to get osCommerce talking to PayPal and making everything work nice and smoothly—easy! Let's run through the whole process step by step so that everything is clear at this point. First, a customer gets to the following stage on the site:

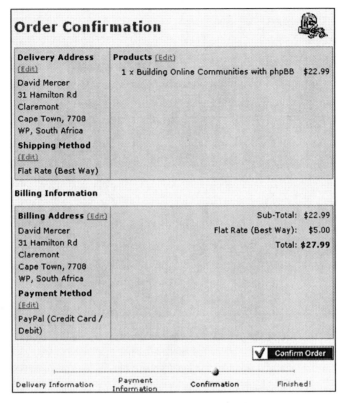

Notice that this is now on the live site: the customer has selected the PayPal (Credit Card/ Debit) payment option, and that the total price of the purchase is $27.99. Once the Confirm Order button is clicked, the customer is redirected to the PayPal site to complete the payment. If, however, we take a look at the admin tool, we see that it has already picked up on the fact that we are, in all likelihood, about to receive a payment via PayPal, and the screen looks like this:

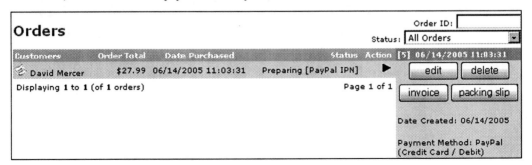

Now, the Status message is set during the editing of the IPN payment module as you have already seen earlier in the table presented. So, at this stage, osCommerce knows what is coming in terms of the type of payment that is being made, and it's waiting on the customer to go through and make the payment. Assuming the customer does just this, he or she will be presented with the following customized page (recall that this setting was also made when editing the IPN payment module):

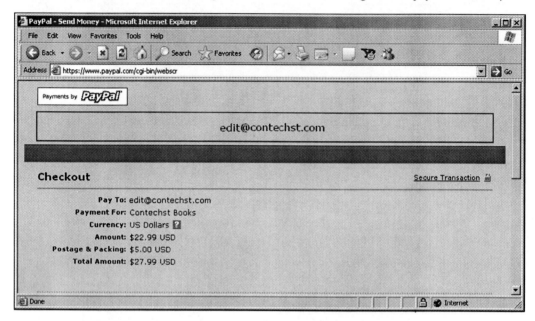

Of course, this is just a demo to show that you can control the look and feel of the PayPal page so that it provides a more seamless transition between your site and PayPal for customers. Once the payment has been made, we can look at the order in more detail. You will notice that there is now a new section, which shows the status of the IPN towards the bottom of the screen:

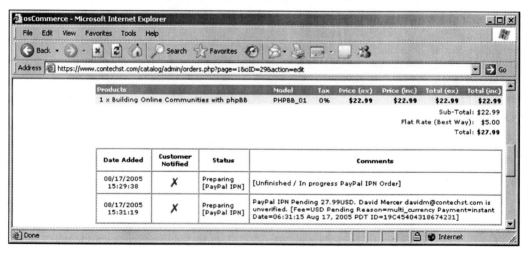

The first two status rows actually get added between the purchasing of the product on the site and the acceptance of payment by the merchant once the customer has paid. Of course, to confirm all this, you should receive an email from PayPal informing you that you have received a payment from a customer. Once the customer clicks Continue to complete their payment, they are returned to your server and will be shown your customized checkout success page:

The story is not quite finished yet; you as the receiver of funds still need to accept payments made. Should you choose to accept the payments, then the following note will be added to the order:

Date Added	Customer Notified	Status	Comments
08/17/2005 15:29:38	✔	Preparing [PayPal IPN]	
08/17/2005 15:31:19	✔	Preparing [PayPal IPN]	
08/17/2005 15:34:11	✗	Processing	PayPal IPN Completed 27.99USD. David Mercer davidm@contechst.com is unverified. [Fee=USD Payment=instant Date=06:31:15 Aug 17, 2005 PDT ID=19C45404318674231]

Notice that at the bottom of the list we now have the latest record (in this case at 15:34:11): the customer hasn't been notified of this development by osCommerce (but remember that PayPal will notify them that their payment has been accepted), the Status of the order has been set to Processing as expected, but the real interesting point is that the Comments section is telling us that the actual process is Completed as opposed to Unfinished as it was initially. This means we have the money, safe and sound.

For the demo site, things were set up like this because we want the opportunity to print out an invoice and packing slip, and then finally set the status of the order to Delivered manually so that the final order page looks like this (note that we also emailed the customer to inform them of the delivery and they can now check the site to view the full order history of this order):

Date Added	Customer Notified	Status	Comments
08/17/2005 15:29:38	✔	Preparing [PayPal IPN]	
08/17/2005 15:31:19	✔	Preparing [PayPal IPN]	
08/17/2005 15:34:11	✘	Processing	PayPal IPN Completed 27.99USD. David Mercer davidm@contechst.com is unverified. [Fee=USD Payment=instant Date=06:31:15 Aug 17, 2005 PDT ID=19C45404318674231]
08/17/2005 16:00:46	✔	Delivered	

Obviously, how you choose to deal with your particular setup will come from what you want out of the site and what you learn as you go along. Having been through this example, though, you should feel pretty good about the process of obtaining payments via PayPal. Of course, there is plenty of testing to do, and you should always ensure that your purchases and stock levels are adjusted as you expect—you can take a look at the Products Purchased report in the admin tool to confirm whether the correct products have indeed been purchased by your PayPal customer.

There is really no substitute for the two things to ensure you have everything set up correctly: practice and experience. Make sure you play around with every aspect of this module so that you understand how it works thoroughly. Then, how to best implement the functionality can be tweaked as you gain experience—you may wish to do things entirely differently altogether.

For example, you may wish to entice customers to actually click on the Continue button when finished with PayPal so that they do go back to your site and are given a confirmation email, instead of logging off and then wondering why no one is talking to them. For this, open up the includes/modules/payments/paypal_ipn.php file and search for the following two lines somewhere about line 330:

```
$parameters['cancel_return'] = tep_href_link(FILENAME_CHECKOUT_PAYMENT, '',
'SSL');
$parameters['bn'] = $this->identifier;
```

Under that line, add the following line so your code looks like this:

```
$parameters['cancel_return'] = tep_href_link(FILENAME_CHECKOUT_PAYMENT, '',
'SSL');
$parameters['bn'] = $this->identifier;
$parameters['cbt'] = 'Click here for email confirmation of your order';
```

Once you have saved that, take a look at the button you get when you are making payments via PayPal. You should see something like the following:

Pretty neat, huh? Apart from this, the other important thing we learned in this section is that we can create custom order statuses to suit our needs in the Localization section of the admin tool. In this case, we set the status to Processing once we were in a position to accept funds. As you will see in Chapter 10, when we deal with the download controller, having a solid approach to naming the various statuses your store encounters is quite important.

That about wraps it up for a live, functional PayPal-based payment system, but you should never leave things as they are. You need to secure everything using encryption, and for this you will probably need access to some sort of certificate and key generation tool—most good web hosts should provide you with this. For now, though, this is good enough, and we will continue developing this example in the next chapter, when we discuss security in depth.

Credit Card Payments

Let's begin this section by stating that there are several caveats to consider when embarking on the journey to credit card payment bliss! The main one is that it can be quite a pain in proverbial back end of your application getting an Internet Merchant Account. This is because Internet transactions are considered to be at a high risk from fraud, and one result is that transaction fees are often higher too. There is not really much help that this book can offer you in terms of obtaining a merchant account—this is between you and your bank and/or merchant account provider.

For more information on obtaining merchant accounts, visit the service providers of your choice, who will have plenty of information about how to use them and how to find your way around the system in general. For example:

- `http://www.authorizenet.com/solutions/merchantsolutions/onlinemerchant account/`

- `http://www.secpay.com/`

- `http://www.psigate.com/merchantaccount.asp`

will all furnish you with plenty of relevant information to help you make your choice.

Secondly, you need to make absolutely certain that you are not providing a platform for hackers to gain access to customer's credit information by not implementing proper security over the entire site. If we were to accept credit card details with the site in its current form, we would certainly be deserving of the term *negligent* in our responsibility to protect client's information, because there is no secure method of information exchange between the clients, us, and the financial institutions that we need to interact with.

> This chapter does not look at how to secure your site in any detail, since all security issues will be covered in the following chapter. While we are setting up payments using credit cards here, you should not consider the job complete until you have implemented security for the payments.

Cheer up, though; it's not all doom and gloom. Apart from what has just been mentioned, the process of getting set up is much the same as it was for PayPal. Before we go any further it might be worthwhile to lay out all the players in the credit card transaction world so that you have a fair idea of what you need to do to get things working:

- **Merchant Account**: Anyone who wants to process credit card payments themselves (as opposed to letting PayPal handle it) will need a merchant account. Further, if you want to provide online payment facilities, you will need an Internet merchant account, and not your run of the mill account. For some businesses it is particularly difficult to obtain a merchant account—however, so long as you stick to retailing fairly tangible goods you should be safe in this respect. Anything that leaves a verifiable trail comes in handy as proof, should the question of fraud arise.

- **Acquirers**: Any institution that issues merchant accounts, often banks, are known as acquirers. For example, HSBC and Barclays are two well known acquiring banks.

- **Payment Service Provider**: These companies, amongst other things, have as their main focus the task of facilitating payment transactions for merchants (such as yourself) via a payment gateway.

You might find that depending on who you work with, your acquirer offers full support for your payments transactions, in which case you may not need a payment service provider. Of course, most of the payment modules available are for use by payment service providers, and not the banks directly.

> Having set up PayPal facilities, customers are already able to pay with their credit cards or bank accounts. Adding credit card facilities here is really an exercise in making non-PayPal customers lives' easier.

So, the process is still the same as it was for PayPal:

1. Sign up with the relevant corporations to obtain a merchant account and/or a payment gateway.
2. Install the relevant module.
3. Test, test, and test again.
4. Make absolutely certain that everything is secure and functional on the live site.
5. Rake in the cash.

Accordingly, there isn't too much to discuss by way of anything new here other than to show a couple of examples in action. We will begin with the Credit Card module and also demonstrate the PsiGate payment module.

The Credit Card Module

You can make use of the Credit Card module if you have a merchant account, which you will use to process payments manually. Basically, the details that are provided on the site by the customer are simply stored in the database, ready for you to process them accordingly. On the surface of things, this seems like a really nice and easy way to do things, but don't be fooled, you can get yourself into a lot of trouble doing things this way. Let's look at how everything works so that it is clearer.

Head on over to your admin tool, and click on install for the Credit Card module and enable the module by setting the first option to True so that your page looks like:

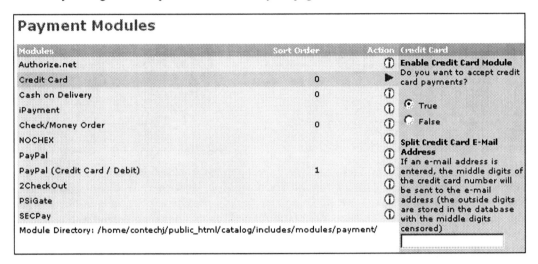

Update that, and head on to the site and make a purchase. When you get to the checkout-payment page, you should now have the option to receive credit card payments; enter the dummy credit card value and add a date later than the current one as the expiry time, like so:

Carry on with the purchase until you receive the checkout success page, and then go to the Orders section of the admin tool and take a look at the information given for this latest purchase. You should have something that looks a lot like this:

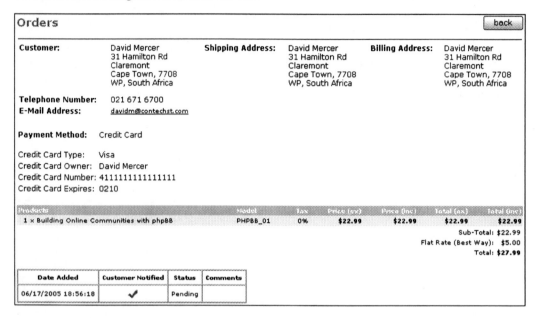

A sight like this will generally have your average security expert in tears because not only are we storing the customer's credit card information in our database, but we are also allowing access to that information bundled up and presented in a nice report format. If anyone ever gained access to the admin tool, they would be able to read off client credit card information from here. Even worse, if a hacker ever gained access to the database, they would now be able to read off all the credit card information directly from the database.

"Sure, but this is all password protected, and we will be adding security later" I hear you say. Well, actually this very module comes with a bit more security, so let's try that out. Go back to the payment module's edit page and add in an email address to which you would like half of the credit information sent. Save that and repeat the process and notice that this time the order page looks like this:

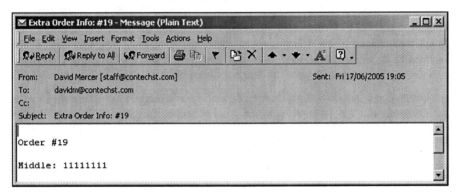

Well, that's slightly better because now if someone gained access to the site, he or she would only be able to get their hands on half of credit card info; the other half is not held on the site. Instead, it has been sent via email to the address you specified:

Now you can simply match the middle numbers to the outer numbers via the order number, which is common to both records, and are thereby able to retain the complete details without running the risk of holding all the information in one place. While this is much better, it is still exceptionally poor in terms of the type of security you should be hoping to implement, because that email has been sent to you in a non-secure manner.

Assuming someone knows that this is going on, they could intercept the unencrypted message and match the numbers up. This might all seem like quite a reasonable risk to take, but bear in mind what is at stake—your livelihood. If customers find out that your site, and therefore their private financial data, has been compromised (and they will because they will notice fraudulent transactions on their accounts), then as a business, your reputation is more or less irrevocably destroyed.

While you could always take the information and encrypt it before emailing it to yourself (which we will do in the following chapter on security), you will still have to work with this information, and somewhere along the line there will be a chink in the armor. Rather don't take the risk at all, and let someone else handle it—there are plenty of reputable businesses who plow far more resources than you or I could into making their services secure, so that you can use them. It may hurt to fork out for the service, but it's nothing compared to the trouble you could land yourself in.

Having seen how the Credit Card module works, let's move on to look at how one of the service-provider modules functions.

The PsiGate Module

It's important to bear in mind before we test this module out, that each gateway service might have a slightly different methodology for processing credit card payments. For example, those of you who try SECPay will notice that at no time does the customer enter credit card details onto the merchant's site—instead, the browser is redirected to a secure payment page on the SECPay server, before being returned to the merchant site once the payment details have been entered.

> Whatever module you choose to use, or even if you choose to write your own application code to handle payments, setting everything up is really all about learning how your gateway service operates and using that knowledge to integrate their service into your application.

PsiGate makes it easy for us to test our application because we can run test values off it without having to register with them first. Consequently, pretty much the only thing you need to do is install the module in the Payments section as you have seen in previous examples, and then navigate to the payments page on your site and run through the payment process as normal.

The astute observer will notice a slight difference in the processing of payments once the PsiGate option has been checked. Let's run through that quickly because it will also illustrate the generic process followed by all the other gateway services (more or less). Suppose you have entered the relevant test info into your site, so that your page looks like this:

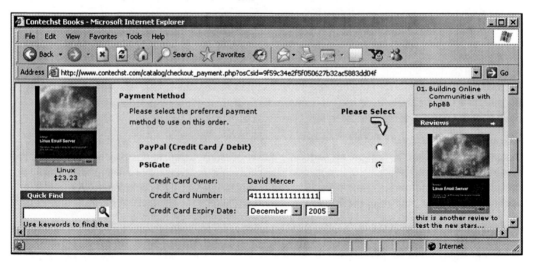

Click on Continue to get to the order confirmation page. This is where things change a bit behind the scenes. Once the customer confirms his or her details are all correct and clicks on Continue, that information is sent to a secure PsiGate server instead of simply being held on your site. You can view the status bar in your browser immediately after clicking on Continue to confirm this, and can also see a quick notice from the actual PsiGate site before it redirects the customer back to your store, like so:

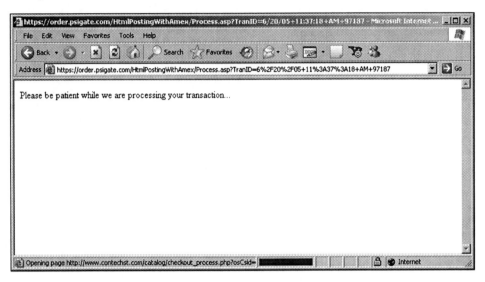

Notice from this screenshot that we are actually executing the `Process.asp` page on the `https://order.psigate.com/` URL, and the target URL, shown in the Status bar at the bottom of the screen is the `checkout_process.php` page back on the store's server. As well as this, the session is preserved because the target also includes the session ID parameter (not quite visible).

So, what has happened here is that your store's server has sent information to the PsiGate secure server, which has processed the information and returned its results. If the transaction has been successful, the customer sees the usual Your Order has been Processed message on the checkout success page (or whatever your equivalent of this is). If the order is not successful, then the error is collected by the payment module and outputted to the customer's screen.

So what type of options do we have to work with? Well, as we did for the PayPal section, here is a table representing all the options and their values and meanings:

Property	Setting
Enable PSiGate Module Do you want to accept PSiGate payments?	Obviously this is set to True if you want customers to be able to use this form of payment.
Merchant ID Merchant ID used for the PSiGate service	This ID will be assigned to you once you have an Internet merchant account. Please see the PsiGate site for more info on this: http://www.psigate.com/faq.asp.

Property	Setting
Transaction Mode Transaction mode to use for the PSiGate service	The first value, Production, should be enabled once you decide to go live. The three that follow are used for testing purposes to ensure your system is behaving correctly. For example, select Always Good to test for successful transactions while testing.
Transaction Type Transaction type to use for the PSiGate service	Setting this to Sale means that PsiGate will treat this as a normal transaction and transfer funds appropriately—use this only if the product reaches the client immediately (in other words, the product is downloadable). PreAuth will ensure the funds are available (reserved), but will not perform the transaction—this is left for you to do manually from your PsiGate Admin section once you have delivered the product. Use PostAuth if you want to settle a PreAuth transaction which reserves funds. You must have the PreAuth order ID and the correct amount to do this—for more info see the PsiGate docs at www.psigate.com/java.pdf.
Credit Card Collection Should the credit card details be collected locally or remotely at PSiGate?	You can choose whether customers will enter their credit card information onto your site or onto PsiGate's site. If in doubt, take the responsibility off your hands and pass the buck to PsiGate.
Transaction Currency The currency to use for credit card transactions	The only two options for this module are Canadian dollars and US dollars since PsiGate only deals with these two currencies.
Payment Zone If a zone is selected, only enable this payment method for that zone.	Once again, you should select the zones you wish this module to be enabled for. For example, you may prefer to use PsiGate in North America, but SECPay in Europe.
Set Order Status Set the value for the status of orders made with this payment module	You can set this to whatever value option you like; however, remember to be consistent in your choice of status because you may wish to programmatically implement features based on the Status of payments at some stage. For example Preparing [PayPal IPN] is not a bright choice because this has nothing to do with PsiGate.
Sort order of display. Sort order of display. Lowest is displayed first.	As usual, you can select the order of appearance using this option.

There are, of course, many other modules that you may opt to use depending on your businesses' needs and setup. The exact manner in which the module implements the payments is really dependent on the gateway that you are using, but what you have seen here is a good outline of what is expected once you have an Internet merchant account against which to run e-commerce transactions.

One final thought before we move on. If you are concerned about the safety of your business and wish to know more about how to prevent or reduce fraud, then visit your payment service provider or acquirer online and look over their fraud-detection software or other such products. With that out of the way, we should briefly look at a few more methods of payment, which might come in handy somewhere along the line.

Alternative Forms of Payments

While credit cards and PayPal payments are probably the easiest and most convenient for a customer to use, not everyone will trust the Internet with their payment details and will instead prefer to use more old-fashioned methods. Ironically, a higher percentage of fraud is associated with check payments than with credit cards from online sales, but there you go.

Be careful with checks and money orders. Some banks will clear the funds in your account immediately when you deposit a check into your account. Acting on good faith, you then promptly deliver the product, only to find that the bank has removed the funds from your account once the check bounced and the customer has either maliciously or unwittingly left you out of pocket. Ouch!!

If you feel that your sales will be adversely affected due to the lack of other payment methods, then by all means, read on…

Checks and Money Orders

This module is about as easy as it comes to set up. Simply go along to the Payments section and click install. Then, edit it appropriately (the settings are self explanatory, or have already been covered several times), and away you go. Obviously, you would not change the status of the order until you received the check/money order, and you certainly would not want to release your products or make them available till you are in possession of the funds.

Another issue you will need to research is whether or not the form of payment is valid for you. Money orders may not be redeemable if you are not based in the US. Apart from doing a bit of background research on the niceties of each form of payment, there are no real concerns about security on the site because no sensitive information is passed between the customer and the store. This makes it easy for you to implement, but an exercise in patience for the customer as they wait for you to receive and process the payments.

Cash on Delivery

If you are going to be delivering the products you sell, then the Cash on Delivery module is probably worth installing. Again, there is nothing complex about this module, and editing should present no problem for you. The only things worth mentioning here are that:

- The chances being fairly high that you only deliver within a single zone, the Payment Zone option becomes far more important because you can enable this option for only your locality.
- Merchants can ship COD using UPS, but there are extra costs involved. See the UPS site for more details: http://www.ups.com.

Shipping

There are six shipping modules currently *shipped* with osCommerce by default, which give you a fair amount of control over how you handle the delivery of your goods. There are also a huge number of modules available, which can augment the default functionality, or provide new facilities altogether. The best thing to do when organizing your site's shipping is to sit back and think carefully about who will be buying what, and where they are likely to be.

Once you have a good idea about where most of your products are going, you can develop a shipping strategy to suit your needs. For example, if you are only going to be shipping to a relatively small geographical area, and your products are more or less the same in terms of size and weight, then a flat shipping rate may be appropriate. However, it is more than likely that you will want a more fine-grained level of control over your shipping charges, so let's take a quick look through the modules that are available (excluding the flat rate module, which is trivial to install).

Before we do this, though, I should point out that while it is pretty simple to install and control each individual shipping module, it is not so easy to actually obtain precisely what you want in terms of shipping charges. What I mean by this is that you could decide to offer several methods of shipping based on the various locations and zones you are retailing to. If you do this, then you have to ensure that each one will cover your shipping costs wherever the customer is based (or is disabled if that option is not viable).

In other words, a flat rate will always be a set value even if someone is purchasing from overseas, and the customer will more than likely choose the cheapest option available regardless of whether you meant them to choose one option or the other. So be careful you don't end up with a situation where the customer is offered several shipping options, one of which is not enough to cover the shipping costs.

Flat Rates

Having said this, you can use flat rates for several different zones, so don't feel you are restricted to only implementing flat rates to one area. To do this, make copies of the flat.php file in the includes/modules/shipping/ and includes/languages/english/modules/shipping/ folders. Then edit these copies, replacing each occurrence of the term flat or FLAT with the name of the copied files. For example, I have named the new files flat1.php in both folders, and replaced each occurrence of the term flat or FLAT with flat1 or FLAT1—a simple search and replace will work here. The result is a new flat-rate module, which can be used to ship flat rates to a different zone.

This is incredibly useful if you want to make flat rates to specific countries without having to bother with zone-rate settings or other forms of shipping. Looking at the shipping options available on the demo store, you can see the following:

It's clear that we now have two flat-rate modules, with the new one only being enabled for the Florida shipping zone, with a slightly higher Shipping Cost to distinguish it from the original flat rate module. Looking at the effect this has on customers who are based in Florida (shown in the following screenshot), we can see that they now have two flat-rate options available (obviously you would only want one rate enabled per zone, but this is left as is to demonstrate the point):

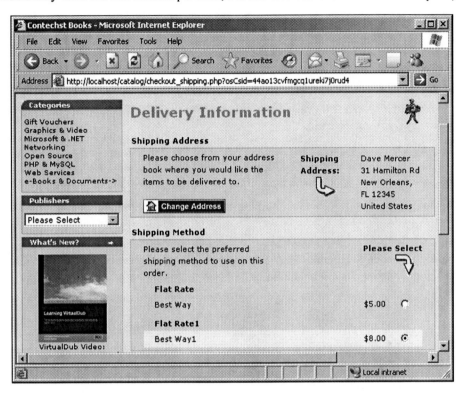

Now, you will probably want to make your new flat-rate modules display more descriptive names such as Flat Rate to Europe or Flat Rate to Australia, and you will need to test to ensure that customers from certain zones, or goods that belong to a certain tax class, get linked to the correct flat-rate shipping method. However, we won't dwell on this any more because you should be able to add as many flat-rate modules (or any other module for that matter) as you like, given what you have just seen here. Just play around and experiment to find what works for you…

Per Item

Once again, this is pretty straightforward. Simply install the module and away you go! osCommerce will multiply the number of items in the customer's shopping cart on checkout and will deliver a total based on that alone. You can set the Shipping Cost you wish to charge per item, as well as a Handling Fee, Tax Class, Shipping Fee, and Sort Order. Of interest here is the handling fee, which applies to all the shipping modules. Adding an amount here allows you to cover other costs such as packaging material and labor, by tacking that amount onto the shipping price.

Of course, this option is probably not ideal if you are selling large number of products per purchase, and packaging them up in one container. Obviously, you need to always think of the most efficient and cost effective way to ship your products so that you can pass those savings on to your customers.

Table Rate

This option gives a lot more control over how you make your charges, through the use of a shipping table. There are two module-specific options here, which you will need to get used to in order to effectively utilize this form of payment.

Shipping Table: This option determines the total shipping cost based on the total cost or weight of items. You can set the charges using a colon- and comma-delimited list as shown here:

25:8.50,50:5.50,100:3.50,500:1.50

This will cause osCommerce to add a charge of $8.50 for the first 25 units of product (units precede the colon, which is followed by the price), from there to 50 units, we charge $5.50, from 50 to 100 units we charge $3.50, and from 100 to 500 we charge only $1.50.

Table Method: This allows you to select whether or not osCommerce should base its calculations on the weight of the products or the total cost.

That's all well and good so far; we have now looked at several shipping methods that we can offer to customers. However, to reiterate the idea that you need to carefully control where each module is enabled, the following screenshot highlights a couple of points:

In this figure, there are two options offered to the customer. Now, it is clear that the customer is going for the cheaper option, which is based on the table rate with the Table Method of the Table Rates option, set to Price, defined such that any purchase over $50 gets delivered free. The Per Item option simply adds $2.50 to the delivery price for every item purchased, so it increases while the other decreases.

The unfortunate thing about both these Shipping Methods is that the Shipping Address is in Africa, and will likely cost Contechst Books a lot more to ship than either quote, assuming Conechst is based in the States. We will look at how this is resolved in the *Contechst Book's Shipping Solution* section later in this chapter.

> Remember that you can enable free shipping for purchases over a certain value by defining this value in the Shipping section of the Order Total Module page (found below Shipping in the Modules category).

It is recommended that you play around with the settings in the Order Total Modules section in order to get a good idea of what functionality it provides. Since it is fairly straightforward, we won't cover it all here, and it is left to you as an exercise to familiarize yourself with the various options.

UPS and USPS

As with the PayPal and credit card modules, you will need to obtain an account with these two service providers before you can go ahead and offer this shipping option—or at least make contact with the provider of the service to confirm orders. Let's begin with UPS…

The big advantage of using UPS is that they are extremely convenient for you, as the business owner, and the customer alike. They, like other large shipping businesses, pride themselves on their reliability and are certainly justified in doing so. If you enable this module, then using the shipping address you entered in the Configuration section, the payment module contacts the UPS server to obtain a quote for the price of the delivery, and will present all the different relevant options available for the customer to choose from.

Using a service like this takes the responsibility out of your hands because it becomes the responsibility of the shipper to live up to their promises. For example, suppose you were based in the States and a purchase was made on your store from somewhere else in the world. Instead of having to work with a combination of complicated shipping rates, UPS would simply give you their worldwide quote, like so:

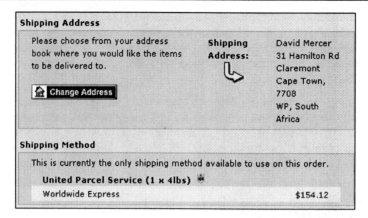

Now, when the customer recoils in horror at the price of delivery, they may decide to provide a shipping address in the US where they can pick up the product during their upcoming visit (for sake of argument). In this case, UPS will use its table rates to calculate the cost and present its different options, like this:

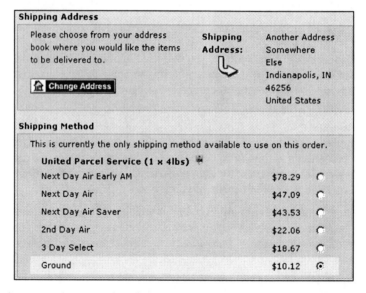

This is obviously extremely convenient for everyone concerned because the only thing left for you to do (assuming the customer decides to use UPS) is get in touch with them to confirm this shipping—ideally, you would get an account with UPS so that you can automate pick up along with a host of other advantages.

Before we leave UPS, you should also take a quick look over the editable options for this module to decide on the method of pick up, whether you want to package products yourself or leave it to UPS to provide material, or whether you are delivering to a residential or commercial address. Of course, UPS itself can help you make these decisions by registering with them or looking up their site, http://www.ups.com.

So, what's the disadvantage? Well, let's face it; you could probably get products to your customers a little cheaper... enough said!

USPS does things slightly differently in that you need to register with them before you can use their servers to automate the shipping process. You can visit them at http://www.uspspprioritymail.com/et_regcert.html in order to find out more about this service. Below is an excerpt from the registration confirmation email, which explains how the service is used:

Your Web Tools User ID and Password to integrate USPS Web Tools are provided above. The User ID and Password are used for testing your implementation of the Web Tools. With these, you may begin sending calls to the test server. The address to the test server is: testing.shippingapis.com and the path is /ShippingAPITest.dll. Use this information in combination with your User ID, Password and your XML string to send a request to the USPS servers. For more details, refer to the programming guides (located at www.usps.com/webtools) for the specific API you are integrating.

A sample test request would look like: "http://testing.shippingapis.com/ShippingAPITest.dll? API=[API_Name]&XML=[XML_String_containing_User_ID_and_Password]"

When you have completed your testing, email the USPS Internet Customer Care Center (ICCC). They will switch your profile to allow you access to the production server and will provide you with the production URL.

Of course, this serves to outline how the service works, but this complexity is hidden from us because osCommerce takes care of all this for us. For example, you can confirm that osCommerce is querying the correct server by inspecting the `usps.php` file in the `includes/modules/shipping` folder:

```
switch (MODULE_SHIPPING_USPS_SERVER) {
    case 'production': $usps_server = 'production.shippingapis.com';
                       $api_dll = 'shippingapi.dll';
                       break;
    case 'test':
    default:           $usps_server = 'testing.shippingapis.com';
                       $api_dll = 'ShippingAPITest.dll';
                       break;
}
```

From this you can see that the correct server and DLL are targeted by osCommerce. Getting everything working is simply a case of inserting your username and password into the module in the admin tool as well as making a few other standard decisions, which are common to all shipping modules.

Zone Rates

This module is quite interesting in that you can select the price of shipping in a specific zone and for specified package weights. The problem is that this is limited to only one zone at the moment, and so is not effective for anything outside that zone. The following screenshot shows the results of using this module when a customer based outside the US makes a purchase:

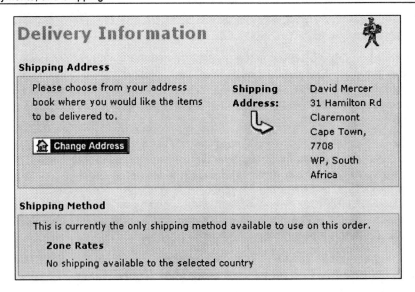

Hmm, none of these options are really ideal by themselves, so what is the solution? The smart money is on a combination of the different modules using zones to enable or disable them. Of course, this won't quite get us to where we want to be in the case of the demo site, because this is a truly global English language technical bookstore.

Contechst Book's Shipping Solution

The majority of Contechst Books' sales come from the United States, so we would like to offer an excellent shipping service, with a variety of options to cater for customers who might be willing to pay the extra amount to have their books delivered ASAP. Accordingly, we will use the UPS module to cater to the national market. However, not everyone in the US might want to pay the slightly higher prices of UPS and may be happy for the package to make its way a little slower but proportionally cheaper. So we need another option to cater for these people—it's easy enough to enable the Table Rate payment module for only the US, so that is what we'll do.

While most of the sales come from the States, areas like Europe, Africa, India, and Australia are also appreciable markets that need to be catered for in our shipping plan. Accordingly, the second shipping method we will make available is the Zone Rates shipping module. But we are still limited to specifying only one zone, which is not sufficient if we want to deliver all over the world, so we need to make a slight modification to the code in order to get the module to allow as many zones as we need.

In the `public_html/catalog/includes/modules/shipping/zones.php` file, you can simply modify the line that reads:

```
$this->num_zones = 1;
```

to something like this (depending on how many zones you need):

```
$this->num_zones = 4;
```

Now, of course, comes the slightly tricky bit. In order for the new settings to take effect properly, you need to reinstall the module. If you reinstall the module, you will lose all your current settings, so remember to make backups of whatever info you need before doing this. Now, when you access the module again, you get something like the following:

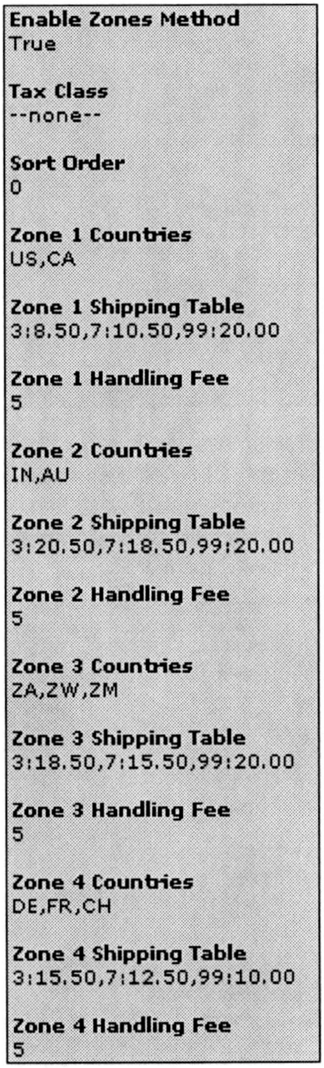

```
Enable Zones Method
True

Tax Class
--none--

Sort Order
0

Zone 1 Countries
US,CA

Zone 1 Shipping Table
3:8.50,7:10.50,99:20.00

Zone 1 Handling Fee
5

Zone 2 Countries
IN,AU

Zone 2 Shipping Table
3:20.50,7:18.50,99:20.00

Zone 2 Handling Fee
5

Zone 3 Countries
ZA,ZW,ZM

Zone 3 Shipping Table
3:18.50,7:15.50,99:20.00

Zone 3 Handling Fee
5

Zone 4 Countries
DE,FR,CH

Zone 4 Shipping Table
3:15.50,7:12.50,99:10.00

Zone 4 Handling Fee
5
```

OK, so the rates aren't too important for us since this is just a demo, but we have a pretty authoritative shipping policy in place, which you can observe by viewing the options presented to customers coming from different areas around the world. So, as we expect (and require), a customer purchasing from Africa has two options available to them—UPS and Zone Rate, which offer different pricing based on how fast they are going to arrive:

Notice that these customers aren't offered table rates, which apply only to the states, and that they aren't offered UPS' specialized quotes for US-based customers, which is just fine. Don't worry about the actual numbers involved for now; you will need to work out what is appropriate for you on the basis of your business model and specific costs. To round this off, the following screenshot shows the options available to a US-based customer:

Shipping Address

Please choose from your address book where you would like the items to be delivered to.	**Shipping Address:**	Another Address Somewhere Else Indianapolis, IN 46256 United States

Change Address

Shipping Method

Please select the preferred shipping method to use on this order.	**Please Select**	

Table Rate

Best Way	$8.50	⦿

United Parcel Service (1 x 4lbs)

Next Day Air Early AM	$78.29	○
Next Day Air	$47.09	○
Next Day Air Saver	$43.53	○
2nd Day Air	$22.06	○
3 Day Select	$18.67	○
Ground	$10.12	○

Zone Rates

Shipping to US : 4 lb(s)	$8.50	○

Now you can see why a combination of shipping options is the best solution, because just as we desired, US customers can choose to use UPS, but now they are also offered the table rate, which is slightly cheaper because we are sending it to them directly ourselves.

Notice that there is a Zone Rates option given here, which is the same price as the Table Rates. These values would diverge if, for example, the zone changed, or the weight of the products changed, but this is not really a concern because the Zone Rates module is used mainly for pricing overseas shipping. If you feel it would be wiser not to offer all three options for US customers, then you could simply enable the Zone Rates module for only those overseas areas that you ship to. This would then provide UPS or Table Rates only to US customers.

Summary

Having a comprehensive payment and shipment policy goes a long way to running a successful online business. After completing this chapter, you should now know exactly what you need to do in order to implement your own store's payment and shipping functionality. Hopefully, you will have decided to take as little risk as possible by handing over your customer's credit information to secure and trusted providers. I should reiterate the fact that you should only use trusted payment service providers—there are a lot of fraudsters out there.

So, by this stage you should have all your payment facilities up and running, with all the requisite accounts working as they should. Further, your calculations of the price of goods should include shipping options with the correct values for your target customers. But the job is not done yet. Recall that we are communicating with PayPal's IPN server without the use of encryption. Even worse, we have not secured any part of the site yet—it is wholly possible that a hacker could gain control of your entire site without too much trouble.

Remember to comprehensively test every conceivable permutation of payments, incorrect payments, shipping details, incorrect addresses, and so on before you consider your payments and shipping to be robust enough to take to the live site. Admittedly, while working on a development machine, your testing may be limited in some respects, but as soon as we have discussed security in the following chapter, you will be able to port your store over to the web host if you are in a hurry to get it up. Otherwise, simply wait till the chapter on *Deployment and Maintenance* to run through this process.

8

Securing Your Store

The term *security* has such wide-reaching implications that it is often quite hard to define in one single sentence. There are a host of different types of security, all of which aim to either validate, protect, or authenticate actions taken on or over your server and ensure that your server remains in a working state. Sorting through the wide variety of security methods and options can take some time and consideration. It is, without doubt, best done with a preconceived plan that has taken into account all the different areas of vulnerability of the application to be secured.

One of the big advantages you will have derived from working on your store yourself is that you now have a fairly good idea of how the site works. Knowing how something works is a major step towards being able to secure it properly, because you intuitively have an idea for where vulnerabilities exist. This by itself is only a part of the security strategy, which should also encompass an appreciation for the value of the information that is being hidden, as well as a firm understanding of the security technologies that you are going to put in place.

Unfortunately, most people balk at the prospect of securing their applications because it can be quite time consuming and, above all, complex compared with the rest of the application. While this certainly can be true, it is not necessarily so. In fact, this chapter aims to provide you with all the information you need to make your retail store as secure as possible without bending over backwards to make it impenetrable.

"Why not make it totally secure?" many of you may ask. Well, the answer is that *total security* does not really exist in the real world. No matter how secure you make your site, if it is accessible on the Web, then it is not a hundred percent secure. The trick is to make something more expensive to break into than the value of the information being hidden. The second you remove the financial viability of breaking into something, it is no longer a worthwhile target. Another reason we don't attempt to make the site fully secure is that implementing security always has performance costs—most customers will not wait 15 seconds for each page to load even if it is in the interests of security.

Relative to you as a potential store owner, security should mean that:

- Your customers can shop safe in the knowledge that their financial details won't be aired to anyone other than the intended parties.
- Some form of encryption is implemented to ensure that information passing to and from your server is not decipherable if it is intercepted.

- Access to parts of your site that are not open to the public is protected by passwords or is not available online.

- A concerted effort is made to close any potential security holes and ensure that data integrity is preserved.

If you have seen to it that the above points are dealt with, then not only will you benefit from peace of mind, but you will also find that you instill confidence in your customers when they notice elements of a well-secured site during their shopping.

Of course, this doesn't make your site invulnerable to attack, so while this chapter will do its best to make things as secure as possible it is by no means a guarantee of any sort. Consequently, you will always need to keep an eye out for any potential threats as time goes by and act on suspected breaches quickly and decisively.

One last point to make note of is that while much of the security you implement on your development machine is useful in terms of learning how to go about making your site secure, it is probably not going to add any benefit to you in the long run. This is because you will find that unless you are your own Internet Service Provider, you have to make use of the technologies and software made available to you by your provider.

What does this mean? Well, for one thing, you can't just install OpenSSL on your live site because you won't have permission to do so. Basically, you need to ensure that your provider has facilities in place to allow you to secure your site as you would like before you go ahead and use that provider. Most providers will do this since they appreciate that any e-commerce site will need some level of security. Treat what you learn in this chapter as the training ground for when you go live—implementing security on your development machine might also not be a bad idea if you are on a network of some sort and not on a standalone computer.

What's all This Security Business?

Hopefully, you have decided to take the advice given in the previous chapter and not deal with credit card details yourself, leaving them instead for the specialist service providers who must comply with the *Payment Card Industry (PCI) Data Security Standard.* Doing this will not only make your security requirements a lot less stringent, but will also allow you to be more flexible in terms of the way you deal with customers and third parties.

> Having said this, we still need to make use of all the basic bits and pieces of software that go into making a secure site, so even if you are storing credit card information on your site, you will still find the information you need in this chapter.

So, where do we begin when we think about how to secure a site? Well, an analysis of all the potential vulnerabilities is a good beginning. You will also find that when it comes to security, it is all but impossible to predict all the security holes at once—don't feel too despondent about this though, because pretty much any piece of commercial software in the world possesses weaknesses. This includes the very operating systems and technologies that everyone uses.

A quick point in case is the HTTP Response Splitting security hole discovered in osCommerce a little while ago (hopefully by the time you read this, there will be a patch, or a newer version that will fill this gap). This hole allows malicious code into the HTTP variables required by osCommerce for user responses. Having a vulnerability like this as part of osCommerce's make up is really beyond your immediate control, and this type of thing won't concern us for the moment.

By the same token, knowing that there is at least one security hole is also no reason to up and move to a different technology—there will be holes in those technologies too. Have faith that the development team at osCommerce will work diligently to provide you with the most secure platform possible. Remember too that having a security hole doesn't automatically mean that your entire site is vulnerable—the hole might allow someone with too much time on their hands to be a nuisance, without actually being too harmful.

From our point of view, we will make the assumption that osCommerce itself is secure. This means that we will assume that the source files contain no malicious code that could open up backdoors or secretly disseminate information. If anything, the threat of this type is more likely to come from software that is not open source and therefore not open to scrutiny by the programming public.

Taking this assumption into account, we should look at the website as a whole (recall we saw a similar diagram in Chapter 3 while discussing Internet architecture) to look at how it works, how information is passed around, where information goes, what it does, and finally how and where it is stored. The easiest way to do this is with a diagram that highlights these main points, like so:

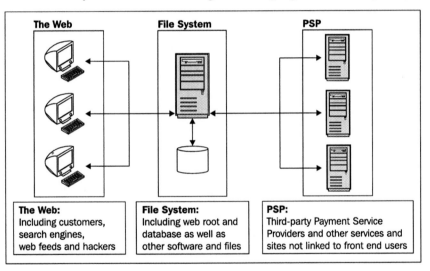

From the above diagram you can see that osCommerce itself is housed within the file system on your host site. This site itself can contain directories and folders, programs and software—pretty much anything you can imagine. However, the only things that are actually accessible directly through a browser are the files within the web root folder. Everything else can be accessed (subject to restrictions) indirectly through the code within the web root folder, including other software like your database(s). One other point to mention is that you might also have an FTP server, which again will be available for access over the FTP protocol—more about this when we come to deployment later on.

The arrows in the previous diagram represent lines of communication between your server, the database, the Web, and third parties such as PayPal, RSS feed sites, web service providers, and so on. Any line of communication that can be set up is a potential threat, and the type of information that is allowed should be closely scrutinized and planned ahead in order to prevent all sorts of rubbish from fouling up your system.

It is critical that you understand the difference between securing a line of communication and restricting the type of information that can pass down that line. For example, it is no good ensuring that communications between you and a customer is totally secure and encrypted when you are going to allow the users themselves to send malicious instructions to your server through the secure channel. A big example of this is generally not ensuring that user input is stripped of SQL commands.

To clarify what I mean by this, let's assume that you have a textbox on your site that allows users to enter their names. This is of course a reasonable assumption because all osCommerce sites have this by default. Now, let's say you encrypt your communications and use a secure server so that no one can eavesdrop on this information being passed between the user and yourself. Now, say your SQL statement goes something like this:

```
insert into customers (customer_name) values ('$HTTP_POST_VARS[name]');
```

This is simple enough to understand: you receive a value from your PHP page, which is held in the superglobal array variable `$HTTP_POST_VARS`, and you stick it into the `customers` table under the column `customer_name`. If the customer enters John into the textbox and clicks on send, then the actual statement can be read by replacing the variable name with its value, like so:

```
insert into customers (customer_name) values ('John');
```

That's absolutely fine! There is nothing wrong with that statement, and the customer's name will dutifully be inserted into your database. The problem comes when someone decides that they would like to destroy your database, and instead of inserting their name they insert the following value into the name textbox on your site:

```
John'); drop database osCommerce; #
```

Your SQL statement now reads:

```
insert into customers (customer_name) values ('John'); drop database osCommerce; #
...
```

Oh dear, the user has finished off your SQL statement for you (by adding a single quote, closing the brace and adding a semi-colon to finish the first SQL statement) and inserted one that has wiped out everything in your database—all your hard work is now gone and you have to re-enter everything.

Why not go try this out on your osCommerce installation and see what happens—what do you think will happen offhand? If you try this you will notice that the string gets stored into the database as a whole, despite adding single quotes—funnily enough, osCommerce was susceptible to this type of attack (called an SQL injection attack) in previous versions. I tried a variety of different methods of breaking the code like this, all without success!

Now, this example is not the whole story; it is merely here to give you a better idea as to the type of thought you need to put into securing your application. It is astounding what chinks in an application's armor can show up when it is accessible from the Web. The reason it is important to show you an example like this is that at some stage during your site's lifetime, you will more than likely want to add extra functionality yourself. If you do, make sure you re-read this chapter first!

Now, back to our assumption that osCommerce provides a secure platform for us to use. If that is the case, then we need not concern ourselves with actively checking the code for problems like these because this is being done on a daily basis by hackers all over the world (this is why open-source products are often very secure). We need to ensure the following things:

- Any sensitive information passing between a browser and the server is secure.
- Any sensitive information passing between the server and third parties is secure.
- Files on the server's files system are properly protected.
- Files that are not intended for public use are not present in the document root.
- Important files and information are regularly backed up.

While this list seems quite short, each point covers a fair amount of ground because the term secure itself can mean a number of things. However, we have to draw the line somewhere in terms of the scope of this chapter; otherwise it could turn into several volumes worth of material. Instead, we will focus purely on the above points without being distracted by bits and bobs that you can easily research yourself.

Before we begin working towards a secure environment, let's meet a few of the common technologies and software utilities that you will use.

The Main Players

As discussed, there are quite a few different methods for controlling a web application's security. No matter how you decide to go about it, though, there are certain elements that *will* probably make an appearance. This is mainly because certain ways of doing things are better than others, and as such, these have evolved into industry standards more or less. This section aims to give you a brief outline of everything you will be using and how it works, before we begin with the actual task of implementing a well-secured site.

SSL

Without getting bogged down in too much detail, the basic outline of how SSL works can be summed up as follows:

In order for SSL to work, the server sends a **public key** and its **certificate** over to the browser, which performs some validation of the certificate before using the server's public key to encrypt its own key. Now, the server is the *only* machine that can decrypt this message, which contains a key from the browser. The server can then use the browser's key to encrypt its information, which is now only accessible to the browser. In this way, the information that is then sent between the server and the browser is encrypted both ways.

> While SSL safeguards information between two parties, it doesn't identify the user who is requesting information in any way. For that you still need a username and password.

Now, don't worry too much about understanding this process in much depth, for the moment—it is all handled automatically anyway. Later on you may have to create certificates and keys of your own so that your server can use SSL to implement secure connections. Even then, you will be shielded from the real dirty work by osCommerce, which can deal with keys for you.

Passwords

Of course, at some stage osCommerce will want to know who it is dealing with, whether it is the site administrator or a customer. For this type of authentication, we revert to the time-honored username and password method. Of course, this can be also used to control access to certain folders as well as simply allow an administrator or customer to log on. This can be done using .htaccess files, which we will discuss in more detail a little later in the chapter.

One of the most important things to remember about passwords is that they are only as secure as the method you use to transmit them. If you are going to send your password as **clear text** (clear text is human-readable format and has no encryption) over a non-secure connection, then you can bet that anyone who is interested in obtaining your password will be able to do so without too much trouble.

Encryption

We saw in the last chapter that, unless we implement some form of encryption between our server and the PayPal server, there is a slight chance that our information can be intercepted. Accordingly we need to ensure that we are encrypting our communications behind the scenes.

There are plenty of different types of encryption, and some have managed to retain a pretty good record in safeguarding their data. Encryption for us as osCommerce users is greatly simplified because we don't really need to concern ourselves with the type of algorithm that we will use to perform the encryption, or anything else for that matter. The main thing to remember is that encryption doesn't prevent our information being intercepted by someone else—like a locked box, it prevents the interceptor from discovering the contents of the messages we are sending.

Securing the Administration Tool

Without a doubt, one of the major potential security threats comes from using the administration tool over the Internet. Should someone gain access to this tool on your live site, they could cause untold mischief, and much wailing and gnashing of teeth will ensue. As a result, we are going to enforce the use of a username and password in order to gain access to the admin folder, as well as ensure that the admin folder is only available over the secure server HTTPS (which uses SSL to encrypt communications).

You might also wish to change the name of the admin folder to something random, which will add a small amount of security in that it may not be immediately obvious to a potential hacker where this web-based tool is housed. If you do so you will need to edit config.php to reflect these changes as none of your file paths should contain the word admin anymore.

Before we do go ahead and secure the admin tool, it is worth considering that forcing communications over HTTPS will slow down whatever interaction we have with the server. Once again, it's a trade-off; if you don't think it is necessary to use SSL for communication with your server, then perhaps simply implement password security—but be warned that it is possible to intercept passwords that aren't transmitted in encrypted form, or over SSL.

Creating Password-Protected Folders

In order to enforce the use of a password on a certain folder, you will need to make use of the .htaccess file. This is either present by default or, if it is not, you will need to create a blank text file called .htaccess (with no other extensions) and place it in the admin folder. Now, there are a few things you need to note with regards to the use of .htaccess:

- .htaccess is for use by Apache, not PHP or IIS or anything else.
- .htaccess will influence the security of all subfolders below the folder it is present in, unless there is another .htaccess file in the subfolder. In this way you can secure an entire directory in one go, or give each subdirectory its own fine-grained security.
- You need to make sure that you can either use this method of securing files, or can make use of the native security system provided by your host.
- .htaccess commands are one line only. Make sure you use a new line for each separate command.
- Please make sure you set permissions on the .htaccess files correctly. If you make it readable by everyone, then your security is compromised. Set it to 644 so that the server can read it, but it is not readable by a browser (More on file permissions a little later in this chapter).
- Setting this up on your *development machine* is recommended for practice, but be advised that it may cause problems with your host's security system (if your host implements security differently) once you have deployed the site.

Now, this really assumes that you will not have access to the Apache configuration file on your host's server, which is more than likely the case. Generally, you should only use .htaccess when you don't have access to the main configuration file (since this is where security should be implemented from) because using .htaccess slows down your site. That said, .htaccess should still give us enough security for our needs without being too much of a drag on performance, so let's continue.

The first thing you need to do is create a password file. Apache comes with the htpasswd utility to create this for us—since we are only going to need to control access to one folder and we only want ourselves to be the administrator, we aren't going to mess around with groups; we are simply going to make *one* user with access to this folder. htpasswd is in the bin folder of your Apache distribution, so you need to make sure your command line can access it. To create a new password file, do the following:

```
C:\Program Files\Apache Group\Apache2\bin>htpasswd -c C:\<path>\password davidm
Automatically using MD5 format.
New password: ********
Re-type new password: ********
Adding password for user davidm
```

The htpasswd utility doesn't like spaces in the directory path, so you might have to surround the file path with quotes. The password file that is created by the above command contains the username (davidm) and an encrypted password as follows:

```
davidm:$apr1$uG1.....$j9vMis9FCwtDgDuzs.VXfO
```

You should leave this file out of your document root so that browsers cannot access it at all. Alternatively, you can simply create your own password file using the following format if you don't have access to the htpasswd utility:

```
username1:password1
username2:password2
...
```

Once this file is set up, you can refer to it in your .htaccess file as follows:

```
AuthType Basic
AuthName "Password Required"
AuthUserFile 'C:\Program Files\Apache Group\Apache2\passwords\password'
Require user davidm
```

This tells Apache that the authentication type we are using is Basic, that the message to be displayed when requesting the username and password is Password Required, that the file to use to check the supplied credentials against is C:\Program Files\Apache Group\Apache2\passwords\password, and that the user we want is davidm.

One last thing to do before this will work is to change the httpd.conf file in Apache to ensure that it checks the .htaccess files, like so:

```
# AllowOverride controls what directives may be placed in .htaccess files.
# It can be "All", "None", or any combination of the keywords:
#   Options FileInfo AuthConfig Limit
#
    AllowOverride AuthConfig
```

You will then need to restart the server so that this setting can take effect. If everything checks out, then each time you access the admin folder you get prompted for a username and password, like so:

This is great! We now have a layer of security added to the site to protect the admin folder from a casual hack or two. There are quite a larger number of things you can do with Apache with regards to security, and you should take a look at http://httpd.apache.org/docs/howto/auth.html for more information concerning this.

While this works nicely for the development server, the demo site's host doesn't allow for this type of password protection—instead the host has a native system that can be used to perform the same task. However, instead of performing any manual settings, the host provides a user interface that can be used to ensure that folders are password protected. So, from the main administrator panel, the option to **Password Protect Directories** was selected, and from there it was simply a case of navigating to the folder to be protected before inputting the relevant information as shown here:

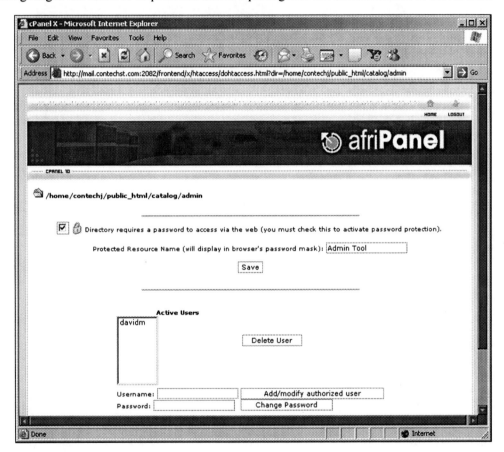

As you might have guessed, this is simply an interface (sometimes called a wrapper) for setting the .htaccess settings in a user-friendly format. As expected, the admin tool on the live site is now password protected. Of course, we don't want these passwords submitted over the Internet without using a secure connection, so now we need to ensure that the admin folder is only available over SSL.

Implementing SSL for the admin Folder

Now, this bit can be quite tricky. If you would like to implement a secure server on your development machine, then you will need to download and install OpenSSL, which you can get at `http://www.openssl.org/`. There are instructions and tutorials available that outline the installation and use of OpenSSL, but we will not go into detail about that here because it is more than likely that the process of securing your live site (which is the important bit) will be done differently.

So, the first step is to find out what SSL facilities are available to you on your live site and how you as the host's client can make use of them. Once you have established that, it should generally be a simple case of implementing that functionality—your service provider will often make this as easy as possible for you, and nine times out of ten it is simply a case of handing over the cash and having SSL enabled for your domain. Be advised that you will more than likely have to pay extra for this facility (and sometimes for extra certificates and so on) but given what you stand to lose if you don't make use of it, the expense is more than justified.

The host for Contechst Books simply enabled SSL, and all that was required was a couple of modifications to the `.htaccess` file in the `admin` folder and to the `configure.php` file in the `admin/includes/` folder. More than likely this is all you will need to do as well, but it is possible that you need to move the admin tool to a secure folder—if this is the case, ensure that you make the necessary modifications to the file paths in the `configure.php` script. Assuming you need not do this, open up `.htaccess` in the `admin` folder and add the following line at the top, like so:

```
SSLRequireSSL

AuthType Basic
AuthName "Admin Tool"
AuthUserFile "path to your password file"
require valid-user
```

This forces the use of a secure server in order to access the folder and its contents. If you now try access the non-secure version, in this case, `http:www.contechst.com/catalog/admin`, you will get a message like the following:

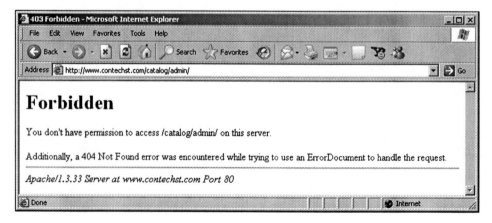

This, of course, is very good news because we haven't even been prompted for a username and password. Now, it is possible to add a few lines to .htaccess to redirect the browser to a page instead of simply showing this message, but since we are only securing the admin tool, and since we are only doing it for ourselves because we are the only ones who will access it, this is fine as it is.

Before we check whether the secure site works as planned, edit the configure.php script in the admin/includes folder like so (obviously, substitute in the values that reflect your site's specifics):

```
define('HTTP_SERVER', 'https://www.contechst.com');
```

This means that instead of trying to access the non-secure URLs when the administrator clicks on a link, the secure site is requested instead. If this setting wasn't changed, then only the admin/index.php file would be accessed through https; everything after that would revert back to the normal server. Having done this, navigate to the secure version of your admin tool, supply your username and password, and then fool around with the links to ensure everything is done through SSL:

It's easy enough to ensure everything is working as planned! Simply check the URL of your page to verify it is being served by the secure server. If you really need proof, then copy one of the page's URLs into a new browser and attempt to access the page—you should notice that you are once again prompted for a password, regardless of the file you are trying to access. You may even want to make a couple of changes to check that uploading and downloading of information works.

It is quite likely that you have noticed a slight delay in the time it takes to serve pages now that we are using SSL and .htaccess. This is quite normal, and is the overhead you pay for adding security, because the server needs to do more work with each page it serves. However, since the vast majority of all the development work should be carried out on the *development machine*, it is an acceptable sacrifice in performance, because we should really have to spend hours and hours making tedious changes to the *live server* through SSL.

That's it! A major potential security hole has now been covered, and provided you use a sensible password (which uses both letters and numbers), you should be reasonably safe from intrusion with respect to the admin tool. There is still a fair way to go before we can breathe a sigh of relief that our store in general is safe—the next task is to use encryption to secure communications between the store's server and third parties, like PayPal.

Securing Payments

A close second in terms of importance is the ability to secure your payments. Why do I say a close second, instead of *the* highest importance? The answer is simply this: if you wanted to ensure your payments don't get hacked online, then you could always ask for bank transfers or some other offline form of payment, whereas there is no way you can maintain your site effectively without the use of some form of online admin tool.

The fundamental goal with respect to securing payments is to make the transmission of sensitive data (which occurs during the checkout stages of a purchase), as well as payment tracking after checkout using IPNs, undecipherable in the event that the transmission is intercepted. Luckily for us, this is the easiest thing in the world to do for the front end of the site, so let's take a look at that first.

The Front End of the Store

Simply open up the `configure.php` file in the `catalog/includes/` folder and make the following SSL-related modifications (read: whatever is appropriate for your domain), if they have not already been set. (Please note that the comments accompanying `HTTP_SERVER` and `HTTPS_SERVER` have been moved to the next line for better readability):

```
// Define the webserver and path parameters
// * DIR_FS_* = Filesystem directories (local/physical)
// * DIR_WS_* = Webserver directories (virtual/URL)
  define('HTTP_SERVER', 'http://www.contechst.com');
// eg, http://localhost - should not be empty for productive servers
  define('HTTPS_SERVER', 'https://www.contechst.com');
// eg, https://localhost - should not be empty for productive servers
  define('ENABLE_SSL', 'true'); // secure webserver for checkout procedure?
  define('HTTP_COOKIE_DOMAIN', 'localhost');
  define('HTTPS_COOKIE_DOMAIN', 'localhost');
  define('HTTP_COOKIE_PATH', '/catalog/');
  define('HTTPS_COOKIE_PATH', '/catalog/');
  define('DIR_WS_HTTP_CATALOG', '/catalog/');
  define('DIR_WS_HTTPS_CATALOG', '/catalog/');
```

Obviously, if you are working on your development server, then the domain will be `https://localhost/`, or, if you have to move your directories and files to be secured to a new folder, then you will have to ensure that you set the correct paths depending on how everything is configured. More often than not, what is shown above will suffice.

Of course, you need to make sure that these changes have taken effect as expected, so navigate to your store—take note of the URL:

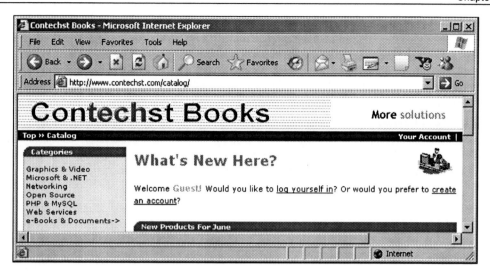

Now try to log in using your customer account. Notice that immediately you are taken to the secure server in order to input your information—this means that customer usernames and logins are as secure as the customer decides to make them. In other words, they hopefully won't simply leave them lying around where someone can find them and use them:

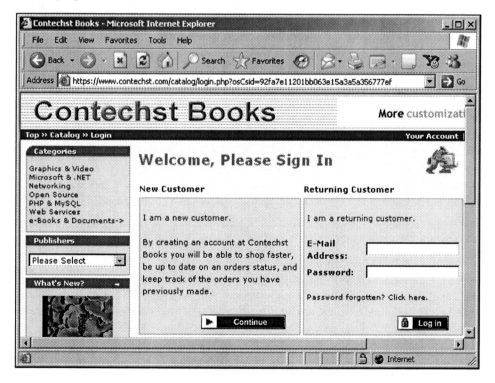

This is really great news for us because pretty much most of the work is done! If you are a new customer, then your registration (as well as your login, if you are a returning customer) takes place over SSL. Now, just because the login has taken place over SSL, doesn't mean the rest of the shopping needs to be done securely—in fact, we don't want it to be secure because it will slow down the site. The next time SSL comes into play is when the customer tries to make a purchase, or to view his or her account information.

What a pleasure! Everything is handled for us automatically by simply making a few settings in the `configure.php` file on an SSL-enabled site. Now, when a customer decides to checkout, the HTTPS server is automatically used to ensure that communication between the browser and the store's server is secure. This is exactly what we required in our stated goals, and that's all that is needed on this side of things.

On the other side of the equation (recall the first figure showing the lines of communication between the store and third-party servers), not quite everything has been done. We'll now take a look at each of the payment methods discussed in the last chapter and ensure that they are all as secure as the front end of the site.

The Back End of the Store

Knowing that a chain is only as strong as its weakest link, it should come as no surprise that we now have to look at the payment process behind the scenes in order to make absolutely certain that there is no chink in the armor, so to speak. This is where some knowledge of how your payment code is actually working comes in handy because knowing how something works will lend you some clues as to how to ensure it is secure. Let's begin with the PayPal module…

PayPal Payments

Having already installed the IPN PayPal module in the previous chapter, it is now time to look at how it goes about ensuring that communications between your store and the PayPal server are secure. A point to bear in mind is the following:

> If you have SSL enabled on your site, then you need not worry about encrypting IPN information, because osCommerce will ensure that your secure server is targeted by PayPal!

You can check up on this by looking at the line in your `catalog/includes/modules/payment/paypal_ipn.php` file, which reads something like:

```
$parameters['notify_url'] = tep_href_link('ipn.php', '', 'SSL', false, false);
```

This tells osCommerce to use SSL if it is enabled on your site, and assuming you have everything working correctly, it will dutifully use the secure server if it is available. If you still want to encrypt IPN communications, then there's quite a bit to do in order to ensure that PayPal and your server link up correctly, so the easiest thing to do is make a numbered list of tasks to follow, like so:

1.   Make sure you have OpenSSL enabled on your website. If not, then you cannot use this module to encrypt your payment data using OpenSSL. We will discuss this situation at the end of this section.

2. Ensure your server has cURL installed. If not, your communications will not be sent using this method of transport and may even be sent as unencrypted information over a non-secure line.

3. Ensure your site has certificate and key generation tools. If not, ensure that you can obtain a private key and a public certificate.

4. Ensure that these keys and certificates are held outside the document root—otherwise you are asking for trouble.

5. Go to your PayPal account page and navigate to Encrypted Payment Settings under the Profile tab. If you don't have this option it may be because you are not yet Verified.

6. Download and save the PayPal Public Certificate to your `certificates` folder (or whatever it is called on your site) on your site's file system.

7. Add your public certificate to the PayPal site and obtain your unique ID.

Once this has all been done, you can now go to the administration tool and finish the settings on the PayPal IPN payment module. The table following shows you the settings used on the Contechst Books site, including a description of what each option does:

Property	Setting
Enable Encrypted Web Payments	Set this to True if you want data that is passed between your server and PayPal to be encrypted. Set this to False if you do not have access to OpenSSL on your site.
Your Private Key	Your path will be something like the following: `/home/contechstbooks/ssl/private/www.contechst.com.pem`. Ensure that this key is not held in the document root and is in .pem format.
Your Public Certificate	Your path will be something like the following: `/home/contechstbooks/ssl/certs/www.contechst.com.pem`. Ensure that this certificate is not held in the document root and is in .pem format.
PayPals Public Certificate	Save PayPal's certificate in your certificates folder like so: `/home/contechstbooks/ssl/certs/live_api.crt`
Your PayPal Public Certificate ID	Obtain this from the PayPal site once you have uploaded your certificate successfully.
Working Directory	The PayPal IPN module needs access to a temporary directory in order to work with files. Set this to be outside the document root: `/home/contechstbooks/tmp`
OpenSSL Location	The location of the OpenSSL binary file that can be used to sign and encrypt your information.

Naturally, you will need to test your site to ensure all this works correctly. However, if you do not have access to OpenSSL, then you will not be able to make use of the encrypted payment notifications using this module. This is not cause for major concern provided you have the ability to use SSL. The reason for this is that the module has three different methods of operation as follows:

1. Use the `openssl_pkcs7_sign` and `openssl_pkcs7_encrypt` PHP functions to sign and encrypt information sent to the PayPal server.

2. Use the OpenSSL tool directly from an `exec` command to perform the same signing and encryption tasks as the previously mentioned PHP functions.

3. Send the information in unencrypted format.

Now, if you have Encrypted Web Payments enabled on your payment module's settings, then it will attempt to perform option 1, followed by option 2. If it is not possible to use OpenSSL and you have enabled this setting, it will kick up an error. If you disable this setting, then option 3 is performed.

It may seem on the surface of things that option 3 is not very secure, but recall that it can be just as secure as the first two options provided you are ensure PayPal is targeting a file on your secure server (HTTPS) for its IPN. If you have SSL enabled on your site, which you should have, then this file is only targeted over SSL (In other words, `https://www.contechst.com/ext/modules/payment/paypal_ipn/ipn.php` or `https://www.contechst.com/catalog/ipn.php`, depending on which version of the contribution you are using), which means that the information coming from PayPal is sent over SSL and is therefore secure.

If you do not have access to SSL, then unfortunately you will have to do without securing the back end of the PayPal payment module. Remember that this is not a train-smash—no credit card details are transferred between sites at any stage. The next section shows how information can be encrypted quite easily before being sent off by email. This could easily be adapted to encrypt whatever type of information you wish, so if you are feeling bold, perhaps you could try implementing your own secure transactions for your payment modules.

Credit Card Payments

There were two types of credit card payment that were discussed in the previous chapter. The first option, storing credit card details on your site, is really not recommended because it turns your store into a target for credit card fraud. That said, we should still take a look at this particular method to ensure that we can, as an exercise, ensure it is relatively secure—after all, any security practice is a good thing. Following that we will look at the PsiGate payment method to see if there is anything we can do to make this more secure.

Now, the first thing to do is look at the process of accepting credit card payments. For a start we already know that the front end of the store is secure because any checkout transactions are done over SSL, which includes the credit card payment methods. This means we can be fairly confident that the customer details will get to us unmolested.

We can now choose whether or not to email the middle digits of the number to a specified email address, or to keep the whole credit card number in the database. Following that, you would use an EFTPOS merchant account terminal, for example, and process the credit card details away from your store. That being the case, there are three areas of concern; specifically, hackers might:

1. Gain access to the administration tool and be able to view credit card details
2. Gain access to the database
3. Intercept emails

Point number 1 is no longer a concern since the administration tool is password protected and runs over a secure server. This is about as secure as we need it to be. This leaves points 2 and 3, of which the first will fall under a discussion on database security, which is to follow in the next section. So that leaves us with the final point to deal with now: what can be done to secure emails sent to us by our online store?

Well, let's take a look at the code that is used to send the email within the credit card payment module:

```
function after_process() {
        global $insert_id;

        if ( (defined('MODULE_PAYMENT_CC_EMAIL')) &&
            (tep_validate_email(MODULE_PAYMENT_CC_EMAIL)) ) {
            $message = 'Order #' . $insert_id . "\n\n" . 'Middle: ' .
            $this->cc_middle . "\n\n";

            tep_mail('', MODULE_PAYMENT_CC_EMAIL, 'Extra Order Info: #' .
            $insert_id, $message, STORE_OWNER, STORE_OWNER_EMAIL_ADDRESS);
        }
    }
```

You will notice that the $message variable, which contains the middle digits, is simply sent as is with no encryption. Obviously, we would like to be able to encrypt that if at all possible. Of course, it is possible, and only takes a minute or so. For example, I have modified this function like so:

```
function after_process() {
        global $insert_id;

        if ( (defined('MODULE_PAYMENT_CC_EMAIL')) &&
            (tep_validate_email(MODULE_PAYMENT_CC_EMAIL)) ) {

            // Added mcrypt functionality to transmit the middle
            // digits of the credit card details in encrypted form.
            $message = 'Order #' . 'encrypted' . "\n\n" . 'Middle: ' .
            $this->cc_middle . "\n\n";
            $key = "Secret Key";
            $encrypted_data = base64_encode(mcrypt_encrypt(MCRYPT_3DES,
                $key, $message, MCRYPT_MODE_CBC));
            $message = $encrypted_data;

            tep_mail('', MODULE_PAYMENT_CC_EMAIL, 'Extra Order Info: #' .
                $insert_id, $message, STORE_OWNER, STORE_OWNER_EMAIL_ADDRESS);
        }
    }
```

Now when you receive an email from an order you will get it in this form:

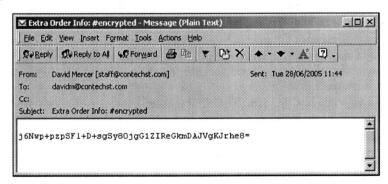

You can now decrypt this using your secret key value quite easily and match the values to the order number that is given in the Subject of the email. Note that there is no point in giving away any information if you are going to use encryption. Passing the order number as clear text gives a potential hacker a interesting piece of information, which is why we haven't done this.

It is quite possible that your host provides similar functionality, so check with your host if there is already something similar in place that you can use. If not, then you will have to install MCrypt on your machine—this can be obtained at `http://mcrypt.sourceforge.net/` for Linux users, or `http://ftp.emini.dk/pub/php/win32/mcrypt/` for Windows users. It is pretty simple to do this; simply copy the library file to somewhere in your path (for neatness' sake, it's probably best to put it in the `ext` directory of your PHP installation) and enable the MCrypt module in the `php.ini` file.

Once you have got this installed, you can make use of the PHP CLI if you are using a recent version of PHP. The script I wrote is shown here:

```php
<?
$key = "Secret Key";
fwrite(STDOUT, "Please enter the encrypted details: \n");
$data = base64_decode(fgets(STDIN));
$decrypt = mcrypt_decrypt(MCRYPT_3DES, $key, $data, MCRYPT_MODE_CBC);
echo $decrypt;
?>
```

This was saved as `decrypt.php` and held in a secure folder on the development machine. The file is used as follows from the command line:

```
C:\secure>php decrypt.php
Please enter the encrypted details:
j6Nwp+pzpSGKaijhyxMo7DgG1ZIReGkmDAJVgKJrhe8=
Order #52

Middle: 11111111
```

As you can see this has reversed the process of encryption and base64 encoding as expected, and spat out the original content of the email, which contains the all-important order number so that we can match the numbers correctly to the order. For more information on MCrypt, please see the documentation at `http://www.php.net/mcrypt`. Now you can proceed to use the details as normal. There are, however, several key things to note here:

1. The secret key used for encoding is contained within the script page. This means that this method is only as secure as the `cc.php` payment module file.

2. Base64 encoding was used to prevent the email client on your development machine from flattening the encrypted string in its raw form. This is why it is necessary to apply base64 decoding to the input string before decryption takes place.

3. MCrypt has plenty of different encryption algorithms to offer, and you are not limited to the ones used in this script. You may also get warning from not using the optional final parameter—please look at the documentation for more information on this if it is a concern.

4. The method shown here can be improved upon by pulling the secret key value from a secure area of your site's file system, and using a proper key rather than a simple password.

5. Decrypting every credit card value may become tedious if you have a large number of orders.

6. You need to ensure that your live site has a version of PHP configured to make use of MCrypt.

If you don't have access to MCrypt, look at what you *do* have. It isn't hard to redo this using GnuPG, for example. Make the most of the resources available to you, and remember to always test, test, test. In this case, you would probably want to be able to catch any errors generated by MCrypt, and store the digits in a secure place instead of emailing them if there is a problem. The administrator would have to sort out the mess manually in this case.

Apart from being able to encrypt information sent within an email, this has also demonstrated how easy it is, with a bit of thought, to implement sufficient security to deter a fair amount of malicious intent. Remember that this is not foolproof just because you now have two files that contain the key used for the decryption—this means that both the server side and the administrator's machine are now in need of some good security to prevent intrusion.

With that done, let's turn our attention to the PsiGate payment module. The PsiGate module does not provide encryption facilities when sending its information to PsiGate, but it does target the secure PsiGate server so that the form information is transferred over SSL. Remember, you can also have customers supply their details directly to the PsiGate server by enabling the Remote option in the payment module's settings. This takes the back-end security responsibilities off your hands entirely.

File-System Security

By now you should not be too surprised to hear that no matter how secure you make your site's communication between browsers and third-party servers, it is all a bit pointless if you don't secure your file system and database correctly. There is quite a lot to think about with regards to the security of both areas, and the only way you will really get to grips with it all is by ensuring you spend time practicing and learning about the different types of loopholes and backdoors that can affect your site.

In general, it is fair to say that the following lists the main points that you should be aware of when thinking about file system security:

*   Who can use the system
*   When and how much can these users use the system
*   What are users allowed to do
*   Monitoring the system
*   Responding to intrusions or attacks

Knowing the answers to the above points gives you a good platform from which you can implement better security. The best way to limit the number of people who can use your file system is to only have one user, which utilizes a good, memorized password—if you must write it down, hold it in an encrypted file offline. Then of course, you need to ensure that no one can physically steal the file, so it's best just to commit your password to memory.

What constitutes a good password? Here is a list:

- Don't use words from a dictionary (of any language).
- Never use your first or last name.
- Don't use your relatives' names, or names of famous characters.
- Don't use your login name.
- Avoid using accessible information about you, such as phone number, license plate number, and social security number.
- Don't use your birth date.
- Make sure that your password is unrelated to any previous password.
- Use a mixture of upper- and lower-case characters along with digits or punctuations.
- Use long passwords, say eight characters long.
- Change passwords regularly and don't reuse passwords.
- Choose a phrase or combination of words to make the password easier to remember.

If you must allow access to other users for whatever reason, then think about exactly what they need to be able to do on the file system in order to achieve their tasks and grant them permissions accordingly. By the same token, don't leave inactive user accounts lying around on your system—have only enough accounts, with just enough permissions set to perform the necessary tasks, and no more.

File permission settings go hand in hand with deciding who can do what, and you should again set permissions so that files can be used in the way they are intended without being susceptible to other, perhaps more nefarious, uses. For example, if you are sure you don't need to modify a file for any reason, then don't allow anyone to have write-access to this file. There are a variety of different methods for setting permissions, depending on how you use your system—the best thing to do here is clarify what the permissions mean so that you can implement this on your system yourself.

File permissions are set using a matrix that determines the final permission value as a three-digit (octal) number, as follows:

- Read permission is worth 4 points.
- Write permission is worth 2 points.
- Execute permission is worth 1 point.

In this way it is always possible to determine the permission settings from the code. The following table shows the permission setting 750, which, as you can see, allows the User to perform any of the three actions, whereas Group can only Read or Execute the file or folder, and World has no access to the file or folder at all:

Mode	User	Group	World
Read	X	X	
Write	X		
Execute	X	X	
Permission	7	5	0

There is another representation of these permissions. Navigate over to the File Manager section under the Tools option in the admin tool—you will notice that these permissions are written out like so:

File Type	User Permissions			Group Permissions			Other Permissions		
	Read	Write	Execute	Read	Write	Execute	Read	Write	Execute
d = directory	r	w	e	r	w	e	r	w	e
l = symbolic link									
s = socket									
p = named pipe									
- = regular file									
c = character (unbuffered) device file special									
b = block (buffered) device file special									

It's easy enough to draw parallels and understand the two representations, but the question now is what do User, Group, and World mean? Well, you can look at it like this: a User is the person who owns or has created the file, a Group is a set of users who share the same group identification number as the user, and World includes anyone who has a valid logon to the system but is not the owner and does not belong to the group.

Why is all this important? Well, the reason is that it is more than likely that at some stage you will need to upload a variety of files to your site, and if you are not equipped with this knowledge it is possible that you might open up some security holes by setting permissions that are too loose. For example, if you enter a new user with a password onto your system (say using .htaccess), then it is a bit silly to allow World to write to that file because it wouldn't be too difficult for someone to access the file and write to it so that they have access to the file system.

Of course, just because you have decided to be careful about who can do what doesn't mean you can sit back and relax. You should always know what facilities there are to monitor your system, and if you are really concerned about this, then there is downloadable software that will help monitor your site for intrusions. Something like Tripwire may be what you have in mind: ftp://ftp.cerias.purdue.edu/pub/tools/unix/ids/tripwire/.

As part of being generally conscientious about your file system, you should find out what facilities your ISP provides as part of your hosting package. For example, the demo site's host has the following security-related utilities:

- Password Protect Directories: .htaccess wrapper for the Apache server.
- Raw Access Logs: Allows observation of who has accessed what.
- Manage OpenPGP Keys: Facility for storing and creating public and private keys.
- HotLink Protection: Prevents freeloaders from linking to your site and using your bandwidth.

- Index Manager: Switching indexes off means that people will not be able to see what files are in a directory that lacks an index file.

- IP Deny Manager: Allows you to block a range of IP addresses to prevent them from accessing your site if you know they are causing your site problems (For example, someone attempting a denial of service attack).

- SSL Manager: Allows you to generate SSL certificates, signing requests, and keys.

Of course, every host is different, but the one thing that all good hosts have in common is that they will be there to offer you support and hopefully advise you on the best software and technologies to use. You should make use of this facility as often as possible—you are paying for the service, after all. Often you will find that you as the client do not have the permissions to make changes as you would like to your own web-based file system. In this case, ensure you get in touch with your provider to discuss how you can either gain those permissions or come to some middle ground.

Knowing all this still doesn't help if you don't *apply common sense* to the server entity as a whole. Many people will diligently secure their web server, ensuring that customers all log in over HTTPS, and that the admin tool runs over HTTPS with server communications secured on the back end. After completing all this they then administer their website's file system by logging in using their administrator password over HTTP without encrypting the password, or worse yet, leave this password lying around. All and sundry can then capture this information, log on to the file system as the administrator, and help themselves to whatever it is they want.

> Secure your administrator's log-on procedure so that it is at least as secure as the rest of your application.

One final thing to mention is that if your file system contains extraneous software then have it removed or disabled so that you don't leave backdoors open. A good example is disabling shells and interpreters that you are not making use of. Doing this will certainly put you on the path to security, but this is not the whole story yet! There are a few other topics that we will need to cover before you have been given the full rundown on file-system security. However, they will only be revealed as we go along since they all pertain to other topics that deserve their own mention. It's time now to look at securing the database…

Database Security

Before we actually do anything with the database, let's consider what it is we want from the osCommerce database in terms of security. To do this, we refer back to the list of considerations given at the beginning of the *File-System Security* section since securing a file system and a database have the same conceptual roots. Combining these considerations with an appreciation for how security is implemented on a database will allow us to come up with a pretty good security policy.

Apart from this, we also really need to know where the database is going to be. This may seem silly at first because you are used to having everything housed on your development machine, but it is possible that your database and your web server are not on the same machine or even at the same address. Separating web servers and mail servers from database servers out into different physical places is a common practice with larger companies, and you might need to ask your host what the deal is with their setup with regards to this. More than likely, though, you are safe in assuming that the web server and the database server at least have secure lines of communication, if they are not actually present on the same server.

A MySQL relational database management system houses zero or more databases, which in turn can house zero or more tables. Access to those databases is granted through defining users who have various permissions set for them. When we first installed the MySQL database on the development machine, we logged in as root, we mentioned way back then that allowing osCommerce root (or administrator) access to the database was poor form. Consequently, we created a user with diminished capabilities on the localhost.

The story on your live site will be slightly different because you will not have root access to that database at any stage. Instead, you will be allowed to create a database and define the permissions you want to set on that database, and that database *alone*. If they allowed everyone to have root access, then you would find that you would be able to modify other people's online databases and vice versa, which is clearly a major security flaw. So, you need only worry about your own database on the live site.

At this stage, it is important to emphasize that you only have a *single* active database user on your site because it is poor security practice to have several inactive user accounts lying around waiting to be picked up. This means that when osCommerce itself connects to the database, there are only so many actions it can perform. Why is this important? Well, remember the SQL injection attack that was shown earlier, where a hacker entered a command to drop the database? If you only have one user on your database, and that user does not have sufficient authority to drop databases, then it is not possible to have this command executed against your precious data.

That's not to say that it is impossible to drop all your data anyway! It is a simple matter of issuing a bad update command, and pretty much the same effect can be achieved. The point though is that setting permissions that are unnecessary can lead to unpredictable security holes, so it's best not to take the chance.

So, we know that we want to create a *single user* who has just enough permission to perform the tasks required of a working osCommerce site. But where can the database be accessed from? It is very easy to access databases on a remote server—this functionality is necessary for applications that are distributed over a large physical area, such as international businesses. As a result, there is a distinct possibility that your database could be accessed from another server. This means that we also need to tell MySQL that it should listen only to one user on only one server.

Unless you have a specific reason to enable access from a different server, your user should only be allowed to access the database from localhost. Recall that there is a slight chance that your database is not on the same machine as your web server, in which case you will need to allow access only from that server. Enforcing this criterion immediately cuts out anyone else trying to access your database from anywhere other than the localhost.

Let's take a quick look at the `configuration.php` file for the `catalog/includes` folder again. The database-related settings are as follows:

```
// define our database connection
  define('DB_SERVER', 'localhost');
// eg, localhost - should not be empty for productive servers
  define('DB_SERVER_USERNAME', 'osCommerce');
  define('DB_SERVER_PASSWORD', 's3cur3pa55');
  define('DB_DATABASE', 'commercedb');
  define('USE_PCONNECT', 'true'); // use persistent connections?
  define('STORE_SESSIONS', 'mysql');
// leave empty '' for default handler or set to 'mysql'
```

Now, these settings are simply used by osCommerce when connecting to the database. If any of the information is wrong, you don't get a connection, or get a permission denied error. Don't confuse this with database security issues we are discussing! This has nothing to do with how MySQL has its access permissions set. For this there are a plethora of SQL commands to attain just about any access configuration you can imagine.

You'll be pleased to hear that there is little point in rattling off a whole bunch of SQL commands when it is likely that your site's host provides you with a wrapper of some sort to allow you to perform these tasks over a web interface. If you are interested in learning more about SQL than what we saw in earlier chapters, then please go to: `http://dev.mysql.com/doc/mysql/en/index.html`. For completeness, knowing what access is allowed and from where, you can use a GRANT statement to ensure that your user has the correct privileges on your database, like so:

```
mysql> GRANT SELECT,INSERT,UPDATE,DELETE,CREATE ON database.* TO
'username'@'localhost' IDENTIFIED BY 'password';
```

This statement is pretty self explanatory, but you should still read over the manual carefully if you intend to work with SQL statements directly as it can be trickier than it looks to get things right. Instead of going through this in depth, let's look at the demo site's database administration page, which should be fairly representative of most sites out there. The page is quite long, so we will discuss it section by section:

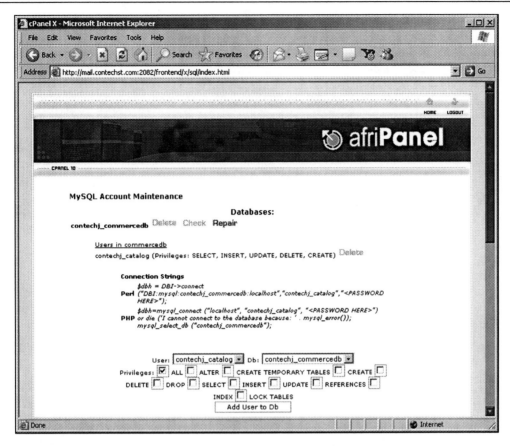

From this you can see that we have been provided (once again) with a wrapper for our SQL commands. From the top, you will see that there is one database called contechj_commercedb, which was created during the deployment phase of the site's development. Below that you can see that there is only one user, as discussed, with the privileges to select, insert, update, delete, and create. Why have the other actions been disallowed? Well, mainly because once your database has been created, there is no need for the other actions, so they are not allowed in case they open up security holes.

> Obviously, you may find that you require more privileges for your user—the main point is not to provide privileges that you don't need at all!

Below that are examples of the correct connection strings to be used within your code. This of course is superfluous information for us, as all connections are handled by osCommerce. It will of course come in handy if you decide to add functionality that needs access to your database. Below that is a set of drop-down lists and checkboxes that are used by the hosts to generate the SQL behind the scenes to grant the chosen privileges to the specified user on the specified database.

If you scroll down the page, you can see that the ability to add more databases is provided (see the figure that follows)—since there is no need for another database, we can simply ignore this—followed by a section that allows users to be added to the account. If you do require more than one user to access a database, you can grant them permissions on that database once their account is created:

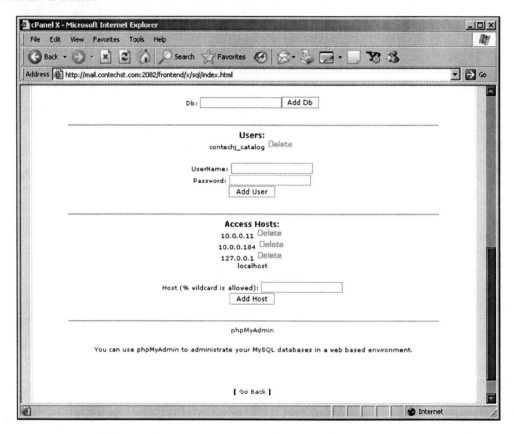

The area that follows then shows us where access to the database is granted from. As discussed, this should be restricted to localhost as shown here. The reason there are three IP addresses given is that this host has multiple servers that are all considered to be part of localhost. Not much can be done about that, but since it is only servers owned by the host (who by definition we have to trust) this is not a huge problem.

Notice that there is a message saying % wildcard is allowed. Under no circumstances should you ever allow this to be entered as a host on your live site because it matches to any address in the world. Basically, you would be giving universal access to your database in terms of where it can be accessed from. Many hosts will simply turn this off trusting that there is no reason you would want to allow the entire world access to your database.

Finally, phpMyAdmin is provided for database administration. We will discuss the use of this tool in the chapter on *Deployment and Maintenance* as it very powerful, convenient and easy to use, and pretty ubiquitous.

Now, as an exercise, you should be able to spot a serious flaw in the security process shown here. Hint: *you can see it in the previous two figures*. Did you see it? The administration tool is being used without SSL. This means that any information being passed between the browser and the server is crying out to be captured by someone else. What's worse is that passwords and usernames are being given out here, so if someone does happen to eavesdrop, we are in trouble because right from the start our security is compromised.

Naturally, all sensitive information like usernames and passwords should be sent over a secure connection!

Disaster Recovery

Making sure that access is properly controlled and that code cannot be subverted for unintended purposes is only a part of the concept of security. Ensuring that you can recover in the event of some unforeseen circumstances or an *Act of God*, as the insurance companies like to call it, is all part of an integrated security policy. I'm sure many of you, as have I, have worked on a document when for no reason the application simply packs up and says something suitably terse like *I am going to close down and ensure that the last three hours of your hard work will never be seen again* <insert evil laugh and fade to blue>.

Well, if this has happened on a document, then you can imagine the amount of anguish you are likely to experience when the last three years of sales information along with your configuration settings and database are erased by a ten year old kid who has breached your security and wiped the slate clean. Without a proper disaster recovery policy it is very likely that you will soon be out of work and unable to feed the mouth of your ten year old computer whizz-kid.

Hopefully, throughout the development phase you have been saving versions of your site at important milestones. If you have, then the principles of backing up your data should be quite familiar to you by now. Let's look at the main issues surrounding disaster recovery.

Back Up Your Files

Just because things like fires, earthquakes, and floods are often not the most threatening of disasters when it comes to computers doesn't mean that disasters can't strike. On average, companies that are reliant on the Internet for a large portion of their income, and do not have any type of disaster recovery plan in place will close their doors in two years after a major disaster, which can range from anything like theft, computer viruses, hardware and software failure, to plain old human error.

Problems can happen more often than one would like to consider. For example, some contributions have been known to damage stores quite seriously on installation. If you haven't taken the requisite steps to protect yourself, then it is no one's fault but your own—as harsh as that might seem. What are the requisite steps then? Well, you should already have several development versions of your site safely zipped up and stored on your development machine, but that is not really enough for a live server.

You should:

- Every now and then, at regular intervals, or before any modifications are made, back up your entire catalog folder plus any other folders on which the application relies. If you want to do this on a regular basis, you may want to consider creating a cron job (known as a scheduled task in Windows). We will look at cron jobs in Chapter 9 when we build the RSS Tech Feed WebPage.

- Store your backups in a location different from your live server. Preferably make copies on CD and keep those in a secure place. You might consider removing the passwords from the stored backups to prevent the theft of those leading to breaches in security.

- Make backups of all your logs files, and store these offsite too. These can be invaluable for tracking how and where things went wrong in the event of a disaster.

Doing this should ensure that in the event of something mangling your live system, it should not take you too long to reconstitute it and get it up and running with little or no fuss. Remember that your host might also implement some sort of backup policy, so make sure you know what they provide too. You will find that no matter what you do, you may lose some data, but this is not an insurmountable problem by any means. Of course, there is little point in backing up the file system without backing up your data, so let's look at that here.

Back Up Your Database

The people at osCommerce realize how important database backups can be for your business, so they have added functionality to the admin tool to take care of this. If you navigate to the Tools section you will see something like the following:

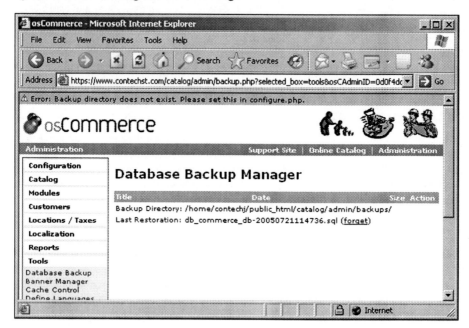

Observe the error message at the top of the page, stating that we don't have a backup directory in place. Most kindly, we are pointed to the configure.php file in the admin section to set this up, so let's do exactly that. If you open up the configure.php file and search for the line that sets the path for the backup files, you will see it towards the bottom of the page:

```
define('DIR_FS_BACKUP', DIR_FS_ADMIN . 'backups/');
```

Well, that looks pretty set, but of course the error might arise because the actual backups folder is not present in the file system, so go ahead and create that under the admin folder, and head back to the Tools section in the admin tool. You might well get another warning like this:

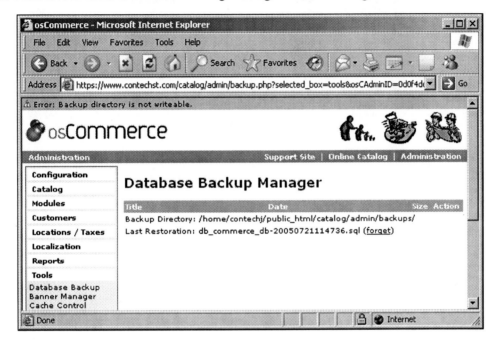

With your newfound knowledge of file-system permissions, go back to this folder and set the permissions on this folder to 777—this will allow osCommerce to write to the folder. Now when you view the Database Backup Manager page in the Tools section, you get the option to backup or restore. Clicking on backup will present you with three options that you can use to determine how the backup will take place—as No Compression (Pure SQL), or compressed with Use GZIP, or instead of keeping the backup on the web server, for Download only.

As an example, this is the type of page you should expect to see if you back up using pure SQL:

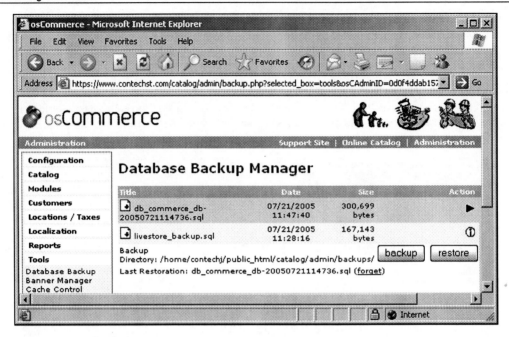

You can of course confirm this has saved the database by looking at the file created in the backups directory. Some sample content from this file is shown here:

```
# osCommerce, Open Source E-Commerce Solutions
# http://www.osCommerce.com
#
# Database Backup For Contechst Books
# Copyright (c) 2005 David Mercer
#
# Database: contechj_commercedb
# Database Server: localhost
#
# Backup Date: 06/29/2005 16:14:42

drop table if exists address_book;
create table address_book (
  address_book_id int(11) not null auto_increment,
  customers_id int(11) default '0' not null ,
  entry_gender char(1) not null ,
  entry_company varchar(32) ,
  entry_firstname varchar(32) not null ,
  entry_lastname varchar(32) not null ,
  entry_street_address varchar(64) not null ,
  entry_suburb varchar(32) ,
  entry_postcode varchar(10) not null ,
  entry_city varchar(32) not null ,
  entry_state varchar(32) ,
  entry_country_id int(11) default '0' not null ,
  entry_zone_id int(11) default '0' not null ,
  PRIMARY KEY (address_book_id),
  KEY idx_address_book_customers_id (customers_id)
);
```

Now, if there is a problem with your live database, you can simply click on the backup file you wish to restore and click restore. This will recreate the database in the form it was in when you made the backup. You can also simply click restore to browse for a backup file on your local machine in the event you have stored the backups off the web server.

> If your site consistently processes a large number of transactions, then it is probably prudent to make a backup of the database each day so that you never lose more than one business day's data in the event of a problem.

This backup utility is not the only one available, and you might find that you want to use your file system's native functionality to make automated backups for you. In this case it is likely you want to set up a *cron* job. More about this later in the book; for now, you have the ability to back up your database, and provided you are using a secure connection, you can take these backup files off your server and store them on disk and so forth.

It may be safer to download your backup directly to your local server if you are using a secure connection. In this case, click on backup and check the Download only box. If you are using IE you will find that you get the following error message:

This is the result of a problem with downloads, sessions, and SSL. In order to fix this you will need to go to the `sessions.php` file in the `admin/includes/functions` folder and modify the file like this:

```
function tep_session_start() {
    session_cache_limiter("must-revalidate");
    return session_start();
}
```

Please be aware that this is only the author's quick fix, and no representations are made that it will not affect anything else adversely—if in doubt, test, test, test! Trying all this again will give you the following window, as expected:

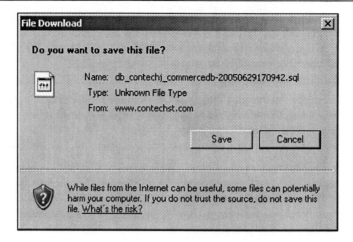

Once the file is safely on your local machine, you can then either encrypt it or store it on a CD or both.

This concludes our discussion on disaster recovery and security as a whole. Before we move on to implementing some of the more exciting and advanced functionality available to osCommerce stores in the following chapter, there is one more thing to remember...

Stay Up to Date

If you are a Windows user, you are probably familiar with the need to constantly update your system with security updates and necessary patches from time to time as weaknesses in the software are discovered. Well, because it is so important for everyone using a particular piece of software to be kept up to date with the latest security fixes, Microsoft has automated the process. In the same way, you need to keep an eye on the forums and security sites in order to stay informed about whether any new security flaws have been found, and if so, obtain the fixes as soon as possible.

Like any software, osCommerce itself undergoes changes, and you should look at upgrading to the next milestone once it is available. Generally, I like to wait for a couple of months before adopting a new version of software on a live site, just so the general community has a bit of time to iron out any wrinkles; you might consider doing the same.

Summary

While much of the material contained in this chapter really applies to your live site, you should have gained a valuable insight into how to approach the problem of securing your live store. You should now be aware of how to look at security as a chain in which each link must be as strong as the next in order to present a seamless shield against the multitude of attacks or flaws that can ruin your application, business, and peace of mind.

Security is a great and very important challenge for any online retailer, and hopefully you will take it very seriously too. Remember that the more reliable online shopping or e-commerce is perceived to be by the general public, the more people will migrate to Internet-based commerce. Everyone who runs an e-commerce site has a responsibility to maintain strict security and protection standards in order to provide a safe and reliable environment for consumers everywhere.

This chapter has put you well on the path to doing precisely this. Specifically, by looking at how to build an integrated security policy that takes into account not only the main areas of security (such as ensuring customers' details are only transmitted over an SSL-enabled server), but also that you as the merchant behind the scenes act sensibly and don't unwittingly introduce security flaws.

By adopting a holistic security-oriented approach to everything you do online, not only will you benefit from a much more enjoyable work environment and peace of mind, but even your business will benefit from the resulting reliability. I'm sure you will agree that while it has certainly been a fair amount of extra work to get everything working properly, it wasn't too bad and certainly worth the effort now that you can honestly be confident in the security of your site.

Let's get on with some more exciting stuff...

9
Advanced Features

In terms of the development of the site, the majority of the heavy lifting has now been completed. This chapter (and to a lesser extent, the one that follows) represents the last of the work that is to be done on the site before deployment. As things stand, you should have a version of your site (in development) that already distinguishes itself from the competition in terms of look, feel, and security—even though you may be waiting for deployment before you can implement your security fully. There are still a few things missing though, before you can say that your site is a good alternative to any of the major online retailers out there.

This chapter will introduce functionality that is intended to bridge the gap between sites like Contechst Books (in other words, those with smaller budgets) and the larger e-commerce sites (that is, those with considerably more resources at their disposal). As a result, we are going to look at several examples of some less common and hopefully impressive and useful features, which customers under normal circumstances might only expect from big sites like Amazon and so on.

To do this, we will turn to the community contributions for help as well as run through the author's own contribution, which we have already done some preliminary work on in earlier chapters. Remember, the urge to add extra functionality must stem from the dictates of your business, and not from a vague feeling that the site should be crammed with gimmicks if it is to succeed. Effectively, you should only add things that add value, and nothing more. To this end, the demo site is going to have the following added:

1. The RSS technology feed
2. Cross- and up-selling features
3. Gift voucher functionality

The idea behind adding the above mentioned features is to give customers a richer and more convenient place to shop online, while benefiting the retailer by being able to attract more people, offer them a better service, and market goods more effectively.

These specific additions have been selected because they are generally in popular demand from today's online retailers. That's not to say you have to implement all of this yourself—instead, use this chapter to learn *how* to add functionality of this nature so that you can implement those new features that best suit your business' needs, even if they are not specifically the ones shown here. As part of the chapter's pedagogy, you will also take home valuable lessons on how to *create* your own advanced features as well as gain experience with regards to using community contributions.

Highlighting a Generic Process!

As mentioned, the most important thing to gain from this chapter is not just the use of these three new features (although, they are very useful in themselves), but rather the process behind adding them. To summarize, you should:

- Think about what you want to add to the site and ensure it relates well with the business goals of the site.

- Perform a fairly in-depth requirements analysis so that you know what type of functionality you are working towards implementing.

- Back up your site before beginning any work on the additional material.

- If you are writing your own code, then you need to plan how everything will fit together before embarking on the coding process.

- Create, write, and/or install the feature.

- Thoroughly test everything about the new feature and confirm that all the wrinkles have been ironed out.

- Analyze any possible security holes and spend some time thinking about how you might try to break this new code. (If you don't, others certainly will.)

- Back up your site with the working addition before moving on to something else.

Admittedly, you might find it hard to perform a full suite of security tests on installed contributions, but in the absence of this you should make up by testing them as thoroughly as possible. One of the great things about using popular community contributions is that you can be quite certain plenty of people have looked over them and that flaws are being detected and corrected all the time. Just so we are clear, this doesn't absolve you of your duty to your customers to ensure that each contribution is working safely—it's just an encouraging thought!

Sticking to the generic process outlined here will ensure that you end up using less time and implementing better code—especially if you are attempting to write your own modules. You will find over time, assuming you work on a lot of contributions, that this process will become engrained, and your life will be made that much easier by following these best practices.

With that said, let's get on with it…

The RSS Technology Feed

We will look briefly at what RSS actually is in a moment, but before we do, it's important to answer a fundamental question first. *What value is this project going to bring to my business?* To answer that in the case of RSS, we can simply say that by providing information that is relevant and useful to the store's target audience, we hope to attract and hold on to a larger share of customers. There are RSS feeds available today to cater to just about any need you can imagine. All you have to do is think about what type of information would be of some interest or value to your customers, and then go and find a web feed that provides that sort of information.

For example, in the case of the demo site, it is entirely possible that programmers (who are visiting the site to purchase technology books) might wish to see a page of technology-related jobs that is regularly updated and can be browsed on the store's site. If this turns out to be a popular choice, then you will probably have succeeded in attracting potential clients, as well as established clients back to your store more often than otherwise. Since it is more likely that people will buy something from you if they are actually visiting your site, this feature adds value on both sides of the coin.

As it turns out, I have decided to use a technology news site to provide up-to-date information on the world of technology, in the hope that this service will provide a more rounded technology experience for the site's customers and encourage people to use the site more often as a result. As you will see a little later on, it is incredibly simple to make use of whatever feed you want, so it shouldn't be hard to provide information on a variety of topics all at once. You are certainly not limited to providing one type of information at a time.

Adding functionality that is not directly related to your site is, in a way, treading on thin ice. Don't go overboard and provide an environment in which people view your site as something other than what it is—an online store. A situation where potential clients visit you to fulfill some need but go to your competitors to actually make purchases would be a terrible waste of your time and especially your money (or lack thereof).

So, using something like this to augment your site without detracting from its overall purpose should really give your site a nice, refreshing flavor, and help foster a loyal and hopefully lucrative customer base.

What's All This RSS About?

First thing's first—what is RSS? In short, it's an XML (eXstensible Markup Language) based method of delivering web content. Some of you might already have heard of XML, but for those who haven't, you can think of it as a more flexible and powerful version of HTML. RSS stands for Rich Site Summary, although you might find that there are a few other definitions out there—we will use this one as it reflects our use of the technology more accurately than any other definition. RSS has only very recently ascended to mainstream popularity, but why is it here at all?

In a nutshell, someone somewhere on the Internet decides they want to create content that they believe will be of interest or use to other people somewhere else on the Internet. So, they write and write and write, but after a while they find that with so many different people trying to access this information, they need a standard way to present it so that anyone can use it. RSS is just such a standardization. You can find more on RSS from *RSS and Atom* by Packt Publishing (ISBN: 1-904811-57-4).

Now, anyone who wants to obtain information from someone else who has created an RSS feed can do so quite easily. But why does it have to involve another technology—in this case, XML? XML is perfect for this type of job because it allows us to create our own tags (just like HTML tags, which you are now familiar with) to describe the information contained within those tags. This meta-information makes it easier to understand what we are looking at and consequently to work with it.

Since it is important that you learn how to deal with an RSS feed so that you can modify the demo code to reflect your own requirements, let's should take a quick look at how an RSS feed is presented. Once you know how it is presented, we will take a look at how to make use of it using some native PHP functionality, and finally put everything together to produce a great looking, informative technology news page for the demo site. To start with, let's look at RSS…

Using RSS Feeds

One of the unfortunate things about RSS is that there are different versions of it which may use slightly different formats. What this means is that once you have decided on a particular feed to use, you will need to ensure that your code will deal with whatever RSS specification the feed providers are using. Whenever you consume an RSS feed using third-party software, or your own homemade scripts, you are aggregating the feed. An *aggregator* is simply something that makes use of an RSS feed, and we are going to be building our own simple aggregator for the site.

For the purposes of this demo, our aggregator is going to make use of RSS version 2.0, which is the latest version of RSS and looks something like this:

```
<?xml version="1.0" encoding="utf-8" ?>
 <rss version="2.0">
 <channel>
  <title>Some News Title</title>
  <link>http://www.thelink.com</link>
  <description>The latest technology news from your feed
provider</description>
  <image>
    <title>someTechFeed</title>
    <url>http://www.theLink.com/logo.gif</url>
    <link>http://www.theLink.com</link>
  </image>
  <copyright>Some Copyright Message. All Rights Reserved.</copyright>
  <managingEditor>theEditor@theLink.com</managingEditor>
  <ttl>60</ttl>
  <language>en-us</language>
  <item>
    <title>Really exciting news story</title>
    <description>Oh boy oh boy oh boy, you gotta read this exciting news.
</description>
    <link>http://www.theLink.com/article1/art=1103</link>
  </item>
  <item>
    <title>Another really exciting news story</title>
    <description>You won't believe this at all...</description>
    <link>http://www.anotherLink.com/anotherarticle.php?art=1230</link>
  </item>
  ...
```

There are quite a few things that you can make note of from observing the above snippet of code:

- The first tag shows the version of XML that is being used, along with the encoding.
- The second tag shows the version of RSS being used.
- Each RSS feed has exactly one <channel> element, which contains the entire feed.
- Following the <channel> tag are several tags containing information about the providers of the feed itself. This includes information such as a description of the feed, links to the site, logo images, the language being used, copyright messages, and who is responsible for the feed, among other things.

- Once that information has been given, the actual feed itself is presented in a series of `<item>` tags. Each item covers one story and contains several other tags, namely `<title>`, `<description>`, and `<link>`, which provide information about the item.

Looking at the above points you can see why we need XML. If we couldn't define our own tags such as `<description>`, it wouldn't always be immediately clear what our content was doing. Furthermore, notice how nicely all the information fits into the structure it is given, and how each item is contained in exactly the same format as all the other items. Doing things this way allows us to use code to automate the retrieval of each item because we don't have to worry about there being random tags popping up all over the show.

Indirectly, this examination of the feed raises some separate issues. One of the most important being that you can't simply make use of a feed without first ensuring you adhere to any conditions of use or copyright. You might find that not all sites allow you to reproduce their material without making it clear that they are the source, or you might find that the content is pay-per-view, in which case you cannot disseminate it for public consumption. If you are in any doubt as to the use of the material, then either contact the producers or use material you know to be safe to use.

Apart from determining how the feed's content can be used, you should also make sure you understand clearly the nature of the content and how often it is updated. Clearly, it is no use connecting to a feed that is only updated every month if you intend to provide up-to-the-minute reports for your customers, and naturally, if the feed is updated every few minutes, you should ensure you build your application to cater for this too.

Planning the Application

As always, we need to plan ahead so that we don't end up doing redundant or incorrect work at a later stage. As you will often find when developing web applications, what appears to be a simple task to begin with, nearly always contains hidden pitfalls under close scrutiny. This is no different! Let's begin by outlining exactly what we want to do (call it a brief requirements analysis), and then examine that outline to ensure we are aware of all the issues.

In short, we want to build a feed aggregator to retrieve news items from a source site and present them on a web page for our customers to view. The web page should show each news item's heading and description, and the user should be able to click on either in order to visit the source site to read the article in its entirety. It will probably help you to visualize the desired outcome by showing you a figure of what the finished product should look like here:

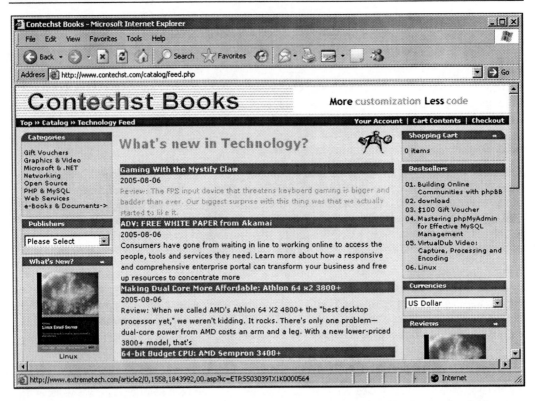

As you can see, we have made use of the `feed.php` file created earlier in the book. The feed page presents the results of the feed aggregation to the browser in a format that complements the rest of the site (in other words, fits in nicely). As you can see from the color of the font in the first article, it is a link, which will allow customers to open up a new page to read the article at the target URL shown in the status bar at the bottom of the browser.

Just looking at this you should notice one issue almost immediately. What happens if there are hundreds of articles? We don't want to have a page length that can be measured in meters, so we will need to paginate the results appropriately. In this case, ten results per page should do just fine, but what other issues should we isolate at this point?

We really only need our news to be updated on a daily basis (depending on what feed you are using, you will need to decide how often to update), so it is pretty wasteful to make each page call fetch information from the source server across the Web. It is very inefficient to download the news every time a customer clicks on the `feed.php` page, especially if the news is really going to remain relatively static over the course of a day.

Instead, what we can do is download the news once (in the morning, say) and store it to our database. Then, the `feed.php` page can query the database for much quicker retrieval because it no longer has to retrieve information across the Web. This will boost the performance of our site, and will reduce the load on the source server as well as the bandwidth of both sites, which is a better deal all round.

In terms of how you should deal with the content of the feed, the following, call it Mercer's Canon of Web Consumption, applies:

> Seek someone you trust to provide you with information... and then don't trust them!

What this means is that you should always get your web feeds from a trusted source—a well respected organization, which is unlikely to introduce any malicious material into its feeds. Even if you trust your source site implicitly, you cannot allow your code to do the same. Remember that you are downloading information from somewhere else and storing it on your database, for display on your site. If someone inserts something malicious, whatever that may be, then it can really affect your business badly.

Hand in hand with ensuring that your application is relatively secure goes the requirement that it actually works. The second you are relying on someone else to do something for your application, you need to consider the possibility that a malfunction could be introduced by them, and cater for that eventuality in your code. This means adding a bit of error-handling functionality to catch problems before they make their way to the customer's browser.

What else can we say about the application before we begin working on it? Well, one final thing to think about is that since we are going to update this information on a regular basis, this task is a great candidate for automation. On a Linux server, which is what your live site will be hosted on in all likelihood, you can automate the running of certain tasks using something called a **cron job**. We will take a brief look at this to automate the updating of our feed table each day.

If we can do all of the things mentioned in this section, then we should come out with an efficient, reliable, and automated technology news web page for our store. Modifying this to present whatever information you desire could mean as little as simply changing the address of the RSS feed source file.

Creating the Feed Table

The first thing to do is decide what information we need to store in the database in order to accomplish our task. This is an easy question to answer if you have already examined the feed. Since the information in the feed is already structured, our table can take its lead from this. The only difference we will make here is adding a date field, which will probably be useful to you in the future even though it is not specifically required by us right now.

The following SQL statement creates the feed table in the commerce_db database:

```
mysql> create table feed(
       > link text,
       > title text,
       > description text,
       > added date
       > );
```

As per the requirements, this gives us a four-field table that can store the link, title, and description sections of the feed, as well as record a date in the event you wish to have some form of timekeeping implemented. (This is a common requirement, even though we don't need it for this example.)

Please note that this is a very simple table, which doesn't have even have a primary key. The only reason we can get away with creating such a simple table is because there is no need to search the records or perform any manipulation on the data that is contained in this table. If you feel that you might need to manipulate information contained in your feed's table at any stage, then it is best to add a unique field and declare it as the primary key so that you can easily locate records. However, for simply storing and retrieving feed items, this is sufficient.

Creating the Aggregator

Thankfully, PHP now comes with some built-in functionality that makes it easy for us to perform some simple operations on XML files. As a result, it only takes one line to hook up to the RSS feed of our choice—the devil is in the details! To begin with, you need to check that you have access to SimpleXML. SimpleXML is provided by default with PHP5, so you should have it on your development machine.

If your host provider doesn't have SimpleXML, don't panic; you can use DOMXML, which your host should provide for working with XML—you will, however, need to make a few modifications to the code provided here to get it working. You can find more information about DOMXML at the following URL: http://www.php.net/manual/en/ref.domxml.php. Since the XML-centric part of the application is relatively simple to work with, we will go ahead and use SimpleXML for demonstrative purposes.

Our home-made aggregator, entitled cronfeed.php, looks like this:

```php
<?
//cronfeed.php: A simple script to insert feed items into a database

require('includes/application_top.php');

$request = "http://rssnewsapps.ziffdavis.com/extremetechreviews.xml";

try {
    $response = file_get_contents($request);
    if (!$response){
        throw new Exception ('Problem accessing feed! Please check the source site
and repopulate the database manually...');
    }
    $xml = simplexml_load_string($response);
    tep_db_query("delete from feed;");

    foreach($xml->channel->item AS $story){

        $link = $story->link;
        $title = $story->title;
        $description = $story->description;
        $description = htmlspecialchars(addslashes($description));
        $link = htmlspecialchars(addslashes($link));
        $title = htmlspecialchars(addslashes($title));
        $time = substr(date('c'), 0 ,10);

        tep_db_query("insert into " . 'feed' . " (link, title, description, added)
values ('$link', '$title', '$description', '$time');");
    }
} catch (Exception $e) {

    $to = "davidm@contechst.com";
    $subject = "Urgent RE: Tech Feed Cron Job ";
```

```
    $body = 'Caught exception: ' . $e->getMessage() . "\n";
    $from = $from = "From: staff@contechst.com\r\n";

    mail($to,$subject, $body,$from);
}
?>
```

The main points to note about this script are the following:

- We still need to include `application_top.php` in the file because we need to ensure that the web page is nicely integrated with osCommerce as a whole. This means that we should query the database using the in-built functions supplied to us by osCommerce, even if it is not strictly necessary.

- We are using the `extremetechreviews.xml` RSS feed published by Ziff Davis Media's ExtremeTech.com. This is stored in the `$request` variable, which is used to retrieve the contents of the file a little later in the code.

- Since we need to know whether we are successfully managing to access and download the contents of the `extremetechreviews.xml` file, we wrap the request in a `try-catch` block and throw an error if there is a failure for some reason. `try-catch` blocks are new to PHP5, so you might have to modify your script slightly to work with earlier version of PHP if your host does not support PHP5.

- Assuming we are successful in obtaining the feed, we load the response into a SimpleXML object, `$xml`, by using the `simplexml_load_string` function, and drop the current contents of the `feed` database to make way for the new feed info since we only want to present one day's news at a time.

- We then use a `foreach` loop to iterate through the contents of the feed and store each item in the database after ensuring that we have properly escaped quotes and removed certain special HTML characters—both the `addslashes` and `htmlspecialchars` functions are provided by PHP for security.

- Finally, if an exception is thrown up during our attempt to access the feed, the `catch` block creates a quick email message, which is sent to the administrator of the site, informing them of the problem. In this case, no actions are taken against the database, which will retain the old feed until it is updated.

While this script has taken into account a variety of considerations in order to make it reasonably robust, it is still not perfect. For example, it is quite possible that the `mail` function could fail, in which case our `catch` block is made redundant. You might consider writing to an error log as well to guard against this. All in all though, you should find that this script will chug along quite nicely in the background, updating your news feed each day according to how you set the cron job (We will look at this in a moment).

Given that it is likely that your host may not be using PHP5 and so will not be able to use the above script as it stands, I list here a modified version, which is PHP-version agnostic. This script makes use of DOMXML, and does away with `try-catch` blocks (which would foul up any system using PHP4 or earlier). The script is called `cronfeed_dom.php` instead of `cronfeed.php`:

```php
<?

/*cronfeed_dom.php: A simple script to insert feed items into a database
without requiring PHP5
*/

require('includes/application_top.php');

$request = "http://rssnewsapps.ziffdavis.com/extremetechreviews.xml";

if (!$response = domxml_open_file($request)){
   $message = "'Problem accessing feed! Please check the source site and
repopulate the database manually...'";

   error_handle($message);
}else{
   tep_db_query("delete from feed;");

   // get the node root and then the children of it.
   $node_array = $response->get_elements_by_tagname('item');

   foreach ($node_array as $childnode) {
      $tag = $childnode->child_nodes();
      // build the array
      foreach ($tag as $value) {
         $array[$value->tagname] = $value->get_content();
      }

      $title = $array['title'];
      $description = $array['description'];
      $link = $array['link'];
      $description = htmlspecialchars(addslashes($description));
      $link = htmlspecialchars(addslashes($link));
      $title = htmlspecialchars(addslashes($title));
      $time = date("Ymd");

      tep_db_query("insert into " . 'feed' . " (link, title, description, added)
values ('$link', '$title', '$description', '$time');");
   }
}

function error_handle($message){
   $to = "davidm@contechst.com";
   $subject = "Urgent RE: Tech Feed Cron Job ";
   $body = 'Caught exception: ' . $message . "\n";
   $from = "From: staff@contechst.com\r\n";

   mail($to,$subject,$body,$from);
}
?>
```

This script works in exactly the same way as cronfeed.php, and you would simply get the crontab to refer to this script instead of cronfeed.php in order to get your RSS feed working. Having already gone over how cronfeed.php works, we shan't repeat that information here—please look over the code file to familiarize yourself with it instead.

So now we have a database table that can accept the feed's information, as well as a script that updates that information. We now need a page that can access that information and display it appropriately in the browser.

Building the RSS Tech Feed Web Page

We have already added the page stub for the Tech Feed page in Chapter 6. So, we have all the navigation boxes or information boxes, along with headers and footers and so forth. All that is required from us is to retrieve the information from the database, and output it in a nice format with pagination. Of course, you don't have to worry about which version of the cronfeed.php script you used because this page only accesses the information in the database—how that information got there is of no concern to feed.php.

In order to properly paginate the feed page, we are going to need to make use of a GET variable called start. This will allows us to determine which page we are on, and display the navigation accordingly. The first piece of the new code block, which should be inserted into the correct place on your feed.php page, goes like this (I have added a few of the preceding HTML lines to give you a clue as to its location in the feed.php file):

```
<tr>
 <td><table border="0" width="100%" cellspacing="0" cellpadding="2">
  <tr>
   <td class="main"><?php

if(!isset($_GET['start'])) {
$start = 0;
}else {
$start = $_GET['start'];
}
```

As you can see, it simply determines whether this variable has been set, and assigns a value to the $start variable accordingly. $start will be used to determine how to navigate in the coming code.

We then need to initialize some of the variables we need in order to navigate and produce the correct queries of the database, as follows:

```
$initval = $start;
$limit = 10;
$now = $initval + $limit;
$back = $initval - $limit;
$next = $initval + $limit;
```

In this case, $initval will be used in the second database query as part of the LIMIT SQL statement. This is needed because we don't always want to retrieve the first ten values from the database; if we want to see the second page, we want the second group of ten values to be retrieved by our SQL statements. The $limit variable simply hardcodes the number of records we want to retrieve per page. You could always add a drop-down list or something similar to the page to allow customers to choose how many records to display per page. $now, $back, and $next are used for navigating, as you will see shortly.

We then need to query the database to find out how many rows we have in total and to return the group of results that we want, depending on the initial value held in $initval:

```
$find_rows = tep_db_query("select count(*) from feed;");
$numrows=mysql_result($find_rows, 0);

$gather_feed_query = tep_db_query("select link, title, description, added from feed limit $initval, $limit;");
```

There are a number of ways to go about this, and you might decide you only want to query for the number of rows once per session. If this is the case, you need to add a session variable that will hold the number of rows for the duration of the session rather than query the database each time. For our purposes this is absolutely fine as it is, since the number of records is never going to be excessive.

Now we want to iterate through the results, outputting each item as a link and with proper formatting:

```
while($query_data = mysql_fetch_array($gather_feed_query)){
    $link = html_entity_decode($query_data['link']);
    $title = html_entity_decode($query_data['title']);
    $description = html_entity_decode($query_data['description']);
    $date = $query_data['added'];

    echo "<a class='feed' href=\"$link\" target='_blank' title=''>$title </a><a
align='right'>$date</a>";
    echo "<br><a href=\"$link\" target='_blank' title=''>$description </a><br>";
}
```

As you can tell, the while statement takes the results of the second database query as an array, and assigns the various values to variables, which are then used in the echo statements that output the HTML links using tags assigned in our stylesheet.css file. It's worth it to show the a.feed stylesheet block (added to stylesheet.css) here quickly since this is what is used to give the nice red stripe for highlighting the title of each item as you saw in the initial screenshot earlier in the chapter:

```
a.feed {
    width: 100%;
    font-family: Verdana, Arial, sans-serif;
    font-size: 11px;
    font-weight: bold;
    background: #FF2626;
    color: #ffffff;
}
```

With that taken care of, all that's left is to add navigation at the bottom of the feed so that customers can search through the different pages. This is where all the variables that we declared initially, and have not used so far, come into play:

```
echo "<table align = 'center' width='50%'><tr><td  align='left' width='30%'>";

if($back >=0) {
    echo "<a href='" . tep_href_link(FILENAME_FEED) . '&start=' . $back ."'>
<font face='Verdana' size='2'>Previous</font></a>";
} else{
    echo "<font face='Verdana' size='2'>Previous</font>";
}

echo "</td><td align=center width='30%'>";

$i=0;
$l=1;
for($i=0;$i < $numrows;$i=$i+$limit){
    if($i <> $initval){
        echo " <a href='" . tep_href_link(FILENAME_FEED) . '&start=' . $i . "'>
<font face='Verdana' size='2'>" . $l . "</font></a> ";
    } else {
        echo " <font face='Verdana' size='2' color='red'>$l</font> ";
    }
    $l=$l+1;
}

echo "</td><td  align='right' width='30%'>";

if($now < $numrows) {
    echo "<a href='" . tep_href_link(FILENAME_FEED) . '&start=' .$next ."'><font
face='Verdana' size='2'>Next</font></a>";
```

260

```
} else{
    echo "<font face='Verdana' size='2'>Next</font>";
}
echo "</td></tr></table>";
```

This section is effectively split into three stages! The first one presents a Previous link, which is only active if the customer is not on the first page. The middle section presents a series of numbers that highlight the current page in red and allow the customer to click on any of the pages other than the current one. The final section presents a Next link, which is operational except when the customer is already on the last page.

Why did we use the `tep_href_link` osCommerce function to format our links for us when we could have simply added the filename `feed.php` to the a `href` tag? This is a perfect example of why you should always preserve the overall structure of the files you are working on. If we had simply given the filename in the link, then the page would have been served as normal, and you would even get all the way to the live site without realizing what the problem is. Can you spot it?

If you don't use `tep_href_link`, then you will lose your session IDs, and any customer who happens to look over the web feed will have all sorts of trouble trying to make a purchase because osCommerce won't know who he or she is anymore. Using the built-in functions, in this case, ensures that the sessions are passed from one page call to the next.

While we are on this topic, some of you may be encountering errors with the navigation code shown above. Why is this? If you look closely at the line:

```
echo " <a href='" . tep_href_link(FILENAME_FEED) . '&start=' . $i . "'>
<font face='Verdana' size='2'>" . $1 . "</font></a> ";
```

you will notice that we assume that `tep_href_link` is passing the session ID as part of the URL. Because of this, we are appending the start variable using an ampersand, &, character. Of course, once you come to deploy your site you will more than likely wish to force the use of cookies in order to store session information because this is more secure (During development it is beneficial to pass the session in the URL so that we can see for ourselves that they are being handled correctly).

As a result, you will need to modify the `echo` statements in the above code to reflect the fact that no session ID is passed with the URL when cookies are activated. This means that your lines change to something like this instead:

```
echo " <a href='" . tep_href_link(FILENAME_FEED) . '?start=' . $i . "'>
<font face='Verdana' size='2'>" . $1 . "</font></a> ";
```

Notice that the ampersand has been changed to a question mark in order to produce a properly formatted URL. Once you have done that, your navigation will work correctly, and you will be able to move between the different pages with no problems.

Talking of different pages, here is what the 21st record looks like, along with the navigation table that follows at the end of each page:

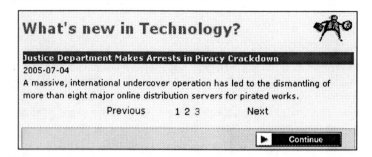

Pretty neat stuff! However, we are not quite done yet, because we need to set the `cronfeed.php` or `cronfeed_dom.php` script to run at midnight every night to update the data in the database. You will need to find out how you can implement this on your host site. In the case of the demo site, we are provided with a wrapper for the crontab file, which is what determines when specified commands are to be run. Before we look at that, let's have a very quick look at how the crontab works...

All the variables set in the crontab are numerical constants, with the exception of the asterisk character, which is a wildcard that allows any value. The ranges permitted for each field are as follows:

- Minutes: 0-59
- Hours: 0-23
- Day_of_month: 1-31
- Month: 1-12
- Weekday: 0-6

You can include multiple values for each entry, simply by separating each value with a comma. The command you wish to issue can be any shell command and can also be used to execute web pages, like the `cronfeed.php` file. The basic structure is shown quite clearly in the following screenshot, which shows the demo site's crontab-editing page:

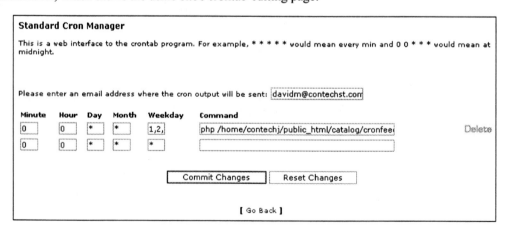

Here you can see that we have set the command `php /home/contechj/public_html/catalog/cronfeed.php` to run at midnight every weekday night (by setting the crontab values to 0 0 ** 1,2, 3, 4, 5), and that any cron output should be sent to `davidm@contechst.com` so that the cron job can be traced—if anything goes wrong (or right) with the cron job, the recipient of the supplied email address will know about it. Of course, you will need to ensure that you are able to run the `php` command on your host site—if the cron job doesn't work with this command, talk to your hosts because it may be that you have enter path information such as `/usr/bin/php` instead.

Before we go any further, there are a few things to discuss with regards to the way things are set up. At the moment, the `cronfeed.php` script is saved within the document root (`/home/contechj/public_html/catalog/cronfeed.php`), which means that someone can access it directly from a browser. They won't get anything useful from the page, but it will cause the script to request information from the RSS feed server each time someone accesses the page. This is not a huge problem unless someone continually (and maliciously) accesses it over and over—eventually this might cause you to be banned from using the feed (which can happen with some of the busier feeds).

A way around this would be to create a `crons` folder outside the document root and place the script in there. If you do this, however, you will need to provide the script with its own database connection facilities because it will no longer be able to use relative filepath names (such as `includes/application_top.php`) that are used to provide osCommerce native database functionality.

Another possibility for preventing overuse of the RSS feed server would be to cache results and only update the cache every day (or hour, minute, or whatever you need). Sadly, the field of feed aggregation is far too large to cover in its entirety here, so it is left to you to modify the code provided to suit your needs. What you have already should work really nicely as is...

With that done, you now have a great value-added feature for your site. Whatever you decide to present on your site can easily be done by changing a single line in the `cronfeed.php` file. For example, if you wanted to show an up-to-date list of programming jobs instead of a news feed, then you could use whatever job-related feed you prefer, provided you ensure that the structure of the document is the same. If each item is arranged differently, you will need to modify the application accordingly.

To demonstrate this, say we wanted to take a look at all the aerospace jobs available on the redgoldfish site: `http://www.redgoldfish.co.uk/RSS/rss_aerospace.xml`. Simply view this file in your browser and take a look at the structure of the file—you will notice that we need to make the following changes to the `cronfeed.php` or `cronfeed_dom.php` files:

```php
<?
require('includes/application_top.php');

$request = "http://www.redgoldfish.co.uk/RSS/rss_aerospace.xml";

try {
  $response = file_get_contents($request);

  if (!$response){
    throw new Exception ('Problem accessing feed! Please check the source site
and repopulate the database manually...');
  }
  $xml = simplexml_load_string($response);
```

```
tep_db_query("delete from feed;");

foreach($xml->item AS $story)
{
  $link = $story->link;
  $title = $story->title;
  $description = $story->description;
  $description = htmlspecialchars(addslashes($description));
  $link = htmlspecialchars(addslashes($link));
  $title = htmlspecialchars(addslashes($title));
  $time = substr(date('c'), 0 ,10);

    tep_db_query("insert into " . 'feed' . " (link, title, description, added)
  values ('$link', '$title', '$description', '$time');");
  }
...
```

I haven't shown the entire file here as only the two lines shown here need changing. But from these two simple changes—which resulted from simply finding a new RSS feed and observing its structure—instead of seeing the technology feed, we have a job board as shown here:

That brings to a close the addition of your very own web feed! Obviously, you are free to modify this code as you see fit—you might wish, for example, to keep more than one day's worth of feed in your database. In such a case, the date fields are already there for you to use, and you shouldn't have too much trouble modifying the scripts accordingly.

It's now time to turn our attention to a few of the community contributions that will also enhance the site, and, particularly the next example, will provide a slightly more intelligent marketing platform for your products.

Cross- and Up-Selling Features

It's a wonderful thing to have a dynamic feel to your website—if there is something new, interesting, and different on every page the customer looks at, then you as the retailer are doing a good job of selling your products. What's more, if you can make the dynamic part of your site show products that are meaningful or helpful to a customer, then your effectiveness as a marketer is increased and so hopefully is your bottom line. But how do you even begin finding out what a customer wants while they browse?

The answer is that you can either track everything they browse and then compare that to what other customers with similar tastes have bought in order to make suggestions, or you can simply apply a bit of knowledge about the products you are selling. As you can imagine, the first option requires a fair amount of effort and cost in order to put into action, but the second might not be quite as difficult. What do I mean by *apply a bit of knowledge*?

Well, look at the demo site. If I wanted to offer customers books that are likely to be more relevant to them while they browse, I need to know first of all what they are looking at. Once I know what they are looking at, I can work out what they might be interested in by deciding which products are most closely related, or complement the product being browsed in some way. If someone is looking to buy a book on PHP programming, then it is likely that they might be interested in a book on Apache or osCommerce too. If this is the case, then ideally I could show them these books at the same time they are looking at the PHP-programming books.

This type of marketing strategy is prevalent nowadays although you have probably become so attuned to it that you don't even notice it anymore. Popcorn with coke for the movie, anyone? Offering related products to people shopping for a given item is called *cross-selling* by those in the know. A slightly more subtle spin-off of cross-selling is *up-selling*, which offers more expensive items to the customer in the hope that they will find these products useful and go the extra mile. It's very clever and it works, otherwise we wouldn't be discussing it here.

So, what is it that we want to do precisely (before we head off and download any contribution that mentions sales)? Well, we would ideally like to be able to link related products together so that when they are viewed, the linked products are also displayed. In this way, we can determine our own marketing strategy with regards to cross- and up-selling, and have it implemented by osCommerce via the links that we determine. Thankfully, there is a contribution that can help with precisely this…

Installing the X-Sell Contribution

The first thing to do is download the contribution from the community website at `http://www.oscommerce.com/community/contributions,1415`—ensure that you download the full version and not just an add-on. Once you have that on your development machine, please ensure that you make a backup of your site before continuing. You can then extract the files to your hard drive and read the installation instructions for both the `catalog` and `admin` sections— there are two sets because the X-Sell feature requires changes to both sides of the application.

One last thing to mention is that for both the coming contributions, we will only cover the installation in English. Installing the contribution in any other languages that are available would add quite a bit of length to this text, and the process for all languages is exactly the same so there is not much point. If you do need to install files for other languages, then simply view the documentation supplied with both contributions to ensure that you do everything as required.

catalog

For completeness, we will run through the installation procedure here quickly, though you should find that there are instructions supplied with the download too. There are few steps that get a bit tricky, so we'll elaborate on those here:

1. Create the new table and fields in the database by using the `products_xsell.sql` script. You can do this by opening up `mysql` on the command line and typing in something the following (substituting the correct path to the `products_xsell.sql`) file:

    ```
    mysql> \. C:\path_to_file\products_xsell.sql
    ```

    You can verify this has created the requisite table by issuing the following command:

    ```
    mysql> describe products_xsell;
    ```

2. Copy the `xsell/catalog/includes/modules/xsell_products.php` file to your `catalog/includes/modules/` folder.

3. Add the following lines to the `catalog/includes/database_tables.php` file:

    ```
    // Added for Xsell Products Mod
    define('TABLE_PRODUCTS_XSELL', 'products_xsell');
    ```

4. Add the following lines to the `catalog/includes/filenames.php` file:

    ```
    // Added for Xsell Products Mod
    define('FILENAME_XSELL_PRODUCTS', 'xsell_products.php');
    ```

5. Modify your `catalog/product_info.php` file to include `FILENAME_XSELL_PRODUCTS` above the `FILENAME_ALSO_PURCHASED_PRODUCTS` entry. To do this, search for this section:

    ```php
    <?php
     if ( (USE_CACHE == 'true') && !SID) {
         echo tep_cache_also_purchased(3600);
       } else {
         include(DIR_WS_MODULES . FILENAME_ALSO_PURCHASED_PRODUCTS);
       }
     }
    ?>
    ```

    and change it to this:

    ```php
    <?php
    //added for cross -sell
       if ( (USE_CACHE == 'true') && !SID) {
       echo tep_cache_also_purchased(3600);
        include(DIR_WS_MODULES . FILENAME_XSELL_PRODUCTS);
       } else {
         include(DIR_WS_MODULES . FILENAME_XSELL_PRODUCTS);
         include(DIR_WS_MODULES . FILENAME_ALSO_PURCHASED_PRODUCTS);
       }
     }
    ?>
    ```

6. Add the following line to the `catalog/languages/english/product_info.php` file:

    ```
    define('TEXT_XSELL_PRODUCTS', 'We Also Recommend :');
    ```

7. Copy the X-Sell file, `xsell/catalog/includes/languages/english/` `xsell_products.php`, to your `catalog/includes/languages/english/` folder.

With that completed, you can now turn your attention to the admin side of the contribution.

admin

In order to integrate the contribution with your admin tool, you will need to perform the following steps:

1. Copy the `admin/xsell.php` file from the contribution to your site's `admin` folder.

2. Copy the `admin/includes/languages/english/xsell.php` file to your site's `admin/includes/language/english` folder.

3. Add the following line to your `admin/includes/filenames.php` file:

   ```
   define('FILENAME_XSELL_PRODUCTS', 'xsell.php');
   ```

4. Add the following line to your `admin/includes/application_top.php` file:

   ```
   define('TABLE_PRODUCTS_XSELL', 'products_xsell');
   ```

5. Add the following line to your `admin/includes/languages/english.php` file:

   ```
   define('BOX_CATALOG_XSELL_PRODUCTS', 'Cross Sell Products');
   ```

6. Add the following line into the array in the `admin/includes/boxes/catalog.php` file:

   ```
   '<a href="' . tep_href_link(FILENAME_XSELL_PRODUCTS) . '"
   class="menuBoxContentLink">' . BOX_CATALOG_XSELL_PRODUCTS . '</a>'
   ```

   Simply add this line at the bottom of the array so that it looks like this (note the extra `<br>` tag and period character in the second-last `<a>` element):

   ```
   ...
   '<a href="' . tep_href_link(FILENAME_SPECIALS, '', 'NONSSL') . '"
   class="menuBoxContentLink">' . BOX_CATALOG_SPECIALS . '</a><br>' .
   '<a href="' . tep_href_link(FILENAME_PRODUCTS_EXPECTED, '', 'NONSSL') .
   '" class="menuBoxContentLink">' . BOX_CATALOG_PRODUCTS_EXPECTED .
   '</a><br>' . '<a href="' . tep_href_link(FILENAME_XSELL_PRODUCTS) .
   '" class="menuBoxContentLink">' . BOX_CATALOG_XSELL_PRODUCTS . '</a>'
   );
   ```

With that done you can navigate to the new Cross Sell Products page in the Catalog section of the administration tool to check out the changes. You should see something like the following:

Cross-Sell (X-Sell) Admin

Product Id	Product Model	Product Name	Current Cross-Sells	Update Cross-Sells	
44	VirtualDub_1	VirtualDub Video: Capture, Processing and Encoding	--	Edit	--
45	PHPBB_01	Building Online Communities with phpBB	--	Edit	--
46	MyAdmin_01	Mastering phpMyAdmin for Effective MySQL Management	--	Edit	--
50	Lin_01	Linux	--	Edit	--
Displaying 1 to 4 (of 4 products)					Page 1 of 1

As things stand, you have not yet made any links between files, so your X-Sell admin page should just list all the products you have in your database, and of course, the Cross Sell Products option should be available in the Catalog section on the left of the page. All that's left to do now is deciding on a cross-selling strategy and then implementing it. Let's take a quick look at how to make use of this tool!

Using the X-Sell Contribution

Making use of the new cross-selling facilities in the admin tool is fairly straightforward. Simply click on a product you wish to work on and then check the products you wish to link to this product in the table that follows. Your page will look something like this (notice that the second product in this case has been checked):

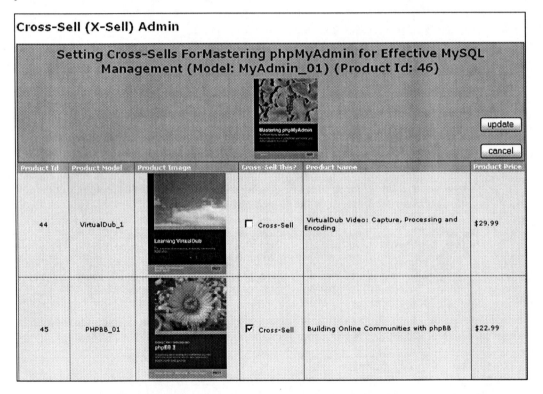

Once you have checked all the products that you wish to link, simply click on update, and you are done! You can confirm everything has worked by observing the green highlighted message along the top of your browser, which should say something like: Cross Sell Items Successfully Update For Cross Sell Product #45. Assuming you get this notice, you can now check the Cross-Sell Admin page again to view the linked products, like so:

Cross-Sell (X-Sell) Admin

Product Id	Product Model	Product Name	Current Cross-Sells	Update Cross-Sells	
44	VirtualDub_1	VirtualDub Video: Capture, Processing and Encoding	--	Edit	--
45	PHPBB_01	Building Online Communities with phpBB	--	Edit	--
46	MyAdmin_01	Mastering phpMyAdmin for Effective MySQL Management	1. PHPBB_01 Building Online Communities with phpBB 2. Lin_01 Linux	Edit	Prioritize
50	Lin_01	Linux	--	Edit	--
Displaying 1 to 4 (of 4 products)					Page 1 of 1

Notice that now the book that has products linked to it has not only the Edit option associated with it, but also the Prioritize option. Clicking on Prioritize brings up a page that allows you to set the sort order for the linked products. In other words, you can control which products get shown first—effectively allowing you to rank products from most likely to least likely to be useful.

When you are happy that all your products have been linked correctly and all the priorities are in the right order, go along to your site and play around by clicking on a few of the available products. Now when a product's information screen is brought up, you should see an extra box recommending other products, like this:

It should be pretty clear that this is extremely useful to you in terms of educating your customers as to the range and depth of your stock. Making intelligent suggestions available to your customers can only bring a more pleasurable shopping experience, especially for those people who are not quite sure what it is they need (this often applies to technically complex products).

Hopefully you are starting to feel that the store is beginning to look more like a competitor to Amazon than a one-person show, and there's no stopping us yet. Time to work on the gift vouchers…

Adding Discount and Gift Voucher Facilities

Another fairly common and useful marketing technique relies on the use of gift vouchers and/or coupons. Since most people should understand how these concepts work in practice, we don't need to discuss in much depth. There are quite a few advantages you can derive from implementing these facilities, such as:

- **Providing a rounded, flexible shopping experience**: Customers wishing to purchase gifts, for example, can instead purchase a gift voucher, which is redeemable by the recipient.

- **Bringing other customers on board**: In order to redeem gift vouchers, customers who might otherwise not visit the site need to come and select a purchase. In this way they are exposed to your store and are more likely to visit it in the future.

- **Marketing**: Handing out promotional gift vouchers and discount coupons is a good way to attract new business to your store.

Once again, we need to ask ourselves what it is we require from the additional facilities in order to fulfill our needs in this respect. We definitely want to be able to maintain fine-grained control over how the coupons and vouchers get used and who receives them, so we need some sort of control panel for administering them. As well as this, the checkout process needs to be modified to allow customers to redeem either coupons or vouchers, and have their totals calculated accordingly.

It goes without saying that the whole system needs to be secure and fool-proof. In other words, the last thing we need is for someone to be able to create their own gift vouchers and redeem them against products in our store at will. Because we are using a contribution to handle this for us, to some extent we have to trust the new code and hope that it doesn't introduce any security holes. Remember too that a large part of the store's security comes from the overall security policy we have already discussed, and so long as we keep up secure lines of communication between the administration tool, customers, the database, and our server, we should be fine.

Naturally, osCommerce has a contribution that can do all of this for us, entitled the Credit Class & Gift Voucher module, and you can download it from: `http://www.oscommerce.com/community/contributions,282`. It is going to be a fairly long process to get everything up and running, so if you haven't yet, perhaps make yourself a cup of coffee before we get going.

Installing the CCGV Contribution

There are two methods of installation available for this module. The first, decidedly easier, way is to simply copy all the contribution files over to your `catalog` folder and add a few lines to the relevant files here and there. The contribution is large, and it is unfortunately quite tedious doing things the other way. The problem with doing things the easy way is that it is highly likely that you will mangle whatever work you have done on your site thus far. Consequently, it is only recommended that you copy files across to your `catalog` folder if you are using a clean installation of osCommerce.

If you have done any work on your installation, then you need to do things the long way. This is not such a bad thing because it will at least afford us a look at the code we are introducing to the store. So, begin by extracting the download to your hard drive and then follow the instructions listed below. I don't need to remind you to back up your current files now…

> When you come across an edit instruction in the material that follows, it means you need to search the contribution files listed for the modifications they have made. These are mostly marked with a series of hashes or the letters CGV—and copy those changes into your current files. *Hint: Copy the entire code block, with comments, across to your new files so you know what you have and haven't added.* Please be aware that often it is not a straightforward case of inserting code, but you might need to replace a line instead. Make sure your code looks exactly the same in the local region as in the contribution.

Before we begin with the file changes, you should create the new tables necessary for this all to work. The SQL commands are contained in a separate `.sql` file, and you should now be able to execute that against the database using the same technique as we used for the last contribution:

```
mysql> \. c:\path_to_file\order_total_gv.sql
```

You should receive several confirmation messages telling you that everything has been created properly, and you can use the following commands to first list all the tables, and then show the ones you are interested in:

```
mysql> show tables;
mysql> describe <table>;
```

Once you are satisfied that all is as it should be, carry on with the following instructions for the catalog and admin installations.

catalog

Good luck! There are plenty of additions and changes to make. Please be very careful that you add or replace material exactly as it is shown in the contribution files—failure to do so will result in errors that can be hard to track down.

1. Add the following files from the download to your `catalog` folder:
    ```
    catalog/add_checkout_success.php
    catalog/gv_faq.php
    catalog/gv_redeem.php
    catalog/popup_coupon_help.php
    catalog/gv_send.php
    ```

2. Edit the following files in your `catalog` folder:
    ```
    catalog/checkout_confirmation.php
    catalog/checkout_payment.php
    catalog/checkout_process.php
    catalog/checkout_shipping.php
    ```

```
catalog/checkout_success.php
catalog/create_account.php
catalog/logoff.php
```

3. Move the following images to your `catalog/images/` folder:

   ```
   catalog/images/gv_100.gif (NEW)
   catalog/images/gv_50.gif (NEW)
   catalog/images/gv_25.gif (NEW)
   ```

4. Edit the following files in your `catalog/includes/boxes/` folder:

   `catalog/includes/boxes/information.php`. (The changes in this file are not marked. You will need to copy the following line:

   ```
   '<a href="' . tep_href_link(FILENAME_GV_FAQ, '', 'NONSSL') . '">' .
   BOX_INFORMATION_GV . '</a><br>' .
   ```

   over to your file. You have already worked with links, so you know to be careful to add <br> tags and periods in the right places.)

   ```
   catalog/includes/boxes/shopping_cart.php
   ```

5. Edit the following files in your `catalog/includes/classes/` folder:

   ```
   catalog/includes/classes/order_total.php
   catalog/includes/classes/payment.php
   catalog/includes/classes/shopping_cart.php
   ```

6. Add the following file to the `catalog/includes/languages/` folder:

   ```
   catalog/includes/languages/add_ccgvdc_english.php
   ```

7. Add the following line to the bottom of the `catalog/includes/languages/english.php` file:

   ```
   require(DIR_WS_LANGUAGES . 'add_ccgvdc_english.php');
   ```

8. Move the following files to the `catalog/includes/languages/english/images/buttons/` folder:

   ```
   catalog/includes/languages/english/images/buttons/button_confirm.gif
   catalog/includes/languages/english/images/buttons/button_redeem.gif
   catalog/includes/languages/english/images/buttons/button_send.gif
   ```

9. Move the following files to the `catalog/includes/languages/english/modules/order_total/` folder:

   ```
   catalog/includes/languages/english/modules/order_total/ot_gv.php
   catalog/includes/languages/english/modules/order_total/ot_coupon.php
   ```

10. Move the following files to the `catalog/includes/languages/english/` folder:

    ```
    catalog/includes/languages/english/gv_send.php
    catalog/includes/languages/english/gv_faq.php
    catalog/includes/languages/english/gv_redeem.php
    catalog/includes/languages/english/popup_coupon_help.php
    ```

11. Edit the following file in the same folder as the previous step (Warning: this code is prefixed with ICW, not GCV):

    ```
    catalog/includes/languages/english/create_account.php
    ```

12. Move the following files to the `catalog/includes/modules/order_total/` folder:

    ```
    catalog/includes/modules/order_total/ot_gv.php
    catalog/includes/modules/order_total/ot_coupon.php
    ```

13. Move the following file to the `catalog/includes/` folder:
    `catalog/includes/add_ccgvdc_application_top.php`

14. Insert the following line into the `catalog/includes/application_top.php` file:
    `require(DIR_WS_INCLUDES . 'add_ccgvdc_application_top.php');`

Thankfully, that is the last of the modifications needed on this side. Hopefully you have managed to add each code snippet or file correctly, and we will test everything out fully once we have the admin side of things up and running. For now, though, you might just want to try to purchase an item just to see whether you have introduced any errors to the code. For example, I encountered this error when attempting to make a purchase the first time:

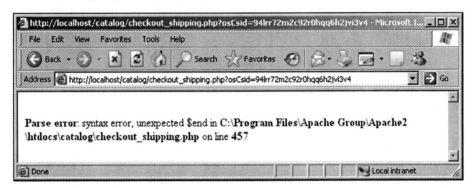

This error was caused by the following modification to the `checkout_shipping.php` file:

```
// ##### Added CCGV Contribution #########
//   if ($order->content_type == 'virtual') {
  if (($order->content_type == 'virtual') || ($order->content_type ==
'virtual_weight') ) {
// ##### End Added CCGV Contribution #########
    if ($order->content_type == 'virtual') {
      if (!tep_session_is_registered('shipping'))
tep_session_register('shipping');
      $shipping = false;
    ...
```

Can you spot the problem? Take a look at the first line after the added contribution code. It is the same as the line inside the addition barring the extra condition. The reason we get an error is because the addition is really supposed to be a *replacement*. You are supposed to remove the original line, otherwise you are opening up two `if` blocks by accident. Since there is now one `if` block that is never closed, PHP reports an error at the end of the file when it doesn't find a closing brace for the extra `if` statement.

Removing the original `if` statement to give you the following code corrects the problem:

```
// ##### Added CCGV Contribution #########
//   if ($order->content_type == 'virtual') {
  if (($order->content_type == 'virtual') || ($order->content_type ==
'virtual_weight') ) {
// ##### End Added CCGV Contribution #########
      if (!tep_session_is_registered('shipping'))
tep_session_register('shipping');
      $shipping = false;
    ...
```

273

Now when you navigate to the `checkout_shipping.php` page, it displays as normal (assuming there is nothing else wrong with the file). We will go over the use of the contribution in its entirety in the section on *Using the CCGV Contribution*. If there are any errors in your setup, they should show up then. For now, let's continue with the installation…

admin

There aren't nearly as many changes to be made to the admin tool, so take heart—you are well on your way to finishing. To continue:

1. Move the following files to the `admin` folder:

    ```
    admin/coupon_admin.php
    admin/gv_mail.php
    admin/gv_queue.php
    admin/gv_sent.php
    admin/listcategories.php
    admin/validcategories.php
    admin/listproducts.php
    admin/validproducts.php
    ```

2. Move the following file to the `admin/includes/` folder:

    ```
    admin/includes/add_ccgvdc_application_top.php
    ```

3. Insert the following line into the `admin/includes/application_top.php` file:

    ```
    require(DIR_WS_INCLUDES . 'add_ccgvdc_application_top.php');
    ```

4. Insert the following line into the `admin/includes/column_left.php` file:

    ```
    require(DIR_WS_BOXES . 'gv_admin.php');
    ```

5. Move the following file to the `admin/includes/boxes/` folder:

    ```
    admin/includes/boxes/gv_admin.php
    ```

6. Move the following file to the `admin/includes/languages/` folder:

    ```
    admin/includes/languages/add_ccgvdc_english.php
    ```

7. Insert the following line into the `admin/includes/languages/english.php` file:

    ```
    require(DIR_WS_LANGUAGES . 'add_ccgvdc_english.php');
    ```

8. Move the following files to the `admin/includes/languages/english/images/buttons/` folder:

    ```
    admin/includes/languages/english/images/buttons/button_confirm_red.gif
    admin/includes/languages/english/images/buttons/button_release.gif
    admin/includes/languages/english/images/buttons/button_report.gif
    ```

9. Move the following files to the `admin/includes/languages/english/` folder:

    ```
    admin/includes/languages/english/coupon_admin.php
    admin/includes/languages/english/gv_queue.php
    admin/includes/languages/english/gv_mail.php
    admin/includes/languages/english/gv_sent.php
    ```

That's it, we're all done! Of course, now comes the moment of truth, when you check to see whether the last few hours of changes bear fruit. The first thing to do is navigate over to your administration tool to see if all is well—assuming it is, you should now have the option to navigate to the Vouchers/Coupons section in the admin tool. Doing so will bring up a page that looks like this:

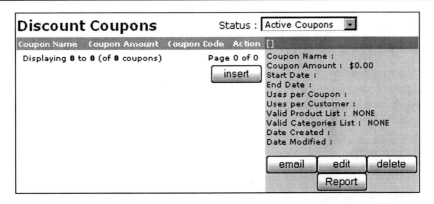

We will explore the use of this tool in just a moment. However, it is important to mention at this stage that if you are receiving error messages then it is in likely that you have implemented one or more of the steps incorrectly. The trick here is to look closely at the message and to ascertain exactly where in the code the error is coming from. Once you know this, you can cross-reference that piece of the code with the appropriate installation instruction and make any changes necessary.

Remember that the code does work in the contribution files, so you should always make sure that your site's file looks exactly the same as the contribution file in the area local to the modification. Assuming everything in the admin tool is ship-shape, we will now begin playing around with vouchers and coupons, and ensure that the catalog side of things works according to plan.

Using the CCGV Contribution

As you might expect, there is a lot of functionality we get in return for the amount of work we had to do to install this contribution. From using gift voucher products to using discount coupons and FAQ pages, there is plenty to *work on*, and above all, to *make work*. We will begin by looking at how to make and administer gift vouchers followed by the same for discount coupons.

Gift Vouchers

One of the most interesting things about this contribution is that it actually treats gift vouchers as a product. In order to create a suite of gift vouchers, you simply create them as products, which can then be purchased like anything else. Say for example we want to offer $100 gift vouchers, which customers can purchase from the store. Simply navigate to the Catalog section in the administration tool and click on new category, and then add a new gift voucher product in that category by clicking on new product.

Create your gift voucher product with the following provisos:

1. The voucher model number must begin with GIFT. I suggest that if you are making a $100 voucher, you call it GIFT_100, and so on for other denominations.

2. Certificate images are provided by the contribution and are found in the catalog/images/ folder. Alternatively you can create your own images and link these to the product on creation. Remember that you should also supply larger images according to the method used in the chapter on customization.

3. Set the weight attribute of the gift voucher to 0 in order to prevent shipping charges being added to the voucher price (assuming you are happy to have these vouchers in electronic format and are not distributing paper copies).

Now when customers navigate to the store, they have the following category page available to them. Notice that I have shown an example of using both the *provided* voucher and a rather extraordinary *home-made* one—simply to demonstrate that you don't have try to fit a standardized image onto your page:

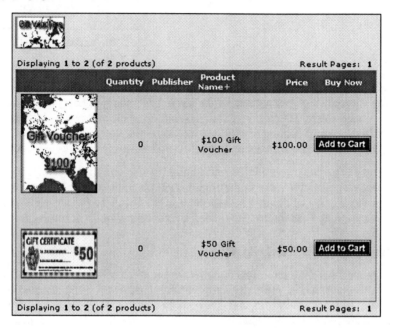

Before we continue, in order to make use of the Gift Voucher and Discount Coupon facilities, you will need to have the modules enabled in the Order Total section of the Modules category of the admin tool. There are some settings that you can play around with on the Gift Vouchers page in the Modules section as follows:

Gift Vouchers	Setting
Display Total	Set this to true in order to display the total—recommended.
Sort Order	740—leave this as the default value unless you have a specific reason not to.
Queue Purchases	true—this prevents fraud by allowing voucher credit to be released manually only after payment is received.
Include Shipping	Set this to true if you want the shipping prices to be covered by the gift voucher.
Include Tax	Set this to true if you want tax to be covered by the gift voucher.

Gift Vouchers	Setting
Re-calculate Tax	Leave as None unless you are compelled by your tax laws to recalculate tax.
Tax Class	Leave as None unless you need this as part of your tax calculation.
Credit including Tax	Set to false unless you wish to deduct the tax amount off the initial value of the voucher purchase.

> Please note that the contribution comes with comprehensive material on how to set your attributes; it is recommended that you make use of that for both the gift vouchers and the discount coupons.

Let's assume that a customer, blinded by the exceptionally loud colors on the $100 voucher decides to purchase one. They dutifully click on Add to Cart and go through the checkout procedure. At the end of the purchase, they receive a notice that the purchase was successful, but there is no notice informing them that the voucher is theirs. Accordingly, you may want to adjust the text for the checkout_success.php page to inform customers that if they have purchased a voucher, then their account will be credited with the amount of the voucher as soon as their payment has been accepted.

This leads us neatly to the next point. How do we release vouchers to customers who have purchased them? It's quite easy; simply go the Gift Voucher Release Queue page as shown here:

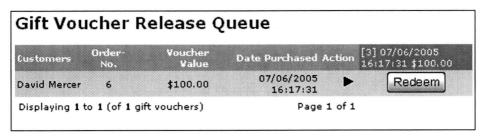

Select which voucher you would like to redeem by clicking on Redeem—you will then be asked to confirm this. As soon as you have confirmed it, the voucher is removed from the queue and the customer is credited with the value of the voucher. Executing this procedure means that when the customer checks their shopping cart, they now see something like this:

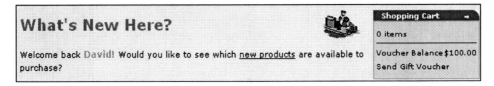

Now they have a Voucher Balance, which they can either use against purchases, or can choose to email an amount to someone else who can then redeem that amount as a voucher. Essentially this has provided a type of currency that is accepted only at your store. Now if a customer decides to make a purchase, they get the following payment page:

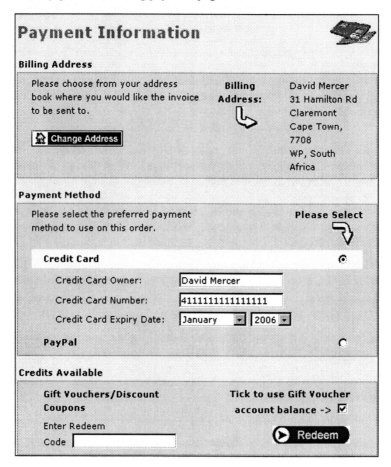

There are three very important things to notice about this upgraded checkout_payment.php page. The first is that you can now use a checkbox to pay for the purchase with your gift voucher. The second is that if you are the lucky recipient of a gift voucher from someone else, then you can enter the code (received with the gift voucher notification email) and use that against the value of your purchase. The third is that we have to rework the Redeem button to fit in with the rest of the buttons on the site.

At any rate, let's say we simply want to use our voucher against the purchase and we aren't redeeming a gift from someone else. We would simply click Continue to bring up the confirmation page, which will show the value of the purchase, and the value of the voucher being used. Clicking on the Confirm Order button will make the purchase, except now the customer is left with only the value of the voucher minus the value of the purchase (as shown in the shopping cart box):

Let's now say that the customer is satisfied with their latest purchase and wishes to send a gift voucher to a friend. In this case, he or she can simply click on the Send Gift Voucher link in the Shopping Cart box, to bring up the following page:

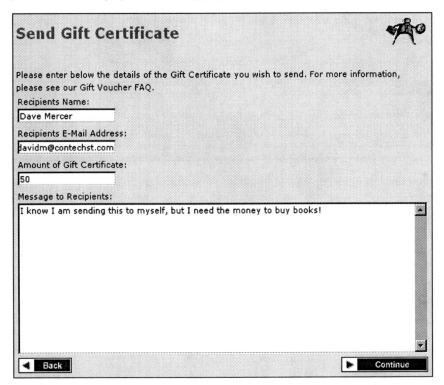

Many of you will find that your page settings have gone a bit strange when opening this page. If you recall, earlier in the book we modified all the pages to contain them all within a width of 800 pixels. Unfortunately, all the new contribution pages we moved across to the catalog folder will now also need to be modified in the same way; otherwise we will end up with un-neat screens. However, these are all simple modifications that you have already seen before; we won't go over all of that again here, but bear in mind that hidden dangers like this lurk whenever you add new code.

In order to send a gift voucher to someone, the customer simply fills out the form shown and clicks Continue. There is a quick confirmation page (with another button to be modified) and after that, the voucher is sent by email, the value of the voucher is deducted from the customer's total, and a voucher code is issued via email, like so:

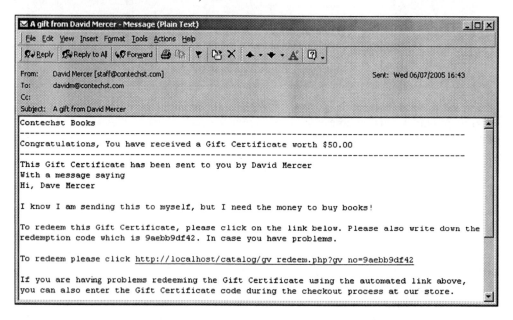

Now the recipient can log on to the site, and enter the redemption code during the checkout process to receive the value of that voucher.

Apart from what we have covered, the administrator of the site can also send gift vouchers via email, using the admin tool. It isn't hard to fill out the form, so we won't mention it further here. Another thing to note in the Vouchers/Coupons section is the Gift Vouchers Sent section. From here you can view all the activities surrounding your gift vouchers in order to keep track of what is going on and where.

The final thing we will look at in this section deals with the configuration section. Take a look in there, and you should see two extra fields added to the list of settings. These control whether you will automatically send a welcome gift voucher, and if so, what the value of that gift voucher should be. By default, no gift voucher is sent, so you don't have to worry about handing out discounts automatically.

I'm sure you'll agree that this contribution is really great stuff! Just bear in mind that you need to test the site in a comprehensive manner, as you never know when little oddities might crop up. For example, I found that much of the content provided in the contribution download was in French—as a result I had to scrounge bits and pieces of code from earlier contributions, to convert it to English.

Discount Coupons

Coupons can be created and maintained through the Coupon Admin page in the administration tool under Vouchers/Coupons. It's a simple enough task to click insert to bring up the coupon-creation page, which provides you with a list of settings in order to define how the coupon will be used as well as its value, and so forth. For example, the following coupon was created to provide a 10% discount on all PHP titles in the store:

Discount Coupons	
2005-07-07	
Coupon Name	Discount!
Coupon Description	Provides a 10% discount on PHP Titles!
Coupon Amount	10%
Coupon Minimum Order	20
Free Shipping	No Free Shipping
Coupon Code	c69134
Uses per Coupon	
Uses per Customer	1
Valid Product List	
Valid Categories List	26
Start Date	07/07/2005
End Date	07/07/2006
confirm	back

The settings are all well explained and not hard to understand. If you struggle to find the cPath value (in the event that you want to restrict the coupon's use by product category), simply navigate to that category in the store and check the URL, which will show you a value for the cPath. For example, you can see in the previous screenshot that the valid categories list is set to 26. Navigating to the PHP & MySQL section of the site shows this URL:

```
http://localhost/catalog/index.php?cPath=26
```

So only the products contained within this cPath will be subject to the discount. Now, let's put this coupon to the test. Hopefully, we will be allowed to redeem 10% of the value of a purchase on PHP books alone. So, the administrator simply emails the coupon to the desired recipients, who receive the coupon code in the body of their email. They then log on to the site, decide what they would like to purchase, and go to the checkout procedure.

> Remember to have your Discount Coupons module installed in the Modules Order Total section of the administration tool.

Now, before we go and take a look at how the payment page works, it is probably a good idea to look over the settings for the Discount Coupons in the Order Total section of the admin tool. The following table highlights the possible settings:

Attribute	Setting
Display Total	Set this to true if you wish to display the value of the discount coupon. (Probably wise!)
Sort Order	Use this to sort the order of display. Best to leave as the default, unless you have a very good reason to change this.
Include Shipping	This is set to false in the demo application as shipping is calculated separately from products' prices in our business model.
Include Tax	This is set to true in the demo site because we want to give customers 10% off the gross price of the product. You will have to set the value according to your business model.
Re-calculate Tax	This is set to None as there is no need for us to do this if we are including tax in our calculation for the coupon.
Tax Class	Select the relevant tax class from the drop-down list when treating the discount coupon as a Credit Note. Obviously, this should hint at the fact that discount coupons can be used to credit customer's accounts in the event they return a product for some reason. The demo site has this set to None.

The default settings are quite sensible, but you should still play around with all of these to ensure that you understand their action and can make the correct settings depending on your own tax laws and preferences. With that said, let's rejoin our customer, who has reached the payment page and now wishes to redeem their discount coupon of 10%. After entering the coupon code and clicking Redeem, they are shown the following page (assuming nothing is wrong):

Order Confirmation

Delivery Address	Products (Edit)	
(Edit)	1 x Mastering phpMyAdmin for Effective MySQL Management	$29.99
David Mercer		
31 Hamilton Rd		
Claremont		
Cape Town, 7708		
WP, South Africa		
Shipping Method		
(Edit)		
Flat Rate (Best Way)		

Billing Information

Billing Address (Edit)		
David Mercer	Sub-Total:	$29.99
31 Hamilton Rd	Flat Rate (Best Way):	$5.00
Claremont	Total:	**$34.99**
Cape Town, 7708	Discount Coupons:c69134:	**-$3.00**
WP, South Africa		
Payment Method		
(Edit)		
PayPal (Credit Card / Debit)		

✔ **Confirm Order**

As you can see, according to the settings we made, the coupon has dutifully deducted 10% (rounded up) of the subtotal, which doesn't include the shipping. If the customer clicks on Confirm Order, then the PayPal payment page confirms that the price they are expected to pay is in fact $31.99, which is exactly what we want. But what happens if someone tries to cheat and enters a code that he or she has made up? Obviously, we expect osCommerce to disallow that transaction.

This is the result that is produced on the demo site:

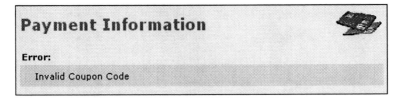

This confirms that the site is working reasonably well. Of course, you will have to do far more extensive testing than we have space to show here. For example, you should try purchasing goods that are not valid for redemption with the coupon. In this case, the total reduction off the value of the purchase should only include those goods for which the coupon is valid. This works fine on the demo site, as you can see from this:

The coupon still only discounts $3 from the total price because the Linux title is not part of the category that qualifies for the discount.

Many of you may have problems with the more info link in the shopping-cart box. If you are experiencing these problems over Internet Explorer, try modifying the following code in the catalog/includes/boxes/shopping_cart.php file, which fixes the problem I encountered:

```
// ########### Added CCGV Contribution ##########
// CREDIT CLASS script moved by Rigadin in v5.13 for compatibility with STS
$cart_contents_string ="
<script language=\"javascript\">
  function couponpopupWindow(url) {
  window.open(url,'popupWindow','width=450,height=280')}
</script>";
echo $cart_contents_string;

  if ($cart->count_contents() > 0) {
    // ########### Added CCGV Contribution ##########
    $cart_contents_string .= '<table border="0" width="100%"
                     cellspacing="0" cellpadding="0">';
    $cart_contents_string .= '<table border="0" width="100%"
                     cellspacing="0" cellpadding="0">';
...
```

Please ensure that you add the period after $cart_contents_string in the if statement as shown in the previous code. However, if worst comes to worst and this still doesn't work for you, simply modify the following line towards the bottom of the same file instead:

```
$info_box_contents[] = array('align' => 'left','text' => '<table
cellpadding="0" width="100%" cellspacing="0" border="0"><tr><td
class="smalltext">' . CART_COUPON . '</td><td class="smalltext"
align="right" valign="bottom">' . '<a href="javascript:popupWindow(\'' .
tep_href_link(FILENAME_POPUP_COUPON_HELP, 'cID=' . $cc_id) . '\')">' .
CART_COUPON_INFO . '</a>' . '</td></tr></table>');
```

This second modification won't solve the problem as such, but will at least allow the info popup to work by calling a different JavaScript function altogether. After all is said and done, the main thing is to test, test, and test. Not only will this prove whether your new contribution is robust, but it will also help you learn how it works. Remember that you can also set a welcome discount coupon in the Configuration section of the admin tool, and that like any other part of the site, this contribution is fully customizable and is programmed in the same manner as the rest of osCommerce to make it easy for you to find your way around.

Summary

You have now seen examples of how to add your own functionality (the RSS tech feed) as well as how to add contributions to your site. There are literally thousands of modifications that you could make to your site, of which we have only covered three. However, these three contributions should have provided you with enough practice to confidently move forward with whatever plans for additional features you may have in mind.

Your site now has some great extra features, which will lend an air of professionalism to your store and will hopefully result in better earnings in the long run. It's time to now look at some less involved, but equally neat tools, tips, and tricks!

10
Tools, Tips, and Tricks

The previous chapter focused on fairly complex additions to the site. While these are certainly important, not all additions need to be large and powerful in order to add value. There are plenty of neat little applications that you should consider implementing in order to tweak the final appearance and functionality of your online store. Like any physical product, a car for instance, you can look at the development of your online store as being more or less completed, with the engine, chassis, and body all in place; it's just a case of adding airbags, windscreen wipers, cup holders, and so on.

As you might expect, over the course of osCommerce's lifetime a huge number of scripts have been written to perform the multitude of tasks each and every store owner has required. Obviously we can't hope to cover all of those in this chapter, but you already know how to make use of the community in order to search for what you want. You also have a good idea how to go about making additions yourself. Accordingly, what this chapter will do instead is discuss the a few tools that come as standard with osCommerce or are commonly provided as part of your hosting package, as well as show a few examples of how to finish off the site nicely.

Specifically, we will look at the following in some detail:

- Banner Manager
- phpMyAdmin
- Low Stock Report
- Download Controller
- PayPal trouble
- Dynamic Box Headers
- Creating Matching Buttons

By the end of this chapter your site will be complete from a development point of view, and after the appropriate testing, you should be ready to deploy everything to its home on the Internet. By and large, what you decide to add or change during this phase of the development process is really something that only you can decide based on the needs of your store and the nature of your hosting package. In all likelihood, you will only find a use, or discover a need, for some of the topics covered here once you have been running a live site for a little while already.

Whatever you decide to use or implement from here on out, rest assured that at the very least your site is already one of the best online store's around. The question of whether you succeed should now be reduced to simple economics and no longer be subject to the fickle mistress that is software development. We're on the home straight, so let's not stop now...

Tools

It's easy to sit back at this stage and consider the site as fit to go live; but consider the revenue-generating possibility of banner ads, which we haven't even looked at yet. Normally, this might be a tricky thing to implement, but osCommerce ships with its own banner manager to help us out. As a result it is important that we look at this quite closely in order to make effective use of the tool and banner ads.

Tools are not all about adding functionality to your site of course. A useful tool, which is ubiquitous in the open-source world, is the phpMyAdmin tool for administering MySQL databases. If your host provides you with MySQL as part of your hosting package, you can be fairly certain that they will also make phpMyAdmin available for your use. If not, ask them why not, because you will find it a lot easier to work with phpMyAdmin than having to manually issue commands every time you need to query your database.

Let's begin with the banner manager...

Banner Manager

Naturally, should your store become reasonably popular, it is entirely likely that you can boost your revenue by providing advertising *real estate* on your site. Since this is a pretty common requirement for e-commerce sites, osCommerce ships with the **Banner Manager** administration tool, which you can find under the **Tools** section on your site. By default, the banner ad is placed at the bottom of the page and contains the familiar osCommerce logo. Some of you may have noticed that the screenshots of the catalog area on the demo site have an advertisement for Packt at the top right of the page instead.

This is because the code that controls the banner ads was moved from the footer.php file to the header.php file so that banners are displayed at the top of the page instead of the bottom where it is more likely that they will be seen. Of course, where you place your banner ads is entirely up to you, and we will take a quick look at how to show different banners in different parts of your site simultaneously using this tool.

Incidentally, the header.php file now looks like this:

```
<table border="0" width="800" cellspacing="0" cellpadding="0">
  <tr class="header">
    <td valign="middle"><?php echo '<a href="' .
tep_href_link(FILENAME_DEFAULT) . '">' . tep_image(DIR_WS_IMAGES .
'contechst_books.gif', 'Contechst Books') . '</a>'; ?></td>
    <!--
    <td align="right" valign="bottom"><?php echo '<a href="' .
tep_href_link(FILENAME_ACCOUNT, '', 'SSL') . '">' . tep_image(DIR_WS_IMAGES .
'header_account.gif', HEADER_TITLE_MY_ACCOUNT) . '</a>  <a href="' .
tep_href_link(FILENAME_SHOPPING_CART) . '">' . tep_image(DIR_WS_IMAGES .
'header_cart.gif', HEADER_TITLE_CART_CONTENTS) . '</a>  <a href="' .
```

```
        tep_href_link(FILENAME_CHECKOUT_SHIPPING, '', 'SSL') . '">' .
        tep_image(DIR_WS_IMAGES . 'header_checkout.gif', HEADER_TITLE_CHECKOUT) .
        '</a>'; ?>  </td>
            -->
          <td align = "right">
        <?php
        if ($banner = tep_banner_exists('dynamic', '468x50')) {
    ?>
    <!--<br>-->
    <table border="0" width="250" cellspacing="0" cellpadding="0">
        <tr >
          <td align="right"><?php echo tep_display_banner('static', $banner); ?>
          </td>
        </tr>
    </table>
    <?php
          }
    ?>
    </td>
        </tr>

    </table>
    <table border="0" width="800" cellspacing="0" cellpadding="1">
      <tr class="headerNavigation">
      ...
```

If you take a look at the footer.php file, you will see that the extra code was simply lifted from there and placed directly into the header file's HTML code with a bit of formatting to align the banner on the right-hand side of its cell. It's as simple as that to create a new banner ad area. Taking a slightly closer look at this code, you will notice that there are two functions used to find and display banner ads. The first, tep_banner_exists searches for whatever banners are available in the stipulated group. In this case, the parameter dynamic tells the function to pick one ad at random, and 468x50 is the name of the banner group to select the ad from.

If you simply wanted to display a banner of your choosing, you would change the first parameter to static and supply the banner's ID. If you are not certain of which banner ID belongs to which banner, you can simply check your MySQL database for the requisite banners with something like this:

```
mysql> select banners_id, banners_title from banners;
```

This will list all the IDs and banner titles that are currently stored in your database, and you can make your selection from here.

The second function, tep_display_banner, has the same options available to it. You can supply it with a first parameter of either dynamic or static, followed by the name of the banner group or banner ID respectively. In this case you can see that the function is called with static, and $banner, which works just fine because tep_display_banner uses the results from tep_banner_exists to display the ad. If you wanted to show one specifically, you could write something like this:

```
        echo tep_display_banner('static', '2');
```

This would dutifully pick out the second banner ad and display it. Remember that is better to keep the code as it was shown in the header file because that will prevent error messages like the following one being shown on your site if you don't first check whether the ad exists before displaying it. Remember that for development purposes it is actually an advantage to see these errors, but it is better to show no ad than to show an error message on the live site:

Play around with the various combinations of parameters until you are happy with how the code works. You should find that at some stage you would like to be able to specify a different banner group for a specific ad to work on. This is where the admin tool comes onto the scene. Let's take a quick look at it to see how to make use of banners effectively.

The Banner Manager page shows a list of all the banner ads you have available, and from here you can activate or disable any ads as well as check up on their performance and usage. Clicking on one of your ads in the Banner Manager will bring up the banner's statistics page, which will show you how many times the banner has been viewed and how many times it has been clicked on.

The first thing you will probably want to do is create a new banner ad, so click on New Banner to bring up the new banner creation page, which looks something like this:

Banner Manager

Banner Title:	Packt Publishing * Required
Banner URL:	http://www.packtpub.c
Banner Group:	468x50 ▾ , or enter a new banner group below
Image:	[ ] Browse... , or enter local file below
	C:/Program Files/Apache Group/Apache2/htdocs/catalog/images/
	contechst_animation_b
Image Target (Save To):	C:/Program Files/Apache Group/Apache2/htdocs/catalog/images/
HTML Text:	
Scheduled At: (dd/mm/yyyy)	18/07/2005 ▾
Expires On: (dd/mm/yyyy)	[ ] ▾ , or at
	[ ] impressions/views.
Banner Notes:	update cancel

This interface is really quite simple, but there are a couple of things to note here, so we'll go over them quickly. The Banner Group is what allows you to specify different types of ads, which can then be used to display adds on different parts of your site. We will see in a moment how this can be put to use.

The Image and Image Target settings are also quite important for the live site because it may well be that you need to download your image from somewhere else, in which case you also need to specify a folder to save it to. Make sure you have the permissions required to write to the target folder, which will hold your uploaded banner files.

The HTML Text option allows you to create HTML-based banner ads, which can then make use of JavaScript or Flash files. Most of the time you will simply be dealing with animated GIF files supplied to you by the advertiser. Finally you can also specify when to start showing the ad and when to stop (depending either on the date or the number of times the ad has been viewed). The result of the settings made in the previous screenshot, combined with the modified header.php code, as well as disabling the default osCommerce banner is shown here. (Unfortunately, you can't tell that this banner image changes, so you'll have to view the live site for confirmation.)

Now, what happens if we want to show a banner ad somewhere else on the page? Let's also say that these ads are unrelated to those that are shown in the header file, so we don't want them to be picked from the same group. Here's how you do it:

1. Ensure you create a new Banner Group and add all related banner ads to this group.
2. Create a new banner ad.
3. Insert the banner code into the correct place on your site.
4. Modify the banner code to check for and display only ads from the correct group.

You will need to pick a standard size to fit your site's layout and ensure that all the banner ads conform to this size. A quick search on Google will reveal the most common banner sizes used today, but remember that there is software now that blocks standard banner ads, so you may consider using your own sizes to counter this.

For this example, I have decided that the Tech Feed information box should display a banner ad of the site from which the information is pulled. This example is chosen simply to demonstrate how to display banner code in a new place and ensure that the right ads are displayed in the right places. So, the eweek.gif banner was added to the images folder in the catalog directory. A new banner ad was created using this image and the relevant URL and title as shown overleaf:

```
┌─────────────────────────────────────────────────────────────────────────┐
│ Banner Manager                                                            │
│                                                                           │
│  Banner Title:       [eweek              ]      * Required                │
│  Banner URL:         [http://www.eweek.com]                               │
│  Banner Group:       [Tech Feed ▾], or enter a new banner group below     │
│                      [                    ]                               │
│                                                                           │
│  Image:              [                ] [Browse...], or enter local file  │
│                                                       below               │
│                      C:/Program Files/Apache Group/Apache2/htdocs/catalog/images/ │
│                      [eweek.gif         ]                                  │
│                                                                           │
│  Image Target (Save  C:/Program Files/Apache Group/Apache2/htdocs/catalog/images/ │
│  To):                [                    ]                                │
│                                                                           │
│  HTML Text:          [                                            ▲]      │
│                      [                                             ]      │
│                      [                                             ]      │
│                      [                                            ▼]      │
│                                                                           │
│  Scheduled At:       [18/07/2005  ▼]                                      │
│  (dd/mm/yyyy)                                                             │
│                                                                           │
│  Expires On:         [              ▼], or at                             │
│  (dd/mm/yyyy)        [0        ]  impressions/views.                      │
│                                                                           │
│  Banner Notes:                               [ update ] [ cancel ]        │
└─────────────────────────────────────────────────────────────────────────┘
```

Once this was created, it was enabled by clicking the green circle on the Banner Manager page in the admin tool. Finally, the following code was added to the Tech Feed information box in order to include the image at the top of the file:

```php
<?php
$info_box_contents = array();
$info_box_contents[] = array('text' => BOX_HEADING_FEED);

new infoBoxHeading($info_box_contents, false, false);
$info_box_contents = array();

if ($banner = tep_banner_exists('dynamic', 'Tech Feed')) {
  $info_box_contents[] = array('align' => 'center', 'text' =>
tep_display_banner('static', $banner) . '<br>' . '<a href="' .
tep_href_link(FILENAME_FEED) . '">' . BOX_FEED_TEXT . '</a>');
  }else{
    $info_box_contents[] = array('align' => 'center', 'text' => '<a href="' .
tep_href_link(FILENAME_FEED) . '">' . BOX_FEED_TEXT . '</a>');
  }
new infoBox($info_box_contents);
?>
```

From this you can see that we first check whether we have any ads in the Tech Feed banner group. If we do, then we display the ad as part of the information box, and if not, we display the information box as normal. Now, instead of seeing the plain old text in the Tech Feed box, the customer can see who the content provider is (or a random selection of content providers, depending on how many different feeds you use) and click on the banner to go directly to the site, or the text below to go to the feed page:

Pretty cool! Once again, getting the hang of how and where to place everything is a matter of practice, and you aren't limited to adding banners to the Tech Feed box. A good place to consider adding banners is down the right-hand side of the page—especially if you are limiting the width of the rest of your site to a specific limit. In fact, we will show how to use this space for another type of advertising in the final chapter of the book, so you will get a good grounding in the potential for ad-based revenue. With that said, let's move on…

phpMyAdmin

Up till now, all database-related tasks that we needed to perform were accomplished by using MySQL directly. Luckily for us, this need not always be the case. Having to learn SQL in order to effectively query a database is a notoriously tricky task—it's one of those things that are easy to learn but difficult to master. phpMyAdmin helps out by providing a graphical user interface, which allows for far easier manipulation of data.

You can find out more information on this extremely popular tool at http://www.phpmyadmin.net/. If you have this tool available as part of your hosting package, then you will probably find the documentation made available to you on the phpMyAdmin homepage, as shown here:

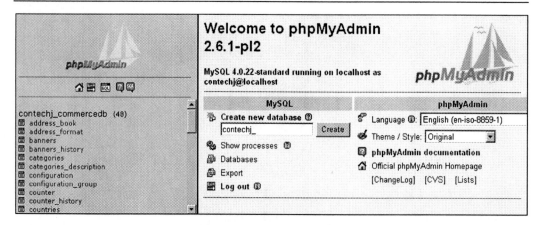

As you can see, all the tables in the commercedb database are conveniently listed down the left-hand side of the page for easy access. On the right-hand side of the page, there are several options, links, and settings, which you will find useful at various stages in your time as an e-Commerce online store administrator. There is quite a lot to learn here, so we will present a whistle-stop tour to give you a good grounding in the basics, leaving it up to you to become master of your own database.

To begin with, if you wish to view the contents of any given table, then click the icon to the left of the table's name. This will bring up a page that shows you the command issued to the database, and a few options for how you wish the data to be presented, followed by the actual results of the query and a few other miscellaneous items, as follows:

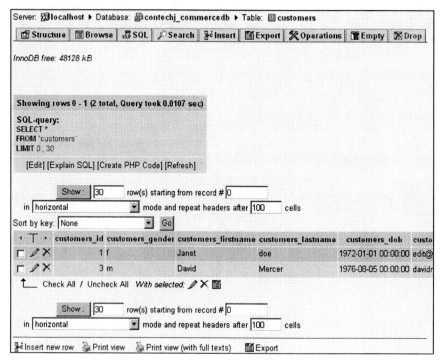

From here you can edit the values in the table or delete and add rows as you desire:

> Be very careful when using phpMyAdmin, because it will allow you to delete records that might still be needed by osCommerce. Deleting records such as order statuses via osCommerce ensures that checks are performed to see whether there are orders that need those statuses—with phpMyAdmin there are no checks of this kind.

You can even export the table, and we will cover exporting data in a moment as you will find it a pretty valuable operation for backing up your database. If you don't want to look at every single row in the table (some of the tables contain a lot of information that may not be immediately relevant to you), you should consider modifying the query by using the Edit option in the SQL-query section of the page.

For example, if we wanted to show only the customer's ID, firstname, and lastname, then we could click Edit, highlight the * character in the query, and insert the desired fields before clicking on Go, like so:

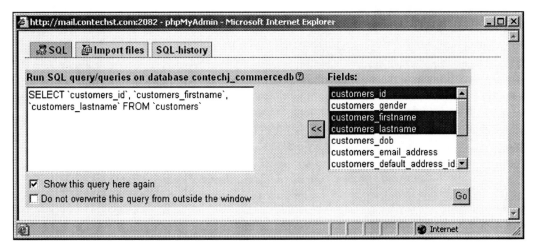

The resulting page then looks something like this:

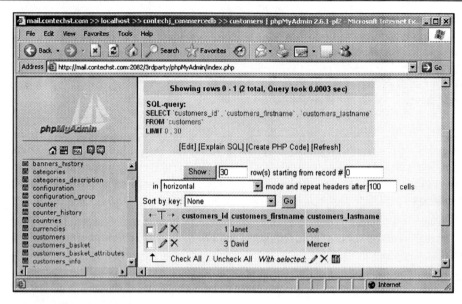

That's all pretty easy to do. Now that you can modify the information contained within the tables, which is more than likely the only operation you should need to perform, what about actually making modifications to the structure of the tables themselves? Well, to view the metadata (or structure) of a table, simply click on the table's name in the left-hand column instead of the icon. This will bring up a page that holds, among other things, field information, index information, space usage, and the ability to run queries against the table.

Recall that in an earlier chapter, we used the EasyPopulate contribution to add information to our database. Well, it is possible to do the same type of thing from phpMyAdmin. Simply create a text file with all the information you need, and run it against the table by using the Insert data from a textfile into table link at the bottom of the table's page. For example, I have decided to add some more publishers to the database. This requires updates to two tables, namely the manufacturers and manufacturers_info tables.

We need two text files that contain the new information, like so:

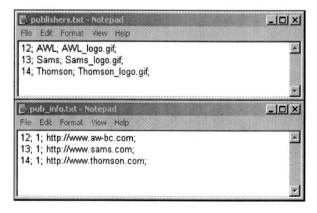

Then we simply click the link, and ensure all the information required by phpMyAdmin is correct in the insert data page, like so:

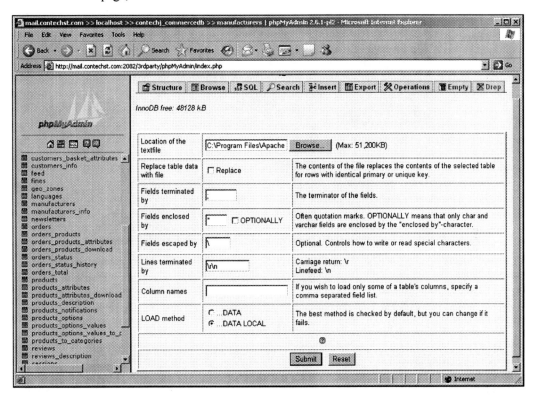

Notice how the structure of the text files relates both to the settings on this page and to the structure of the table itself. If you look at the manufacturers table, you will see that the date fields are allowed to be NULL valued, which is why we could get away with only supplying three values in the first file instead of all five. Assuming that nothing is wrong with your files, clicking on Submit will bring up a confirmation page, which will notify you of how many rows were modified. You can then ensure that the correct changes have taken place by viewing the table.

Let's take a look at the export option available in phpMyAdmin. This is a great piece of functionality, which you can use to back up your database in parts or completely at any time. You can export your entire database by clicking on the Export option on the phpMyAdmin homepage, or you can export individual tables by clicking on Export once you are viewing the table's information page. To be safe, let's try export the entire database...

Go to the phpMyAdmin homepage and click on Export. This will bring up the export options page, which should contain a list of all available databases in the Export text area. Make your selection and leave all other options at their default values, and click on Go. You will find that a large file containing a huge amount of SQL commands is generated—simply save this file in a safe place, and voilà, your entire database is backed up! All you need to do in order to restore this database is click on the SQL icon above the table list in phpMyAdmin, and then click on the import files tab at the top of the pop-up window, which will allow you to browse for the exported file, as shown here:

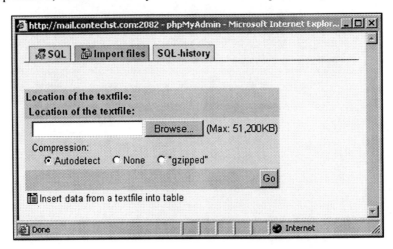

Once you have located the file in question, simply click Go, and all the SQL statements that were created during the export will be run against the database to recreate everything exactly as it was. Apart from working on individual tables, or making backups, it is also possible to view the entire database structure by clicking on the name of the database, which appears above the list of tables in the left-hand column. This will bring up a page that looks something like the following:

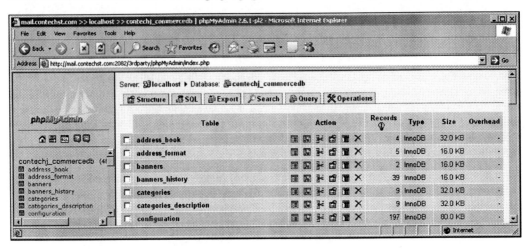

From here you can perform a variety of different actions on each table, including emptying or deleting them entirely, so please be very careful.

Always make sure you have a recent back-up copy of your database or tables before you attempt to modify or delete data.

Notice too that there is a navigation bar above the list of tables, which you should search through in order to familiarize yourself with what is available (you'll find the Search function pretty useful as and when you misplace a record or two). You already know how to create basic SQL queries, but you will find that your ability to create more complex statements is aided by the graphical nature of the phpMyAdmin tool. Any problems you encounter should hopefully be remedied by reading through the documentation, which is supplied with the tool and is available from the homepage.

Here endeth the whistle-stop tour of phpMyAdmin! There is enough functionality in this tool to fill an entire book, so please do make sure that if you have access to this tool you practice enough to become proficient in using it—doing this will ensure you work efficiently in all things to do with data administration.

Tips and Tricks

As with any project, it is always nice to add *finishing touches*. This section will take a look at a grab-bag of different scripts or modifications, which will hopefully add a certain style or flavor to your already fully functional website. It should be stressed that none of these are essential in any way to the working of your site, so if you are in a hurry to get everything up and running, then it may be better to skip ahead to the deployment chapter, which follows.

If your need to begin earning online is not overwhelming, then it will definitely benefit you to take a bit of time to look at what's here. Even if there is nothing you decide to implement yourself, it may give you ideas for your own innovative changes (which hopefully you will share with the community some time).

Low Stock Reports

By default, osCommerce comes with a few reports, which you can use to monitor your site. However, in all likelihood, at some stage you will find you want either better or different reports and report formats. Because of this, it is a good idea to install one of the report contributions, which is useful for maintaining good inventory control by alerting you to the fact that you might have certain products running out.

You know the drill by now, so make a backup of your site and then navigate to http://www.oscommerce.com/community/contributions,1245/ in your browser to obtain a copy of the contribution. While you are there, you may as well browse around the other report contributions to see if there is anything that might also be of use. The low stock reports contribution is pretty simple to install! Follow these steps:

1. Copy the `admin/stats_low_stock.php` contribution file to `admin` on your site.

2. Copy the `admin/includes/languages/english/stats_low_stock.php` contribution file to the `admin/includes/languages/` directory on your site

3. Add the following to `/admin/includes/languages/english.php`:

    ```
    define('BOX_REPORTS_STOCK_LEVEL', 'Low Stock Report');
    ```

4. Edit `/admin/includes/boxes/reports.php` by replacing:

    ```
    '<a href="' . tep_href_link(FILENAME_STATS_CUSTOMERS, '', 'NONSSL') . '"
    class="menuBoxContentLink">' . BOX_REPORTS_ORDERS_TOTAL . '</a>');
    ```

with the following:

```
'<a href="' . tep_href_link(FILENAME_STATS_CUSTOMERS, '', 'NONSSL') . '"
class="menuBoxContentLink">' . BOX_REPORTS_ORDERS_TOTAL . '</a><br>' .
'<a href="' . tep_href_link(FILENAME_STATS_LOW_STOCK, '', 'NONSSL') . '"
class="menuBoxContentLink">' . BOX_REPORTS_STOCK_LEVEL . '</a>');
```

5. Edit `admin/includes/filenames.php` by adding the line:

    ```
    define('FILENAME_STATS_LOW_STOCK', 'stats_low_stock.php');
    ```

That's it, you are all done! Now if you go along to the Reports section in the admin tool, you will notice that you have a new Low Stock Report option, which, if clicked, will bring up the following page:

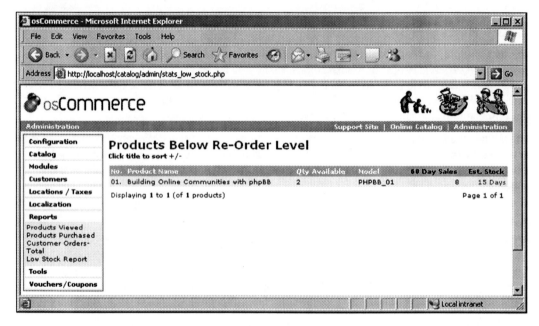

From this screenshot you can see that there is one product that has a stock less than the re-order level, which is set in the Configuration section of the admin tool on the Stock page. Two nice features of this report are that it shows the purchase history of the product for the last 60 days as well as an estimate for the amount of time it will take to deplete the remaining stock. In this case we have made eight sales in the last 60 days, and have about 15 days before we run out of this particular book totally.

Another thing to note is that if you have set up your stock control to allow checkout to go through even if a product is out of stock, then this report can show a negative value for the Qty Available column, meaning that you have these products on back order. Of course, if you have set the Allow Checkout setting to false, then it is not possible to get negative values here.

Working with Downloadable Products

Some of you may have had a nagging feeling that you shouldn't be allowing downloadable products to be downloaded until you actually have the payment in your account. You are obviously quite correct to be worried about this, because as it stands, the default behavior of osCommerce's download functionality will ruin you quite quickly.

Basically, what we want from the store is to only make a download available once a payment (be it PayPal, credit card, or whatever) has a certain order status. Now, what this means is that you need to look closely at all the payment methods you accept, and come up with an integrated policy that will allow you to make a call on whether something is downloadable or not with relative ease.

This probably sounds a bit confusing at the moment. It helps to think about it in terms of how a payment is processed. Recall that in Chapter 7 we used the PayPal IPN payment module to implement payments via PayPal. We had several statuses set for this type of payment, ranging from Denied, Preparing [PayPal IPN], to Processing, and even Delivered. Recall too that while the status was set to Preparing [PayPal IPN], we had not actually received the funds in our account. It was only once we had accepted the funds that the status changed to Processing. It was then left to us to set the status to Delivered manually.

It should be clear to you that we don't want to make the download available when the status of the payment is Denied, or even when it is Preparing [PayPal IPN], because it is likely that the customer can download the product without ever forking out the cash. So in this case, we really want the download to be available only once we have reached the Processing or Delivered status.

Thankfully the Download Controller found at `http://www.oscommerce.com/community/ contributions,135` can be of assistance here.

Installing the Download Controller

There are quite a lot of changes to make to your files, so back everything up now. One of the big problems with using this contribution is that it may well affect other contributions you already have installed. As a result, we have to make the modifications to altered files manually instead of replacing the files entirely.

The following instructions will get the controller working on your setup:

1. Add the following files:
    ```
    /catalog/includes/modules/shipping/freeshipper.php
    /catalog/includes/languages/english/modules/shipping/freeshipper.php
    /catalog/includes/modules/payment/freecharger.php
    /catalog/includes/languages/english/modules/payment/freecharger.php
    /catalog/images/icons/shipping_free_shipper.jpg
    /catalog/languages/english/images/buttons/button_download.gif
    /catalog/includes/functions/downloads_controller.php
    /catalog/includes/functions/webmakers_added_functions.php
    /catalog/includes/languages/webmakers_added_languages.php
    /catalog/includes/languages/english/downloads_controller.php
    /admin/includes/functions/webmakers_added_functions.php
    /admin/includes/languages/english/downloads_controller.php
    ```

2. Edit the following files:
    *   `/catalog/includes/application_top.php`:

Replace the line:
```
// Shopping cart actions
```
with:
```
// BOF: WebMakers.com Added: Functions Library
include(DIR_WS_FUNCTIONS . 'webmakers_added_functions.php');
// EOF: WebMakers.com Added: Functions Library
// Shopping cart actions
```

- /admin/includes/application_top.php:

  Add to the very bottom of the file just before the last ?>:
  ```
  // BOF: WebMakers.com Added: Functions Library
  include(DIR_WS_FUNCTIONS . 'webmakers_added_functions.php');
  // EOF: WebMakers.com Added: Functions Library
  ```

- /catalog/includes/languages/english.php:

  Add to the very bottom of the file just before the last ?>:
  ```
  // BOF: WebMakers.com Added: All Add-Ons
  require(DIR_WS_LANGUAGES . 'webmakers_added_languages.php');
  // EOF: WebMakers.com Added: All Add-Ons
  ```

- /admin/includes/languages/english.php:

  Add to the very bottom of the file just before the last ?>:
  ```
  // BOF: WebMakers.com Added: All Add-Ons
  require(DIR_WS_LANGUAGES . 'webmakers_added_languages.php');
  // EOF: WebMakers.com Added: All Add-Ons
  ```

As well as these edits, you will also need to go through the following list of files and implement the changes between the contribution files and your store's files as shown.

3. Modify the following files by comparing the contribution file with the file in your store, and then incorporating the differences (you may wish to use some sort of comparison software such as Beyond Compare, which you can find at http://www.scootersoftware.com/, for this):

    ```
    /catalog/includes/modules/downloads.php
    /catalog/checkout_process.php
    /catalog/checkout_shipping.php
    /admin/orders.php
    ```

The actual changes aren't going to be listed in the text here because they will take up a fair amount of space and won't mean much to you anyway (you can always look at the files directly if you want to view the code for yourself). You should try to implement the changes, failing which you can view the actual modified files on the demo site.

I will give you the following handy hint though: you will probably get a MySQL error if you don't remove the following line from the contribution's code before you make use of the checkout_process.php file:

```
'comments' => $order->info['comments'],
```

This is because there is no comments column in the orders table. Apart from this, it is a case of going through each of the files in the previous list and carefully making changes or replacements as necessary.

Once that is all completed, it is time to get the contribution up and running so that you can start allowing downloadable products onto your site.

Working with the Download Controller

In order to make the download controller effective, you need to understand how it works. The most important thing to remember here is that a product will be made available depending on the value of its order status. The first thing to do is sort out your order status values by going to Orders Status in the Localization section of the administration tool and adding or removing statuses according to your needs.

Based on the needs of the demo site, the following settings were created by deleting all but Pending, which is the default, and adding the new statuses in order:

```
Command Prompt - mysql -uroot -p commerce_db                       _ □ ×
mysql> select * from orders_status order by orders_status_id;
+------------------+-------------+----------------------+
| orders_status_id | language_id | orders_status_name   |
+------------------+-------------+----------------------+
|                1 |           1 | Pending              |
|                2 |           1 | Denied               |
|                3 |           1 | Preparing [PayPal IPN] |
|                4 |           1 | Processing           |
|                5 |           1 | Delivered            |
|                6 |           1 | Updated              |
+------------------+-------------+----------------------+
6 rows in set (0.00 sec)

mysql>
```

This shows you the command used to display the order statuses that have been saved on the system, using the MySQL client. Depending on what you need, you might decide to use different statuses, or simply different status IDs. As it stands on the demo site, we really want to allow downloads to be made available only for orders that have a status of 4 and above, because all others allow a customer to obtain the download without us first getting payment.

> Note that you will need to recheck the settings of your payment modules if you have just added these statuses to your system now. This is because the modules will probably still be picking up the old status ID values and giving you the wrong status!

In order to tell the download controller that it should only allow downloads based on these criteria, open up /catalog/includes/languages/english/downloads_controller.php and implement the following changes:

```
define('DOWNLOADS_AVAILABLE_STATUS','4');
```

As well as this, we need the Updated status to help the contribution perform a couple of actions needed after updating download settings on an order—the contribution also sends an email to the customer notifying him or her of this. To do this, simply go to /admin/includes/languages/english/downloads_controller.php and implement the following change:

```
define('ORDERS_STATUS_UPDATED_VALUE','6');
```

Obviously, if the order_status_id of your Updated status is not 6, then you would change this to reflect the value you have in your orders table. What this means is that if for some reason a customer had a problem with their downloads and you decided to allow him or her to try download it again, you could update the order status to Updated, and then set it back to whatever status is normal (say Delivered for argument's sake), and the customer would find that they are able to download the product again because the number of days and downloads that are available to the customer are refreshed.

The last thing we should do in order to make things as easy as possible on us is to remember that downloadable products do not weigh anything. If you have a product that is downloadable, then set its weight to 0 when you add it to your catalog. If a product has zero weight, then the shipping charges are not added to the product, which is exactly what you expect.

With everything set up, it is now time to test out the new download contribution.

Testing the Download Controller

The first thing you need to do is add a downloadable product to your database. So, if I wanted to sell an article for download, I would add it as per the instructions in Chapter 4 in the *Download* section, remembering to set the weight to zero. Once this has been done, we need to try to purchase this downloadable product using each and every one of the available payment methods.

For example, the following result was obtained directly after purchasing a downloadable item using PayPal:

This is perfect because the download is not available yet as we hoped. Note the highlighted message at the bottom of the screen, explaining that the download will not be available until we confirm the transaction. In the case of the demo site, the PayPal IPN module needs to set the status to Processing before the customer can download his or her product. This in turn only occurs once we have accepted the PayPal payment in PayPal itself.

Of course, you can set your downloads to deal with purchases however you see fit. There is quite a bit more to the download controller contribution that we don't have time to cover here since it has already provided us with what we initially needed it for. It is left to the reader to poke around and find out what else there is.

PayPal Trouble?

This section has been added because if you're like me, you might have experienced an infuriating niggle with regards to receiving PayPal payments. At some stage during testing, I noticed that instead of being returned to the `checkout_success.php` page after a successful purchase, the browser was directed to the log-in page. What's worse, if I logged in as the same customer, my shopping cart was still full, which would be terribly confusing for customers who were under the impression they had just paid for goods. Obviously not a good situation to have...

What in the world could be wrong with osCommerce? Actually, the answer is, "Nothing!" In this instance, osCommerce is actually working perfectly. The problem comes from using the button provided by PayPal, which returns the customer's browser back from PayPal to the osCommerce store. For some reason, it destroys the query string part of the URL by appending its own name. What does this mean?

Well, the target URL given in the page's source code (which you can view by clicking on View | Source in your browser) is something like this: `http://www.contechst.com/catalog/ checkout_process.php?oscsid=2dg33kffiuhfr435j55jmr9r`, which is perfectly correct. The idea behind returning the URL with the session ID in the query string (the query string part of the URL is everything after the question mark), is so that osCommerce can check whether the request for the page is being made by someone who has logged in and so on. Cutting and pasting this URL into your browser will result in the correct `checkout_success.php` page being displayed.

So why is this not getting through when the customer clicks on Return to Merchant (or in our case, Click here for email confirmation of order!)? If you are sneaky and add a bit of code to the top of the `checkout_process.php` file, then you might afford yourself a glance at what is being passed back to osCommerce by PayPal instead. In my case, I wrote the following:

```
if(!isset($_GET['oscsid'])){
   print_r ($HTTP_SERVER_VARS);
   die();
}
```

This simply tells osCommerce to print out all the server variables that are hanging around and die. Lo and behold, I noticed that instead of having a query string like:

```
?oscsid=2dg33kffiuhfr435j55jmr9r
```

I had something like this:

```
?=Click+here+for+email+confirmation+of+order
```

Oh dear! This is a bit embarrassing. For some reason PayPal is appending the value of the button to the query string instead of leaving the `oscsid` in place. This explains why the customer was redirected to the login page—osCommerce wasn't being passed a session ID, so it simply referred the customer to log in.

What can we do about this? Luckily for us, we don't have to use the GET request method, which is the one used here by default. I tried using the POST method, and to my delight everything worked out just fine—in other words, the session ID, `oscsid`, remains intact. The solution, assuming you are suffering from this problem too, is to add the following line to the PayPal IPN module:

```
$parameters['rm'] = '2';
```

Your paypal_ipn.php code should look like this:

```
    $parameters['cancel_return'] = tep_href_link(FILENAME_CHECKOUT_PAYMENT,
'', 'SSL');
    $parameters['bn'] = $this->identifier;
$parameters['cbt'] = 'Click here for email confirmation of your order';
$parameters['rm'] = '2';
```

I am not sure why PayPal has done things the way it has. Hopefully by the time you read this, PayPal will have sorted it out and the payments will work without hassle. What this section has demonstrated however, is that you should be aware of the fact that errors can be introduced outside of your application, even if those errors come from entities which provide an otherwise excellent and reliable service.

Regardless, I am sure you will be glad to have this information at hand if something similar ever goes amiss again...

Dynamic Box Headers

Sometimes, it is quite striking to add unassuming animations to your page—although you must be careful not to constantly distract the customer. In this case, I wanted to give the site a kind of *being built as you browse* feel. To this end, I added a little GIF animation to the info box headers, which makes it look like they are hurriedly being painted red as the page loads. This is a bit of a gimmick, so you may prefer not to do something like this, or you may prefer to use your imagination and come up with something totally new.

Whatever you choose to do, remember to keep the file sizes very, very small, so that you don't slow down browsing appreciably. Another important point is to remember not to overdo gimmicks, especially if your market is likely to be sophisticated people who aren't impressed by cheap tricks. Doing something like this will suit a fun-loving, younger audience.

The first thing to do is create your animated GIF file. For this, I used Paint Shop Pro's Animation Shop, as shown here:

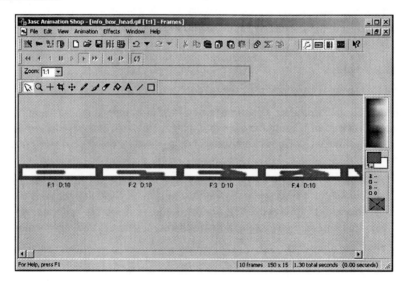

Of course, you want to make the size of the image fit the area of the screen exactly, and preferably only use a few colors to keep the size down. You can see from the consecutive images in the screenshot that the GIF file will simply paint the background from transparent (it must be transparent so that the image doesn't make your site look un-neat by initially being a different color from the background) to the standard red of the information box headings.

This file is tested and then saved in the images folder as info_box_head.gif, following which we simply need to modify the stylesheet setting to reflect our required output as follows:

```
TD.infoBoxHeading {
    font-family: Verdana, Arial, sans-serif;
    font-size: 10px;
    font-weight: bold;
    /*
    background: #FF2626; */
    background-image: url(images/info_box_head.gif);
    color: #ffffff;
}
```

Now, when each page is loaded, there is a half-second where the info box headings appear to be quickly painted in, before the animation stops and the customer can browse as normal. It's as easy as that! The real trick comes in finding something that has relevance and/or meaning with regards to your specific site, and doesn't become irritating or distracting for your customers. Provided you can do that, you should have a great time playing around and experimenting with different methods of animating your site.

Creating Matching Buttons

Many of you will want to change the style of the buttons that are provided with osCommerce by default. If you do want to create your own set of buttons, then there is a good way and a bad way to go about it. The most important thing to do is simply create a button template, and once you have it, keep it safe and make sure it is never modified. If you need to create a new button, make a copy of this template, and write on it the new word that describes the button's function.

Recall that when we added in the CCGV community contribution, we ended up having buttons dissimilar to the default ones we installed earlier. Well, you might find you run into this sort of problem quite often, so it really pays to develop your own button template, which you can then easily use to create whatever new buttons you require.

For example, some of you might like a plain old rectangle button, which looks nice and neat. If that's the case, then simply create a rectangle of the desired dimension, give it a border, and buttonize it. Whatever other effects you decide to add later on, you can. For example, the following button template was created and then included in the includes\languages\english\ images\buttons folder:

Now, the only thing that you need to do is create a copy for each type of button you need, add the appropriate text in using whatever font, style, or color you like, and save it with the correct name so that osCommerce picks it up. The following example shows the button template being used for the Continue button on the login page, button_continue.gif, like so:

Remember too that you need to ensure that your buttons' file sizes are small—anything over 2kb, and it's probably too big. I'm sure you can come up with a better template yourself, and it's definitely worthwhile doing so in order to realize your site's own look and feel—it's also really fun! One thing to keep in mind is that you should keep your template in .bmp format or whatever is best for you, so that you can work with, and resize, the image properly. If you save the template as a GIF file, your options are limited, especially if you need to resize or create special effects.

If you want to be fancy, you might consider animating the buttons using Flash, but this isn't necessary, and sometimes ends up making the site look gaudy—it's really up to you!

Summary

Having finished this chapter you are now able to effectively manage and implement an advertising campaign using banner ads. This of course is not the end of the story, and we will discuss what advertising and marketing policies will be most effective for you, and how to then implement and integrate those policies into your website in the final chapter on advanced issues.

We also looked briefly at phpMyAdmin, an important tool in the fight to maintain accurate and relevant data. Since this tool is used almost everywhere, there is a high probability that you will come into contact with it during the course of running your online business. This chapter has shown enough of how the tool works for you to get a good grounding and move from there to mastering the tool and effectively managing your data.

Finally, we did a bit of fun stuff, creating small animations, working on button templates, and so on. This part of web development is always great fun for the creatively minded entrepreneur, but don't get too carried away and end up with a gimmicky store. Remember that you should only ever incorporate those things that actually add value in some quantifiable way.

Not only has this chapter finished off the discussion on tools, and provided you with a few handy hints for further development, but it has also rounded off the development phase of your online store. By now you should pretty much be able to do whatever it is you wish in terms of adding and removing pictures, boxes, writing, buttons, banners, and so on. There is one last major hurdle to overcome before your site can begin raking in some well-earned cash—deployment!

11
Deployment and Maintenance

The big day has finally arrived! By the end of this chapter your site goes live, and only a few minor deployment issues now stand in between you and the millions of online customers out there. Well, actually that's not quite true. Making sure you deploy your store properly is quite an involved process and you really need to keep your thinking cap on over the course of this chapter. To qualify this last statement, I should make it clear that there's nothing particularly complex about deployment, it's just that you need to keep on top of a lot of different issues. Making silly errors at this stage can have dramatic effects on the final product because we are dealing mainly with configuration issues when we deploy a fully developed application. Of course, making errors is not the end of the world, because we are going to test everything very thoroughly.

It seems a bit unfair that you can have a perfectly working site on your development machine, but a miasma of problems rear their ugly heads after deployment. Well, as you should know by now, the worst of the problems can be avoided entirely by following a proper process. For this reason, this chapter will look at each step in the process, and highlight important points to consider along the way. Don't be too worried about the *miasma of problems* thing too much. Sure, problems *can* occur, but it's a given that you have followed a good development process and that your site should be well designed and robust, which is about the best starting point you can hope for.

At first glance, deploying an online store like osCommerce has got to be pretty easy—it's just a case of copying the `catalog` folder over to the new server! Or is it? Actually, there are a number of concerns that go hand in hand with ensuring everything goes smoothly during the transfer. What about security, for example? If you transfer across all your files using FTP, there's a chance someone might intercept the information and read usernames and passwords out of the configuration files. The database will also have to be rebuilt exactly as it is on the development machine—I'm sure that since most of you have spent some time configuring everything and populating tables, you'll be anxious to not have to do everything all over again. Apart from this, there are the connection parameters and security settings to think about…

Because of the large number of steps to perform during the deployment process, we will do something slightly different in this chapter, and present a few checklists towards the end of each section to allow you to tick off the most important tasks, which will make things easier. Be warned, however, that it's not possible to discuss *every* little issue that could crop up over *all* the different deployment situations, so you'll still have to do plenty of your own testing.

Specifically, the chapter looks at how to:

- Get everything ready for deployment
- Transfer the files to their new home
- Set up the site, including the database
- Test everything thoroughly

Once all the deployment issues have been covered, we will look at what type of administrative tasks you can expect to perform over the course of running an e-commerce site, as well as how to best maintain a healthy online store. Chins up, we're nearly at the end; and it hasn't been all that bad, has it? I for one might just jump on the bandwagon and become an online retailer myself!

Getting Ready to Deploy

First things first! Are you sure you are completely happy with your site as it is? While it is not a huge problem to make modifications to your site after deployment, there is no point in making things hard for yourself by having to recode some pages or make design changes then, when you can get them done now. If everything is in order, then we can begin with the preparation process.

Preparation comes in three stages. First, we need to ensure that we have a nice, clean, working version of the site. We also need a nice, clean, working copy of the database, and finally, a nice, clean file system ready for the files on the host site. Once you have all three, read on…

Make Sure the Host is Ready

Intuitively enough, the first thing to do is to make sure you have an adequate host. By this I mean you have a host on which you can create a MySQL database, and which allows access to the file system, and whatever other goodies you think you may need. To make your life easy, you should also ensure that you have an FTP account available so that you can transfer files across to the host file system. More often than not, you should be able to log on to your FTP account with your administrator's username and password automatically. If you're not sure what all this is about, then try the following URL in your browser (assuming your browser supports FTP):

```
ftp://ftp.your_domain_name.com
```

If you are prompted for a password or are shown the contents of your home directory, then congratulations, you have an FTP account. If you don't have one, then you should consider getting your host to give you one, or finding out from them how they upload files. Incidentally, instead of being prompted for your username and password every time you use your FTP account, you might want to send them in the URL, like so:

```
ftp://username:password@hostname/
```

If you're worried about security (by this I mean: you *are* worried about security), then it's best to leave out the password and simply pass the username, because otherwise this can cause security problems if URLs are logged in a non-secure place. Remember that this information is already being passed in an unencrypted format. If you wish to do everything securely, you should speak to your host about how to secure file transfers.

Now, once you have made sure there is somewhere to upload your osCommerce files too, and something to do it with, you need to create a database. Goodness only knows how many different ways this can be done in, so I will demonstrate on the demo site's hosting package how a database is created for use by our store. Hopefully the process you follow will be quite similar. If you get stuck, get help from your host's support team; that's what they are there for.

The demo site has an interface for MySQL database creation, like this (you might find that your host provides our good friend phpMyAdmin):

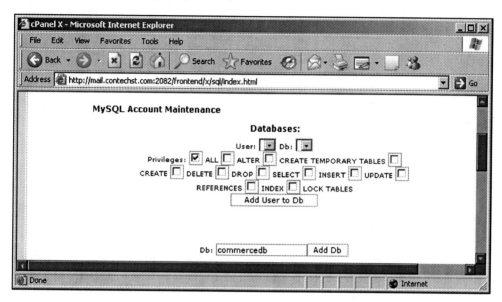

Entering a database name and clicking Add Db brings up a confirmation page. Now we have a database to work with, so we're getting somewhere. Of course, we need to specify a user for this database, but in doing so, let's not forget the security lessons we learned—think closely about the types of permissions we are going to eventually set. The following user is created and then added to the commercedb database:

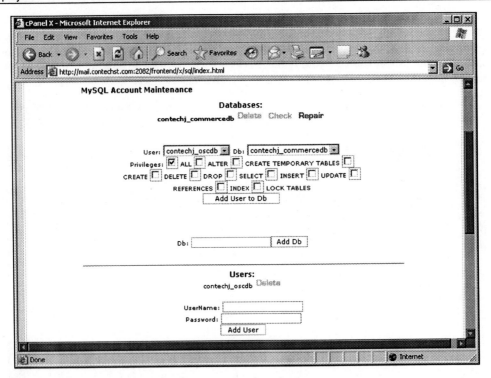

For the purposes of installing the database, we will temporarily allow this user All privileges to the databases. Once all the tables are properly installed, we can reduce the privileges to only those that are needed by osCommerce to operate.

> Notice in the previous screenshot that the host automatically prepends something (in this case contechj_) to the user and database names. Your host will likely do this too. If so, make a note of it, as you will need this when configuring your connection variables in osCommerce.

Perfect! We now have everything set up on the host server, so let's look at the files on our development machine and ensure they are fit to be transferred across to the host.

Get the Files Ready

Before you do anything, you will need to make a master copy of the site before deployment. Make sure you zip up the exact version you send across and save it somewhere safe—preferably onto a disk that you can hold somewhere. This copy then represents the version you will work on if you need to make any major modifications to your site in the future (assuming you haven't modified the online version to such an extent that you need to use it as the new development copy). Before you do that, though, you may as well clean up the catalog folder properly so that you don't end up saving erroneous files.

If you're like me, then you probably create backups of all the files you modify as you work. As far as Windows machines go, they will place the backup files, denoted by `.bak`, in the same folder as the original file. If this is the case, then you probably have a ton of backup files lying around the place. Make a backup of your `catalog` folder before deleting anything, just to be safe. Then remove all backup files from the osCommerce folders.

While it might seem a bit excessive to do this at the moment, there are a couple of good reasons for it. First, having any sort of unused files lying around on your host file system is poor security practice. Second, why clutter up your brand new installation with files you don't need? You will find that it is a constant battle to keep everything neat and tidy as you go anyway—so start as you mean to go on. Finally, if you have worked on a lot of files over the course of the development phase, you are adding a lot of unnecessary size to the upload.

Once you have swept osCommerce clean of backup files, you should move on to any other type of erroneous file. Figuring on the top of the list of types of files to be removed are unused scripts. During development, you might have written a few scripts to help perform certain tasks, or downloaded extra code to help with development. These scripts, which you no longer need, must not be left lying around—again, for security reasons. Other types of files to look out for are unused image files, which are generally quite large; you don't want to upload a whole bunch of useless images, which take up disk space and increase upload time. If you are not using all the default languages, then you don't need to hold on to all the other language files either, so you can get rid of those too at this stage (remember to remove them from the Localization | Languages section of the admin tool too).

Next, open up the configuration files and remove all usernames and passwords. As you can probably deduce, your current database name and password will change to the ones you set in the previous section, but there is no point in transferring any type of sensitive information like this—especially since people often prefer to use the same username and password for a variety of things. While these usernames and passwords may not be of any use for your osCommerce database connection, they might be the same ones you use for your banking, and it would be a disaster if someone found them. I take it, you don't use the same username and password for more than one site, right?

The two main files you should look at cleaning up are the two `configure.php` files—one in `catalog/includes/` and the other in `admin/includes/`. If you have any other sensitive information in other files, consider removing that for the time being too. I suppose I should point out that this security precaution is only of value if you have a secure connection to your server over which you can edit files. Otherwise, you may as well send everything through as is, because you would only have to perform your settings over a non-secure connection anyway.

While this next task is not entirely necessary, you may as well do it here; you will need to work on it once the files have been transferred anyway. Remove any `.htaccess` files that you have set up, because they will not work on the new file system. If you don't remove them now, or at least edit them so that they don't require authentication for access, then you could be letting yourself in for a hair-pulling, teeth-gnashing time if the `.htaccess` files do require authentication and reference a password in a file that is not on the host server. See Chapter 8 for more information on `.htaccess`.

Once this is done, you just have to add one more file (discussed in the next section) and you can then make a master, compressed copy of osCommerce—call it RTP (Release to Public) or something similar to distinguish it from other versions. If you are working on a Linux box, you can tar and gzip your files if you wish—it will obviously help with the upload time. If you are developing on Windows, then you might want to make sure that your host can unzip .zip files since they will be using a Linux server—there shouldn't be a problem, however. In the unlikely event that there is, the best thing to do is download and install a gzip utility for Windows at http://www.gzip.org/, which you can then use to zip up your files in the .gz format.

Get the Database Ready

As it stands, the database holds plenty of configuration information as well as product and customer information. You might find that the dummy customers you have used for testing are no longer necessary, or that you don't want the 35 purchases you made of one item during testing, to feature on the site. If this is the case, you should consider getting rid of any data that you know will be unnecessary. There's no hard and fast rule here; just make sure you don't delete anything without first making a backup.

Talking of backups, that is really the main point of this section. In order to deploy your database, you will need to make a backup of it. It is this backup file that is then transferred across to the host site and used to create a new database there. There are several ways to go about this. One way would be to download phpMyAdmin and use the export facilities, which were discussed in the last chapter. Alternatively, if you don't want to download and install new software, you can use the database-backup facility provided by osCommerce in the Tools section of the administration tool. Recall you were shown how to use this in Chapter 8 on *Securing Your Store*. Since you already have all the information you need regarding phpMyAdmin and the database backup tool provided by osCommerce, we will look at a third method here.

If you want a bit more flexibility in the way you create backups, then the mysqldump utility is what you need. It is important to look over this tool because it provides you with a great deal of flexibility in how you store database or table information. For example, you might not want to transfer data at all, and might just wish to transfer a database's (or specific table's) structure. Using this tool makes it easy, and you are referred to the documentation for more information on how to go about it.

mysqldump is held in the bin directory of your MySQL installation, so if you have set your PATH variable accordingly, you can access it from anywhere on the command line. If not, simply use the command line to navigate to the relevant directory and then perform the following:

```
C:\> mysqldump --help
```

This will print out a whole list of useful help topics should you be inclined to learn about how to use the utility—it's probably useful to do so because you may well need it in future. If you are simply interested in creating a usable backup copy of the database, then type in the following command (remember to swap the username and password for your own values):

```
C:\> mysqldump -u username --password=p4ssw0rd > livestore_backup.sql
```

This command will create the livestore_backup.sql file in your current directory. You should open this file up to confirm that it has been created and contains a ton of SQL commands to re-create your database on the other side. Whichever way you choose to create you database backup, make sure that it is held within your osCommerce file structure somewhere where you will find it again. The most logical place is in the `admin/backups/` folder of course, but anywhere will do provided you can find it again.

With that, you are now ready to begin transferring files across to your host.

Transfer the Files

You should now have a final, clean version of your online store all zipped up and ready to go. Assuming you have images and a fair bit of data held within your site, you can be sure that the size of the upload is quite substantial. For this reason, you need a reasonably high speed connection—dial-up connections can be slightly erratic over long periods of time, so it may even be worth using a friend's computer or your office connection to send the files to the host site.

By far the easiest method would be to use a native upload feature from your host's file manager over a quick connection. If this is available to you, simply use it to upload the archive file across to the host server. Alternatively, assuming your site has an FTP account enabled, the following two methods represent a quick and painless method of uploading files with FTP.

FTP Drag and Drop

Windows users can open up the host file system using Windows Explorer or Internet Explorer and simply drag the `catalog .zip` folder from their file systems over to the host site, as shown here:

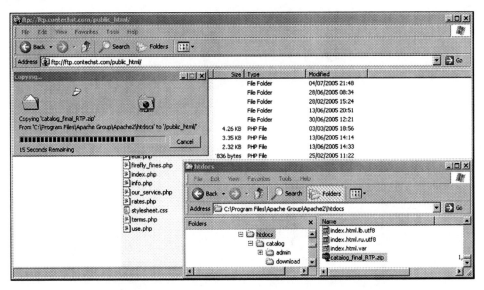

There are a few things to note about the above screenshot. First, even though you can't see it, I had to log on using my administrator's username and password. You should make sure that anonymous FTP access to your file system is disabled. In fact, once everything has been deployed and is up and running satisfactorily, you should disable your FTP account altogether until you need to make use of it again. Second, you can see that the file is being copied to the `public_html` folder. This will give the `catalog` folder a web address of `http://www.domain.com/catalog` once it is extracted on the other side.

The final point to note is that I had an estimate of about a minute for the total transfer time. This transfer was done over an ADSL line, which is fairly fast—if you don't zip the files up, you can expect a seriously long upload time because the FTP utility has to create all the files and folders itself on the destination server. Remember, that it's not only the speed of the connection, but also the speed of the FTP utility being used, that can affect upload times.

FTP Utility

Not everyone will be able to do things this way, so for those of you who cannot make use of drag and drop facilities, the next thing to do is make sure you have an FTP client. Linux and Windows machines all ship with one by default, so simply open up a command shell and type in:

```
C:\> ftp --help
```

This should bring up a help file, which you can browse over to get a feel for things. Now, this utility works in a fairly intuitive manner. You need to make a connection to the host, and then tell the FTP utility to send over the files you want to upload. This can be achieved in a number of ways depending on the type of FTP utility you are using—some have graphical interfaces and others don't. For the purposes of this chapter, we'll simply look at the command-line version. To log on to your site, simply enter the host name, username, and password (which should be required), as shown here:

```
Command Prompt - ftp www.contechst.com
C:\>ftp www.contechst.com
Connected to www.contechst.com.
220 ProFTPD 1.2.10 Server (ftp.contechst.com) [10.0.0.185]
User (www.contechst.com:(none)): contec
331 Password required for contec.
Password:
230 User contec logged in.
ftp>
```

Once you have made a connection you can simply upload the archive file to the site using the commands as shown here (these may differ depending on how your FTP utility works):

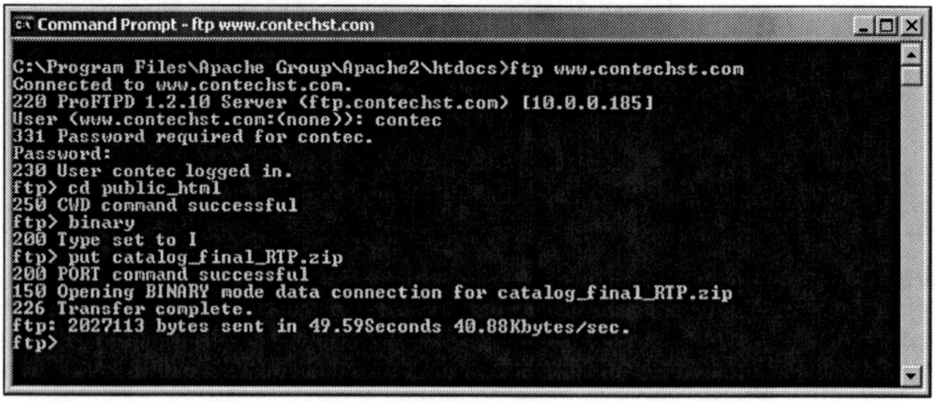

```
Command Prompt - ftp www.contechst.com
C:\Program Files\Apache Group\Apache2\htdocs>ftp www.contechst.com
Connected to www.contechst.com.
220 ProFTPD 1.2.10 Server (ftp.contechst.com) [10.0.0.185]
User (www.contechst.com:(none)): contec
331 Password required for contec.
Password:
230 User contec logged in.
ftp> cd public_html
250 CWD command successful
ftp> binary
200 Type set to I
ftp> put catalog_final_RIP.zip
200 PORT command successful
150 Opening BINARY mode data connection for catalog_final_RIP.zip
226 Transfer complete.
ftp: 2027113 bytes sent in 49.59Seconds 40.88Kbytes/sec.
ftp>
```

You can see that we have done the following:

- Logged on to the FTP account by supplying a username and password.
- Changed the remote working directory to `public_html`; this is where we would like the file to be uploaded to.
- Set the transfer type to `binary`, because we are uploading a `.zip` file and not a plain text file (which would use `ascii`).

Your FTP client will then let you know how things turn out, and from the screenshot you can see we get a report of success. The files have been transferred without a hitch. So far so good...

Before we move back to the host site and begin unzipping files, setting up permissions, configuring the database, and a whole host of other things, it's worth quickly looking at one other method for getting your files across to your host.

FrontPage Extensions

If you are really struggling to get this working and you are a Windows user, then check whether your host site has FrontPage extensions installed. If it does, then try the following:

1. Open up FrontPage and create a new Empty Web.
2. Clear out any folders that FrontPage adds, so that this Web is totally empty.
3. Click on File/Import.
4. Click on Add Folder, select the `catalog` folder, and click OK.

This will import the entire site into your new FrontPage Web. Once this is done, you need to ensure that your host site has FrontPage extensions enabled (not just installed)—it's usually just a case of clicking Enable FrontPage Extensions from your administrator panel. If that's done, then simply click on File/Publish Web, and you should get something like the following screenshot, once you have selected the destination to be published (of the form `http://www.domain_name.com`):

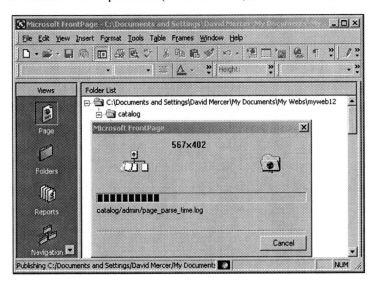

If everything goes according to plan, FrontPage will report the following:

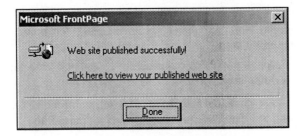

There is little point in looking too closely at the published website because nothing is going to work properly at the moment. However, from the point of view of transferring files, we have been successful. Remember to disable FrontPage extensions as soon as you are done using them, if you have used this method. As well as this, you might need to fiddle around with some .htaccess files, as FrontPage tends to do a lot of things itself, and this can mess up your authentication. It is recommended that you try to get the FTP installation working before resorting to FrontPage. Now we need to go back to the host site to set everything up.

Setting Up the Site

At this stage, you should have a working database and be aware of what the username and password are for that database. You also have your archive file uploaded to the host site, or alternatively, you should have everything installed via FrontPage. We'll leave the FrontPage people for a moment, as the archive people have a quick job to do in order to catch up first.

Set Up the Files

First thing's first, you will need to extract the archive file to your public_html folder. Clicking on it in your file manager should bring up the option to do just this, as shown here on the demo site's file manager:

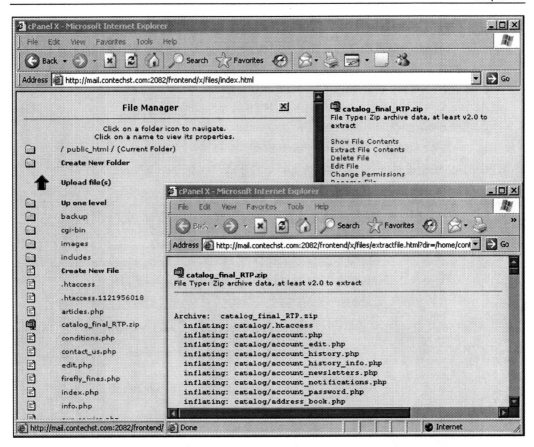

With these files extracted, you should now have a replica of the development machine `catalog` folder on your host's site. Check this by browsing through the `catalog` folder on the live site. You should also find that if you attempt to browse one of the pages from a web browser, you no longer get a page-not-found error, but some other type of error—most likely a MySQL error because we don't have a database connection yet.

> If you find that you are being prompted for a password when browsing the `catalog` folder, but no matter what you enter you aren't given access to the page, then the problem most probably lies in the `.htaccess` files that you have ported over to the site. Remove `.htaccess` from the `catalog` and `catalog/admin` folders for the time being, and try again.

Now that we have the `catalog` folder freshly installed, let's install the database.

Set Up the Database

If you have access to phpMyAdmin on your host site, then open it up and follow along:

1. In the left-hand panel on the phpMyAdmin home page, click on the name of the database you installed earlier.

2. In the new page that opens up, click on the SQL tab along the top.

3. Click Browse under the Location of Textfile option.

4. Locate the file you would like to run against the database, and click Go.

If all goes according to plan, you should get something like the following page:

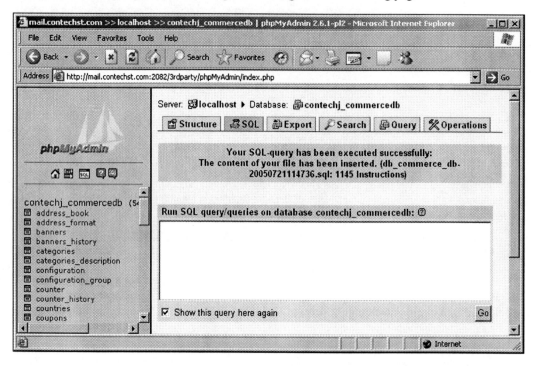

From here you can peruse all the new tables and confirm that everything has been set up as it should be. Notice that I used the backup file created by osCommerce here, and not the sqldump created by MySQL. The reason for this is that at first, the following error cropped up:

```
✕ Error

SQL-query:

CREATE TABLE `address_book` (
  `address_book_id` INT( 11 ) NOT NULL AUTO_INCREMENT ,
  `customers_id` INT( 11 ) NOT NULL DEFAULT '0',
  `entry_gender` CHAR( 1 ) NOT NULL DEFAULT '',
  `entry_company` VARCHAR( 32 ) DEFAULT NULL ,
  `entry_firstname` VARCHAR( 32 ) NOT NULL DEFAULT '',
  `entry_lastname` VARCHAR( 32 ) NOT NULL DEFAULT '',
  `entry_street_address` VARCHAR( 64 ) NOT NULL DEFAULT '',
  `entry_suburb` VARCHAR( 32 ) DEFAULT NULL ,
  `entry_postcode` VARCHAR( 10 ) NOT NULL DEFAULT '',
  `entry_city` VARCHAR( 32 ) NOT NULL DEFAULT '',
  `entry_state` VARCHAR( 32 ) DEFAULT NULL ,
  `entry_country_id` INT( 11 ) NOT NULL DEFAULT '0',
  `entry_zone_id` INT( 11 ) NOT NULL DEFAULT '0',
  PRIMARY KEY ( `address_book_id` ) ,
  KEY `idx_address_book_customers_id` ( `customers_id` )
) ENGINE = INNODB DEFAULT CHARSET = latin1
```

MySQL said: ⓧ

```
#1064 - You have an error in your SQL syntax.  Check the manual that corresponds to
your MySQL server version for the right syntax to use near 'DEFAULT CHARSET=latin1'
at line 17
```

This problem arises because of the phrase DEFAULT CHARSET=latin1, which causes problems because *earlier* versions of MySQL used latin1. You can either specify the default character set to be utf8 when you use the mysqldump utility (with the --default-character-set=utf8 option), or alternatively, run a simple search and replace of the .sql file to remove all occurrences of the offending phrase and then it will work like a charm. Despite this little hiccup, it is still recommended that you get to know your way around the mysqldump utility because of the power and flexibility it provides.

Configure the Site

With the database in place, go back to your two configure.php files in the catalog/includes/ and admin/includes/ folders and alter them according to your setup. This section will list the two configure.php files as they are for the demo site. They have been tested for the demo site, and should work with only minor modifications on your site. The demo site's configuration file in the catalog/includes/ folder looks like this (comments in the script have been wrapped for better readability):

```php
<?php
/*
  osCommerce, Open Source E-Commerce Solutions
  http://www.oscommerce.com

  Copyright (c) 2003 osCommerce

  Released under the GNU General Public License
```

```
*/
// Define the webserver and path parameters
// * DIR_FS_* = Filesystem directories (local/physical)
// * DIR_WS_* = Webserver directories (virtual/URL)
  define('HTTP_SERVER', 'http://www.contechst.com');
  // eg, http://localhost - should not be empty for productive servers
  define('HTTPS_SERVER', 'https://www.contechst.com');
  // eg, https://localhost - should not be empty for productive servers
  define('ENABLE_SSL', 'true'); // secure webserver for checkout procedure?
  define('HTTP_COOKIE_DOMAIN', 'www.contechst.com');
  define('HTTPS_COOKIE_DOMAIN', 'www.contechst.com');
  define('HTTP_COOKIE_PATH', '/catalog/');
  define('HTTPS_COOKIE_PATH', '/catalog/');
  define('DIR_WS_HTTP_CATALOG', '/catalog/');
  define('DIR_WS_HTTPS_CATALOG', '/catalog/');
  define('DIR_WS_IMAGES', 'images/');
  define('DIR_WS_ICONS', DIR_WS_IMAGES . 'icons/');
  define('DIR_WS_INCLUDES', 'includes/');
  define('DIR_WS_BOXES', DIR_WS_INCLUDES . 'boxes/');
  define('DIR_WS_FUNCTIONS', DIR_WS_INCLUDES . 'functions/');
  define('DIR_WS_CLASSES', DIR_WS_INCLUDES . 'classes/');
  define('DIR_WS_MODULES', DIR_WS_INCLUDES . 'modules/');
  define('DIR_WS_LANGUAGES', DIR_WS_INCLUDES . 'languages/');
  define('STORE_SESSIONS', 'mysql');
  define('DIR_WS_DOWNLOAD_PUBLIC', 'pub/');
  define('DIR_FS_CATALOG', '/home/contechj/public_html/catalog/');
  define('DIR_FS_DOWNLOAD', DIR_FS_CATALOG . 'download/');
  define('DIR_FS_DOWNLOAD_PUBLIC', DIR_FS_CATALOG . 'pub/');

// define our database connection
  define('DB_SERVER', 'localhost');
  // eg, localhost - should not be empty for productive servers
  define('DB_SERVER_USERNAME', 'contechj_oscdb');
  define('DB_SERVER_PASSWORD', '********');
  define('DB_DATABASE', 'contechj_commercedb');
  define('USE_PCONNECT', 'true'); // use persistent connections?
  define('STORE_SESSIONS', 'mysql'); // leave empty '' for default handler or
set to 'mysql'
?>
```

The highlighted code in the previous script shows the main settings that are relevant to the file's new environment. The HTTP and HTTPS servers have both been defined along with the fully qualified path to the catalog folder on the file system. Of course, the most important settings show that the new database names and passwords have been put into effect.

> If you have found that you are unable to enforce the use of cookies on your site without the browser being redirected to the default cookie error page, then in all likelihood this is because you have not entered your cookie domain correctly. The previous code listing shows the correct cookie domain for the post-deployment demo site.

You will need to do the same sort of thing for the admin tool too. The configure.php file for the admin tool looks like this (comments in the script have been wrapped for better readability):

```
<?php
/*
  osCommerce, Open Source E-Commerce Solutions
  http://www.oscommerce.com

  Copyright (c) 2003 osCommerce
```

```
        Released under the GNU General Public License
    */

    // Define the webserver and path parameters
    // * DIR_FS_* = Filesystem directories (local/physical)
    // * DIR_WS_* = Webserver directories (virtual/URL)
      define('HTTP_SERVER', 'https://www.contechst.com');
      // eg, http://localhost - should not be empty for productive servers
      define('HTTP_CATALOG_SERVER', 'http://www.contechst.com/catalog');
      define('HTTPS_CATALOG_SERVER', 'https://www.contechst.com/catalog');
      define('ENABLE_SSL_CATALOG', 'true'); // secure webserver for catalog module
      define('DIR_FS_DOCUMENT_ROOT', '/home/contechj/public_html/');
      // where the pages are located on the server
      define('DIR_WS_ADMIN', '/catalog/admin/'); // absolute path required
      define('DIR_FS_ADMIN', '/home/contechj/public_html/catalog/admin/');
      // absolute pate required
      define('DIR_WS_CATALOG', '/catalog/'); // absolute path required
      define('DIR_FS_CATALOG', '/home/contechj/public_html/catalog/');
      // absolute path required
      define('DIR_WS_IMAGES', 'images/');
      define('DIR_WS_ICONS', DIR_WS_IMAGES . 'icons/');
      define('DIR_WS_CATALOG_IMAGES', DIR_WS_CATALOG . 'images/');
      define('DIR_WS_INCLUDES', 'includes/');
      define('DIR_WS_BOXES', DIR_WS_INCLUDES . 'boxes/');
      define('DIR_WS_FUNCTIONS', DIR_WS_INCLUDES . 'functions/');
      define('DIR_WS_CLASSES', DIR_WS_INCLUDES . 'classes/');
      define('DIR_WS_MODULES', DIR_WS_INCLUDES . 'modules/');
      define('DIR_WS_LANGUAGES', DIR_WS_INCLUDES . 'languages/');
      define('DIR_WS_CATALOG_LANGUAGES', DIR_WS_CATALOG . 'includes/languages/');
      define('DIR_FS_CATALOG_LANGUAGES', DIR_FS_CATALOG . 'includes/languages/');
      define('DIR_FS_CATALOG_IMAGES', DIR_FS_CATALOG . 'images/');
      define('DIR_FS_CATALOG_MODULES', DIR_FS_CATALOG . 'includes/modules/');
      define('DIR_FS_BACKUP', DIR_FS_ADMIN . 'backups/');

    // define our database connection
      define('DB_SERVER', 'localhost');
      // eg, localhost - should not be empty for productive servers
      define('DB_SERVER_USERNAME', 'contechj_oscdb');
      define('DB_SERVER_PASSWORD', '********');
      define('DB_DATABASE', 'contechj_commercedb');
      define('USE_PCONNECT', 'true'); // use persistent connections?
      define('STORE_SESSIONS', 'mysql');
      // leave empty '' for default handler or set to 'mysql'
    ?>
```

Once you have set your configuration settings appropriately for your site, you can save the files and then try browsing some pages on your site. With a bit of luck you will see everything more or less as it was on the development machine. If that is the case, take heart that you are on the right track. However, the battle is far from over.

An Interesting Problem

For those of you who have problems at this stage, read what error messages you receive very carefully and try to track down what the problem is from there. If you are getting a database error, then more than likely one or more of your configuration values are incorrect. Some of you may not even know you have problems because everything seems to be A-OK! Well, that's just what we are going to find out in the next section, when we test everything thoroughly. Just in case you are curious, the first time I browsed the catalog folder I got this result:

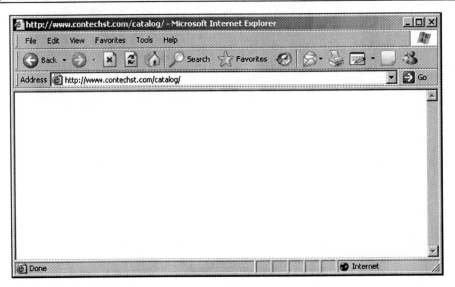

Can you work out why? It took me a little while to figure it out—what had me stumped was that while nothing was showing up on the screen, there were no errors being reported either. The answer will follow in the next section, but use your imagination and think why this could be—I'll wager at least a few of you are suffering from the same problem.

Testing

What is the goal of testing in this instance? Well, between now and the end of the chapter, we want to go from where we are to a fully functional, and most importantly, live and operational site. In order to get there, we need to ensure not only that everything works as expected from the customer's point of view, but also that the site's security is properly implemented and that we can administer the site properly from the administration tool. Knowing this, we can break this section down into three main phases: testing the online store, re-implementing security, and testing the administration tool.

Once you have completed the testing phase, it is probably a good idea to make a backup of your live site because this now represents the only working live copy you possess. Sure, you can easily redo everything from the RTP copy you saved earlier, but why take the chance of having to redo your security settings, or any other changes you may have already made? Bear in mind that some of you will encounter problems that will need to be sorted out—if you don't back up your site after the corrections have been implemented, they will be lost in the event of a disaster of some sort. That's enough of the doom and gloom for the moment though. Let's get on with testing everything…

Test the Online Store

In the earlier section of this chapter, entitled *An Interesting Problem*, I showed a screenshot of the live catalog index page being totally blank, devoid of content and error messages. It took me a little while to figure out what was wrong—during the course of my somewhat frustrating day, I used a series of techniques that are standard programmer's issue for debugging (incidentally, Appendix A will discuss how to effectively debug your applications). None of them worked, and try as I might I could not get any sort of response to show up in the browser.

When I realized that the admin tool was working through the browser, I knew that something was applied only to the catalog folder, and had not been applied to the admin tool. The culprit as it turned out was the page compression, which was not being rendered properly in the browser—recall, in Chapter 4 on *Basic Configuration* we discussed gzip compression of pages. Disabling this from the Configuration section of the admin tool corrected the problem, and the site worked fine thereafter. While this seems like a very simple solution (which it is), the problem can be insurmountable if you don't know where to look. I highlighted this glitch specifically because the nature of it prevents you from seeing any error messages, which are usually what guide programmers during the testing phase.

Before we even look at a catalog page, I should stress that it is quite smart to use to different types of browsers when testing your web pages. Not all browsers are created equal! Since you need to cater for everyone in the world, you should make concessions for all types of browsers, provided those concessions don't hinder your store's functionality or appearance excessively. For example, the demo site was tested using IE from Microsoft, as well as an open-source browser called Mozilla Firefox (which is available at: http://www.mozilla.org). Of course, you are free to use as many as you like.

Now, having thoroughly tested your development site, you should already have a fair idea of how to go about testing the live site. Again, this is a big task; so break it down into smaller more manageable chunks, and stick to a solid and comprehensive methodology. There is no substitute for a methodical progression of tests; despite what gimmicky hosting deals may tell you about having a live store in 30 minutes, you can't assume something works unless you have actually done it yourself.

As tempting as it is to try to fix each and every problem as you go along, it is recommended that you make a list of problems to deal with on your first run. Many problems have related causes, and with a full list of glitches, you can often be more efficient at solving problems with an overall picture. For example, if you find a problem with a payment module, rather flag it up and come back to it once you have tested the admin tool too. This of course doesn't count if you have a problem that completely prevents you from testing the rest of the site:

Store Front Checklist

Use at least two different browsers.	One browser may implement some features that others do not—you might find that something you rely on heavily works on your browser of choice but not on others.	[ ]
Resize your browsers for a variety of pages.	This helps to determine whether you have HTML elements that have not been set correctly. For example, some section may use the full page width, while others expand only to a certain limit.	[ ]

Access pages from fast as well as slow connections.	You might find that certain pages load very slowly over a dial-up connection. This might mean you need to rethink image and page sizes.	**[**	**]**
Check all links— Text and Image.	Often, links break during deployment because of differing file paths and so forth. You should:		
	• Check all product links in the Categories box		
	• Check all links and buttons on each page		
	• Check all links on each info box		
	• Check all links to information pages in the Information box	**[**	**]**
	• Check breadcrumb and navigation links in the navigation bar		
	• Check that both large and small images display appropriately		
	• Check that banner ads link correctly		
Check that all images display correctly.	Remember that it is possible for osCommerce to not display broken image links, so be wary on this one.	**[**	**]**
Check each page's look.	Important, because not all browsers can render certain stylesheet settings.	**[**	**]**
Use each page.	This is vital for ensuring that customers can:		
	• Create and manage accounts		
	• Manage their shopping carts		
	• Select payment and shipping methods that suit them, and which are displayed only if available		
	• Checkout		
	• Make use of the contributions—in this case, they should be able to purchase and use gift vouchers	**[**	**]**
	Ensure that:		
	• The search engine works correctly		
	• Reviews can be written up without problems		
	• Contact emails can be sent properly		
	• Privacy and conditions of use are shown along with any important copyright information.		

| *Try to break the site.* | Just as important as ensuring everything works properly (if not more important), is ensuring that nothing can be broken at will:

• Try cheating the store out of money

• Try cheating the store out of vouchers

• Try breaking the checkout process with huge orders

• Try hacking the site and gaining access to a customer's account or the administration account

Once again—if you don't, someone else will! | [ ] |

If you can perform everything listed in this checklist with several browsers, with no problems, then you can be reasonably certain that your store will hold up when it goes live. Of course, you will need to monitor the site very closely for the first few months of its operation to make sure that nothing drastic goes wrong. Providing a webmaster's email address is a good way to let customers complain if they run into problems on your site. Open lines of communication between you and your customers will help foster strong ties and improve your service.

At this stage, you should be satisfied that there is nothing wrong with the site and that it is robust and stable. Either that, or you should have a list of problems that will need to be solved once you have implemented your security policy and tested the admin tool.

Re-Implement Security

As it stands now, you most probably don't have SSL enabled, nor do you have any password authentication. If this is the case, then you need to revisit Chapter 8 on security, and refresh your memory over what needs to be done. The checklist that is being provided now should be used in conjunction with a coherent set of security tests, and is not meant to list the *only* security checks you perform:

Security Checklist

| *Ensure the admin tool is password secured and accessed only through a secure server.* | Not only must the landing page `catalog/admin/index.php` be password protected over an SSL connection, but all subsequent links under the `admin` folder should also be performed over a secure connection. | [ ] |
| *Secure customer login and payments.* | Whenever a new customer tries to create a new account, or when a registered customer tries to log on, a secure connection must be provided. As well as this, all checkout transactions should also be done over SSL. | [ ] |

Communications with third-party servers meet with the dictates of your security policy.	Adding security here will help safeguard against fraud. Make sure you implement as much security as you can reasonably muster.	[	]
Set file-system permissions appropriately.	Don't give yourself up cheaply to hackers. Provide settings that are just enough for the file to be used as intended, and no more.	[	]
Set database permissions appropriately.	We have already set up one user for the database. You should now: • Reduce that user's privileges • Restrict access from other servers	[	]
Disable any unused tools, utilities, and scripts.	This goes for those created or used by yourself, as well as those provided by your host. Basically, have only what is required for your site to operate, and nothing more!	[	]
Try hacking into, or breaking your site.	If you don't try… someone else will!	[	]
Implement your database and file-system disaster-recovery policy.	Make sure that right from the start you have an automated backup system (perhaps weekly to begin with, but keep it flexible to reflect your site's usage).	[	]

Your site should hopefully be stripped down to the bare minimum, with no erroneous files lying around, and no tools that could be usurped and used against you. Hopefully you will never have any real need for much of the security that has been put in place. However, having it there is a great deterrent in itself, and if you do have the need at some stage, you will be glad you went to the trouble.

With the security policy implemented *and* tested, you can now turn your attention to the final part of the deployment phase—testing the administration tool.

Test the Administration Tool

Thankfully, testing the admin tool is not too much of an arduous task because most of the settings contained in here are held in the database and will not have changed during deployment. In reality, you simply need to make use of each facility in order to ensure it is working just as it was on the development machine—the caveat here is that you should have removed any test setting you had on the development server. The last thing you want is to offer all your clients a 100% discount on all goods because you forgot to remove this from your development version. Remember to test all changes you make to the admin tool with the corresponding changes to the store front—for example, if you email a customer, ensure that the mail actually gets there.

In the interests of completeness, here is a list of the more important checks to be performed before you can relax and congratulate yourself on a deployment well done:

Administration Tool Checklist

Ensure the admin tool picks up settings correctly.	Effectively, this is really testing whether the database connection is working properly. If your catalog is picking up the products correctly, but your admin tool is not working, then recheck the admin's `configure.php` file.	[　]
Add, edit, and remove products and categories.	This is important to make sure that updates to the database are executed without problems.	[　]
Modify product attributes.	For completeness, these and a number of other tests ensure that all of the tables in the database are used in testing.	[　]
Test all contributions and modules thoroughly.	Not all contributions are as robust as osCommerce. For example, some may have version issues that were not apparent during development. As well as this, all payment and shipping modules should be checked to ensure that they are set as you want them for your *live store* and not as they were during *testing*.	[　]
Add and remove manufacturers.	This tests, among other things, whether file images can be uploaded properly.	[　]
Add, remove, modify, and email customers.	Ensure that your customer-handling facilities are all in place, and test out the state of your administrative emailing capability.	[　]
Use each tool in the Tool section.	This will give you a comprehensive overview of all the tools and will help to iron out any wrinkles that may have appeared between the development phase and the live site.	[　]

If you did encounter problems during the course of your testing, then now is the time to look at them and attempt to fix anything that may have gone awry. *Appendix A* will give you some help in this regard. As soon as you are confident that there are no *wrinkles* left to iron out, make a backup of your site and save it somewhere safe.

With the completion of the deployment-phase testing out of the way, I extend my warmest congratulations to you, the newest member of the e-commerce world. I trust that with the requisite hard work and a solid business idea, your store will blossom into a success and provide you with a base from which to grow your business to meet your ambitions, whatever they are!

If you haven't been driven to the bar for drinks several times during the development and deployment phases, you may as well take a break and pop into the local bar for a celebratory drink before worrying about maintenance or marketing issues. Your site can now look after itself for a little while without you having to worry about anything.

Maintenance

You may be forgiven for thinking that your shiny new website is now done and dusted, and that you simply need to keep it filled up with new products in order for it to keep going forever. Well, it will certainly go for some time like this, but what you really need to do is keep on top of maintenance chores right from the start, in order to keep your site uncluttered, efficient, and neat. Doing this will make working with your site a far more pleasant and efficient process as time goes by. But what are the actual goals of a maintenance plan?

Fundamentally, your maintenance-based goals must relate to the fact that you want to keep your store as up to date and relevant for your customers as possible. A secondary requirement of your maintenance plan is to keep the site well-ordered behind the scenes so that the administration process is kept effective and efficient. From this we can derive a kind of three-pronged attack on the system's entropy, which can be summed up with the following tenet:

> *Out with the old, in with the new! And what else?*

What this means is that whatever is no longer needed must be removed from the site entirely. New content must be added whenever it is needed, and if anything else that is of great use has come about since the initial deployment, it should be implemented. This rather terse philosophy should be implemented for every aspect of the site's maintenance, since it applies to the upkeep of images, just the same as it applies to software updates.

The best way to act on this philosophy is to engrain a built-in process for performing everyday tasks which fulfils this tenet. So for example, the process for adding a newer version of a product for one which has been discontinued goes from:

1. Add new product to the relevant category.
2. Upload and link product's image to the product.

to:

1. Search for newer products that customers will find useful.
2. Remove discontinued product from the product list.
3. Remove product's image from the file system.
4. Clean up any other product-specific references that may appear on the site.

5. Add new product to the relevant category.

6. Upload and link product's image to the product.

7. Update any cross-selling or features necessary to integrate the product into the site.

As you can see, the second option is quite a bit more work, but it is work that is really necessary in order to keep your store on the cutting edge. For example, the process of finding new products moves from a passive one (for example, you might receive product updates from manufacturers) to an active one (you watch manufacturer's sites for any new products and respond accordingly). You also prevent your site from becoming cluttered up with useless information as time goes by, as well as ensuring that each new product is properly integrated into the site from the moment it is added.

As well as performing this kind of conscientious update for your site on a task-by-task basis, you should also schedule a periodical maintenance update in which you perform a number of checks and tasks to ensure that everything is working smoothly. The type of checks you perform will really be based on the type of store you are running, but one of the things you should always keep an eye out for, regardless of how your store works, is *what's new on the block*. Remember that as time goes by, new updates are made available and new technologies make things better and faster. Keeping up to date with the latest trends will ensure you don't get left behind.

Two good examples of this are the fact that PHP5, the latest version of PHP, is the version of the native programming language that hosts will eventually upgrade to. osCommerce itself is due for another milestone release and you should make sure you keep an eye on what advantages it can offer. If at any stage, you decide that it is worth upgrading your store, then you must work on the development machine again.

> All major development should be done on the development machine! Only minor changes should be made directly to the live store.

Simply back up your live site, send it over to your development machine, and begin working on the new additions/upgrades. Once you are entirely satisfied that everything is working as it should be, find a time when you store is the least busy (and so unlikely to affect customers) and re-deploy the site. If you are always busy, then it may be prudent to post a notice informing customers that there will be some downtime.

In addition to the methods for site maintenance outlined here, the following list of considerations might come in handy in guiding you as you go. Since every site is different, I couldn't hope to make this list authoritative and exhaustive, but you should be able to use this as a platform from which to work:

- **Modification and addition of website content**: Ensure that you update dates and references on a regular basis. Your site's copy might also need to be upgraded from time to time in order to keep it relevant.

- **Image manipulation and addition**: Always ensure that the images you are adding to the site are small so that they don't slow things down. Make sure they also fit in with the site's look and feel so that you don't lose your site's graphic appeal. Finally, make sure you remove any old images, to prevent clutter.

- **Newsletter and email list maintenance**: Obviously, regular updates are required—especially if you operate a monthly newsletter or send out other news or information that needs to be timely and relevant. Ensure that broken email addresses are removed from your lists.

- **Product updates**: Depending on the nature of your business, you should ensure that your site reflects the latest possible product information that your site can fulfill. Don't advertise the latest available product from a manufacturer if you can't yet get your hands on it.

- **Update announcements, articles, and so on**: Keep your customers informed of important goings on—especially when it comes to things like upgrades that might impact on your site's performance.

- **Addition/removal of pages**: From time to time you will find that you need to add pages to cater for new services or facilities. In such a case, ensure the page is developed and tested on the development machine before it is ported over to the live store.

- **Database maintenance**: Ensure that any old, out-of-date content is removed. This is more important than simply maintaining a clean database—if you fail to remove old information, you could experience unwanted effects such as outdated information appearing in your search results.

- **Update product information**: No more need be said—don't allow a gap to form between the products you provide and the information presented on your site.

- **Ensure orders are kept up to date and dealt with efficiently**: Depending on your setup, you will probably find that it is necessary to update your orders on a regular basis. Doing this is an important part of your site's accounting, so don't fall behind on this.

- **Update emails**: Emails form an important part of your site's relationship with customers. Ensure that this relationship doesn't become stale with old emails.

- **Ensure all banners are up to date, and remove old ones**: Keep your advertisers happy and your advertising relevant by ensuring that your banner ads are always shown at the right times.

- **Check search engine is still working quickly**: While this is not something you have to check up often, you might find that you run into problems as your database becomes large. Make sure that this doesn't affect your customer's shopping experience.

- **Update and maintain discounts and vouchers**: Vouchers and discounts can form an integral part of your site's marketing and appeal. Keeping customers excited about your store with new deals will certainly boost your revenue-generating potential.

- **Ensure you keep up to date with all site-related payments**: This is pretty self explanatory—losing your domain name would be about the most disastrous thing that could happen, because it would leave someone else to collect on your business's good name.

- **Keep up to date with new patches, security updates, and changes**: As discussed earlier—keeping abreast of developments will ensure that you don't fall behind.

If you can stay on top of things by using an effective maintenance plan right from the start, then the benefits in terms of the service your site provides to customers as well as the savings in time derived from a streamlined, well organized site, will make your life that much more pleasant. With that, our little foray into website maintenance is at an end…

Congratulations once again on the deployment of your new business venture!

Summary

For a task as important as building an online e-commerce site, it is necessary that you spend a lot of time considering your options, and developing and testing your site. Since it is not really feasible to do this sort of work on the live site, you need to employ a development machine to aid you. Because of this, the topic of deployment is an important one in the overall scheme of things because it is deployment that actually links your finished development to the live store that customers can use.

This chapter outlined a solid process for preparing for deployment, followed by several of the most common methods for transferring files. Of course, it was also necessary to set up a new database on the host site, but this should be relatively easy because any good host should make the task fairly simple by providing a tool like phpMyAdmin to work with the database.

Hopefully you came to realize that the deployment process itself is not particularly complex for an osCommerce site, since the only real configuration work that needs to be done is adding a page worth of configuration parameters to the two configuration files used in the `catalog` and `admin` folders. Having the complexity of the site's deployment reduced to configuring a couple of files is a real advantage for osCommerce users. This simplicity makes it easy to then concentrate on ensuring that security measures are properly in place.

Of course, while the actual deployment of the site is fairly simple, it was shown that there were quite a few issues to deal with, and not the least of them is testing. It is critical that a full suite of tests is carried out on any site before it goes live—losing customers to silly errors is the last thing that any start up business can afford. This chapter then has given you the grounding you need to successfully turn a development site in to a live site that will generate revenue reliably for some time to come.

12

Building Your Business

So you find yourself sitting with a well developed, sophisticated piece of online retail software, which is fully capable of selling to hundreds of thousands of customers all over the world. You have a great product, which you just know is going to be popular if only everyone out there knew about it—but nobody does. Your main consolation in this situation is that you are not alone. In the US, each year thousands of new Internet startups fail because they simply cannot generate enough revenue from their online sites. The reasons for this can be varied, but whatever they may be, you can be quite sure that one of the main factors is the site not gaining enough exposure.

The difference between success and failure is really a numbers game, when it comes to dealing with e-commerce. Unless you already have a select, loyal client base from which you can draw enough sales to keep you going, you are going to have to market and advertise and do just about anything else you can to get people to visit your site. Actually, even that is not enough nowadays, because you more often than not have to pay to get visitors (or traffic), and the last thing you want to do is pay for a hundred thousand visitors, none of whom have any interest in your product.

Ideally, what you want is to have more of the *right* people coming through your site. What do I mean by right people? Well, the right person is someone who is in some way predisposed to buying your products. This is a basic principle of marketing, which holds true for any product big or small—advertise to people who are potential buyers of your product. In other words, don't try selling fridges to Eskimos!

But how in the world are you supposed to tell whether or not someone browsing your store is predisposed to buying your products? The simple answer is *you can't... but other people can.* The Internet is a vast virtual world inhabited by devilishly clever people, who are all looking out for the best and most efficient way to provide services for people like you. I should say that unlike many open-source projects, these services are really designed to earn money for the companies who provide them.

It is unfortunately a reality that if you want to make a success of your business, at some stage you will have to spend money to make money!

Don't feel too down about this last quote. While it is certainly true that you will spend some money, you should be able to manage the expense and offset it against the gains in revenue. If there is one thing you can say about marketing and advertising on the Internet, it's that you can at least obtain an accurate appraisal of the performance of your investments. As well as this, the task of separating yourself from the vast number of other stores and shops is without doubt a difficult one, but it is not impossible. All you need is… you guessed it, a solid process. This time, your process has to be mixed with a dash of patience and long-term planning.

We all hear about the marvelous overnight successes of Internet businesses all the time, and certainly these rags-to-riches stories do happen, but to be realistic, you can't plan for that to be the case. As a result, you need to make advertising and marketing your priority for the time to come. (Incidentally, if you do make millions overnight, feel free to help out this poor author :)

While I feel a pang of guilt for not bringing it up earlier in the book, the monumental task you face, of bringing revenue to your site, is more than likely the one that will make or break your business as a whole. To this end, this chapter will give the best possible starting point for you to make an impact and capture your market. Specifically, we will look at:

- Marketing
- Advertising
- Dropshipping
- Search engine optimization

Don't be fooled by the fact that there are only four distinct topics listed here. Each one covers a lot of ground and hopefully you are raring to learn about how to gain the customer base you *deserve*. The wording of this last sentence is quite important. Remember that while making a living is tough in today's economy, it is generally even handed, and you should get out of a business what you put in. That said, I certainly hope that all of you reading this will enjoy huge success. Let's begin…

Marketing

The concept of marketing is a very broad one, which is often not fully appreciated by the average person, or even people in the advertising industry itself. Most people assume that because advertising is the most visible result of an attempt to attract customers, it must be the most important part of attracting said customers. This is unfortunately a fairly blinkered view of things because if you take the time to think about it and ask a few questions, you will quickly learn that without marketing intelligence, it is all but impossible to create and deliver effective advertising.

The concept of marketing therefore covers a lot more ground than advertising, in that advertising can be viewed as part of a marketing campaign, not vice versa. Both can be summed up in the following definitions:

- **Advertising:** The paid promotion of goods, services, companies, and ideas by an identified sponsor
- **Marketing:** The management function responsible for identifying, anticipating, and satisfying consumer requirements profitably

The reason I am stating the definition of each term is that understanding the difference between the two helps clarify the nature of each, and, as you should know by now, we don't start working on anything unless we already have a fairly good idea of what we are doing. Knowing that you first need to identify demands in your market, find creative ways to satisfy those demands, and then implement your marketing strategy based on this knowledge will go a long way to helping you develop a coherent advertising and promotional policy, which ultimately should outstrip your competitors and grab market share.

Research

It's time to change out of developer mode and adopt a business-oriented attitude from here on out. Begin by doing a lot of research into how your business fits into the overall economy and how your products relate to consumers. Understanding these two points will lead you on to more specific questions (and hopefully, some answers) like "How can I identify myself uniquely with my target consumers above my competitors in my sector of the industry?"

How do you go about finding out this information? Well, there is an easy way, and a hard way. The easy way is to simply pay a research company to release its data to you, but this can be quite costly if you are paying for fresh research to be done, and it is not always guaranteed that you will get precisely the information you need if you are paying for research that has already been completed. We'll leave that option here because you can be pretty effective on your own if you are imaginative enough.

The other way is the good old fashioned hard way—in other words, do the work yourself. You basically need to know the following things about your target market:

- Who they are
- Where they are
- How much money they have
- How do they like things done

How you find out this information is really up to you. For example, if you are selling computer books like the demo site, you would probably want to join chat forums that cover the same topics as your stock. Chatting and getting to know the type of people who use the technology is a great way to get a feel for who your average customer is going to be. You would most certainly want to look at other successful businesses in your market and see how they are doing things. The advantage in doing this is that you should be able to deduce what it is they know about their clients from the way they do things. Be careful not to go overboard on this one—you want to find out *why* these businesses are successful, and not simply copy *what* they are doing.

Take a look at sites that are not doing well (it can be hard to tell, I will admit) and try and deduce why they are not successful. Combine this knowledge of your direct competitors with news and industry information—read magazines, blogs, journals, newspapers, and so on to get a good overall perspective of what your industry *looks* like. For example, if I (as the owner of the demo store) read that a certain cell-phone manufacturer had released a new phone a few months ago, which has taken the market by storm because of its versatile use of mobile applications, I have an indication that I should be selling at least a few books on programming for mobile devices over the next few months.

This last example, should implicitly demonstrate that marketing is an ongoing process and not something you do at the outset of your business career. Let's continue with our cell phone example. If I believe that there will be a growing demand for programming for mobile devices titles, then I should approach the manufacturer of the phones in order to find out details of how they work, so that I can make an informed decision about what to stock. While I am chatting to their marketing director, it is probably also a good idea to see if we could somehow both benefit from mutual cooperation since our goals in this instance are aligned.

What type of cooperation are we talking about? Well, whatever you can imagine you can put forward. You could decide to cross market products with reciprocal links. This would mean that people visiting the manufacturer's site to buy phones see a link to your store, which offers them a book on how to program for the phone, and vice versa. You could decide to offer promotional packages together; you could get one of their technical gurus to write an article for your site in return for a banner ad linking to their phones. Finding and exploiting gaps is one of the most interesting parts of business precisely because the rewards can be great—often in terms of the relationships you build rather than direct revenue generation.

I could go on and on about this, but I am sure you get the picture.

> Know your audience, and look for the gaps to exploit. If you can do that, backed by solid products, you are bound to be a success.

So now, you have your site set up, you have done your research, and you know who and where your audience is. You also have relationships with manufacturers or other businesses that can add value to your enterprise. Now you need to let people know about it. Although this is not the end of the story for marketing, it is where advertising comes in. The following sections will look at different types of advertising, followed by a few other important marketing opportunities available to us through the Internet.

Advertising

There have been quite a few methods for determining the value of advertising on the Internet over the years. One of the most common methods of advertising—one which we all have come to know and hate—is **spamming**. As much as you may detest being spammed, the fundamental fact is that if it wasn't profitable, then people wouldn't do it. While it is most certainly not recommended you become an agent for spam, email certainly is a useful tool for providing advertising, and you might want to think of some sort of email-based strategy for promoting your products.

What is very popular in the advertising world, however, is the payment-per-clickthrough method, whereby a micro payment is made every time a browser clicks through to a target site from an ad. Cost per clickthrough can really vary, and depends on the value the advertiser places on getting traffic from the site where the ad is placed. What you are ideally looking for is an ad that attracts a large number of people, with a high percentage of those actually following through and making purchases.

But how do you go about finding out where to place your advertising? Recall that I said earlier that effectively it is not possible to tell if someone browsing your store is predisposed to buying your products. Well, this is true if you don't know where the customer has been. If you know where your type of customer hangs out, then you can advertise there in the hope that they are already happy to buy your products without any additional effort required on your part. For example, if you were selling car part spares, then advertising on a used-car dealer's site would probably be quite beneficial to you—as opposed to advertising on a pet store site.

If we act further on the implicit assumption that people who are already using specific types of information are predisposed to buying related products, then we find ourselves, after a logical extrapolation of the idea, ending up with advertising on search engines. This is because someone using a search engine is giving away valuable marketing information every time he or she initiates a search.

For example, if someone types spark plugs into a search engine, it is fairly safe to assume that they are more predisposed to buying spark plugs than someone who types in ballet shoes. Since our car part spares store sells spark plugs, they should ideally place an ad on the results page that comes up every time someone types in car parts, spark plugs, and so on. This is what is known as targeted advertising, and is really quite effective. The drawback is, of course, that you will have to pay for it—finding a good balance is half art, half science, and is the topic of the *Generating Revenue from Your Site* section a little later in this chapter.

Before we look at that, though, it is important to realize that advertising works both ways. Remember that if you have a successful site, then it is very likely that others will be willing to pay you to advertise their products or businesses on your site. This means that there are two channels for generating revenue on the Internet. One relies on gaining sales from advertising, and the other relies on gaining revenue from providing advertising. We will discuss how to generate revenue from advertising on your own site after the following section.

Using Google AdWords

Once again, how you choose to advertise your site on the Net is really limited only by your imagination, and you should explore as many avenues as possible in this regard. Sadly, we don't have space to talk about each and every possibility, so we will instead focus on one of the more popular and effective advertising campaigns around. As you know, we are going to be looking at Google AdWords, and you can find them online at: `https://adwords.google.com/select/` should you wish to sign up.

Before you do sign up, remember that you will have to pay for these ads. However, Google provides pretty fine-grained control over how much you spend on a given ad campaign, and it is recommended that you create an account and learn how the system works even if you aren't entirely convinced this is the route to go at the moment. The reason I say this is that Google won't oblige you to pay a minimum amount or stay registered for a minimum time. This means you can back out at any time if, after learning how you can benefit from this service, you don't think it is the right way to go.

First thing's first, go to the sign-up page and register. Google actually runs through the whole process of setting up an ad and choosing target search words during account creation, so we will discuss that here by way of demonstration. You will initially be asked to make a few selections about what language you would like to use and the geographical area you would like your ads to cover. Naturally, you should select this based on the needs of your business. For example, if you are shipping all over the world, then you should select Countries as the customer location area. The following page allows you to be more specific in that you can select specific countries or regions. Once that is done, click Continue.

The next page looks like this:

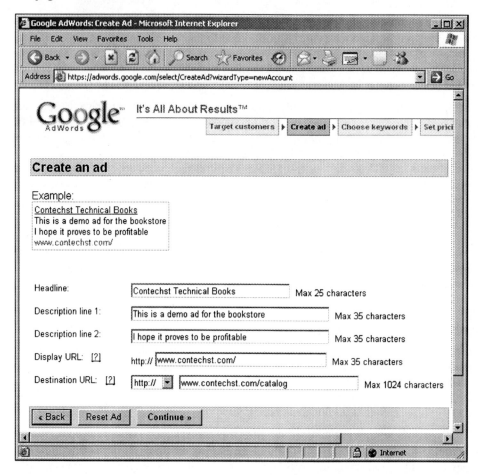

It's actually harder than it looks to write a good Google Ad. You want to try to get across as much important information about your site as possible, but you are limited to a headline followed by a 70-character description. Try to reduce the essence of your site into a single sentence—remember, there will be competing ads all around you, so you need to convince the user that your store will cater for their needs better than anyone else's. If you find you can't get across everything you need to say, then don't panic—you are allowed to create more than one ad, though only one will be shown at a time.

Try your hand at making an effective ad, but don't spend too long ruminating over this—it's very easy to modify ads from the Google AdWords Campaign Manager once you have registered. When you are satisfied, click Continue. You will notice that Google then checks your ad to ensure that it complies with its rules. Google provides guidelines for you to use in order to not fall foul of its checks—view them at https://adwords.google.com/select/guidelines.html. Assuming your ad is accepted, you are then asked to choose some keywords.

Keywords are words or phrases that you believe will most accurately indicate the type of user who would find your store of interest. For the sake of speeding things up, type in something related—in this case, we'll go with technical book—and then click Continue. You can then decide on which currency you would like to use as payment, and following that you can choose the CPC (Cost Per Click) that you are prepared to pay for your ad.

Before you dash to select the minimum amount, remember that there will more than likely be competitors who also want to display their ads for these keywords. Obviously, if they are prepared to pay more, then their ad will likely appear above yours. If there are lots of people targeting certain keywords, your ad might not even appear on the first few search-result pages unless you are prepared to fork out a goodly amount to have its ranking improve. By the same token, you don't want to offer twice as much as anyone else either.

> Choose a CPC that you are prepared to pay, and then monitor your ranking in the ads for your keywords and adjust accordingly depending on if you are always too low or always first!

I should stress at this point that you will only be able to work out exactly how much to pay, how many ads to use, which keywords are the best, and what to set your daily budget to, by keeping a close eye on the performance of your ad campaign over time. Don't spend too much time worrying about settings here because everything can be very easily modified at any stage, and you will be better qualified to make these changes once you are able to view some data about how many clicks you are getting, how many views you are getting, and so on.

Next, you can set your daily budget. Once again, you should pick a value that you are comfortable with paying. Remember that you will not necessarily reach your daily budget, but you will never exceed it. In other words, it is only an upper bound. Once your daily target has been reached, your ads will no longer be displayed, so you will need to spend some time analyzing your ad's usage and relate it to your overall budget. For example, setting your CPC and daily budget to the same value is pretty silly because you will only, at most, get one visit a day from your Google AdWords campaign.

Google provides some tools that will be of some assistance to you, and you can view these at the bottom of the current page. The Traffic Estimator, shown here:

Estimates for the maximum CPC: 1.50 ZAR					
Keywords	Avg. Position	Clicks / Day	Cost / Day	Avg. CPC	Status
Overall	2.0	< 0.1	0.07	0.76	-
technical book	2.0	< 0.1	0.07	0.76	Normal

Estimates for these keywords are based on clickthrough rates for current advertisers. Some of the keywords above are subject to review by Google and may not trigger your ads until they are approved. Please note that your traffic estimates assume your keywords are approved.

will give you a rough idea of your ad's rank, the number of clicks you will get a day, the cost of using this keyword per day, and the average CPC. From the previous screenshot you can see that for a maximum CPC of R1.50, the ad's rank will average out to second, but will really not get many clicks per day. But this is because I initially chose to only show the ad in South Africa. If I now click on Change your customer targeting to include the US and the UK, I get the following results:

Estimates for the maximum CPC: 1.50 ZAR					
Keywords	**Avg. Position**	**Clicks / Day**	**Cost / Day**	**Avg. CPC**	**Status**
Overall	2.3	2.9	2.58	0.89	-
technical book	2.3	2.9	2.58	0.89	Normal

Estimates for these keywords are based on clickthrough rates for current advertisers. Some of the keywords above are subject to review by Google and may not trigger your ads until they are approved. Please note that your traffic estimates assume your keywords are approved.

As you can see, my average position has dropped (no doubt because there are more advertisers wanting to use these keywords), but my clicks per day as well as my CPC have increased. You should be getting the feeling that it is quite a balancing act to choose the most effective keywords and pay the right price for them. If you are, it is a good sign, because you will need to work on this to get everything just right. As you will see in a moment, Google will provide you with plenty of historical data from which you can make deductions and refine your campaign.

When you are finished playing around with your ads, keywords, and CPCs, click Continue. You will be taken to a review page where you can check out the results of your work. If you are happy, then click Continue to Sign Up. You will then go through the process of signing up, which involves supplying an email address, confirming it, and then logging on to your new account. You will find that your account will not be activated until you have provided your payment information.

After you have supplied your billing information, you will have access to the campaign manager in its entirety. From here you can create new campaigns, which in turn contain ad groups. A typical page looks like this:

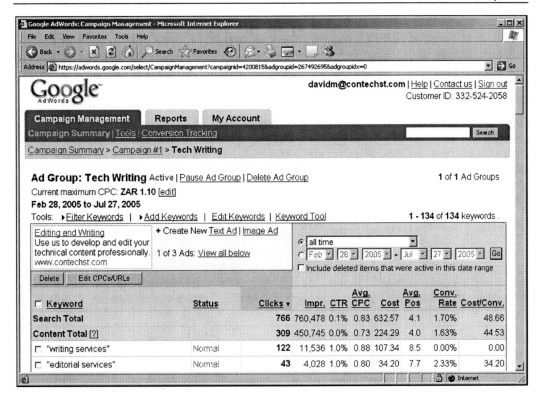

As you can see, you can:

1. Create new text or image ads.

2. Edit your maximum CPC.

3. Add, edit, remove, or filter keywords.

4. Pause or delete ad groups.

5. View all historical data for your keywords.

6. Make use of reports.

Several important points are raised by the previous list.

The first one is that by clicking on the Reports tag at the top of the page, you can create a selection of reports in order to help you keep track of your campaign's performance. You can even automate these reports and have them emailed to you. All the instructions on how to do this are presented in links on the Reports page, so it is recommended that you play around with this once you have built up a bit of data to work with.

Second, you can view the Status of each of the keywords in your campaign. It is important that you keep an eye on the status of all your keywords because Google will disable your ad group if your campaign goes too long without being administered. If you want to find out more about how the status of your keywords is determined, then see: https://adwords.google.com/select/status.html.

Finally, you may have noticed that there is something called Conversion Tracking. A **conversion** occurs when a click on your ad leads directly to user behavior you deem valuable, such as a purchase, signup, page view, or lead. This is an extremely helpful tool, which is definitely worthwhile using. Simply click on the Conversion Tracking link at the top of the page and read through the documentation in order to get it up and running. In the previous screenshot you can see the extra statistics on the far right of the table, which deal with conversion rates and cost.

There are more features and facilities than we have space to cover here, but once you have an account, you will find that everything is very well explained and documented and you shouldn't have too much trouble in customizing your campaign to suit your needs. Remember too that Google is not the only channel that can be utilized for this type of advertising, and to some extent you can integrate your advertising between channels. For example, Google provides a cross-channel tracking tool for just this purpose.

Generating Revenue from Your Site

There are a myriad of schemes and programs available for you to take advantage of in order to generate income. The first and foremost thing to remember is that you will only have to worry about this once you have enough traffic coming through your site to justify going to the trouble of setting everything up. If you are only getting a couple of hundred hits per month to begin with, then focus all your efforts on getting more traffic and forget about advertising on your site for the moment.

If you do decide to go ahead, then you can do one or more of the following:

- Use your banner manager to administer ads throughout your site
- Use a third-party ad provider such as Google ads
- Sell sponsored content
- Add popups
- Sell *opt-in* traffic

Using the banner manager is a really good option because it gives you total control over how much screen real estate you wish to hand over to advertisers. Obviously you don't want to crowd out your own store with a multitude of banners because this will lead to a decline in traffic, which in turn leads to a decline in revenue from ads and purchases. The main point to remember here is that you need to develop a relationship with your advertisers, and it can be a bit of a trick to do this if you are starting out. There is also help to be found by employing companies that specialize in precisely this sort of thing—a quick search on Google will unearth hundreds of them.

Google ads is a good option too because it also gives you plenty of control over the look and feel of the ads you place. The difference here is that Google determines which ads will be the best for your site. While Google may not get it right all the time, the approach at least saves you from having to go and develop relationships with advertisers yourself. It's basically a money for nothing scheme provided your site can generate a fair number of clicks.

If you are interested in using Google ads, then visit `https://www.google.com/adsense/`. Since you have already seen how to use set up an AdWords account, we won't go into the account-setup details here. You will find that everything is well documented and explained, and you should have no trouble setting everything up. Remember that when you are generating a new set of Google ads, you should keep in mind how your site is going to change as a result.

You might find that you need to alter a bit of HTML in order to accommodate the script that Google provides in order to insert the ad. Talking of which, inserting your ad is simply a question of making a series of selections such as the color, size, and dimensions of the ads you wish to show, and pasting in the resulting script. For example, the following script was generated for the demo site by Google in response to my selection criteria:

```
<script type="text/javascript"><!--
google_ad_client = "pub-0173529661079174";
google_ad_width = 120;
google_ad_height = 600;
google_ad_format = "120x600_as";
google_ad_type = "text_image";
google_ad_channel ="";
google_color_border = "FF2626";
google_color_bg = "E0E0E0";
google_color_link = "000000";
google_color_url = "F79418";
google_color_text = "000000";
//--></script>
<script type="text/javascript"
  src="http://pagead2.googlesyndication.com/pagead/show_ads.js">
</script>
```

and after fitting it into the HTML on the catalog's index.php page, which involved resizing the width of the page to 930 pixels from the original modification of 800, the resulting page looks like this:

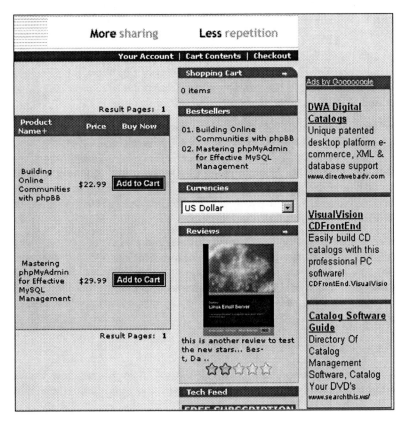

Now there are a couple of things to make note of with respect to the way these ads are presented. First of all, the site was specifically designed to be 800 pixels in width precisely because of the intention to advertise along the right-hand side of the page once everything was in place. As you can see, the addition of the ads in no way affects the customer's browsing experience, and they can even be removed from their screen by resizing the window if they so choose.

Next, the ads have been customized to fit in precisely with the look and feel of the site. As an online shopper myself, I tend to avoid sites that I find unpleasant on the eye—having a mish-mash of different colors and ads bundled helter-skelter gives a disorderly impression and is the sign of a lax business outlook. Make sure the quality of your site is not affected, because after all, the people using your site are already customers, and to lose them to pushy or un-neat advertising is bordering on criminal.

Once again, you will really need to play around in order to gain experience and get a feel for what is and isn't effective for your business. It is my recommendation that you always treat advertising as unimportant relative to the primary goal of your site, which is to provide customers with an excellent environment for shopping. If you can provide targeted advertising that is unobtrusive and even helpful, then you have achieved a good, but exceedingly rare, balance.

Going back to the list, the next item is *selling sponsored content*. You will find, assuming that you have enough traffic going through your site, that some companies are willing to provide content, which contains a credit and a link, in return for money. Once again, this is really up to you to seek out and implement, and you shouldn't worry about this until you have taken care of your primary source of revenue first.

The final two items on the list are mentioned only because they are revenue-generating schemes. However, it is not recommended that you *add popups* to your site. Many people employ popup blockers or find them irritating. Since you are trying to foster a loyal community of customers, the last thing you want to do is bombard them with popups.

For exactly the same reason, don't ever use the final option of selling *opt-in* traffic unless you have expressly been given permission to do so. An opt-in is where you add a checkbox to your site saying something to the effect of *I, the customer, agree to receive communications regarding various products and promotions*. You then take this agreement and sell the email addresses to companies that then bombard them with spam. In fact, given the amount of spam nowadays, it is probably more valuable to add a notice to your site affirming your commitment to never release customers' email addresses to third parties.

At the end of the day, determining the advertising strategy that suits you best will probably take some time. You need to build up a picture of *who* is using your site for *what*, and *how many* use it *where*, *when*, and so on. Once you have a clear picture, you can tweak your policy to reflect your knowledge. Remember at all times to treat the customers you already have like gold, and don't subject them to mind-numbing ads in an attempt to squeeze every last cent off them—they will move on if you do.

Affiliate Programs

Many businesses generate revenue through affiliates. An affiliate program, also known as an associate or referrer program, is any type of revenue-sharing program where an affiliate website receives a portion of income for delivering sales, leads, or traffic to a merchant website. There are a staggering number of different programs and schemes out there, and not all of them are reliable, so be careful and look for people who are established and have good reputations. Not sure how to go about this? Try asking on the osCommerce forums—you can be sure that there are other community members who use affiliates.

From your perspective, cash can be generated in two different ways by using affiliates. You can either deliver sales and leads to affiliate sites from your site and take a percentage of the profits, or you can ask affiliates to generate sales and leads for your sites, pay them a percentage of the profits, and keep the rest for yourself. In both cases, you need to make sure that the sales are actually made.

What I mean by this is the following: Consider two affiliate programs, one offers you 50% commission on all goods that you had a hand in selling, and the other offers 25%. At first glance, you would probably select the first one because that should mean more money. Unfortunately, this is not always the case, because no matter what commission is offered, customers still need to make a purchase. Customers will only purchase if the goods offered are good quality, meet their needs, and so on, which is why you have to pick your affiliates carefully. On the flip side, there is no point in setting up affiliates to sell your goods if they are unlikely to attract the right type of people (in other words, people who are predisposed to purchasing your goods).

> Effectively, affiliate programs are best used by stores that have a reasonably high profit margin on their goods. This allows them to share profits while still maintaining a healthy bottom line.

By and large, if you are careful and don't rush into anything you don't fully understand, you can use affiliate programs to grow your business, and earn extra revenue. In fact, this technique is so popular that a quick search on Google will reveal thousands and thousands of affiliate networks or programs, which deal with pretty much any product you can imagine. Just make sure you only get involved with products or schemes that are aligned with your own goals as a business. For example, don't offer links to gambling sites if you are trying to hold on to a family-based clientele.

Of course, osCommerce comes with its own affiliate program community contribution, osC Affiliate, which is available at `http://www.oscommerce.com/community/contributions,158`. Remember that since this contribution requires some modifications to your core code as well as addition to the database, you must use the development machine to get everything working before you attempt to use this on your live store. Since you are already familiar with how to get contributions working, we won't cover the installation here, but it is recommended that you try it out as well as look at some of the major affiliate networks out there. You might want to look at:

- Commission Junction: `http://www.cj.com`
- Affiliate Window: `http://www.affiliatewindow.com`

Whatever route you choose to take, remember that fundamentally you need to focus on your main source of income—your online store. Don't bog down your site with tons of links and ads, which will ultimately choke your own business in favor of gaining commission from others. Of course, from the other side of the fence, the more reliable affiliates you can get to sell on your goods, the better.

Become Active in the Community

This section really goes without saying. Becoming known as the person to speak to in your given industry is uncountably valuable in terms of word-of-mouth recommendations. Make sure that you get involved with forums and lists and in discussions. Write articles for other sites and ensure that you get some sort of recognition for yourself and your business in return. Even go so far as to venture offline in your efforts—attend conferences or become involved in committees that are related to what you do. Sponsor charities or other organizations, and earn both exposure and goodwill.

The list goes on and on, and is really as long as you intend to make it. Whatever spare time you have should be utilized by promoting your business and getting people to know you and your store.

The world of marketing is vast and you should learn as much as possible in an attempt to effectively reach your customers. The harder you work, the more likely you are to succeed because you will cover more ground than your less hard-working competitors—especially when it comes to marketing your business.

Search Engine Optimization

One of the most common goals for today's e-commerce community is to appear high up on the big search engine rankings. As you should know, having a high ranking increases the chances of potential customers finding your site among the mass of other sites. So what is it that you can do to make your site rank as highly as possible without actually having to pay anyone to do it for you? Well, there is no straight answer to this, unfortunately, and many people will give you just as many different answers. However, there is a core set of things you can do that are known to help—they might vary in importance, but it is probably worth performing all of them. The following table highlights the most important optimizations or tasks, which you should consider performing:

Optimization	Explanation
Write web-enhanced copy	IMPORTANT: Think about how your target customers would find your store. What type of words would they use to find a shop like yours? Once you have come up with a list of key words and phrases, ensure that the writing on your site makes use of these phrases whenever possible.
	If you are using Google AdWords, then you can check the popularity of various search terms yourself—simply put them forward as potential target keywords and check on their stats, which Google provides before they are added.
	For example, if you are selling cellular phones, and you wanted to make the phrase cellular phone a term that you rank highly on, then instead of writing something like:
	This product can be used to call other people, you should write:
	This G1 super **cellular phone**, can call any other **cellular phone** from wherever you are.
	In other words, without destroying the readability of your website copy, fill it with relevant search terms. In this example, your copy went from not containing a single key phrase to containing two, without damaging the readability of the sentence in any way.

Optimization	Explanation
Use meaningful file names	While this is not as important as the first point, it certainly will help to have everything named meaningfully, because search engines do look at file names. Instead of naming a page `product_1.html`, you should name it something like `G1_cellularphone.html`. Don't go overboard on this because it is not too important.

Use meaningful anchor text	IMPORTANT: Search engines, in particular Google, place a large amount of emphasis on the anchor text used in links. As a result, make sure all your links have meaningful text associated with them. For example, you would rewrite the following sentence:
	
	`Buy our new G1 Cellular Phone <a href ="<yourlink>">here</a>.`
	
	to:
	
	`Buy our <a href ="<yourlink>">Cellular Phone</a> here.`
	
	The reason for this is because that the word here is not particularly meaningful to a search engine, even though humans can easily make the connection. For the sake of your rankings, simply move the link to the key phrase Cellular Phone to place more emphasis on it for the search engine.

Write meaningful metatags	As many people will tell you, metatags have become less and less important as time goes by. However, they are still useful, and you should at least go to the effort of filling them out properly. The two metatags that you should consider making use of are the keyword and description tags. For example, the following shows a possible tag for a cellular phone store: `<meta name="keywords" content="cellular phones cellphone phone mobile">` Metatags have been the subject of some abuse, and you should view the W3C consortium's guidelines for their usage: `http://www.w3.org`. The Header Tags Controller community contribution might be of interest to you here because it allows you to specify the title, keywords, and description on a per-page basis. You can find it at `http://www.oscommerce.com/community/contributions,207`.
Manage your links	IMPORTANT: A high level of importance is placed on the perceived popularity of a website. Search engines can judge the popularity of a website by looking at how many links there are to the site, and how popular the sites that link to it are themselves. For this reason, you should ensure that you link to and link from only sites that you feel are suitable partners. Effectively, you should search for as many relevant reciprocal link pages as possible, or actually speak to the relevant sites to determine whether you can provide mutual links. The more links you have from popular sites, the better your ranking will be. You can also try to get one-way links to your site—these are also rated highly by search engines.

Write meaningful `alt` tags for images	Search engines don't see pictures like humans do, so there is nothing you can do about images... or is there? Instead of naming your images `02_03.jpg`, you might consider giving them names like `G1_cellphone.jpg`. Don't stop there either. Instead of adding an image like this:
	
	`<img src="G1_cellphone.jpg">`
	
	write it like this:
	
	`<img src="G1_cellphone.jpg" alt="New super G1 cellular phone">`

Use meaningful URLs	osCommerce comes with several contributions that convert the standard osCommerce URLs into being more meaningful and search-engine friendly. If you decide to implement these, be sure to do so on your development machine, as the forums indicate a large number of problems associated with these contributions for highly modified sites. You might try `http://www.oscommerce.com/community/contributions,2823`.

Optimization	Explanation
Submit your site to search engines and online directories	Make sure your site is listed wherever possible. Most hosting packages provide an automated SE-submission facility, which will automatically forward your site to search engines for indexing. Otherwise, look for other SE web page submission tools, or search out your own lists and directories to become part of.
Read up on lists, forums, and online tutorials	There is a lot of helpful information out there. Make sure you do your own research and come up with an SEO policy that is right for you.

Of course, all of this work can be bypassed by getting a professional company to do this for you. However, if you are prepared to put in the time to develop your links and constantly upgrade your site, you will eventually recoup the benefits that accrue over time. However, don't expect everything to happen overnight!

Dropshipping

Dropshipping is an ideal way for new or small businesses to increase the size of their inventory, or reduce their shipping costs. Sound too good to be true? Generally, when things sound too good to be true, it's because they are. In this case, however, the benefits arise because dropshipping makes use of the fact that Internet stores are *virtual*. This means that the products you show online to your customers don't necessarily have to be in your warehouse. Not only do you not have to have them in store, you don't even ever have to lay eyes on them.

Take, for example, the demo site, which sells technical books from a variety of different publishers. Let's say each publisher delivers free of charge all over the world and ships within 24 hours. Now, this is probably far better performance than the demo store as a small business could manage running its own inventory. But wait a second! Instead of ordering in bulk, shipping all the titles to a warehouse, paying for the transport and storage and then packaging and shipping along the way, what if you didn't bother actually physically getting a copy of the book at all?

If this was the case, you would sell a book to your online customer, and receive payment. You would then purchase that book from the publisher and ask them to ship it to your customer with your return address. Assuming you had a dropshipping agreement with these publishers, your customers could benefit from the free, 24-hour delivery anywhere in the world, and you could save a huge amount on storage and transport costs—in effect, you would only earn your markup above the publisher's price on the book, but there is little to no hassle involved in making a sale.

From the customer's point of view, you have sold them a book, received payment for it, and have delivered the book to them. They have no idea that the order has been fulfilled by someone else. Doing something like this (there are different forms of dropshipping) is a great way to boost the size of your online inventory without having to incur real costs. An example of a dropshipper can be found at Quality Books: `http://www.qualitybooks.com/dropshipping.htm`.

Before we round off, a quick caveat! Remember that you as an online store will only be as reliable as your dropshippers, so be very selective and careful about who you choose for backing up the promises you make. Again, use dropshipping as a tool to advance your business if you feel it is right for you, but keep your core focus—if you become a pure middleman, without any real products, you might find yourself in a fairly tenuous position at some stage, and not one that could be considered too reliable.

Summary

Taking an active role in growing your business from the time it goes live until the time (hopefully) you retire wealthy is a critical responsibility, which must be taken seriously if you are to succeed. At all times keep an eye out for opportunities and keep abreast of all the latest trends and advances in technology, business, and business in technology. Provided you are prepared to put in the time and effort to do things properly, you should find that you come out on top in the end.

Because building an online store is not the end of making a success of your business, this chapter ended the book by looking at the more practical and business-oriented issues surrounding osCommerce stores and e-commerce sites in general. You should now have a firm grounding in how to go about marketing your business, as well as how to use the latest tools to advertise your wares.

Of course, the Internet being the place it is, opportunities for businesses are staggering and you should be aware that not only can you advertise your wares, but you can also trade on your success as a business to earn revenue through advertising for others. At the end of the day, you should always maintain your focus on your business as providing an environment in which customers can purchase goods, and place any advertising schemes second in this respect.

Building a healthy business is not just about advertising; the Internet has spawned a number of innovative new processes that can be utilized to maximize your exposure and turnover. To this end, we looked briefly at affiliate programs, which increase the size of a merchant's sales force in return for a share of the profits. This performance-based profit sharing is a popular method of gaining market share and new business. As with all things in life and in business, though, it should be approached carefully, and you should always deal with only *the right people*. Who are the right people? Well, your success will depend in part on how well you are able to determine this for yourself—look for reliability, honesty, and loyalty.

Next, an interesting spin-off advantage of having a virtual retail store was explored in the section on dropshipping before the final part of this chapter looked at how to increase your store's profile on search engines through the use of search engine optimization. Ensuring that you have a high page ranking for your particular key terms is a very important factor in determining how much traffic your site generates. Think of the analogy like this: A high page ranking equates to having a high street store, where everyone walks past and peers in the window every day. Having a low page ranking is like owning a shop down a dark back alley where it is unlikely people will suddenly drop in.

Without doubt, owning and running an online business is one of the most multi-tasking, multi-discipline business opportunities that the modern world has to offer. The fundamentals of economics haven't changed though—work hard and look for the gaps, and you will do just fine.

Congratulations on finishing this book, and I wish you every success in your endeavors!

Troubleshooting

At some point in your career, you might experience problems with your code; no matter how diligently you try and work, errors do creep in. So common are errors (most often called bugs), in fact, that any big corporation nowadays has to implement comprehensive testing and debugging plans for months on end before it can consider new software to be fairly stable. Even then, as you have probably experienced, there are problems that slip under the radar and require patches or updates.

Since bugs are a part of life, it is better to learn how to deal with them properly than to hope to avoid them completely. This appendix will provide a few neat methods, as well as reiterate the best process for dealing with bugs. Remember, though, that if worst comes to absolute worst, and your site is beyond repair for one reason or another, then simply erase and fall back to your latest backup.

Types of Errors

Recall from Chapter 1 that there are three common types of errors that you will encounter:

- **Syntax error**: These will prevent PHP from actually running your code, but on the plus side should be relatively easy to locate if you have proper error reporting in place on your development machine – the php.ini file is the place to control error reporting levels. Of course, once your site is live, you don't really want the internal errors in your system being reported to the screen, because this can often allow malicious users to glean information about your system.

- **Run-time error**: These are slightly worse than syntax errors because they are not quite as obvious, or easy to pin down. There are different ways in which a run-time error can occur, and many of these can only be caught by thorough testing on your live site as well as your development machine. For example, file paths may change between your development machine and your live site, breaking links, losing files, or disrupting connections. While these errors won't show up when the PHP script is *parsed*, they will show up when it is executed.

- **Logic error**: These are quite sneaky in that they won't really show up at all. It is incumbent on you to decide whether your site is performing as it should. For example, accidentally typing a plus (+) sign instead of a minus (-) won't show up as either a run-time error or a syntax error, but will obviously affect the result of a calculation, which could have disastrous effects if it is part of your invoice calculator.

It is important that you are able to decide for yourself what type of error has occurred. Often, it takes a bit of experience to realize what an error message usually means, because PHP can't always isolate the exact place an error has occurred. If you have already found yourself suffering from seemingly cryptic error messages, then read on to the *Debugging Code Yourself* section for help on a variety of issues.

An Effective Process for Dealing with Bugs

Whenever you encounter a bug that has a nontrivial or non-obvious solution, engage the following process to get it fixed:

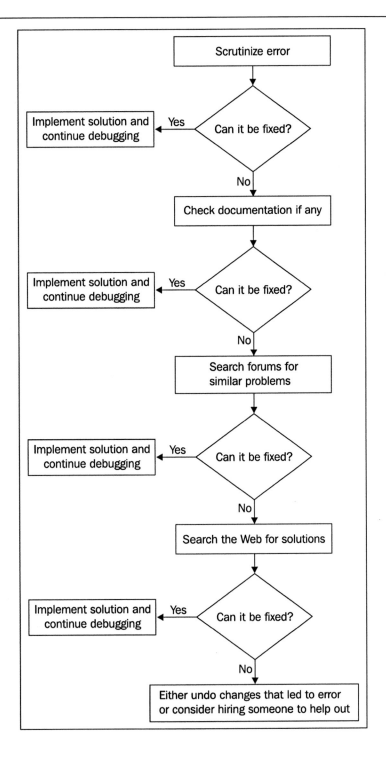

As you can see, the outlined process begins by trying to solve the problem yourself, and in the event that you can't, it incrementally increases the scope of the search for solutions. Ideally, however, you don't want to have to upgrade the problem to hours of searching on the Internet if at all possible. You simply want to be able to deal with the problem yourself and move on. In order to be able to do this with any sort of confidence, you need two things:

- Experience
- A toolkit for solving problems

Unfortunately, you can't gain experience from a book, so the next section will focus on giving you the tools to complete the job—how much experience you gain is really up to you. Once you have a few tricks of the trade under your belt, you will find that solving problems becomes, more often than not, a satisfying occupation. Remember, that every time you attempt to solve a problem in your code, you are learning more about the software, which will in turn help you the next time round.

Debugging Code Yourself

Let's begin with a couple of the easier-to-solve syntax problems. PHP will kick up a variety of different errors depending on where and how the syntax problem has caused an error in the script. For example, if you added a line to your code in order to perform a task (perhaps you added an extra echo statement), but get the following screen when you run the script:

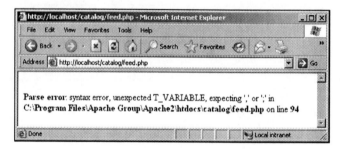

Looking at this error, you can see that on line 94 of the feed.php script, the PHP interpreter expects to find a , or ;, but instead it has come across something called a T_VARIABLE. A T_VARIABLE is simply PHP's name for a variable defined in your script. So the English translation of this error is:

I have come across one of your variables instead of what I expected, namely a comma or semi-colon, on line 94 of the feed.php script in the C:\Program Files\Apache Group\Apache2\htdocs\ catalog directory.

If we take a look at that spot in the code, we see the following:

```
} else{
    echo "<font face='Verdana' size='2'>Previous</font>";
}

echo "</td><td align=center width='30%'>"
$i=0;
$l=1;
for($i=0;$i < $numrows;$i=$i+$limit){
```

Can you see the error? We simply forgot to insert a semi-colon to finish off the echo statement so PHP didn't realize the line had ended and ended up coming across $i unexpectedly. Adding one fixes the problem, and the script runs as normal. So far so good, but what about other types of syntax error? What can we expect to get from PHP if, for example, we miss out a brace two lines above the echo statement? Reasonably, you could assume that it should report that there is a missing brace on line 92 (since the closing brace is two lines above the echo statement from the previous example), couldn't you?

Well, removing the closing brace from the else statement in the previous code snippet gives the following error message:

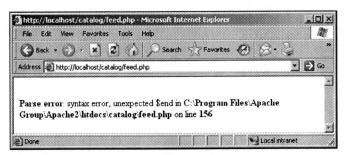

Oh dear, this is not very helpful; line 156 is the very last line of the script, and we happen to know already that it is line 92 which is causing the problem. How have things gone wrong, and what is PHP trying to tell us? The problem here lies in the fact that PHP doesn't really know what your program does, It simply takes it for granted you know what you are doing. So when you open a brace, it will treat everything that follows as part of that code block until it finds a matching closing brace—even if this is not what you intended. In our case, there is no matching closing brace, so PHP is telling us:

I got to the end of the file, but that is unexpected because you haven't finished your script properly.

This is where having a good PHP editor comes in. If you are using something like the Zend development environment, then the script editor is PHP-aware and can often help pinpoint problems like this because it automatically indents code so that it is a lot easier to see problems like this by simply looking at the file. Which is easier to understand, this:

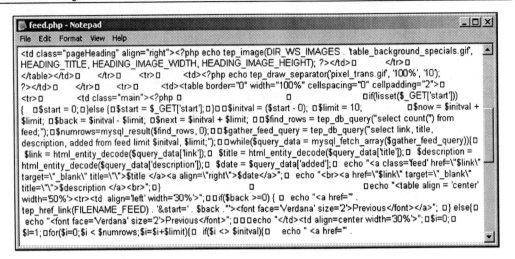

Or this:

As you can see, a proper editor makes life a lot easier because from this screenshot, we can see that there should be a brace inserted after the fourth visible echo statement, but before the fifth. How? Well, Look at the code indenting, if the fifth echo statement was part of the else block, it would also be indented. Of course, this is slightly contrived, but you get the picture—make sure you have a reasonable code editor before you attempt any serious debugging.

What about slightly more tricky problems, such as errors in the code's logic? Perhaps you have noticed that while no errors are being thrown up by PHP, your web page doesn't behave as you expect. Problems like this require a slightly more sophisticated approach. Let's say, for example, that when viewing the `feed.php` page in the browser, you notice that the navigation at the bottom of the page is not working properly—an example is shown here:

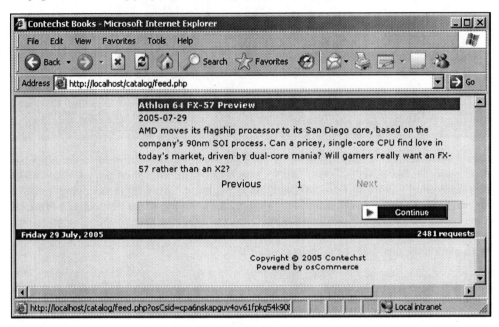

The above screenshot also highlights why it is so important to test everything thoroughly. Can you spot the problem? Well, the navigation links at the bottom of the feed page show that there is only one page, yet as you can clearly see, the Next button can still be activated, implying that there are more than ten items in the feed. This is a bit of a problem: either there are only ten items in the feed, in which case the Next button should not be active, or there are more than ten items in the feed, in which case there should be more than one page of feed items.

So what do we do in this case—there are no fatal errors or warnings to guide us, so we are on our own. Well, luckily for us, a large part of the analysis of the problem has been done for us already, because we know how this part of the application should behave. In other words, the problem is simple to understand—this doesn't necessarily mean it has a simple solution, but knowing what we want to achieve is an important step to rectifying any problem.

Furthermore, we have already advanced two plausible explanations for the problem. Either the Next button is not behaving properly or the pagination display is not working correctly. What's the next step? Do we jump in and try to fix the code? Not yet; there is something else we can do to further clarify the problem. Since we have access to the database, let's find out how many records there actually are—this will tell us whether we should have more pages than we do.

A quick visit to the MySQL command line tells us the following:

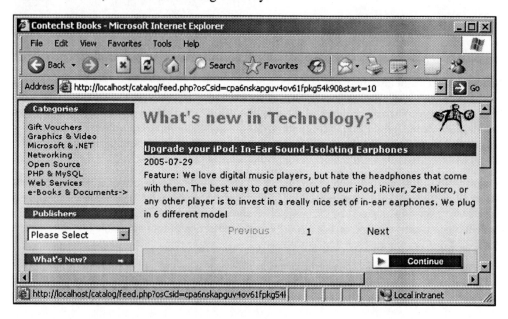

We have eleven items in the feed table, which means that the pagination display is definitely not working correctly. Do we go fix it yet? Not yet; just because the pagination display is not working, doesn't automatically imply that the Next and Previous links are. Let's test those quickly before we do anything. With 11 rows in the database, we expect the first page to have an inactive Previous link and an active Next link. If we click the Next link, the following page should have an active Previous link, an inactive Next link, and only one item. Trying this all out confirms that under these circumstances, the links are working correctly:

Before we go any further, there are a few considerations to point out. First of all, the pagination and links may work for the given number of items in the database. Just because they do, you shouldn't assume that they work for any number of items. The page should be tested with a wide variety of item quantities to ensure they work correctly. Second, if the Previous and Next links didn't work, then there was nothing you could assume about the nature of the problem, because either there is a separate source of error for the pagination and the links, or there is a common link causing the errors in both—you can't tell with the information you have.

> When debugging, try to keep your mind completely free of assumptions about the nature of the error.

OK, so we can consider the problem to be fairly well analyzed now. We understand how the code is supposed to work, and we have gathered information to help us eliminate certain possibilities as well as confirm certain suspicions. Having done all this, we should still try keep a clear view of things, because often problems can have very unexpected or subtle causes, which are hard to find if you act predominantly on assumption. With the analysis done, we now need to begin examining the code in order to understand the nature of the problem.

This is where certain tricks come into play. Two of the most common questions a programmer needs answered are:

- What values are being held in variables at a given point of program execution?
- How is the program being executed?

Now, at this point it is probably worth mentioning that you can obtain something called an Integrated Development Environment (IDE) for developing and debugging code. Zend, the people who make PHP, have a development studio available, and you can look over their products at `http://www.zend.com/store/products/zend-studio/`. This comes with a suite of facilities to help you sort out problems like this. For example, you can expect:

- A Code analyzer
- Code completion
- Syntax highlighting
- A Project manager
- A Code editor
- A Graphical debugger
- Wizards

All of these work together to help you create better code, and debug and analyze any code that you already have. If, however, you don't feel the need to fork out cash to work on your projects, then you might want to consider something like the freely available Dev-PHP, found at `http://devphp.sourceforge.net/`. However, you can do a fairly useful job of discovering variable content and program execution all by yourself by employing the following methods:

- `echo` variable contents to the screen
- `echo` program execution markers to the screen

Let's take a look at how this can help us to solve the feed page problem.

Knowing that we are most likely looking at a pagination display problem alone, let's focus our efforts on seeing what is happening under the hood. Hopefully, this will reveal where the flaw is occurring so that we can modify it and solve the problem. First thing's first, Let's find the relevant section of code:

```
$i=0;
$l=1;
for($i=0;$i < $numrows;$i=$numrows+$limit){
   if($i <> $start){
      echo " <a href='" . tep_href_link(FILENAME_FEED) . '&start=' . $i .
"'><font face='Verdana' size='2'>" . $l . "</font></a> ";
   } else { echo " <font face='Verdana' size='2' color='red'>$l</font> ";}
      $l=$l+1;
}
```

This snippet is responsible for outputting the pages. The first thing we notice is that it makes use of the $numrows variable, which is declared elsewhere. Let's go look for that declaration, so we understand what type of value it should contain. Looking up the page we find:

```
$find_rows = tep_db_query("select count(*) from feed;");
$numrows=mysql_result($find_rows, 0);
```

Ah ha! Notice that $numrows should contain the number of records in the database. Recall that earlier we used the same SQL query to determine this value. We are also making use of the $limit and $start variables, which we need to find as well. Searching earlier in the code, we find:

```
if(!isset($_GET['start'])) {
$start = 0;
}else {
$start = $_GET['start'];
}

$limit = 10;
```

From this we can see that the $start variable contains the value of $i, which is the iterator variable for the for loop, and $limit is simply the number of items to show per page. Since we are not getting the right number of pages printed out to the screen, let's take a look at how the for loop is working in more detail. In order to do this, we want to track the values of the variables being used as well as the program execution. Accordingly, we can use a debugging modification like this:

```
$i=0;
$l=1;
for($i=0;$i < $numrows;$i=$numrows+$limit){
   echo "We are in the for loop here: <br>";
   echo '$i = ' . $i . "<br>";
   echo '$l = ' . $l . "<br>";
   echo '$numrows = ' . $numrows . "<br>";
   echo '$limit = ' . $limit . "<br>";
   if($i <> $start){
      echo "  We are in the if statement here: <br>";
      echo '  $i = ' . $i . "<br>";
      echo '  $l = ' . $l . "<br>";
      echo '  $numrows = ' . $numrows . "<br>";
      echo '  $start = ' . $start . "<br>";

      echo " <a href='" . tep_href_link(FILENAME_FEED) . '&start=' . $i .
"'><font face='Verdana' size='2'>" . $l . "</font></a> ";
   } else { echo " <font face='Verdana' size='2' color='red'>$l</font> ";
      echo "    We are in the else block: <br>";
```

```
    echo '     $i = ' . $i . "<br>";
    echo '     $l = ' . $l . "<br>";
    echo '     $numrows = ' . $numrows . "<br>";

    $l=$l+1;
  }
}
```

Generally, you don't need to be quite as verbose as the above statements. If you have a fairly good idea of what is going on, you simply need to echo one or two values to the screen to find out what is happening. Looking at the results of the above modifications, we see that for the first page our results are:

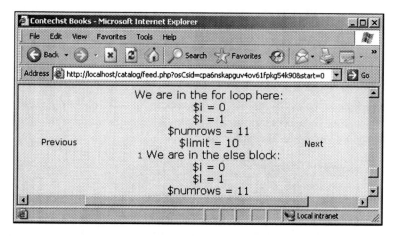

Straightaway you should get the nagging suspicion that something is wrong, because we are only going through the loop once before finishing. What's worse, our if condition never evaluates to true before the for loop ends its single iteration. The values we have outputted all seem to be in order for what we would expect for the first iteration of the for loop, so immediately we should suspect that something is wrong with the actual for loop conditions. Let's take a closer look at them here:

```
for($i=0;$i < $numrows;$i=$numrows+$limit){
```

Agh! What a silly mistake! Looking at the for loop condition from a structural point of view, we have asked it to do the following:

1. Begin the loop with $i equal to zero.

2. Test if $i is less than $numrows.

3. If it is, then execute the code block.

4. Evaluate the final expression $i = $numrows + $limit.

5. Repeat steps 2 to 4.

From the output of our echo statements, shown in the previous figure, we can see that initially:

```
$numrows = 11
$limit = 10
```

So, when step 4 is evaluated, $i is assigned the value 21. Moving to step 5 redirects us to step 2, which asks us to test that $i (21) is less than $numrows (11), which it quite clearly isn't, so the for loop breaks out, and we move on without performing any more actions. To be honest, this example is slightly contrived because an experienced programmer would have immediately noticed that $numrows + $limit > $numrows because $limit > 0.

For the purposes of learning how to monitor program execution, this is perfect because we noticed an unexpected result in that the for loop was only executing *once*. So, we need to modify the for loop so that it executes the correct number of times. In order to do this, we need to think carefully about what it is we want the loop to achieve. Effectively, we need it to take the number of items there are in the database, and divide by the record limit per page in order to decide how many pages to create. Then for each page, it needs to create a numbered link to those results, except for the current page, which is not a link.

Modifying the third condition of the for loop to the following:

```
for($i=0;$i < $numrows;$i=$i+$limit){
```

fixes the problem because whatever the value of $numrows, the for loop will iterate the correct number of times because we are increasing the value of $i by $limit each time. Trying the debugged code again gives the following results:

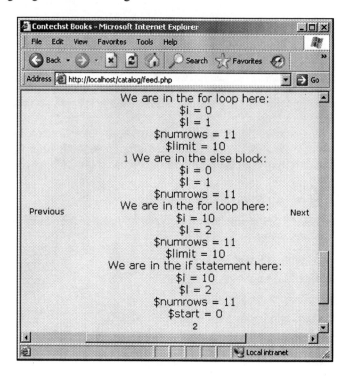

Looking closely at this output, you can see that there is now a 2 outputted at the bottom of the screen. This is as we would expect, because there are two pages required for eleven feed items. The `for` loop finishes after the first `if` statement (not counting the initial execution of the `else` block) because after that `$i` has a value of 20. To complete our debugging exercise, we can now remove the code we added to aid us in our debugging to view the results.

Next, you can see that the second time we enter the `for` loop, `$i` has a value of 10. Because of this, we enter the `if` statement because `$i` (10) is not equal to `$start` (0) because we are on the first page. This means we output a link to the second page and set the value of `$start` to 10 by appending it to the URL of the link.

Summary

While there is really no substitute for experience, you cannot really join the fray without some tools to help you on your way. This appendix has shown you how to deal with a few of the more common and simple errors, which occur reasonably often. Following this, a good process for dealing with more complex problems was outlined by way of example using the feed page code, which was added in Chapter 9, *Advanced Features*.

From this you have learned to gather information and analyze a problem before diving into the code. Once you have established what you expect the code to do (make sure you understand enough to have the correct expectations), you can go about determining possible causes. Following which, you learned a few tricks for helping illuminate the program's execution so that you provide yourself with important debugging information.

Remember that many development environments provide all sorts of features that can make your life easier—if you find that you don't have time to invest in doing things manually, then using one of the PHP IDEs on the market is certainly a worthwhile alternative.

Index

Thank you for buying Building Online Stores with osCommerce: Professional Edition

Packt Open Source Project Royalties

When we sell a book written on an Open Source project, we pay a royalty directly to that project. Therefore by purchasing *Building Online Stores with osCommerce: Professional Edition* Packt will have given some of the money received to the osCommerce project.

In the long term, we see ourselves and you—customers and readers of our books—as part of the Open Source ecosystem, providing sustainable revenue for the projects we publish on. Our aim at Packt is to establish publishing royalties as an essential part of the service and support a business model that sustains Open Source.

If you're working with an Open Source project that you would like us to publish on, and subsequently pay royalties to, please get in touch with us.

Writing for Packt

We welcome all inquiries from people who are interested in authoring. Book proposals should be sent to authors@packtpub.com. If your book idea is still at an early stage and you would like to discuss it first before writing a formal book proposal, contact us: one of our commissioning editors will get in touch with you.

We're not just looking for published authors; if you have strong technical skills but no writing experience, our experienced editors can help you develop a writing career, or simply get some additional reward for your expertise.

About Packt Publishing

Packt, pronounced 'packed,' published its first book "*Mastering phpMyAdmin for Effective MySQL Management*" in April 2004 and subsequently continued to specialize in publishing highly focused books on specific technologies and solutions.

Our books and publications share the experiences of your fellow IT professionals in adapting and customizing today's systems, applications, and frameworks. Our solution-based books give you the knowledge and power to customize the software and technologies you're using to get the job done. Packt books are more specific and less general than the IT books you have seen in the past. Our unique business model allows us to bring you more focused information, giving you more of what you need to know, and less of what you don't.

Packt is a modern, yet unique publishing company, which focuses on producing quality, cutting-edge books for communities of developers, administrators, and newbies alike. For more information, please visit our website: www.PacktPub.com.

Printed in the United States
76274LV00005B/141-150

9 781904 811145